W9-ART-158

The Worlds of MAURICE SAMUEL

WORKS BY MAURICE SAMUEL
Principal Publications

NON-FICTION

You Gentiles
>   Harcourt, Brace & Co. New York, 1924

I, the Jew
>   Harcourt, Brace & Co. New York, 1927

What Happened in Palestine: The Events of August, 1929, Their Background and Their Significance
>   The Stratford Co. Boston, 1929

King Mob: A Study of the Present-Day Mind
>   [Frank K. Notch, pseud.] Harcourt, Brace & Co. New York, 1931

On the Rim of the Wilderness: The Conflict in Palestine
>   Horace Liveright. New York, 1931

Jews on Approval
>   Liveright, Inc. New York, 1932

The Great Hatred
>   Alfred A Knopf. New York, 1940

The World of Sholom Aleichem
>   Alfred A. Knopf. New York, 1943
>   Vintage Books. New York, 1973 (paperback)

Harvest in the Desert
>   Jewish Publication Society of America. Philadelphia, 1943
>   Alfred A. Knopf. New York, 1944

Prince of the Ghetto
>   Alfred A. Knopf. New York, 1948
>   Schocken Books. New York, 1973 (paperback)

The Gentleman and the Jew
>   Alfred A. Knopf. New York, 1950
>   Greenwood Press. Westport, Conn., 1972 (reprint ed.)
>   Behrman House. New York, 1977 (paperback)

Level Sunlight
 Alfred A. Knopf. New York, 1953
Certain People of the Book
 Alfred A. Knopf. New York, 1955
 Union of American Hebrew Congregations. New York, 1977 (paper-
 back)
  D'muyot me-Sefer ha-Sfarim (Hebrew translation). Massadah. Tel Aviv,
  1960
*The Professor and the Fossil: Some Observations on Arnold J. Toynbee's "A Study of
 History"*
 Alfred A. Knopf. New York, 1956
Little Did I Know: Recollections and Reflections
 Alfred A. Knopf. New York, 1963
  V'Anokhi Lo Yadati (Hebrew translation). Dvir. Tel Aviv, 1968
Blood Accusation: The Strange History of the Beiliss Case
 Alfred A. Knopf. New York, 1966
 Weidenfeld and Nicolson. London, 1967
  L'étrange affaire Beiliss (French translation). Stock. Paris, 1967
  Krovavi Navyet (Russian translation). Waldon Press. New York, 1975
  (paperback)
Light on Israel
 Alfred A. Knopf. New York, 1968
In Praise of Yiddish
 Cowles Book Co. Chicago, 1971
 Henry Regnery Co. Chicago, 1975 (paperback)
In the Beginning, Love: Dialogues on the Bible
 With Mark Van Doren, edited by Edith Samuel. The John Day Co.–
 Thomas Y. Crowell. New York, 1973
The Book of Praise: Dialogues on the Psalms
 With Mark Van Doren, edited by Edith Samuel. The John Day Co.–
 Thomas Y. Crowell. New York, 1975

FICTION

The Outsider
 Duffield and Co. New York, 1921
Whatever Gods
 Duffield and Co. New York, 1923
Beyond Woman
 Coward-McCann. New York, 1934
Web of Lucifer: A Novel of the Borgia Fury
 Alfred A. Knopf. New York, 1947
  Das Netz des Bösen (German translation). Humanitas Verlag. Zurich,
  1949
  Avotot S'tanim (Hebrew translation). Massadah. Tel Aviv, 1950

The Devil That Failed
Alfred A. Knopf. New York, 1952
Victor Gollancz. London, 1953
The Second Crucifixion
Alfred A. Knopf. New York, 1960
Victor Gollancz. London, 1961

TRANSLATIONS

The Jewish Anthology by Edmond Fleg
(From French). Harcourt, Brace & Co. New York, 1925
Behrman House. New York, 1933
Greenwood Press. Westport, Conn., 1975 (reprint ed.)
Selected Poems of Chaim Nachman Bialik
(From Hebrew). The New Palestine. New York, 1926
Union of American Hebrew Congregations. New York, 1972
(new illus. ed.)
The World in the Making by Count Hermann Keyserling
(From German). Harcourt, Brace & Co. New York, 1927
Europe by Count Hermann Keyserling
(From German). Harcourt, Brace & Co. New York, 1928
Childhood in Exile by Shmarya Levin
(From Yiddish). Harcourt, Brace & Co. New York, 1929
Youth in Revolt by Shmarya Levin
(From Yiddish). Harcourt, Brace & Co. New York, 1930
The Arena by Shmarya Levin
(From Yiddish). Harcourt, Brace & Co. New York, 1932
The Plough Woman, edited by Rachel Katznelson Shazar
(From Hebrew). Sharon Press. New York, 1932
Herzl Press. New York, 1975 (paperback)
The Sinner (Yoshe Kalb) by I. J. Singer
(From Yiddish). Liveright, Inc. New York, 1933
Harper & Row. New York, 1965
The Brothers Ashkenazi by I. J. Singer
(From Yiddish). Alfred A. Knopf. New York, 1936
The River Breaks Up by I. J. Singer
(From Yiddish). Alfred A. Knopf. New York, 1938
Roosevelt: A Study in Fortune and Power by Emil Ludwig
(From German). Viking. New York, 1938
East of Eden by I. J. Singer
(From Yiddish). Alfred A. Knopf. New York, 1939
The Nazarene by Sholem Asch
(From Yiddish). G. P. Putnam's Sons. New York, 1939

Heil Hunger: Health Under Hitler by Martin Gumpert
  (From German). Alliance Book Corp.–Longmans, Green and Co. New
  York, 1940
The Lights Go Down by Erika Mann
  (From German). Farrar & Rinehart. New York, 1940
Theodore Herzl, A Biography by Alex Bein
  (From German). Jewish Publication Society of America. Philadelphia,
  1941
What I Believe by Sholem Asch
  (From Yiddish). G. P. Putnam's Sons. New York, 1941
Children of Abraham by Sholem Asch
  (From Yiddish). G. P. Putnam's Sons, New York, 1942
Haggadah of Passover
  (From Hebrew). Hebrew Publishing Co. New York, 1942
The Apostle by Sholem Asch
  (From Yiddish). G. P. Putnam's Sons. New York, 1943
Forward from Exile: The Autobiography of Shmarya Levin
  (From Yiddish). Jewish Publication Society of America. Philadelphia,
  1967.

The Worlds of

Edited and with an Introduction by
MILTON HINDUS

Foreword by Cynthia Ozick

MAURICE SAMUEL

Selected Writings

THE JEWISH PUBLICATION SOCIETY OF AMERICA

Philadelphia 5737/1977

Acknowledgment is gratefully extended to Edith Samuel for permission to use excerpts from the works of her late husband, and to the publishers named below for granting permission to reprint the following material by Maurice Samuel:

"My Virgilian Uncle," "The Twig Is Bent," "The Eruption," "Chaim Weizmann," "Founding Fathers," and "The Maggid," from *Little Did I Know: Recollections and Reflections.* Copyright © 1963 by Maurice Samuel.

" 'Returning' Home" series originally published in *The New Palestine,* issues of July 25, 1924, August 8, 1924, and August 15, 1924.

"Liberating the Fellah," from *On the Rim of The Wilderness: The Conflict in Palestine.* Copyright © 1931, 1959 by Maurice Samuel.

"The Haunted Land" and "Digression on an Astronomer," from *Harvest in the Desert.* Copyright © 1944, 1971 by The Jewish Publication Society of America.

"The Beginning of the Snarl," "The Snarl Thickens," "The Claim," "The Occupants," and "The Diaspora of the West," from *Light on Israel.* Copyright © 1968 by Maurice Samuel.

"Suppressio Veri," "Suggestio Falsi," "The Nature of Jewish Monotheism," and "The Ethos and Techniques of Survival," from *The Professor and The Fossil: Some Observations on Arnold J. Toynbee's "A Study of History."* Copyright © 1956 by Maurice Samuel.

"The Evasion," "Fury and Fable," "The Birth of Bugaboo," and "The Collusion of Your Churchmen," from *The Great Hatred.* Copyright © 1940, 1967 by Maurice Samuel.

"Echoes after Fifty Years," from *Blood Accusation: The Strange History of the Beiliss Case.* Copyright © 1966 by Maurice Samuel.

"Meir of Kikkle," from *Meyer Weisgal at Seventy: An Anthology* edited by Edward Victor. Copyright © 1966 by George Weidenfeld and Nicolson Ltd., London, England. Reprinted by permission of the publisher.

CONTENTS

part seven
WRITER AND READER

FOREWORD *Cynthia Ozick*

When exactly this took place I cannot now recall. I see a plain wood table, a full water pitcher, a small bright space; a lofty Viking of a man; a squarish, briefer man. There is an audience for this so-called "symposium," and I, in my hungry twenties, am in that moment enduring the first spasms of a lasting blow; afterward the blow will be recognizable as an ambush by the Idea of a Jewish history.

It is more than a mere lacuna, it is a poverty, not to be sure of the place. In those years I used to follow Maurice Samuel from lectern to lectern, running after whatever it was I thought I might get from him. I ran after others, too: poets, story-writers, novelists, everyone who might be in possession of a volcanic pen. I supposed the pen itself made volcanoes; I had a perfect faith, common to the literary young, that imaginative power is contained in the mastery of words.

The place, after all, may have been the art gallery of the Ninety-second Street Y in New York—a compromise-hall. If the audience is not large enough to fill the Y's auditorium, the speakers and their loyal little flocks are packed into the smaller hall, to huddle on metal folding chairs and pretend they are a crowd. For speaker and for audience there is always something slightly (and secretly) diminishing about the more modest room; it is as if those two elements of the scheme, teller and told, have together failed of permanence and eminence and are designated, even before the first word falls, to the evanescence of a puny event.

The event was not puny. There they stood, the courtly pair, beginning with the same obsession: the history of the Jewish people. One of the two was Erwin Goodenough, the Yale scholar; the other was Maurice Samuel—an uncategorizable presence, thickly though unsatisfactorily labeled: essayist, novelist, activist, thinker, historian, polemicist, (not least) public lecturer. Nor is "Yale scholar" good enough for Goodenough: stand before the row of his books, and you ponder a library. Something in his figure suggested the high monument of his work: the great learning, the ordering, erudite, deeply honest brilliance—the mind, say, of George Eliot sans the novelistic surge.

These two had come together as "discussants," not as antagonists; but afterward they parted in a state of—how to describe it?—metaphysical separation. Not that they disagreed; they did not disagree. What was clear history for the Yale monument was clear history also for the public lecturer. What the noble gentile scholar, unfolding the centuries, saw, the steady Jewish thinker, though implicated in those dense unreeling scrolls, saw with an equal eye. Eloquence for eloquence, they were a match; grandeur for grandeur, sensibility for sensibility, mind for mind, wit for wit. The room—whatever place this was, Y or other place—swelled to the size of an endless peopled meadow. Before that, and especially afterward, I would find myself a molecule in vaster audiences than this, halls as wide as some Roman plaza: as the years passed, throngs came to witness the fabled speaking fame of Maurice Samuel. All the same, it was in this narrower space that the huge Idea opened.

I do not now remember how the argument came to its crux, by what turnings or challenges; but now, thinking back on it, I see how like a clash of a pair of archangels it was—secular archangels—each intent on hammering out the meaning (or unmeaning) of Jewish history.

"The history of the Jews," Goodenough began, "is what the Jews have done, and what has been done to them."

"The history of the Jews," Samuel said, "is that. And something else."

"There *is* no something else," Goodenough said. "There is only what has been. The history of any people is coextensive with that people."

"The history of the Jewish people is coextensive with the Idea of the Covenant," Samuel said.

Then Goodenough: "The Covenant is *ought*. For history, *is* is all there is."

Then Samuel: "For Jewish history, *ought* is all that matters. Without the Covenant there is no Jewish people."

Goodenough: "Jewish history is history made by Jews."

Samuel: "The Covenant made Jewish history. If a Jew worships an idol, is that Jewish history?"

Goodenough: "Yes."

Samuel: "No. If a Jew worships an idol, that is one Jew worshipping an idol, but it is not Jewish history."

Goodenough: "And if a thousand Jews worship an idol?"

Samuel: "Then that is a thousand Jews worshipping an idol, but it is not Jewish history."

Goodenough: "History is the significance of data."

Samuel: "History is the significance of data. And more."

Goodenough: "History is what has happened. Nothing else."

Samuel: "History is what has happened. And also a judgment on what has happened."

And so on. Obviously I have made up the words of this dialogue, but I have not invented their direction. When the debate halted, it was plain that Goodenough had won it on the ground of "logic." But Samuel had won it on lesser, or maybe higher, ground: on the ground of stiff-neckedness, which has something to do with the way Jews receive the struggling light of holiness. What had come between them was not the force of fact, but this small persistent flame.

What flew up out of that archangelic exchange was Samuel's buried theme—the covenantal nature of the Jew. It was a buried theme because so far as his hearers and readers can tell he never again referred to it overtly. It was a volcanic theme because it taught that idea and imagination are the same; and that the imagination of an idea can successfully contradict what is truly known.

Yet Samuel's subject, by and large, was what is truly known— flat history, history exactly as Goodenough would have it: a record left by a people, not an afflatus divinely breathed, still less a Voice. Samuel was on the side of the pragmatic and the concrete: the "real." He was not in the prophetic line, in however minor a fashion; he gave public lectures to uneven audiences (every age, every "level"), and he did it, in fact, for a living. He was called, and did not mind calling himself, a *maggid*—an itinerant preacher. But he was no more a *maggid* than he was a contemporary lesser prophet; he did not preach, or exhort, or redeem; perhaps, now and then, he reminded. Even his reminders were informational, not clerical. He was learned, but he had taught himself. He was scholarly, but the excuse for this was a fevered need to know. He revered language, but he loved idea more. He was meticulous, but his range kept widening. He was, in short, not a closed system. If, as a public speaker, he had no title and arrived on every scene without an official description or affiliation, and was neither preacher nor professor, and not quite performer either, what exactly did he *do?*

His métier was thinking: thinking aloud. In his autobiography Samuel distinguishes between "reciters"—cautious types who declaim a fixed text—and genuine lecturers like himself, who evolve, or discover, a text. But perhaps there has never been another lecturer as daring as Maurice Samuel. He set out like a climber negotiating a ledge; he hit on a point, sometimes an obstacle, sometimes a gratifying piece of good fortune; whatever it was, he assessed it, grappled with it, took his victory, and sprang on to the next peak. Along the way he tossed in his talismans of erudition, irony, and above all the long view. He was quick, he was fleet, he was dogged, he made connections. And still, having described all this, nothing has been described. What did he do? What was his job?

His job was to address a generation and to explain. In essence he was an argumentative explainer. This is different from *maggid,* prophet, sage, teacher—they all, in their several degrees and guises, have the kind of authority that emanates from their persons. They are *beings,* voices, conscious of speech and the effect of speech, conscious of themselves as representing value, tradition, core. They know they are there to *be;* and that by being, they will transmit. But an explainer is out to give an explanation, not a tenet. The explainer thinks aloud; he is not thinking of his role; he has no expected, usual, given role. An explainer hurls himself into his story. He becomes the story. How does he do this? By joining himself with its elements, by taking sides with its various parts. By sorting out. By setting aside error and misapprehension—only after first entering into their spirit.

In brief: through polemics. Polemics is the chief instrument, the illustrious and ancient mode, of the explainer. Through polemics, as through no other means, an idea can be beaten out. Polemics is a hammering, a hacking into the flanks of imagination. It has the furious relation of stone to sculpture; there is no serenity in its progress. It begins with what is deformed, and only after the ringing and the smashing does it lead to grace. But the aesthetic analogy does not go far enough. Polemics is thinking in the furnace of antithesis. Polemics sees the adversary as an outrage, but also as an advantage. One reason it is inappropriate to define Maurice Samuel as *maggid,* or prophet, or sage, or teacher, is that not one of these avatars commands the antiphonal as a *necessity.* Wisdom-teaching, whatever its devices, goes in a straight line; it knows what it knows and is not really required to look over its shoulder at what does not pertain. In that sense it may be more correct for tradition to have assigned Moses the epithet "our polemicist" instead of "our teacher." "Thou shalt not" is as concerned with the antagonistic culture as it is with the ideal culture and is perpetually looking over its shoulder at alien practices: to shun is to see.

Maurice Samuel is above all a polemicist, assuredly the best of our time. Leo Baeck is a consummate polemicist, but only once (though that once is a pinnacle), in his essay "Romantic Religion." Walter Kaufmann, Baeck's translator and the author of *Critique of Religion and Philosophy,* is a more consistent polemicist, though more often from the standpoint of idiosyncratic, rather than Jewish, thought. But Samuel is a polemicist from beginning to end: which is to say an unrelenting critic of thought—and always from the Jewish standpoint. For Samuel the Jewish view is almost never yielded up through simple declaration or exposition; it is wrestled out of the engagement with, and finally a disengagement from, an alternative world view. *The Gentleman and the Jew* and *The Professor and the Fossil* are only the most emphatic of such demonstrations.

Nothing serves Samuel's powers better than Arnold Toynbee's misrepresentations, errors, and contradictions. It will not do to say that if Professor Toynbee had not existed, Maurice Samuel would have had to invent him: given the actual history of the West, there is no way for Professor Toynbee *not* to have existed. He is the classical anti-Semite in scholar's clothing, as was Apion (died 45 c.e.) before him. The same can be said of the configuration of the "gentleman." There is no way, given the actual history of Europe, for the "gentleman" idea, with its code of honor, heroism, and valor based on bloodshed, *not* to have manifested itself in contradistinction to the Jewish code of moral decorum—*mitzvah.* But in both instances the polemicist must have not merely significant mastery but complete mastery of the code, cult, culture, and overriding concepts of his antagonist. Indeed, he must *include* in himself his antagonist. A polemicist must first embody that which he hopes to expel. It must be a version of self he casts out.

Without a Manchester childhood devoted to the consumption of English schoolboy novels, without a period of rejection, or at least indifference to, parental heritage, without a phase of passionate allegiance to "universalism" (the kind that de-Judaizes)—without, in short, having brought himself up as an ideal Englishman—Samuel

could not have taken on Toynbee, or the principle of the "gentleman," or the opponents of the Zionist idea. If Moses, nurtured in
Pharaoh's palace, was as much polemicist as lawgiver, it was because
he knew the priests who administered the idols firsthand, and knew
how to beat these royal magicians at their own game. And the case
for Theodor Herzl, the Viennese journalist and boulevardier, is of
course open and shut: the modern State of Israel was founded on the
tongue of an imaginative polemicist. Maurice Samuel did not come
from so far over on the other side—he is closer to his Uncle Berel the
tailor than he is to the English playing fields—but for a time he
traveled toward the allure of what he later called "the brilliance and
attractiveness of . . . a frivolous world," and he was drawn in that
direction early enough to understand profoundly, and from the inside, what it was he ultimately opposed.

"He was the teacher of a generation," the people who were in
his audiences say of him, remembering the rigorous lectures—they
were not entertainments—and the remarkable radio dialogues with
Mark Van Doren. "He is my teacher," his readers say, preserving
both the sense of individual possession and the present tense—readers' privileges. But both memory of the lectures (corruptible though
instructive) and familiarity with the books (continuing and renew-
able) offer finally a static sort of homage if they address themselves
only to Samuel as teacher. It will not do—not simply because, unlike
a teacher, he did not primarily intend to shape any of us. Sitting rapt
among his hearers, observing how (in those "question periods" that
follow public lectures) he did not suffer fools gladly, it seemed to me
even long ago that he hardly cared whether his voice touched fools
or gods. He was grappling not with *us* but with certain footholds,
difficult to ascend to, just above his line of sight; impossible to posit
rationally that the footholds are *there.* That strange wrestling in a
small space with the scholar of Yale remains a paradigm of Samuel
as writer, thinker, imaginer. What he was after was the Idea that
would separate itself out from all other ideas, as a single hammer can
go to work on all the flanks of so many stones; the stones split, the
hammer beats on. He neither wrote nor spoke wholly for our sake,
as prophets and teachers and *maggidim* do. Instead, much of it was for
the sake of that hammer—the one that knocks to pieces idols and
other well-made falsehoods. Polemicist's hammer: steadily it breaks,
just as steadily it builds.

In these chapters the hammer beats on.

INTRODUCTION *Milton Hindus*

Maurice Samuel was born in Macin, Rumania, on February 8, 1895, and died in New York City on May 4, 1972. He was the author of more than a score of books in a variety of genres and translated many others from French, German, Hebrew, and Yiddish. A forceful, popular lecturer who traveled extensively throughout the world to address Jewish audiences, he also reached many more thousands of listeners in the course of twenty years of regular national radio broadcasts and telecasts.

In an early book provocatively entitled *I, the Jew,* Samuel traces his family line back as far as his great-grandfather, who had moved from Poland to Rumania. During his early childhood his family emigrated to Western Europe, and he spent a large part of the fifth and sixth years of his life in Paris, where he laid the foundation of the excellent knowledge of French that was to prove valuable to him later. Eventually the family settled in Manchester, England, and it was there that he received his formal education, first in the elementary schools and later at Manchester University. He was an exceptionally able and diligent student who competed successfully for a number of scholarships. In retrospect, however, he blamed himself for not having learned more than he did from two famous professors at the university: the Nobel Prize-winning physicist Ernest Rutherford and the chemist Chaim Weizmann, with whom the more mature Samuel was to form a personal, political, and literary bond in the Zionist movement. Despite his excellent record as a scholastic competitor, he reacted strongly against the idea and the strain of such competition, indeed against the competitive life in general, and he abandoned his studies at the university after three years without taking his degree.

Samuel's intellectual precocity at first drew him away from the Jewishness of his background. Like so many uprooted children, he formed an intense attachment to the adoptive country of his parents: "England was my nurse, my cradle, my home. I appropriated my surroundings as my natural right. English games, English moral slogans, English institutions—all were mine. English heroes, in all the changes through which my perception of heroism passed in my boyhood and youth, were my heroes. . . . When my awakening taste for literature asked for something more than simple epic narrative, it was Chaucer, Malory, Spenser, Shakespeare, Milton, Byron, Shelley, Keats, Browning—down to Thomas Hardy and a host of moderns." The rhetoric of this account is no doubt touched with irony, but the basic sincerity of the sentiment is hard to doubt.

The naive excess of his patriotic phase quickly gave way to its opposite extreme: internationalism, rationalism, universalism. "Around the age of thirteen," Samuel notes wryly, he was a full-fledged "Socialist and atheist." Confirmed thus in what was then becoming a fashionable intellectual "faith" (which he would later outgrow), he quickly blossomed into an eloquent boy-orator able to arouse the enthusiasm of English workers. It was here that he became aware of himself somewhat disconcertingly as a young Jew whose foreign birth and family background set him even further apart from the crowds of born Englishmen whom he addressed than did his superior education or the social class to which they belonged.

Spending the summer holidays of 1914 in Paris, Samuel witnessed the outbreak of World War I and the beginning of that period of violence which has lasted with some interruptions for over sixty years. By chance, he was sitting at a café table and heard the shot that felled the leader of French Socialism, Jean Jaurès, an incident he vividly recalls in a chapter of his autobiography, *Little Did I Know* (included in this collection). After the war broke out he returned to Manchester for a few months but disappointed his shoemaker father (who had once served in the Rumanian army) by not joining those who were volunteering to serve with the British Expeditionary Forces. Out of a mixture of disaffection with his home, disappointed love, and a youthful desire to see the New World, he embarked for the United States in November. Three years later, in 1917, he was drafted into the American army, where he helped train recruits who understood Yiddish better than English, and he returned to France with the A.E.F. His knowledge of French led to an assignment with the intelligence section of the American army in Bordeaux. There, in his free time, he undertook to recover the knowledge of Hebrew forgotten since his childhood. (The Balfour Declaration had just been issued, and a Jewish homeland with Hebrew as its spoken tongue now became a possibility.) In America he had refreshed his knowledge of Yiddish, briefly met Sholom Aleichem, and looked forward to the realization of the Zionist dream.

After the Armistice in November 1918, Samuel was transferred to Paris. In the summer of 1919 he was asked to serve as an interpreter for an American government commission appointed to investigate pogroms in newly-independent Poland. This commission was headed by Henry Morgenthau, who had once been President Wilson's ambassador to Turkey. Observing the indignities and terror to which Polish Jews were subjected moved Samuel deeply and, as he writes, "had a permanent effect on my already developed Jewish interests." He was harshly critical of Morgenthau and of the euphemistic and misleading report that the commission eventually submitted. He published his views on the matter in the Zionist journal *The New Palestine* and later amplified them in his autobiography.

In 1921, after his return from army service in Europe, Samuel was naturalized as an American citizen. The commitment was a profound one, and more than forty years later he commented: "I would like to write a long essay on my relation to America, the country without which there would hardly be a Jewish people today and therefore no Jewish homeland." For seven years he was an employee of the Zionist Organization of America. In addition to serving as a member of the American Zionist administration, he served for a year on the Actions Committee of the World Zionist Organization. He quit this post in 1928, about a year before the Great Depression struck the country, and he remarks ruefully that, had he anticipated such hard times as followed, he might well have reconsidered his decision. It was not disagreement with the Zionist idea that led him to break with the organization, for he remained a devoted Zionist to the end of his life; his resignation sprang from the feeling that "if there is anything I am supremely unfitted for, it is day-to-day political work." That was why he decided to risk the exchange of a regular salary for the uncertainties of the life of a freelance writer and lecturer.

Samuel was generally so independent in his opinions and outspoken about them that self-employment was far better suited to his nature than organizational work. Though he classed himself self-deprecatingly with professional Jews—"except that they are on fixed salaries while I peddle piecework"—in reality he was in a class by himself. His irrepressible individualism, buoyancy, and ready wit gave flavor and piquancy to everything he wrote and said. Yet somehow he managed to yoke together a pair of seemingly contradictory attributes: he was at once "his own man" and a representative Jew of our time. From 1928 to 1972 his life is largely a record of the books and articles he wrote, the translations he made, the lectures and broadcasts he gave. His devoted activity in all these respects earned him the moral right to reproach gifted friends (like Shmarya Levin, for example, in a selection included here) who were less disciplined and diligent or succumbed to the temptation to fritter away on trivialities the time which they might have put to more productive use.

"He has enthusiasm: without that, what is a man?" Walt Whitman once asked his friend Horace Traubel rhetorically. The question is devastating to the claims of the ordinary teacher or writer, but it points to the source of Samuel's strength. It would be possible to guess the truth that lay behind his dynamism even if he had never declared it openly:

If I did not have to lecture for a living I would be running around offering to do it gratis. I still love with all the passion of my boyhood the feel of an audience and the challenge of oral exposition. I still cannot come across an interesting idea without wanting to tell everyone about it . . . and it has been my wild good fortune that, unlike most compulsive talkers, I have found people willing to pay to listen to me. If I had to stay on at a regular job, with regular responsibilities, I would have gone to pieces under the pressure of my primary compulsion, that of the writer. . . .

The facility with which he wrote and the wide variety of subjects to which he addressed his attention might have made him suspect had he been satisfied to be merely superficial on any of them. But he was never one of those content to contribute to what Whitman called "the rivers and oceans of very readable print" which are destined from the outset to be ephemeral. What is the difference between such journalism and real writing? Gertrude Stein may have grasped it when she said to Ernest Hemingway early in his career: "If you keep on doing newspaper work you will never see things, you will only see words and that will not do, that is of course if you intend to be a writer." With all of Samuel's love of language, it is clear that *things* (reality, substance) were still more important to him. His account of the origins and development of modern Zionism, *Harvest in the Desert,* written in 1943, still strikes the knowledgeable, after more than thirty years, as both a penetrating and pertinent treatment of its subject. *The Professor and the Fossil,* Samuel's polemic against Arnold J. Toynbee's treatment of the Jewish people in *A Study of History,* is impressive for the vast amount of learning it displays and for the acuteness with which it argues the case. Samuel's detailed investigation of documentary material about the frame-up of Mendel Beiliss in *Blood Accusation* was meticulous enough to win the commendation of authorities like George Kennan and Isaiah Berlin.

Indeed, Samuel's work is often characterized by a scholarly quality of a high order, which could have taken him far in a traditional field of academic endeavor had he so chosen. But he seemed to regard formal academic scholarship with some of the same skepticism he felt for other occupations that fitted into conventional rubrics. For the individualist and nonconformist, they were temptations to be avoided. His real vocation was that of the essayist. Despite his contention, supported by an elaborate scaffolding of rationalization, that the category of "the gentleman" was at odds with that of "the Jew," he combined a surprising number of the attributes of both in his own person. His attitude to literature was that of a free man, as defined by Socrates in one of the Platonic dialogues, "a gentleman of letters" who would not allow himself to be enslaved by the demands of a fickle audience in the marketplace. His choice of subject was determined by his own enthusiasms; what sets him apart from other writers is his preoccupation with style and the unexpected flashes of humor and poetry which transfigure his pages.

Samuel had a rich vein of the very quality that he admired in Sholom Aleichem. There is a sharp edge of amusement in his exposition of some of his favorite subjects:

The compilers of Proverbs, and ben Sirach after them, were excessively occupied with the dangers of women and of politics, but especially of women. The one famous passage in praise of a woman presents her as a formidable combination of go-getter and home-factory foreman. Otherwise she is a snare, a corruption, a torment, and a calamity generally. A wise man keeps away from women and from revolutionaries: "My son, fear thou the Lord and the king, and meddle not with them that are given to change."

The complement of this quality is an unaffected eloquence which aspires, not vainly, to the plane of the sublime. An illustration of it is a passage telling of his initial journey to Palestine under the British Mandate in 1924:

Late one night an intermittent glimmer rose below the rim of the faintest stars ahead of us and to the left, and grew slowly into the regular alternating flash of a lighthouse. It was Cape St. Vincent, the furthest outpost of the Iberian peninsula, known to the ancient Greeks as the Hesperides, the lands of the sunset, to the Hebrews as Sepharad, and to us as Spain and Portugal. In the full darkness there was nothing visible but the circling light, which is set there as a warning to ships, but which for me, there and then, shone like a memorial and a sign. For I thought then that Sepharad was sunk in the sea, and I remembered the story of hope and disillusionment, of momentary splendor and swift decline, the story which is wholly Spain's and partly ours.

In his later years Samuel sometimes spoke gloomily of "the oblivion awaiting my name." It was not for nothing that from his early years one of his favorite philosophers was Schopenhauer. But even in these pessimistic moods, one at least among his many accomplishments seemed to him likely to withstand devaluation, and he declared his contentment with going down to posterity if in no other way than as "the herald of Sholom Aleichem in English." It was in 1943, at the very time when the world of Sholom Aleichem was being finally destroyed in Europe, that his threnody to it appeared in America. In time it begot a not inconsiderable progeny, though none of the off-spring was a real match for the parent. *The World of Sholom Aleichem* continues, after these many years, to be his most popular book, and it has never been allowed to go out of print.

But it took a long time before Samuel found the proper form for presenting the life and culture of Eastern European Jewry to readers of English. At first he was simply the translator. A translator, to be sure, whose sensitivity and perception set him apart. No one who has not tried his hand at such translation can rightly appreciate how ingenious, yet seemingly simple and inevitable, are some of the locutions devised by Samuel to serve as the English equivalents of Yiddish idioms. If one compares in detail his version of a story with some others that are extant, one becomes aware of how often Samuel accomplishes quietly and without strain what the others are trying to do without quite succeeding. His successes in straight translation, however, left Samuel dissatisfied. He grasped intuitively the sound-ness of an observation that had been made as long ago as 1888 by Bernard Berenson in an obscure article, "Contemporary Jewish Fic-tion," in a church publication, *The Andover Review*. Berenson had written: "Take up almost anywhere a Jewish romance, and it is so thoroughly Jewish that to one not minutely acquainted with Jewish life it is not very intelligible. That makes it very hard to bring Jewish romance before the world, ignorant as it is of Jewish life. The humor and sarcasm in which the romances abound would be lost. We need only try to recollect how much there is that is unintelligible to most of us in Heine's 'Jehudah Halevi,' in his 'Disputation,' and in his 'Apollo-God' to understand how unintelligible the Jewish romance would be."

Sixty years later, Samuel came to a similar conclusion and stated it explicitly in *Prince of the Ghetto,* a companion work to *The World of Sholom Aleichem,* dealing with another great Yiddish writer, Y. L. Peretz. Here is how he puts the principle informing both books: "Now I, the returned stranger, must explain the work of this complex figure [Peretz] to other strangers. As in the case of Sholom Aleichem, I must do it in a roundabout way. It is useless to present the reader with a body of translation and say: 'There you have the man. Judge him for yourself.' The most characteristic language of Peretz cannot be translated outright. Honest attempts have been made—again as in the case of Sholom Aleichem—and they may be read for what they are worth. These men must be interpreted. One must talk *about* them, and around them, and around their people and its problems; one must retell their stories, one must hint and allude, interpolate, digress, find analogies; their work must be introduced as it were incidentally and by way of illustration, even though it is actually the purpose, and constitutes the bulk of the enterprise."

It was Maurice Samuel's pioneering and, to my mind, his still unsurpassed studies that prepared the way for the spate of notable expositions of Eastern European Jewish culture that followed: *Life Is with People* (by Mark Zborowski and Elizabeth Herzog), Abraham J. Heschel's *The Earth Is The Lord's,* Lucy Dawidowicz's *The Golden Tradition.* His influence can even be traced in such popular works as Leo Rosten's *The Joys of Yiddish* (indeed the author indicates explicitly his indebtedness to *The World of Sholom Aleichem*), *Fiddler on the Roof,* and Ronald Sanders's *The Downtown Jews.* More indirect, yet significant, is the connection between his work and the numerous academic histories, studies, translations, and textbooks of the Yiddish language and literature that have been published in the last thirty years. He helped to create the atmosphere in which Roman Jakobson could write, in his preface to Uriel Weinreich's *College Yiddish:* "There cannot be approximate knowledge of a literary language for its users. Full mastery or illiteracy—*tertium non datur.*" This statement may be compared with one of Samuel's in *In Praise of Yiddish:* "A generation ago it was fashionable among 'modernized' Jews to pretend *not* to understand [Yiddish]; today it is the fashion to make unfounded claims to a knowledge of it."

The love in which this achievement is grounded can be felt in the passage of his autobiography in which he writes: "There is much talk today of the decline and approaching death of Yiddish; it is, I think, exaggerated; but whenever I hear it I think with a pang of the loveliness that must be locked away forever in forgotten languages." That his achievement is capable of receiving more than intramural recognition should be clear from the description of Samuel by John Murray Cuddihy (in his *Ordeal of Civility*) as "the great historian of the *shtetl* and of Eastern European Jewry." In the same vein David Daiches, writing on the occasion of a recent (1974) British edition of *The World of Sholom Aleichem,* records his discovery of this "remarkable book . . . an unusual and . . . brilliant achievement," the achievement he admires being the contribution of "Samuel's own historical knowledge" to an appreciation of the stories of Sholom Aleichem.

My own first meeting with Samuel took place shortly after World War II when I was teaching English and humanities in the college of the University of Chicago. I had by that time published a number of critical essays, some poems, and many book reviews. I had also been asked by Sholem Asch to translate into English his "epistle to the Christians," which he called *One Destiny.* Samuel had been my immediate predecessor as the translator of Asch, and his versions of *The Nazarene* and *The Apostle* had been much admired and set a high standard. *The World of Sholom Aleichem* had also convinced me that its subject was on an intellectual level suitable for serious academic and literary study and that this subject might eventually be incorporated into the curriculum of schools which were neither sectarian nor parochial. I was interested in exchanging ideas about this with Samuel himself. During one of my trips from Chicago to New York, he invited me to come and see him in his hotel room on the Upper West Side, where we talked of Asch and the academic potential of Yiddish.

Samuel and I did not meet again till some years later at a party in Ludwig Lewisohn's apartment at Brandeis University, to which I had come from Chicago in 1948. That second meeting has left me with a vivid memory. Learning from Lewisohn that I was engaged in writing a book on Marcel Proust, Samuel astonished us by quoting from memory a long passage from the celebrated Scott-Moncrieff translation of *A la recherche du temps perdu.* He had been in France in 1919 when a controversy developed over the award of the Goncourt Prize to Proust, and he had savored the intricate style of the work in French before the book was available in English. Because of his own deep concern with the problems of translation, he was particularly interested in how Moncrieff had coped with the challenges of the Proustian style.

Samuel's memory remained astonishingly retentive to the end. I remember that in the course of one of our conversations before he entered the hospital for the last time he recited flawlessly a beautifully balanced paragraph from Gibbon's *Decline and Fall of the Roman Empire* and invited my attention to the minute points of the style which produced the impression of its classical perfection and polish. Such feats throw light on his own superior style, which sometimes has the effect of making his translations vie in distinction with the original text. They sprang from the intensity of his affection for all the languages he knew and for language in general and its hidden powers. That love is preserved in his essay "My Three Mother-Tongues," also included in this book, which was written not long before his death and constitutes a kind of literary and linguistic testament.

Over the years, except toward the end, we met more often at Brandeis than in New York. Occasionally we exchanged letters on one subject or another. At Brandeis I heard him address conventions of Hillel and of the American Jewish Historical Society. I witnessed the impressive convocation in which the university awarded him an honorary degree. After the death of his friend Lewisohn (at whose memorial service he spoke), he visited less often, though he had a standing invitation to do so whenever he could.

During the last year of Samuel's life, when it was clear that his health was failing, I saw him whenever I came to New York. One of these visits occurred during an extended period of treatment that he underwent at Mount Sinai Hospital. Though his heart was obviously faltering, his spirit was not, and in his wit and alertness he was not diminished. He spoke of death openly, with philosophic calm, detachment, and even good cheer. His faith, like everything about him, was an individual variant upon traditional and conventional models, but clearly it was working to insulate him from despair. Later on, when my wife and I visited him at his home during a remission of his heart ailment, he told us that despite the precariousness of his physical condition he was conscious of never having felt more contented in his life. He then proceeded to enumerate matter of factly the various ways in which the burden of care and responsibility had been lifted from his mind.

The light of Maurice Samuel's reason was not only undimmed but seemed indeed sometimes to burn more intensely toward the end of his life. His usually voracious curiosity and intellectual enterprise in seeking out excellence in writers who had somehow escaped his notice were as strong as they had ever been. During one of our conversations, for example, I mentioned one of my own favorite authors of the twentieth century, the Triestan master Italo Svevo. Svevo had been discovered by James Joyce (whom Samuel once met and had read and reread since the 1920s), and he is supposed by some critics and biographers to have been one of the models for Leopold Bloom in *Ulysses,* a character who for obvious reasons had always fascinated Samuel. I sent Samuel one of Svevo's masterpieces, *The Confessions of Zeno,* and almost at once I received a letter from him filled with the excitement of personal discovery. Here was a new luminous star for the literary astronomer to add to his own map of the modernist firmament. Reading Svevo, he wrote me, had been "an eye-opener," though he felt he had not gotten "deeply enough" into him as yet. How, he asked, could he have missed such a phenomenon? One felt, between the lines of his letter, that if only life were granted him long enough, he might add an essay on the assimilated Triestan Jewish writer to the ones he had written earlier on Thomas Mann, Marcel Proust, James Joyce, and Saul Bellow.

Passages from various notebooks he was keeping toward the end of his life express some of the thoughts and attitudes back of the calm flow of his familiar talk:

To be old and not to meditate on death is to miss the rounding out of life's experience. It is the same as to have been young and never to have been in love. I do not know whether I agree with Samuel Johnson's saying that it concentrates the mind wonderfully to know that you will be hanged in a fortnight, but a certain clarity or seeming clarity comes with the knowledge that I will, in all probability, be dead in three or four years time. . . . The insights I may thus acquire will be of no earthly use to young people. Perhaps a few old ones will derive a kind of mumbling satisfaction from them. . . . The thoughts that come to you are not new. You met them in your youth. But now they are cleansed of rebelliousness and impatience. . . . You no longer cry out. . . .

Age gets into you. Whatever you've liked to do you can't do as often. It takes you longer and it isn't as good. Then it stops altogether. . . . It has never happened before that in the midst of writing a book I should often stop and think "I may not live to finish this." Now it is happening. . . .

I am making a quiet exit from the world. . . . I look at these words and I am filled with a mild astonishment. My mind is alert and active. The reports of mankind's headlong rush toward self-annihilation keep pouring in on me from all over the world, and here I am, detached from them in an incomparable calm. I am not benumbed by terror, nor am I in a state of terminal euphoria. It is only that certain matters which may seem to be irrelevant to the vast agitation all about me keep pressing for my attention, and with the habit of over sixty years I write them down as fast as my fingers can guide my pen. . . . I shall be seventy-seven on my next birthday. Seventy-seven is only a moderately long life span, but in my family it seems to mark a limit. None of my numerous uncles and aunts and neither of my parents reached it. There was a fabulous grandfather on my mother's side who went on living till no one was sure how old he was when he died. I was in my late twenties when I last saw him, and I do not remember anything unusual about his later years except their uncountability. . . . But I do not like the idea of growing into an edifying example of longevity. . . .

The unflinching astringency of such realism is the same as that which so distinguishes his autobiographical writings.

Ideally, every work of art and intellect strives toward a universal significance. Yet a place must be reserved in all national "collections" worthy of the name for expressions of a particular spirit or a particular moment in the history of a people which are meaningful to it alone. This volume, which above all forms a penetrating exploration of Jewish particularity, also demonstrates the universality of Maurice Samuel's appeal. During his lifetime Samuel laid claim not only upon the attention of his own people but upon that of sympathetic strangers as well. It is to be hoped that the work before us, in addition to refreshing the memories of an older generation of readers, will also serve to introduce Maurice Samuel to new readers.

The selections that follow have been drawn from a dozen of Samuel's books published over a span of forty years. The earliest of these is *On the Rim of the Wilderness*, published in 1931 and containing reflections provoked by the Arab riots of 1929; the latest, *In Praise of Yiddish*, the final demonstration of Samuel's love of the Yiddish language, was published in 1971, a year before his death.* The bulk of

*A word should be said at this point about the transliteration of Yiddish words in this volume. By and large we have taken our cue from Maurice Samuel himself, who in *Prince of the Ghetto* noted: "I have been at a loss as to how to deal with the transliterations. There are certain scientific rules familiar to scholars, and to few

the selections derive from the period of Samuel's full maturity, from about 1940 onward, when he produced the series of works for which he is perhaps best known: *The Great Hatred* (1940), *The World of Sholom Aleichem* (1943), *Harvest in the Desert* (1943), *Prince of the Ghetto* (1948), *The Gentleman and the Jew* (1950), *Certain People of the Book* (1955), *The Professor and the Fossil* (1956), *Little Did I Know* (1963), *Blood Accusation* (1966), and *Light on Israel* (1968). The other selections include hitherto uncollected essays, verse, and travel impressions contributed over the years to such magazines as *Commentary, Midstream, The Menorah Journal,* and *The New Palestine. The Worlds of Maurice Samuel* gives both old and new readers some indication of precisely how unique a phenomenon Samuel was among Jewish writers of our time. We are not likely soon, in America, to see his like again.

As editor of this volume, I should like to acknowledge the valuable counsel and suggestions that I received from Edith Samuel and from Maier Deshell, editor of The Jewish Publication Society of America. I am grateful to Edith Samuel for her generosity in making available to me the whole range of her husband's published writings and some of the unpublished ones quoted in this Introduction.

---

others. I thought it would be a nuisance to introduce them here. I decided to trust to my ear, and to use the ordinary English reproduction of the sound of Litvak Yiddish." The "scientific rules" have been observed where Samuel so ordered, most particularly in the selection from *In Praise of Yiddish.*

part one

Maurice Samuel's non-fiction writings, dealing predominantly with matters of general Jewish concern, were marked by a strong autobiographical strain. Writing in many cases directly out of his own intellectual experience, he produced a body of work that forms a kind of spiritual autobiography. The tendency to self-revelation is to be noted in such books as *You Gentiles, The Gentleman and the Jew, Level Sunlight,* and *I, the Jew,* which otherwise constitute systematic treatments of their respective subjects. In his sixty-eighth year Maurice Samuel published a more formal collection of memoirs, *Little Did I Know: Recollections and Reflections.* The selections that follow, recounting certain memorable experiences of his early years, are taken from this affecting work.

BEGINNINGS

1 MY VIRGILIAN UNCLE

Among the people who rise out of my past to claim first mention, my Uncle Berel is the most persistent. This would have surprised him. He played only a brief role in my life and had no idea that it was of any importance. He must have supposed—if he ever thought about it at all—that when he was dead and gone I would call him to mind affectionately now and again, but less and less frequently, less and less clearly, as the years passed; and that by the time I reached his age he would be among the ghostliest of my memories. I, for my part, surely did not look so far ahead; but now I am much older than he was at the time of our intimacy, and I find myself thinking about him more and more frequently, and seeing him more and more clearly. It is, in fact, impossible to disallow his claim.

So there he is, Uncle Berel, my mother's brother, Berel Acker, the tailor, who does very little tailoring, making most of his living, such as it is, from repairing, cleaning, and pressing. I usually see him in profile, at his work table before the window facing north on grimy East Fifteenth Street, between First and Second Avenues, while I sit at his right, and we carry on long conversations which on his side are punctuated by what are known as Bronx cheers. He is in the late forties; he has a squat figure, a round, brown, wrinkled face with Tartar cheekbones and overhanging mustaches. He chews an extinguished cigar stump, and his little brown eyes twinkle when he turns to make a point. The Bronx cheers are not derisive; they are modest, mechanical, and professional; he produces them by taking a sip of water from the glass on his left and, with a circular flourish of his bowed white head, spraying from between pursed lips the skirt or pants he is pressing by hand. He ought to have a pressing machine, but for various reasons he has never managed to save up the price; and among these reasons is an admitted disquiet of soul in the presence of a New World innovation which would sever another bond between him and the good old days in Rumania, where he was born and grew up.

There is a constant tug of war between Uncle Berel and me. He wants to talk about things he thinks I know, and I want to hear him on things I know he knows. He would like me to clarify for him once and for all how they measure the circumference of the earth and the earth's distance from the sun; or how a microscope magnifies; or how one can reconcile the obvious uncertainty of man's life with the obvious solvency of insurance companies. I keep steering him toward the details of his occupation and his memories of Rumania.

Uncle Berel is a mixture of shrewd realism and uncontrollable sentimentality. He is a meditative man from two consecutive and contradictory causes. His wife (I barely saw her in America, she died soon after my arrival) was homicidally talkative and threw him back on himself; now he is a not disconsolate widower and much alone. He is a sharp observer and a close reasoner; but he also has fantasy. He hangs his customers on the rack in provocative combinations: Mr. Michelson the grocer next to Mrs. Tuchverderber the matchmaker, a priest's soutane next to a rabbinic caftan. He would make a good novelist, though he did not get more than a *cheder* (elementary Hebrew school) education, has never made a formal improvement on it, and speaks only Yiddish and Rumanian. When I suggest in all seriousness that he could produce, if not a novel, then a new and homely *Sartor Resartus,* and explain that it is a sort of philosophy of clothes, he says: "Beh! A philosophy of *shmattes,* rags, maybe, if I were a writer like you." For I am already a writer, a fact attested by an impressive collection of rejection slips.

"Very good, Uncle Berel! A philosophy of old clothes. There have been so many Jewish old clo' men; it's a tradition."

"Maybe you're having a little joke with me," he answers. "And yet what I do here is no small matter. Here comes an old suit, a beggar, a scarecrow, fit for the garbage can. I take nothing in my hand, as you might say, just a spit of water and a hot iron. I neither add to the cloth nor subtract from it, I make a flipflop with the iron and hopla! there's your suit, a regular gentleman"—but he says "gentledendle" to indicate disesteem—"not to be recognized. A resurrection for the sleeper in the dust, as the *siddur* (prayer book) says. And the things I learn about customers, even if I've never met them and somebody brings their clothes to me, the things I learn—oh, ho! Black coffee beans in the pants pockets—he chews them to cover his breath because he drinks and he's afraid of his wife; cigarette butts in the vest pockets—a miserly soul; chewed toothpicks—nervousness, bad manners, and close-set teeth. And the stains! A world of stains, from the lapels to the pants cuffs; and what they sometimes tell you isn't fit to be spoken of. Has your writer friend—"

"Carlyle—"

"Has he anything to say about that?"

"Not that I remember."

He removes the cigar stump, sips water, and swoops down over the table like a benevolent hawk, reminding me of Dante's "Ha! Ha! Thou stoopest!" Emptied, he tries to switch the conversation; if not Carlyle, then something about actuarial tables; but my Yiddish is defective, I am relearning it after years of alienation; and I was never very good at mathematics. I push him back to his old clothes. It turns out that in his own way he feels actuarially and has formulated for himself a version of Emerson's Law of Compensation.

He feels himself to be a sort of economic barometer, or, rather, a recorder of barometric readings. Mr. Michelson's grocery store is the barometer, and the mercury Uncle Berel watches is represented by Mr. Michelson's suits. When the operators, cutters, hatmakers, pressers, and salesgirls on the block are out of work or on part-time, their diet is low in lox and high in potatoes; then Mr. Michelson's takings are poor and his suits lose heart and acquire luster in longer absences. When times are good and lox is again in the ascendant, Mr. Michelson's suits pick up *joie de vivre* and come in as often as every other Thursday. But there is more to it than that.

"I tell you," says Uncle Berel, "it is a marvelous world. I stand here and reckon it out. When people are out of work they don't have their clothes mended and pressed very often, and therefore I too earn less, which is only right. Good! But you might think I am in danger of starving to death. Not at all! For if people have no jobs they can't buy new clothes; so the suits and skirts grow older and older, and it has been cleverly arranged that the older they get the more often they need mending and pressing. The mind of man can't look through the deepness of it all."

On certain subjects Uncle Berel and I are so hopelessly divided that we have dropped them by tacit consent. I am a newly converted —self-converted—Zionist. I believe that some day, all going reasonably well, we shall have a Jewish homeland in Palestine. It depends largely on us. Uncle Berel is immovably skeptical. The division, to mix a metaphor, is an impasse. "Yes, we will." "No, we won't." "Why won't we?" "Beh! For one thing, they won't let us." Who are "they"? Uncle Berel makes an impatient gesture with the flatiron, giving it a little rapid clockwise and counter-clockwise flip before he plumps it down; that is all he can do, for though his emotions are strong the flatiron is heavy. "Everybody!" But his skepticism is not hostile. When the issue was first raised between us he admitted that he too had once dreamed dreams, but they had faded away, or rather had been extinguished suddenly.

"Once upon a time, years and years ago, when Theodor Herzl" —he pronounced it "Todder"—"was alive, I thought for a moment, yes, maybe it will happen. There is a man who is received by kings and sultans. That must have meant something. They knew him for what he was. A prince. It was a sudden light, and it went out. That's the kind of luck we have. Now it's *farfallen,* done for, not *bashert,* not destined. Today—tremendous nations locked in a life-and-death struggle"—it was the winter of 1914–1915—"where do we *Yiddalach* come in? I respect you, you've been to college, but on this matter, if you'll pardon me . . . Who's going to lead us now?"

I too revered the name of Herzl, though I knew little, at that time, about the personality—royal indeed—fusion of sophisticated Viennese journalist, messianic prophet, and master organizer—who within a decade of his death had become folklore. But I gave Uncle Berel names, which he shrugged off. "Do you call that a Herzl?" The greatest among the Zionist leaders who were then arising I did not mention, though I had met him in person. My ignorance of the Zionist movement was extensive. I had no idea of the role Chaim Weizmann had played and was playing in it. How, then, was I to guess that a still greater role awaited him, or, even more remote from probability, that he would admit me to his friendship and exercise a far-ranging influence on my life?

Another subject I soon learned to avoid with Uncle Berel was socialism. Here I cannot speak of a division; Uncle Berel simply wasn't interested. My fierce insistence on the equality of all men elicited from him not a repudiative squiggle of the flatiron but a meditative "Mm—nn—yeh!," neither approving nor disapproving, followed by a long silence. At that point, I believe, Uncle Berel's respect for my college education was weaker than usual. I left it at that.

I think of Uncle Berel as Virgilian because he was for a period my guide through various limbos of folk and family memories. I responded to them as a fascinated outsider, for though they were mine I was detached from them; nearly half a century had to pass before those of the memories which I shared with him (I migrated in 1900, at the age of five, from Rumania, where he was a frequent visitor at our home) became something more than disconnected little pictures in a gallery, and fused into a deep-toned, mysterious, and magic interior totality. When I was nineteen my childhood seemed to me to have been somebody else's, and it is only recently that I feel it to be more visibly and palpably mine than it was then or during the intervening years. There was, to be sure, much talk at home, in Manchester, about Rumania; Uncle Berel, however, did not merely talk about it; he conducted me into it.

He had a ritual. Every Saturday night, whether his barometer stood at Fair or Foul, he went to a "service" at a certain little Rumanian Jewish restaurant on the Lower East Side. (I have forgotten its name, and it surely closed its doors long ago.) It was nothing like Moskowitz's famous rendezvous, then on Houston Street. The premises were a basement four steps below the dirty street level; there was no instrumental music; the prices were modest. Uncle Berel's fellow-celebrants were all Rumanian Jews, elderly tailors, shoemakers, candy-store keepers, machinists, pressers, who knew each other from of old by first name and the name of the town or village of origin: Leibu of Macin and Itzik of Pitchiniagu and Getzel of Barlad and Moishe of Glodorlui and Chaim of Podoturk and Mendel of Fokoshan. Ostensibly—and, as far as their consciousness went, genuinely —they assembled to eat *karnatzlech, beigalech, mamalige,* and *kachkeval,* to drink what they called and apparently believed to be Rumanian wine, and to play *sixty-six* and *tablenette.* They spoke Yiddish peppered with Rumanian phrases, and the conversation reverted in rhythms to old times. They remembered the Chismijui of Bucharest, and the Red Bridge of Jassy, and the *shool* (synagogue) of Vaslui. (But they said *sheel* for *shool,* whereas I, relearning my Yiddish among Litvaks— Lithuanian Jews—here in America, said, and still say *shool;* I also say *man* [husband] instead of the Rumanian Yiddish *mon,* and *veib* [wife] instead of *vab:* I sometimes even slip into *die* before *veib,* that is, I use the feminine article instead of the neuter, Litvak Yiddish having no neuter article and *veib* being perversely neuter in Rumanian Yiddish, as in German.) From time to time Uncle Berel took me with him, and I enjoyed it intensely, as observer rather than as participant. To my uncommitted and unenchanted palate *karnatzlech* were simply cigar-shaped rolls of chopped meat, overspiced and underdone; *beigalech* (not to be confused with *beigel,* which has been described as a dough-nut dipped in cement) were merely meat patties, *mamalige,* a corn-mush cake, *kachkeval* a rank cheese, none of them particularly appetiz-ing. To Uncle Berel and his cronies these foods were sanctities; it was not an ordinary eating and drinking; they ate and drank time, they smacked their lips over the pathos of distance and irretrievability; their tastebuds had transcended their neural functions, serving as ministrants to the sweet melancholy of divided and uprooted souls.

I have long wanted to write about these and other spiritual-associational values of food. It is not language alone, or even chiefly, that distinguishes man from the animals. A goat crops the grass but a man ingests the landscape and the heavens above it, and even a solitary meal can be an *agapë.*

One would have thought that these emotions were associated for Uncle Berel and his cronies with the exile's vain longing for the land of his birth, with remembered joys of a time and place, both lost forever. In Uncle Berel's case it was certainly nothing of the sort. He hated Rumania and never had a good word for it. He had grown up in a period of mounting Rumanian anti-Semitism. When he was a young man thousands of Rumanian Jews were being driven from the country by poverty and repression. (Oh, idyllic, halcyon days, when Jews were driven from a country instead of being incinerated in it—if only Uncle Berel could have known how considerate the Rumani-ans were!) Many of those who could not buy railroad tickets, or even hire a horse and cart, had formed into large groups which wandered westward on foot, begging their way, singing songs which have now become a little segment of the folklore. Uncle Berel had started out with one such group and had turned back, but whether it was his feet or his voice that gave out I do not know. He became a tailor, made enough money to buy passage for himself and his family as far as England, and later was helped on to America. Why did he, like the other frequenters of that restaurant, seem to hark back to a time of good eating and drinking, a time of high living and contentment? It was a psycho-optical illusion. These were the foods they had loved and never had enough of; what they harked back to was simply their youth.

Uncle Berel put up a fight against the illusion. "What black year is it," he asked, wrathfully, "that makes me want to shed tears of love for Rumania when I hear a Rumanian song? *Vulech gonef!* (Wallachian rogue!) who didn't let a human being live! *Vulech gonef!* With his 'Hey, Zhidan!' (sheeny!) and his 'Don't stand here!' and 'Keep out of there!'" And once he flabbergasted me by an extraordinary outburst quite out of keeping with his native good humor. There was a fat woman singer in our little restaurant. She sang Yiddish and Rumanian songs, without accompaniment; the former I understood, and some of them, like *A Brievele der Mamen* (Send Your Mother a Letter) and *Eli, Eli* (My God, My God, Why Hast Thou Forsaken Me?) were dreadful; others, from Goldfaden and the folk repertoire, were often beautiful. The Rumanian songs I did not understand, and why on that evening that particular song did what it did to Uncle Berel I shall never know. I was watching him and saw his eyes becoming moist; suddenly he stood up, drew a fifty-cent piece from his pocket, and hurled it across the room through the open door onto the steps, whence it bounced back with a shrill ringing. *'Na dir, kurveh!*—take it, whore!" howled Uncle Berel. The woman continued to sing as she made for the coin, and Uncle Berel sat down, quivering.

He resented Rumania's shameless gate-crashing into his loving reveries of the past; it was a parasitic and defiling intrusion. But once he was launched on a sentimental binge Rumania always nicked in for an utterly unmerited place. He saw it, and was helpless to prevent it. It was as though a refugee from a German death camp, sole survivor of a large family, were to hear a performer in a cabaret singing an innocent German folk song, and weep because it reminded him of his childhood. Uncle Berel also chided himself, with the same clear-sighted helplessness, for his disinclination toward a pressing machine. He was a believer in Americanism and progress, but his heart was stuck in the past; and what sharpened his resentment was his view of Rumania as the very embodiment of willful backwardness and moral beastliness.

"A stinking land!" he said. "Not the land itself, which is lovely enough—such a year on all of us!—but the people. No, not the people, the *cham*, the *tzaran* (peasant), the stupid mass, but the *preetzim* (the aristocracy and the rich), the government, which keep them ignorant and brutish. Not for nothing did your mother carry on to make your father leave the country, so that your brothers and you wouldn't have to be Rumanian soldiers. Ask your father what *that* meant."

I knew something about "that," but there was an odd difference-in-agreement between my father's way of telling it and Uncle Berel's. My father had served in a Rumanian cavalry regiment called (as he pronounced it) the *Rawooshoren.* There were at home, in Manchester, two photographs of him in uniform, and in the larger, tinted one he was heroically mounted, resplendent in uniform, saber and all. He had risen to the rank of sergeant, a considerable achievement for a penniless Jew. As a child I had not been able to reconcile the dashing hero on horseback with the rather grim and frustrated shoemaker who was my father. The stories he told of his service were hair-raising and if only half true more than justified my mother's terrors and Uncle Berel's animadversions. The savagery of the non-coms toward the privates was equaled by the contempt of the officers for both. An unbridled sadism passed for discipline, and the quartermaster's service was corrupt through all its levels, so that the uniforms were ragged and the food, poor enough by regulation, was tampered with. I grew up with the notion that the Rumanian army was a hell. I suppose it couldn't have been as bad as all that—and yet a strange incident interpolates itself at this point.

I was in Paris, on leave, in the spring of 1919, a sergeant in the A.E.F., waiting for my demobilization. Coming late one night out of the Rat Mort on the boulevard Clichy, I was accosted under a lamp by two Rumanian officers. Their lips were rouged, their eyes ringed with mascara. I had the impression that they wore corsets. They said something to me in Rumanian, and I recognized an obscene word I had heard from older people in our Manchester group. I started back with such terror and loathing that they in turn started back from me and made off, laughing vilely. I wanted them to know that I had understood them, and I wanted also to insult them. So I shouted after them: "Hey, *Zhidan!*" It was the only offensive Rumanian word I could think of. There may have been a second purpose, to this effect: "And you're the people who despise Jews and call them *Zhidan.*" It is of course absurd to base one's judgment on a few reports and individual episodes—but I am recording my experiences and nothing more.

With all his acknowledgment of the ghastly conditions in the Rumanian army, my father remembered his soldier days with pride. And when England declared war on Germany in 1914, and I as a pacifist refused to join up, my father was contemptuous of me. I also refused to remain in England while others were enlisting (conscription did not come till two years later). In November 1914 I left for America; my mother rejoiced; Uncle Berel, for his part, approved wholeheartedly.

"You couldn't have done a more sensible thing. I only wish the Jews could all get out of Europe, instead of having to shoot at each other, *mir nisht, dir nisht,* because *goyim* like to fight. They've always been at it, and they always will be. *Ich hob zei alle in d'rerd*—they can all go to hell."

By the spring of 1917 my views had changed and my pacifism was tottering. I had become anti-German, and though not an American citizen, I could see where I would stand if America entered the war. I had to prepare Uncle Berel; so there were sharp exchanges, and it almost came to a quarrel.

"What do you mean, Germany is the aggressor?" asked Uncle Berel. "What kind of language is that from *you?* England has a lot of colonies, Germany has hardly any, and she wants her share. You're a socialist and a Zionist, aren't you? You believe all men and all nations should be equal."

"There shouldn't be any colonies, Uncle Berel."

"Right. But there *are* colonies. What difference does it make to you who has them?" He would break into the peculiar Yiddish sing-song of logical discourse which has passed from the Talmudists to the folk. "I-if there were no colonies at all, and i-if Germany were going out to get some, I would say that Germany had to be stopped." He added, hastily, "Maybe," fearing he had yielded a strong interior position on which he might have to fall back later. "As it is, you want to defend an old thief from a young thief."

"Let it be so, Uncle Berel. I say an old thief is better than a young thief. He's tired, and his conscience bothers him, and he wants to make amends and be respectable. When he dies and there's no one to inherit he leaves his money to charity. He even practices charity before dying. A young thief has a fresh appetite; you can't let him start the whole dirty business all over again."

"I don't see your old thief in such a state of exhaustion," said Uncle Berel, sarcastically. "According to the papers, he's giving as good as he's getting."

That was how the main arguments went, Uncle Berel repeating *"Ich hob zei alle in d'rerd"* and I insisting that "they" were not all alike. I had forebodings about Germany, though perhaps not clearly on Jewish grounds. We skirmished on the question of "atrocities," which Uncle Berel laughed off as propaganda. Behind the spoken arguments were emotions we could not refer to; Uncle Berel was as fond of me as I of him; he trembled for me, and he felt some responsibility toward my mother. I knew I was going to disappoint and grieve both of them.

Then America entered the war and I had to make my decision. I did not want to return to England, nor could I bring myself to enlist in the regular army; I was afraid of making myself ridiculous among professional soldiers. When the draft law was passed I took out my first papers so as to come under its operation, and to my immense relief my number was in the first batch—eight hundred and something. I received my training at Camp Upton, Long Island, and there Uncle Berel, dispirited but affectionate, would visit me, bearing always a gift of salami and black bread. I could not convince him that we were not only well fed but perhaps overfed; and he never became reconciled to my decision.

One Sunday morning I took him round the system of trenches we had dug—a replica of a section of the Western front—and were learning to storm and defend. Uncle Berel looked long and earnestly, then turned to me. "These holes in the ground—you're supposed to let yourself be killed rather than give them up?" "Yes, Uncle Berel, that might be the order." *"Vey, vey,"* he mourned, "can human lunacy go further? Fool! If the other man wants them so badly that he's prepared to kill for them, let him have them! Go away and dig yourself another lot of holes."

He took a horrified, almost morbid interest in the details of my military activity. He conceded that the American army was nothing like the Rumanian, but the whole thing was mad anyhow. One circumstance made a peculiarly painful impression on him. My regiment, the 307th Infantry, had a large contingent of New York East-Siders, some of them recent arrivals in the country with very little knowledge of English. I was in Company F, and my captain, a likable lawyer named Davis, asked me whether I would not take over two squads of the newcomers and teach them the rudiments of close-order drill in Yiddish. It was a request rather than a command, and in an evil hour I accepted. My Yiddish had improved considerably in the last three years; I was reading the classics with enjoyment and already entertaining thoughts of translating Sholom Aleichem, Yal Peretz, and Mendele into English. (I had made the personal acquaintance of Sholom Aleichem shortly before his death in 1916.) Uncle Berel had been indescribably delighted by my increasing proficiency in the language, but he was profoundly shocked by the use to which I was now putting it. He was also puzzled; where did I get the military terminology? He had never heard of such a thing in Yiddish, Jews had never fought in that language.

I told him that I gave the commands in English and explained

their execution in Yiddish, with illustration. *"Ven ich zog* 'Te-en-*shun!'*
you must stand up straight, *ot azoi,* like this, feet together at an angle,
ot azoi, shoulders drawn back," and so forth. I confessed to Uncle
Berel that I found the assignment not at all to my taste. The men
didn't take me seriously because of my Yiddish. They were willing
enough to be soldiers, but they looked on me as an impostor. They
argued with me, and one man, Strauss, a thickset Russian Jew, was
particularly objectionable. "Look, Samuel, I've been standing and
walking on my feet for over twenty years, and I haven't fallen down
since I was a baby. I can stand like this, and I stand like this"—he
took up various postures—"and I'm still standing. Give me a gun and
I'll shoot all the Germans you want, but for God's sake *fardrei mir nisht
a kop*—don't drive me out of my wits with that rubbishy left right,
left right! Just tell me where to go and you'll see, I'll get there."

"Strauss," I said, "I'm teaching you what I have to teach you. Go
tell the captain."

"And another thing," answered Strauss. "You want to say 'Attention'? Say it. Don't shout 'Te-en-shun!' and get red in the face.
You want to say 'Forward march'? Don't yell 'Faw-waw-*harch!'* Say
it plainly, reasonably, like a human being."

"Isn't he right?" asked Uncle Berel, and went back to his lament.
"Vey, vey, you take a beautiful language like Yiddish, a dear homey
language, and with it you not only want to teach men to kill, you also
want to turn them into idiots. For the sake of a hole in the ground.
Feh!"

I look back nearly half a century and wonder how far Uncle Berel
would have carried his principles. Would he have agreed with Epictetus, who says: "If a man steals your lamp it is your fault for having
a lamp"? I also wonder how in his brief Zionist interlude Uncle Berel
the pacifist foresaw the emergence of the Jewish homeland. I dare say
it was somewhat as follows: a large number of Jews would realize,
under the magic of Herzl's persuasion, that the time had come for
them to rebuild their country; some would go there, others would
help them; the nations of the world, under the same spell, would
applaud; the Arabs would receive the Jews with open arms: a Messianic picture. . . .

Philosophers will tell you that what has not happened could not
have happened—a wonderful expression of the self-assurance of
hindsight. But many things looked possible in 1919 to men of good
will, and if their hopes were disappointed it does not prove that the
pessimists were wiser.

In the course of the decades the things I learned about Rumania from
and through Uncle Berel, and those I heard of at home, in Manchester, and those I recall myself, have become submerged in the uniformity of that strange, clear, submarine light that now rests on all
my childhood memories. Transpositions may have taken place;
things told may, by repetition, have acquired the intensity of things
lived; things lived may have fused with things told; all are equally
"factual."

The Jews of Rumania used to have a reputation as *lebeyungen,*
high-livers, short on learning, much given to the world and the flesh,
if not the devil. They, and to some extent Ukrainian Jews, also from
a fat land, were contrasted with the lean and hungry intellectual
Litvaks. It may be an individual accident—my birth into a low economic stratum, the family destiny, my mother's temperament—but
my personal memories do not bear this reputation out. Rumania is
touched with sadness for me. In Uncle Berel's restaurant I once heard
from the entertainer a song that had been a favorite with my mother,
about the miseries of the Jewish conscript. I recall it very clearly:

> How many bitter tears my parents shed
> Before they saw me grown to man's estate;
> Now far from home I must lay down my head,
> The road is closed and bolted is the gate.
>
> So sing this song with me, my brothers dear,
> Your youth is gone, the happy time is done.
> Now you have reached your first and twentieth year,
> The next three years you are King Carol's son.

Doleful enough words, and a doleful melody went with them;
but even when she sang a song of cheer (I mean, as far as the words
went) there was a disconsolate catch in my mother's voice that would
have infused a cosmic dejection into "A-hunting We Will Go!" Uncle
Berel told me that as a girl my mother had been a jolly and lively
creature, which was as difficult for me to reconcile with my image of
her as it had been to identify the dashing cavalryman in the resplendent uniform with the careworn, overworked, embittered mender of
old shoes who was my father. It appalled me also to learn that once
upon a time my mother had been able to read and write, and had
corresponded with my father in their courtship days. I knew her
always as an analphabet, though wonderfully intelligent. Years of

sickness and the struggle for a livelihood, especially after we migrated from Rumania, first to France and then to England, had beaten
her down and atrophied, by disuse, such literacy as she had once
possessed.

My mother had a sweet voice and knew many songs. In her
girlhood in Jassy, and then during a stay in Bucharest, she had been
a frequenter of the plays and operas of Abraham Goldfaden, the
founder of the modern Yiddish theater. Besides those arias of his
which had become Yiddish folklore (he was a kind of higher-level
Stephen Foster to Eastern European Jewry), like *Rozhenkes un Mandlen*
(Raisins and Almonds), *A Pastuch Iz Amol Geven* (A Shepherd Once
There Was), and the like, she had memorized passages which have
not caught on in the same way, and which I have not heard again
except at long intervals, when there has been a Goldfaden revival.
(Just a few years ago, on the West Coast, a Hadassah group which
I addressed put on an excellent performance of Goldfaden's *Shulamis,*
and ladies on either side of me, seeing me wipe my eyes furtively,
said: "This must mean a great deal more to you than it can to us."
It did.) Whatever my mother sang was flooded with melancholy. The
cheerful Pilgrim's Chorus from *Shulamis* became a funeral march, so
that, when I heard it rendered with the swing and high spirit Goldfaden had undoubtedly intended for it, I was shocked as by an act
of irreverence. As to what my mother did with the intentionally
doleful passages, I can only say that by comparison the heartbreaking
recitative of Jeremiah's Book of Lamentations on the eve of the Black
Fast sounded like an epithalamium.

Uncle Berel told me that my mother began to change when she
had to settle in the village of Macin, where my father had set up a
shoe-repair shop. She was a city girl, accustomed to the movement
and gaiety of sizable places like Jassy and Bucharest and Braila. I
remember, with a vividness which places the experience beyond
suspicion of dream or the recounted incident, how my mother used
to sit on the stoop of our house in Macin and bewail her fate. Dead
from the front of the house the dirt road ran off toward the Primeria
(town hall), with Todoracu the barber on the right and *Sooreh die
blecherke* (Sarah the tinsmithess, i.e., the tinsmith's wife) on the left,
and farther along, also on the left, the synagogue and the *mikveh*
(ritual bathhouse). Our street, which was the dead end of the Primeria street, stretched one way to the Turkish quarter and the crossroads lantern which was the pride of Macin, the other way to the
glittering Teena (Danube), which made a bend and came round to the

back of our house. Across more than six decades I hear my mother keening as she stares away, holding my head in her lap: *"Gevald, vus bin ich farkrochen in der veest*—God help me, how did I land in this wilderness? Fields and fields and fields, peasants and peasants and peasants. And the nights! Death itself!" It is from that childhood experience, I sometimes think, that I have brought over my aversion to the deep countryside. I cannot bear its special silence. I am overcome by a shudder of fear when I have to walk alone at night along a deserted country road. It is not the fear of assault, or of some mishap, and certainly not of ghosts; it is an unnamable horror which sends me at top speed toward the light of a house and human company.

The memory of those locations—town hall, crossroads, synagogue, Turkish quarter, lantern—I checked with Uncle Berel long ago, and more recently with my older brother, Mendel, who was in Macin until the age of eleven. But the sound of my mother's voice and the words she uttered I shall never be able to check with anyone. The impression she left on me is in one sense a private affair, but in another sense the very opposite; for it is of the *Golus,* the Jewish Exile. Those words: *"Vus bin ich farkrochen in der veest!"* That voice, that sense of the lost and the exiled!

There comes over, from my mother, from my childhood, I should even say from my infancy, and also from my youth and from Uncle Berel, a feeling of the dominant spirit of *Golus* desolation, and behind it, faintly, I hear the wailing of the muezzin on the minaret which was visible from our yard. Uncle Berel's "Beh! They won't let us" seems in my recollection to echo a general hopelessness and listlessness with regard to the Jewish condition among the Jews of my early years. "They won't let us" and "Who are we to undertake such an extraordinary enterprise?" As my mother had lost the ability to read and write, so the Jews I grew up among seemed to have lost, also through transmitted disuse, their faith in themselves as the creators and managers of a Jewish homeland. For a moment Herzl had broken through the paralysis; then, with his death, ancient habit had reasserted itself and—as I was to learn in the Zionist movement—it would take decades of agitation and frightful cataclysms to rouse the will and establish the self-confidence of the Jewish people. I call to mind the legend of Tarquin the Proud and the nine Sibylline Books. The Erythrean Sibyl offered them to the Roman at a certain price; he refused; thereupon she burned three of them and offered the remainder at the same price. He refused again, and again she burned three books and offered the remainder at the same price. In the end Tarquin bought the three for the money which would have got him nine. So with the Jews; they dallied until they had to build their homeland after the two most vital Jewries—those of Poland and Russia—had been either destroyed or cut off from the rest of the world.

We Zionists talk in our propaganda of the electric shock which passed through world Jewry when England issued the Balfour Declaration in 1917, supporting the plan for a Jewish homeland in Palestine. Yes, the reaction was vivid. I also remember out of my childhood how Herzl's brief and blazing career produced a similar effect in our humble, uninstructed corner of the Jewish world, and how his sudden extinction plunged us into mourning (the cliché is in this case a literal description). However, I also remember that the wonder and worship that blossomed round Herzl had had no practical results in my environment—they seemed to be waiting for him to do everything himself, like a Messiah—nor were the results impressive anywhere outside the little band of passionate devotees. The masses did not move at Herzl's call, and they did not move even after the Balfour Declaration. And yet, speaking for the world I grew up in, and the world round Uncle Berel, it was not a fundamental indifference. It was in part distrust of the world at large ("They won't let us"), in part distrust of self ("Who are we, etc?") and in part that messianic attitude in a secular form. For Herzl had been a genuinely messianic apparition, secular in externals, folkloristically sacred in essence, and thwarted by death.

Uncle Berel was "electrified" and confused by the Balfour Declaration. I was at the time of its issuance already a soldier. I had by then worked for, among others, the Zionist Organization of America, the Jewish Education Bureau of New York, a raincoat manufacturer in Cleveland (that lasted two days: I left unobtrusively after having sewn some dozens of sleeve tabs into the armpit ends of the sleeves), and in the pit of the Goodyear Rubber plant in Akron (that lasted some months). I had done some hoboing in the Middle West and had written two novels, the manuscripts of which I was fortunate enough to lose, thereby saving myself a small fortune in stamps alone, and I had published several short stories in Mencken and Nathan's *Smart Set*. On one of my leaves I went with Uncle Berel to his restaurant. He wavered that evening between gratitude for the Balfour Declaration, suspicion of duplicity, distrust of destiny, and above all doubts as to the capacities of the Jewish people.

"A *nes*, a miracle," he said. "Excellent, *anshtendig*, decent," and so on, diminuendo. "Let's suppose that England means it and the other allies agree. Is it *bashert,* destined, and can our *Yiddalach* do it? *Es leigt zich nit oifn seichel*—it somehow doesn't make sense."

Somewhere along the line, in centuries of exile, humiliation, and everlasting displacement, the Jews seem to have formed an attachment to their misery. The sense of earthly futility, too, was to them part of Jewishness. There was not only acquiescence in their status, there was also a lachrymose enjoyment of it. On the evening to which I refer, the entertainer sang a Rumanian refrain I had heard from my mother. All I remember of the words is:

> *O saracu Plevna nostra,*
> *Ah, aman aman, ah, aman aman. . . .*

The first line means: "Alas, alas for our Plevna," and I take it to refer to the famous battle or battles of Plevna in the Turko-Russian war of 1877, in which Rumania had had a part ("Old, unhappy, far-off things and battles long ago"), and what the second line means I do not know. But I remember that in the song occurred the names of Osman Pasha and Skoboliev, and when she uttered them my mother made a gesture of horror. The song is also associated in my mind with one of the earliest, perhaps *the* earliest visual recollection out of my childhood—a squad of soldiers in dusty, gray-white uniforms marching past our house toward the Turkish quarter. In my mother's singing there was a great compassion for the soldiers, and a touch of despair at the bloody antics of the *goyim* in which Jews were compelled to join *mir nisht, dir nisht,* as Uncle Berel used to say. And both Uncle Berel and my mother had a deep-rooted if unformulated conviction that the world, with its privileges and triumphs, was not for the Jews until something like a messianic transformation had taken place.

From *Little Did I Know* (1963)

2 THE TWIG IS BENT

Statistically I am dead several times over. If Uncle Berel had been an actuary, he would have known that anyone born in 1895 in such advanced countries as England and America had an even chance of being alive at fifty; it was less than an even chance for one who was born and continued to live in Rumania. My mother bore nine children, three of whom died in infancy; two little brothers, Aaron and Naphthali, I never knew; I remember as in a vivid dream a sister called Bessie, and I remember the pall that fell on the house with her death. As regards the family, then, I had two chances in three of surviving my infancy, but that is only the beginning of the list of hazards.

I was born together with a twin sister, Hannah, who died in 1955. When we came into the world my mother had three infants and two youngsters to look after, and the double addition was too much for her. I was put out to a Turkish wet nurse who nearly settled the problem when I was a few months old. In letters my father wrote me shortly before his death in 1924, he told me how I peaked and pined and was discovered, on an unexpected visit, in such filth and misery that I was snatched back home. In respect to that episode alone, I overcame a ten-to-one hazard.

Now suppose my mother had not nagged my father to leave Rumania and I had stayed on there for the rest of my undetermined life; what would have been my chances of surviving the Hitler time, to say nothing of intervening dangers? Or suppose we had settled permanently in Paris, where we stayed for nearly a year before proceeding to Manchester, and suppose I had been a French conscript in the First World War; or suppose I had served in the British army instead of the American; or, serving in the American army, suppose I had been sent to the front instead of getting no nearer to it than the advanced zone, whence I was recalled to serve in G II, counterespionage. There were also many private narrow escapes in my life, though these are perhaps part of the general statistical table; once I nearly stepped into an elevator shaft on the twentieth floor when the elevator was not there, and once a farmer in Ohio shot at me when I was stealing peaches from his orchard. It was night, and he missed, but I heard the bullet like a mosquito near my ear, and I ran like mad. However I look at it, I am astonished at being here.

On the other hand, if I had defied statistics till now, statistics will turn their tables on me in the end. I shall assuredly die before my time. We all do, with an uncollected statistical life expectancy.

A more subtle statistical puzzle lies in the fact that I grew up into me and not somebody else. The probabilities pointed at a kind of me that depresses the me I became. For, granting me a normal span of life, what would have been my opportunities had my family stayed on, as the majority of Jews did, in Rumania? "Fancy," I often say to myself, "not having the treasures of the English language and literature to ransack! Fancy not to have known at first hand the greatness of England and America. All that I have read, all that I have seen,

> cities of men
> And manners, climates, councils, governments,

(a little exaggeration here), the spiritual and intellectual excitements which have not yet ceased to visit me, would have remained unrealized.

I became a socialist and atheist around the age of thirteen, whether before or after my *bar mitzvah* I cannot remember. Probably after, because, being a contumacious youngster, I would no doubt have refused to go through with the ceremony if I had considered it "intellectually dishonest."

But the evil seed sprouted before the ceremony; during my last months at *cheder* I was, with my pointed questioning and challenging of sacred things, the affliction of my *rebbe,* a large, fat, and decent man with a vast black beard, a hypochondriac wife, and no pedagogic skill whatsoever. That Manchester *cheder* on Waterloo Road might as a matter of fact just as well have been in Rumania for all the relationship it bore to the surrounding world: the front room of my *rebbe*'s house, thirty to forty boys between the ages of six and thirteen jammed into it, various groups chanting their lessons separately, a marvelously organized bedlam. And yet I am still troubled by my wicked behavior toward my *rebbe,* and if it sounds queer that one should brood occasionally on boyhood sins more than half a century old, we have St. Augustine's warrant for it; he in maturity remembered with passionate weeping how at the age of sixteen he had stolen some pears, not because, like me in Ohio, he had been hungry, but just for the hell of it. How much of "just for the hell of it" lingers in us till the end!

My *rebbe* was a man of learning and in some respects not more than two or three centuries behind the times. He taught me Hebrew so badly that I quickly and willingly forgot whatever I had picked up in seven years of *cheder* attendance. He was, however, a gifted storyteller, and when he went into the *midrashim* (the ancient, extra-biblical homiletic and folkloristic literature), he held us fascinated. He was equally effective when he expounded the *Pirke Avot* (Ethics of the Fathers, a section of the Talmud). But the *midrashim* and *Pirke Avot* came only once a week, the Saturday afternoon treat. He also expounded then the beauties of the ancient Jewish moral and civil codes; he dwelt on the laws of *Pe'ot,* the leaving of the corners of the harvest field to be gleaned by the widow, the orphan, and the stranger, and of the fruit that lay on the ground after a windfall. From the *Pirke Avot* I learned at the age of eight or nine that I would avoid sin and egotism if I remembered what my origin was—a putrid drop; also that he who puts on flesh is only providing food for worms. I must say that my *rebbe* did not seem to me to be troubled by this last bit of information. He was overweight and very fond of cookies and tea between regular meals. During the week he tried to drum *Chumash* (the Pentateuch) and Rashi (the great medieval commentator) into us by the brute force of repetition.

When I became a socialist, the laws of *Pe'ot* outraged me. Why should some men be so well off that the poor could subsist on their leavings, and why should the Law countenance this situation and even enable the rich man to collect heavenly merits by its means? I understood only much later that there was being implanted in me a deep regard for the moral element in ancient Jewish prescription and legislation, and I regret that I was not able to tell my *rebbe* of my change of view.

My conversion to socialism and atheism was the unexpected end result of an event that occurred when I was twelve and a half years old. I won a scholarship to the Manchester Secondary School. I think I was the first in our clan and in our whole Rumanian Jewish colony, then fairly new in Manchester, to perform the feat. It was a very good scholarship; free tuition for five years and an "Exhibition" of five pounds for the first year. My parents were awestruck by the generosity of England; they contrasted my good fortune with the melancholy experience of my two older brothers, who had topped their classes in the village school of Macin and had been harassed and insulted for their Jewish pushfulness. As for me, I celebrated the event by a revolution in my reading habits and in my thinking.

Until then I had devoured weekly ten or a dozen boys' magazines: *The Boys of St. Jim's, The Boy's Friend, The Boy's Leader, The Union Jack, The Gem, The Marvel,* and the like. Since these magazines used to cost an English penny (two cents) each, and my weekly pocket money, delivered every Saturday afternoon, was a ha'penny (half-penny), I had to enter an organization of twenty boys or more, nearly all from homes as poor as mine, and all equally addicted to this type of literature. Two of us bought one magazine and twenty of us would have ten magazines to pass around. Occasionally double-numbers were issued in gorgeously colored covers, price twopence, and if ordinary numbers were musts, double-numbers were double-musts. We usually managed somehow, and gorged on the thirty-two-page issues. When the news arrived that I had won the scholarship, I was filled with a sudden horror of my wasted life. I made a solemn vow to put away folly and frivolity and to prepare myself for greatness.

Whether or not I immediately began to ply my *rebbe* with outright socialistic and atheistic questions I do not, as I have said, remember; if I did not, I sailed very close to the wind, an exceedingly ill wind, for this I do remember: my *rebbe* foretold that I would come to a spectacularly bad end, and that in my downgoing I would involve large numbers of Jews, if not the entire Jewish people, and probably a contingent of Gentiles as well. In our Manchester-Rumanian semi-ghetto, socialism and atheism were blindly but not quite unjustly yoked together, and with them, not quite so justly, a disrespect for the decencies and for the welfare of Jewry.

It was a predominantly unhappy time for me, though shot through with ecstatic interludes. I was frustrated in my search for knowledge. The new reading material I hankered for was expensive, and the juvenile section of the public library did not carry it. There was in those days a publishing enterprise called The Sixpenny Rationalist Reprints—Herbert Spencer, Ernst Haeckel, Joseph McCabe among others. But who had sixpence? The bloated rich. There was also a secondhand bookstall in an alley near Shudehill, where tattered copies of the Reprints could be had for twopence. Twopence was my weekly allowance after I had won the scholarship, and though I earned or cadged a few pennies now and again, I never had enough. In this new world I had entered there were no companions with whom to pool resources. I used to borrow the Reprints at a penny a time; I also used to borrow surreptitiously. I have long been convinced that the cadaverous young man who ran the bookshop knew all about my unpaid borrowings, and it has occurred to me that such business practices accounted for his cadaverous appearance.

I resented my poverty and was in some ways ashamed of it. I could not make friends with more prosperous fellow high-school students. The front room of our house was used by my father as his shoe-repair shop, while everybody else's front room was a parlor. There wasn't a room for talking in.

My deepest source of unhappiness was spiritual. I wrestled in the usual adolescent fashion with ontological problems which gave a nihilistic background to my social and moral thinking. I also dabbled in, rather than studied, astronomy. I managed to get hold of an ancient telescope with a one-and-a-half inch aperture, and constructed a clumsy hand-worked equatorial which moved so jerkily that it was worse than nothing, except for the pride it gave me in my workmanship; but I never went beyond the mathematics of the three Keplerian laws. It was all loosely observational, a sidereal Cook's tour, watching for Halley's comet and sketching the mountains of the moon and looking for nebulae and asteroids. I had unforgettable moments, and I never see the Pleiades without recalling the cry of terror and bliss that escaped me when I first turned my ramshackle little telescope on them. But as I probed the heavens I saw our planet, our solar system, and our galaxy shrink into insignificance. The clockwork of the stars and planets was reflected back for me into human affairs, exposing will and purpose as illusions. Life was meaningless and all our striving a vain gesticulation: slogans, movements, dreams of human improvement, martyrdoms—nothing but a predetermined jigging of matter. The greatest thinkers of the ages were in no better case than the most benighted clods, and to the wisest I conceded at best only a superior sophistication in self-delusion.

Among the first paperbacks I bought—I shall return to the occasion—were certain works by one Robert Blatchford, a widely admired socialist and science popularizer, and those that left the profoundest impression on me were his *Merrie England, Britain for the British,* and *Not Guilty, a Defense of the Bottom Dog.* Blatchford's name was always linked with two others, Victor Grayson and H. M. Hyndman. They were the terrible trio of revolutionary England fifty-odd years ago. Grayson was a young socialist member of Parliament, Hyndman was the elderly intellectual leader of the British Labour Party, which had just begun to make a respectable showing in the House of Commons. To me they were the Trinity, and their fates were various. Grayson disappeared from England and not much later died obscurely in a little town in Australia. Blatchford, who at one time edited the socialist daily, *The Clarion,* became a reactionary and a spiritualist after the First World War. Only Hyndman, the most substantial of the three, carried on consistently until his death in 1921. By then much had happened to me. I had settled in America and established my friendship with Uncle Berel; I had done my two years in the American army, I had been a secretary on the Morgenthau Commission which investigated the Polish pogroms of 1919. I had been demobilized in Paris, where I had opened a public stenography office for Americans, I had served as interpreter on the Allied Reparations Commissions in Berlin and Vienna, I had mastered Yiddish and was learning Hebrew, I had married, and I had returned to America with my first publishable novel.

But to go back. Blatchford's effect on me in my adolescence was shattering. He was a Sinaitic voice and everything he said was law. I remember, fifty years after I last read him, phrases of his which were like hammer blows. On the irreconcilability of interest between worker and employer he quoted a Hindu proverb: "I am bread, thou art the eater, how can peace be between us?" On the unsuspected dormant strength of the working classes he said: "They are like the lions in the zoo; every keeper knows that they can, with a sudden effort, break the bars of the cages; but the lions don't know it." On the problem of the lowest kind of labor in a socialist state and who would do it, he said: "We can make it attractive by shortening the hours. But at least we won't see fat aldermen guzzling oxtail soup at dinner while factory girls starve." I am not sure of the exact phrasing, but I am sure of the key words. I went about repeating them somberly to myself. "Fat aldermen guzzling oxtail soup!" What a revolting picture! And the juxtaposition with starving factory girls! I took it that oxtail soup was the most luxurious and expensive kind of soup in existence; not necessarily tasty, but gratifying to the sense of power and exclusiveness, like peacocks' noses at Roman banquets. That aldermen were fat, and that they guzzled, was self-understood; I was filled with indignation and disgust. Equally self-understood, because Blatchford said so—also because it was such an appealing thought—was the lion's tragic unawareness of its own powers; and I tagged on to Blatchford's scientific discovery some lines from Shelley:

> Rise like lions after slumber,
> In unvanquishable number;
> Ye are many, they are few.

At thirteen I became a stump speaker for the Socialist Party, stupefying the neighborhood and vindicating my *rebbe*. I also went out, as a prodigy, to neighboring towns: Oldham, Wigan, Altringham, Irlam o' the Heights (pronounced Irlamathites, like a sect, or a Biblical tribe). At street corners near and far I thundered in a treble against Winston Churchill when, having been promoted to a cabinet post in Asquith's government, he contested a by-election in Manchester. I defeated him. But it was his Tory opponent, Joynson-Hicks, who got in, and not the socialist I had supported, a certain Daniel whose second name I have forgotten. The Churchill supporters sang, to the tune of "Tramp, Tramp, Tramp, the Boys Are Marching":

> Vote, vote, vote for Winston Churchill.
> He is sure to win the day.
> Don't be fooled by Joynson-Hicks
> And his dirty Tory tricks. . . .

I sang with the socialists:

> Dare to be a Daniel,
> Dare to stand alone. . . .

(which we pretty nearly did) and:

> The people's flag is deepest red,
> It's shrouded oft our martyred dead;
> And ere their limbs grew stiff and cold
> Their heart's blood dyed its every fold.

What the victorious Tories sang I do not remember.

At one point in my earlier socialist career I was a fiery supporter of Lloyd George, the Liberal, because he advocated the nationalization of land. The Liberals had a quite extraordinary song which even today would smack of extreme leftism if not of barricades. Like many English political songs, it was borrowed, as to melody, from America —this time "Marching Through Georgia":

> The land, the land, 'twas God who made the land!
> The land, the land, the ground on which we stand!
> Why should we be beggars with the ballot in our hand?
> God made the land for the people.

My high-school and university years were filled with political and intellectual excitement, and with extremes of mood that were almost manic-depressive. I got to know the Lancashire weavers and their clog-and-shawl-wearing wives, and I conceived an enduring affection for certain little places and groups—warm, eager, hopeful talk, kindly faces and bad teeth, fish and chips after the meetings, or sometimes only chips carried out of the chip shop on a piece of newspaper. But I was not at ease in my early socialist phase. I suffered from recurrent longings for a Jewish way of life. I was troubled less by my atheistic than by my socialist philosophy. "Jewish atheist," while obviously unorthodox, was somehow not impossible; "Jewish socialist," with its implication of cosmopolitanism and rejected Jewishness, was. I lived in a marvelous muddle, which I shall describe further on.

In my post-high-school socialist phase I was acutely uncomfortable for other reasons. At the university, to which I won a three-year scholarship at sixty pounds a year (a large sum in those days), my socialist comrades exasperated me by their dogmatism, by their intellectual bullying (I was all persuasiveness, of course), and above all by their addiction to the phrase: "For the simple reason that . . ." The simple reason was never satisfactory; besides, "simple" was a reflection on my intelligence; worst of all, they were always implying that a good socialist never asked fundamental questions.

Among my comrades in those days was a volcanic, diminutive redhead, Ellen Wilkinson, who ultimately became a cabinet minister in the Labour government. Another was a tall, lean young man with a death's-head face, J. T. Walton-Newbold. He told us that he was going to die soon of consumption, and he looked it. He broke that promise and many others. He, too, entered Parliament and later went from socialism to Communism, from Communism to Fascism. Wilkinson and Walton-Newbold were ready to stake their lives on the prophecy that no great war would ever be fought in an industrialized area; the proof was the last imperialist war, the Russo-Japanese, which had been fought out in the empty spaces of the Far East. War, they said, there would be, but not where productive property would be endangered; the *Pax Capitalisma,* an echo of the *Pax Romana,* forbade it.

I, on the other hand, was ready to stake my life, or at any rate talk others to death, on the thesis that there would not be any kind of war any more. Let a war be declared, I said, and the workers, the toiling masses, would rise in their might—workers never rose in anything else for me—and pull the imperialist conspirators from their place of power to establish universal and everlasting brotherhood and peace.

My sharpest disagreements with my fellow socialists were provoked by their rigid historical and economic determinism. I agreed that socialism was the only conceivable moral order, but how could that which was automatically inevitable also be moral? I continued to chant loyally: "The nationalization of the instruments of production, distribution, and exchange," but in spite of despondent lapses into a wider mechanistic philosophy—during which I hadn't the slightest interest in mankind's future or my own—I found the "inevitability" of socialism not only incompatible with a theory of morals, but personally offensive as well. If the world was moving to perfection under an iron law and at its own pace, it needed no help from me; I was making a fool of myself arguing with people to bring about what they could neither accelerate nor delay. "Inevitability" took the heart out of me.

This frustration did not face me in Zionism. Herzl had, to be sure, declared the Jewish state to be a historic inevitability, but Zionists were not as a rule given to historic determinism. We believed that a Jewish state ought to be created in Palestine; to work for it was right and proper whether or not we succeeded. We differed in our estimates of our chances, but we were content with a belief in the feasibility of our program. Those that went beyond—and there were many—appealed to faith, not to historic determinism.

In New York I discovered for the first time that there was such a thing as a socialist-Zionist movement. There may have been a branch of it in Manchester, but I do not remember coming across it. The Zionists I knew were anti-socialist, the Jewish socialists anti-Zionist. But more pleasing was the discovery that one could be a socialist within the general Zionist movement, which was strongly tinged with liberalism. One could, through the Zionist congresses and funds, support socialist-oriented enterprises in Palestine, and thus work for socialism at large by creating a socialist Jewish state. I did not join the socialist-Zionist party. I had had enough of "inevitability."

In our few exchanges on Zionism and socialism I prophesied to Uncle Berel that a Jewish homeland would, when it came into being, play its part in making a better world, and in my new-found passion for the Bible I quoted: "For from Zion shall go forth the Law and the word of God from Jerusalem." I kept my fingers crossed, as it were, for the second half of this famous verse, for after all I was an atheist. I interpreted "Law" in my own way, the law of economic equality.

Well, here we have a Jewish homeland, which was something of a mirage fifty years ago. It is a remarkable phenomenon—certainly, despite many defects, a progressive force in world affairs; but it is not socialistic or ever likely to be of its own free will. Nor do I want it to be, for I no longer believe that "the nationalization of the instruments of production, distribution, and exchange" is the best managerial formula for a country's affairs—or even a good one. I don't believe it to be workable, at least not until human beings are at such an advanced moral stage that system is irrelevant. What is more, I don't believe that "the toiling masses" want all-round economic equality; they want a decent life, a sufficiency with security, and freedom spiced with the play of reasonable differentiations; and if they can get all this without economic equality, they will gladly concur.

In this they are morally right, with a profound intuitive and practical rightness. I see the problem now in a totally different light. It is a destructive baseness which impels men to say: "This is what I want for myself, and I won't let others have more."

Long after I had seen Uncle Berel for the last time I came across a passage from Karl Marx which helped me to crystallize permanently my rejection of economic egalitarianism:

A house may be large or small, but as long as the surrounding houses are equally small, it satisfies all social requirements of a dwelling place. But let a palace arise by the side of this small house, and it shrinks from a house to a hut. The smallness of the house now indicates that its occupant is allowed to have either very few claims or none at all; *and however high it may shoot up with the progress of civilization,* if the neighboring palace shoots up in the same or greater proportion, the occupant of the small house will always find himself *more uncomfortable, more discontented. . . .* [My italics. M.S.]

What a ghastly indictment of human nature, what a despairing prospect for the human species! I know it is not easy to define "sufficiency," but I am sure that if a man has to survey his neighbor's portion before he can decide whether his own is adequate, the very concept of "sufficiency" disappears; the principle of measurement has ceased to be appetitional satisfaction and has become envy. But envy is unappeasable; it is watchful, touchy, self-promoting; it discovers differences where there are none, so that if objective economic equality could be enforced, the feeling of it would not follow. Thus the demand for an unattainable feeling of equality becomes the enemy of an attainable satisfaction; it is the sacrifice of humanity on the altar of a nobly immoral principle.

Together with the chanted "nationalization of" etc., other slogans of the early days have taken on a hollow sound. "Workers of the world, unite! You have nothing to lose but your chains . . ." When the slogan was coined, a hundred years ago, it was a barely permissible propaganda exaggeration; by the early part of the twentieth century it was a disastrous falsehood. The German and Italian workers had something to lose, and they lost it to Hitler and Mussolini. The workers of Russia had less to lose, except in prospect, and it will be some time before they realize what they lost unnecessarily in order to improve their condition.

But I have more than that to say about the socialist movement. If its theoretical base now looks to me like nonsense, I am still filled with admiration for its practical achievements and with gratitude for the part it has played in my life. The modern Western world would today be a charnel house if the socialist movement had not intervened. Its courage and idealism, if accompanied by wrong reasoning, sprang from the right moral instinct. Imperfect our modern Western world certainly is, but one can only think with horror of what it would have been without the great socialist movement. The classic capitalists were mostly horrible, conscienceless men. Their historic function was to make the breakthrough, to squeeze out of the workers the indispensable accumulation of investment capital. Driven by obsessive greed and lust for power, they performed their function with furious—and unnecessary—brutality. The pace could and should have been slower; the withholding of surplus profit need not have been so extortionate. When the breakthrough came, the capitalists had no intention of calling a halt; they wanted the accumulation to go on forever, to their own undoing and that of society. Their kind is still with us, an unteachable, irreclaimable minority; they are the blind troglodytes who fought the New Deal at every step and, ragingly impotent to nullify it, will continue to fight its extension. (To use an Irishism: there are some people who will not thank you for saving their lives until they are dead.) But if they are a minority today, that is due to the socialist movement and its wide peripheral influence; and if the socialist movement is everywhere in decline, it is because the creative changes it has forced through have outdated it.

What a scurvy trick history has played on the Communists, and no wonder they loathe the socialist movement with a convulsive loathing. It was their original hope to step in where the capitalists had done all the dirty work and take over as angelic liberators. But, being able to seize power only in pre-capitalist countries, they are forced to do their own dirty work, and they are doing it no better than the early capitalist commissars. No, they are not doing it as well; they are forcing the pace even more brutally, and they have repressed the inventiveness and resourcefulness of individual competitive greed.

I remember with even greater admiration the socialist-Zionists who, under infinitely difficult conditions, prevented the nascent Jewish homeland from developing into an early-capitalist exploitative state based on cheap labor. Israel would not have its place among the world democracies had it not been for the primitive *kvutzot,* the later *kibbutzim* (it is well to note that this word is now international), and the workers' cooperatives. In Israel, too, the socialist movement has completed its mission. The labor leaders of Israel still call themselves socialists, but it is an honorific title; they have no program for universal nationalization. The *kibbutzim* themselves are becoming village corporations with equality for all members, a decent form of life which somehow, to the distress of the "socialist" leaders, is not spreading. And in America the socialist-Zionist movement which is committed to the support of "socialist" Israel is entirely middle class.

What remains in me of my one-time socialism? Only the moral element and a certain, informed alertness to capitalist hypocrisies and dodges. My social philosophy is an amalgam of what my *rebbe* and the prophets (it is a long time since I have winced at "the word of God") taught me and what I have read, from my youth onward, in leftist books, including Karl Marx and Engels. I am what Communists call a "reformist" and a "rotten liberal." My views on the techniques of social amelioration come from a layman's acquaintance with economics, history, psychology, etc. My instincts are with the worker as against the employer simply because the employer is as a rule better off. But I no longer believe, as I used to, that the worker is always right vis-à-vis the employer; and I am grateful that workers have now improved their condition to the point where they can sometimes be in the wrong.

I also brought out of the poverty of my childhood and youth, and out of later economic hardship, a distaste for rich people, though, like the anti-Semite with regard to Jews, I make exceptions. Some of my best friends . . . Also a distaste for expensively elegant women and women who like to have men spend money on them, either from greediness or as a lift to their vanity. I could never afford their company, which I would not accept as charity. I have no pleasure in posh hotels and restaurants. Most of all I dislike "easy spenders"— who are seldom easy givers; they show a contempt for money out of excessive deference to it; they stand treat to those who have no need of it because they want to be appreciated "on a higher plane." And that contempt of theirs for money is in more ways than one a contempt for human beings—for the careworn who must watch their pennies, for the fools who are impressed by easy spending. Easy spending and easy giving are psychologically as well as arithmetically in conflict; an easy spender wants to be surrounded by good humor and good fellowship, the sight of misery upsets him without moving him.

I often wish I could have talked all these things over with my *rebbe,* Kalman Moskovitch. It is not unlikely that if I had argued with him from the moral postulates he taught rather than as a "scientific" socialist, we would have found much in common; but the only time I saw him after I left Manchester was not propitious for leisurely discussion.

It was in 1929, in Palestine, as it was then called, two days after the bloody anti-Jewish riots of that year. On August 25 I set out with Colonel Frederick Kisch, the Palestine chairman of the Jewish Agency, on a tour of the cities and settlements. I had put on my old American uniform, hoping to impress, if not intimidate, any Arabs we might encounter on the road, and we carried revolvers. We went north from Jerusalem, visited Beth Alpha and Hephzibah, the two little *kibbutzim* at the foot of Mount Gilboa that had stood off an Arab invasion of the Valley of Jezreel. Then we proceeded to Safad in Galilee, where a number of old people had been murdered.

I knew that my *rebbe* had settled some years before in that ancient and sacred city of the Kabbalists, and when I asked Colonel Kisch whether we might not spend ten minutes looking for him, so that I might send a message to Manchester, he readily agreed.

We found him in one of the narrow, crooked, sloping alleys on whose gray, crumbling walls centuries of Jewish learning, piety, poverty, and messianic conjuration are almost visibly encrusted. When he came to the door I recognized him at once, though his beard was now completely snow-white. He stared at me, puzzled, until I said, in my recently acquired Sephardic Hebrew—a pronunciation he would associate with Christian priests: *'Rebbe, eincha makir oti*—don't you recognize me?'' Then his eyes brimmed over, he uttered a loud cry, and answered in Yiddish (for like all religious Jews in those days he reserved Hebrew only for prayer and study): *''Moishe! Redst takke loshen koidesh, ober fort vi a goy*—you do indeed speak Hebrew, but it's still like a Gentile!''

From *Little Did I Know* (1963)

3 THE ERUPTION

The city of Paris has been a recurrent marker in my life. I was there first from my fifth to my sixth year in transit to England with my family; a second time in the summer of 1914; a third from 1919 to 1920, during and following the negotiations of the Versailles peace treaty; a fourth in the summer of 1939, at the outbreak of the Second World War. These are the sojourns with significance; there have also been many brief visits.

I give the first place to my 1914 sojourn, which occurred in my twentieth year, when I left Manchester for Paris because I was going to be a Writer. I did not make the decision to be a Writer; it had made itself in my boyhood, probably in the fifth grade of school. I could of course have been a writer anywhere, but a Writer only in Paris. What kind of Writing was I going to do? Well, poetry, novels, essays, short stories, plays—I was good at everything. I was prepared to wait for recognition, even anxious to; immediate success would have been a reflection on my genius. I did not, however, aspire to the supreme tribute of lifelong starvation and obscurity; a year or two in a garret would satisfy my self-esteem and add the indispensable cachet to my life story.

From this point of view the beginning was inauspicious; I did not come within hailing distance of starvation. The day after my arrival in Paris in June 1914, with two shillings or so in my pocket, I was able to write home that I was profitably employed not by one newspaper but by two, and under conditions—which I did not describe—the most conducive to my literary freedom. I was, in fact, selling the Paris editions of the *Daily Mail* and the *New York Herald* mornings at the

Gare St. Lazare where the suburban trains brought in the American and English commuters. I cleared seven or eight francs a day for an hour's work (nearer three with the coming and going), and the rest of the day I was free to read, write, gulp in life, invoke the ghosts of Murger and de Musset and congratulate humanity and myself on our successful rendezvous. The sinister omen escaped my attention: selling newspapers in one's youth *might* be the prologue to the acquisition of great wealth, the tradition did not link it with high literary achievement.

Thirty-five to forty francs a week and no work on Saturdays and Sundays! It was more than a competence in the Paris of that time; it was affluence. At 33 rue des Ecoles, just off the boulevard St. Michel —beg pardon, the Boul' Miche' (and where else would I be living?) —I paid seven francs a week for a room on the fifth floor, and had my shoes shined every morning, no doubt to their great astonishment, unaccustomed as they were to more than a flick of the brush every week or two. Breakfast, a buttered croissant and coffee, was fifteen centimes; lunch eighty, with tip; supper a franc ten, *pain à discrétion* (all the bread you wanted). Total, rent included, three francs five centimes a day, leaving me with a discretionary surplus, as I think they call it, of over two francs a day. Newspapers cost me nothing, I read my own. But there was in the France of those days a kind of Haldemann Julius enterprise, the French classics in newspaper form at ten centimes each, and I bought and devoured three or four a week. What else did I need? Writing paper and pencils and, yes, a bottle of *pinard* daily, at seventy-five centimes. I could also afford an evening *apéritif*.

Every morning, after work, I wrote; and every afternoon, except when it rained, I lay in the grass in the Jardin du Luxembourg and read, and sipped, and made notes, or broke off to meditate, or to watch the puppet showman delight an audience of juveniles in the charge of mothers and nurses with a performance of *Jean le Redoutable.* I would have liked to come close enough to enjoy the show itself, but I was ashamed to betray my infantile taste, and I would have had to drop something in the puppeteer's hat. On rainy days I was perched in my garret—infinite room in a nutshell. And there were times when I needed infinite room, when I felt I was about to explode with sheer joy into the dimensions of a sizable nebula.

There was a history behind that onset of euphoria. I had just finished college, that is, I had come to the end of the three-year scholarship awarded me by the city of Manchester, and I had not taken a degree. Not that I had been wanting in application; it was only that I had applied myself with immense if unsystematic industry to anything but the subjects I had enrolled for (French perhaps an exception). I had learned by heart scores of pages of poetry, not one page of physics formulas; I had read Shaw, Wells, Bennett, Galsworthy, Conrad, Rolland, Hamsun, Hauptmann, instead of *Beowulf* and Langland. I had had fits of Plato, Kant, Bradley, Hume, and there was my political activity. All this not because physics or *Beowulf* bored me, but because I was in reaction from competitive study.

From my thirteenth year on, when I got my scholarship to high school, I had hounded myself for good marks because there was no other road for me to an education. At fifteen I had been awarded a "bursary" of fifteen pounds a year for two years; without that six shillings a week I might have had to leave school. I used only one year of the bursary, for at sixteen I won the *Grand Prix* of our junior academic world, three years at the university with sixty pounds a year, enough to keep me and pay for my books. By that time my soul had become warped with the anguish of waiting for examination results.

This is not an exaggeration. When even today I read of a student committing suicide because of failure in an examination, a throb of retroactive terror goes through me. I remember coming home from important examinations, creeping upstairs and lying down on my bed sick in all my body. Or I would walk for hours in unfamiliar streets, muttering. I had failed! My papers had been starred with idiotic answers, and they sprang up before me the moment I left the examination hall. On bad nights I still have nightmares of a peculiar kind which have their origin in that post-examination misery, and I come out of them in a sweat. When, a few years ago, I saw a similar experience portrayed with great skill in Ingmar Bergman's *Wild Strawberries,* I trembled with terror.

I did not actually fail at the university; it was simply that my credits did not add up to a degree, and at the time it seemed a terrible thing to me that I should have to go through life without a B.A. after my name. Against this, however, and overwhelming it completely, was my graduation into freedom. I was no longer a schoolboy, watched and weighed and graded at regular intervals. The world was my examiner now, and I didn't have to be *better* than anyone now; I just had to do my best.

There was another reason for my happiness, deeper, revealed to me later. I was coming out of the phase of philosophic materialism

I have described, alien to my type of mind. I had never accepted it completely or consistently, but there had been enough of it to bring on periodic depressions. My love of poetry was one expression of my rejection of it. I was going to find my spiritual roots before long, but for the time being I was at large, bursting with unchanneled mental energies and reacting to intimations of approaching self-discovery. Some years were to pass before I committed myself to Jewishness, much nourishment had to come up from the roots; I had to learn much in the way of Yiddish and Hebrew and Jewish history, subjects in which I was an illiterate. Thus, my first published books were not on Jewish themes; those waited for almost a decade.

When I look back at those 1914 summer months in Paris, it seems to me that all unsuspecting I was acting out in person a charade of the general self-deception of the time. I was living blithely in a world that was about to burst apart, never to be reassembled. Under our feet tremendous pressures were at the detonation point, and not the slightest tremor reached our consciousness. There were of course criers of doom; but there always are, and one never knows when the cries are timely. There are always Columbuses, real and fake, and they look alike. If you pick out a real one it is largely by luck, which you later represent as shrewdness, or vision. So one plays it safe, one closes one's ears, and as a rule one is of course right. It seems that thus far human history has been unable to proceed in any other fashion. Besides, even the Columbuses themselves never know where they are going.

In that fatuous world of June and July 1914, so complacent, so self-assured, in that massively self-deluding world, I was playing my own silly little game of make-believe. Murger and de Musset! Why, their world was deader than a doornail in 1914—that is, if it had ever been alive. The Latin Quarter, like its imitators everywhere, was largely a sham; the streets swarmed with poets, painters, sculptors, musicians, writers; perhaps one in a thousand meant business. As with the Columbuses and the political prophets, there was no distinguishing between the young dedicated artificer and the windbag. I ought to add that five years later, when I was again in Paris, I still believed for a while that to be a Writer one simply *had* to be in Paris.

I have often wondered why my childhood year in Paris, in 1900 and 1901, has left with me nothing more than factual little memories, unattended by nostalgia. We were very poor there, but not poorer than during our first year or two in Manchester. I remember going in 1914 to the rue Joseph Dijon, in the Clignancourt district, where we had lived, but I was not stirred. We had occupied a room and a half on the ground floor of Number 23; in the half room at the front my father had worked and slept; in the living room at the back my mother and the four children had slept. My mother used to take in sewing and work late into the night; I can still see the shadow of her hand sweep up and down the wall. Hannah and I used to get free lunches at school (Dora was too young for school) and I loathed them; they made me sick—all except the potato soup, and how relieved I was when that came round.

I must have known a lot of French by the time we went to England, but it faded out; I had to learn it all over again, but, as with my Yiddish, there was no doubt a permanent residue. Blocks of meaningless syllables were lodged in my mind, such as my brother Mendel saying: *"Lepattronnaypalla,"* which I have deciphered as *"le patron n'est pas là."* There was a snowfall, and we sang in school:

> *Larnairzher, larnairzher,*
> *Tombofflonker, tombofflonker*

That, I have decided, must have been:

> *La neige, la neige*
> *Tombe en flocons, tombe en flocons*

One look at the rue Joseph Dijon was enough. I cannot recall having gone that summer to the Louvre, or the Tour Eiffel, or the Sacré Coeur, or any other of the sights. My pictures are of the entrances to the Gare St. Lazare, of my tiny room, of the swarming boulevard St. Michel, and above all of the lawns in the Luxembourg Gardens; and all of them are etched in my mind with a surrealistic sharpness which has survived all subsequent returns to them.

When the explosion came, its significance was, as everyone remembers or has read, recognized or guessed at by only a few. War! Ridiculous and unbelievable! All (as we chanted in chorus) because of a shot fired in Sarajevo; because of bumbling, panicky politicians, Austrian, German, Russian, French, English, prisoners of antiquated modes of thought, with antiquated institutions called armies at their command. Hadn't Norman Angell just proved conclusively in *The Great Illusion* that war was an anachronism, as costly to the victor as to the vanquished, and that colonies were liabilities? I myself had made many speeches to that effect to my socialist audiences. This thing was simply inadmissible. In a few weeks, a few months at the outside, the peoples would come to their senses; the damned foolishness would be over by Christmas; the workers would rise in their might; we would take up where we had left off. You couldn't stop the world's progress, you know.

My indiscriminate memory retains words, phrases, scenes, incidents. At street corners crowds on their way to work in the early morning would stop for a short songfest (a lovely Parisian custom) led by a man on a box selling sheet music. One of the instantaneous successes of that time is still with me.

> *Un bruit frappe l'espace,*
> *C'est celui du canon,*
> *Qui vient avec audace*
> *Troubler les nations.*
> *Vont-ils longtemps,*
> *Ces Allemands,*
> *Nous entraîner vers la fournaise?*
> *Mais sans broncher*
> *Sachons marcher*
> *Quand retentit la Marseillaise!*

On the wall of the Sarah Bernhardt theater someone had scribbled in chalk:

> *Aux abeilles les fleurs,*
> *Aux Français l'honneur;*
> *Et pour ne rien perdre*
> *Aux Allemands la merde*

A paroxysm of war fever gripped the country, or at least the city, which I was able to observe at first hand. Good God! What was happening to common sense, to the working class, to civilization, to my *vie de bohème?*

On the evening of August 2 I sat at an outdoor café on the boulevard des Italiens. I had been sitting at another café nearby, a day or two earlier, when I heard the shot that killed Jean Jaurès, the great socialist, one of my idols, for his opposition to the extension of the conscription period. On that second evening I was remembering the agitation that boiled along the streets, the incredulousness, the rage —and with them the consolatory cries: "This does it! This will show the world what kind of people warmongers are. Jaurès! With your martyr's death you have crowned your life work. There will be no more war!" This I was remembering, and war was here.

A black, roaring mass came down on us like a flood from the direction of the Porte St. Martin. It stretched from wall to wall, sweeping back the traffic, upsetting, smashing, and trampling on chairs and tables, carrying along those who did not escape into doorways or side streets. A tremendous rhythmic howling went up from it:

Hein-hein-hein! Hoo! Hoo!
Hein-hein-hein! Hoo! Hoo!

(The rhythm was that of *Al-gé-rie Française!*)

I was not among those that escaped. I wanted to know what this thing was, and what the howling meant. I found myself linked arm in arm with two young Frenchmen, of whom I remember only the one on the right, an undersized boy, with thin face and bulging eyes. The

Hein-hein-hein! Hoo! Hoo!

resolved itself into:

A Berlin! Tous! Tous!

and out of politeness, out of timidity, out of whatever it was, I began to chant with them, feeling like a fool.

A Berlin! Tous! Tous!

As we drew close to the Place de l'Opéra, another chorus swelled on us from behind, mingling with ours and overwhelming it. At first it sounded like:

Ombébého! Ombébého! Ombé:
Ombébého! Ombébého! Ombé!

That resolved itself into:

Conspuez Guillaume! Conspuez Guillaume! Conspuez!

A curious and beastly tickling of excitement, which made me feel like an even bigger fool, was manifesting itself in my viscera. The boy on my right flung his head from side to side. In another minute

or two, I thought, I too was going to have a fit. As we turned off into
the rue Royale, a third chorus was sent forward to us from the rear:

C'est l'Alsace et la Lorraine,
C'est l'Alsace qu'il nous faut!
Ah-ah-ah-oh!

Other crowds, converging from the Left Bank and down the
Champs Elysées, joined with ours in the Place de la Concorde, and
a wild demonstration was staged before the statue of Strassburg,
which had been in mourning for over fifty years.

I had been at demonstrations before, election crowds and political rallies. I remember how, when it was a question of increasing the
Royal Navy by eight battleships, there was great agitation, and at one
very large political rally a speaker who opposed the increase was
silenced for several minutes by an audience which chanted nothing
but:

We want eight!
And we won't wait!

I remember other, similar occasions, but I had never known anything
quite like this. The beastly tickling in my stomach was spreading
through me; it threatened to develop into a maniacal seizure. I fought
it down, I fought it back, repeating to myself something like: "Idiot!
You need Alsace and Lorraine like a hole in the head!" And it was
amazing how this obvious fact refused to stay put in front of my
mind, how it kept wriggling away out of my grip, as if it suffered
acute anguish when it was looked at.

The mob! That was where I first met it in its naked form. The
mob! At its most "useful" it is like a gangster whom we hire to rid
us of another gangster, and who takes over in his place, remaining
a gangster still.

I am prone to read premonitions into my memories; I may be
wrong in thinking that this incident in Paris gave me my first conscious feel of mob psychology; but I cannot be wrong in thinking that
the incident was to stand out for me in years to come as the prototype
of all the mob scenes, all the mob forces, that have been involved in
the shaping of recent history. Not that the mob is a new thing. Moses
several thousands of years ago sternly warned his people against it!
"Thou shalt not follow a multitude to do evil." He did not, by way
of balance, issue the positive command: "Thou shalt follow a multitude to do good." Goodness cannot issue from mob intoxication.

Before the twentieth century, mob manipulation had not become a science, with psychologists and scenarists at its command. What I saw in Paris that evening was primitive and, I believe, relatively spontaneous. What we have seen and heard of since then in the way of mobs is almost in another category; and what our children and grandchildren may yet see is something we seldom think of; for though there is much proper concern about the feeding and housing of a world population of six billion, or ten billion, little thought is given to guarding against mob psychology when America will have a population of half a billion and China of a billion and a half.

I used to think that creators of mob psychologies—and for that matter nearly all those who held what I considered reactionary views —were consciously wicked men, *salauds* (sons-of-bitches, Sartre's favorite word). I was still of that conviction five years later, during my second long stay in Paris, in 1919, when in American uniform I was working in the Hôtel Crillon, one of the headquarters of the peace delegations. But I was myself in a mood of mob enthusiasm for Wilson and the League of Nations, and of hatred of Clemenceau and Lloyd George (Orlando made no impression on me). I had a genuine personal hatred of Lloyd George for his Khaki Election campaign, held soon after the victory (Hitler was to write admiringly of Lloyd George as a master demagogue in *Mein Kampf*). But the chief focus of my fury and contempt was a certain Sir Eric Geddes, one of Lloyd George's lieutenants, because of the powerful slogan he coined at the time: "We're going to squeeze the Germans until the pips squeak!"

That stunned me. I held Germany to be more guilty than the Allies, I thought some reparation was due if only in token of this fact, but I asked: "What kind of man can this Geddes be? What does he think he's up to, and what kind of contribution does he think he's making to the stabilization of Europe and the world after 'the war to end war'?"

These were rhetorical questions. I had the answers; he was a wicked man, a low man. He did not see himself making, he did not want to make, a contribution to the stabilization of Europe and the world. On the contrary . . . I thought: I'd like to get hold of that man; I'd like to look him straight in the eye and ask him: "What the hell are you driving at, sir?"

But there wasn't much likelihood that I would ever get hold of Sir Eric Geddes; I was a sergeant in the A.E.F., and he was a knight and a minister in His Britannic Majesty's Government.

Life, in the peculiar way it has, arranged a meeting. I had a long and friendly chat with Sir Eric Geddes on Christmas Eve, 1933, in

Khartoum. We had flown up together from Johannesburg, and I sat with him for an hour or so before dinner. He was an attractive and knowledgeable man. I had been watching him for three days, admiring his massive head, his unself-consciousness, his graceful carriage. He talked easily, a man secure in achievement and reputation, first about the oddity of the scene—Christmas decorations near the equator and black men hanging up artificial holly. "Though after all," he said, "the Christian part of Christmas originated nearer the equator than we usually remember." Then he spoke about Christmases he had observed in other parts of the world. He boasted pleasantly: "I've been in every one of your forty-eight states." A man of wide experience, solid intelligence, admirable culture, serious, personable, attractive. A wicked, low man? A *salaud?* Ridiculous! I turned the conversation strategically to the need of a supranational outlook on world affairs.

"Oh, yes," he said. "We must have a new system."

"Especially in our teaching of the public," I suggested.

"In that above all."

I had my opening. "Sir Eric," I said, "may I ask you a rather personal question which goes back a number of years?"

He looked a little astonished. "By all means."

"In the Khaki Election you coined a slogan: 'We're going to squeeze the Germans till the pips squeak.' What were you thinking of?"

He leaned back and laughed delightedly. "You know, I've been asked that question, one way or another, several times. I didn't think I'd meet it in Khartoum."

"And what did you answer, Sir Eric?"

"I answered: 'Yes, wasn't that a perfectly silly thing to say!' "

I didn't know what to make of that. In a way, I still don't. There is something about it so disarming—in the literal sense of the word. I wonder what I would have felt and said if I had gotten that answer from Sir Eric in 1919.

In those days life and human beings and the course of history didn't look to me as complicated and baffling and recalcitrant as they do now. My optimisms of early 1914 had not only survived the Great War, they were livelier and more self-assured than ever. Mankind had at last learned its lesson. A benevolent supranational organization was going to take over the management of human affairs, the Clemenceaus and Lloyd Georges and Sir Erics and Senator Lodges notwithstanding. Yes, a new era was dawning. Little nations as well as big ones, the Jews and all other peoples, were to have their wrongs righted, their future secured, by a high-minded World Authority. There would of course be an interim period of turbulence here and there, but that was only natural.

Chaim Weizmann was then in Paris, heading the delegation that was presenting the Zionist cause to a sympathetic Peace Conference. He was by then—and would remain for the rest of his life—a world figure. I saw him once or twice at a distance, and my heart swelled with pride. (I did not dare to approach him; I took it for granted that he had forgotten me,* and was glad of it.) This man was the architect of the Balfour Declaration of 1917; if the Jewish claim to a homeland was now on the international *ordre du jour*, Weizmann's role in placing it there overshadowed everyone else's. But the homeland was not all. The Jewish minorities of Eastern Europe, like all other substantial minorities, were to be safeguarded by international law in the enjoyment of their cultural identities. What more could one ask?

To be sure, there had been murderous outbreaks against the Jews in Poland, and it made one sick that after more than a century of foreign occupation and oppression a country should celebrate in this fashion the new-found freedom which others had bestowed on it. But I was willing to allow for a turbulent interim period. Pockets of unregenerate prewar viciousness, backwardness, and stupidity were bound to linger here and there. They would soon be flushed out by the triumphant forces of progress. I wince as I set down this bombast; but that is the way I thought and talked.

Two important episodes belong to that Paris time: a seven-week spell as secretary-interpreter on the Polish Pogrom Commission headed by Henry Morgenthau senior; a twelve-month spell as interpreter on the Reparations Commissions in Berlin and Vienna. The visit to Poland fell within the period of my army service; on the Reparations Commissions I worked as a civilian. Each commission separately strengthened me in the conviction, long since abandoned, that the world's troubles come solely from the wickedness of men at the top.

I was demobilized in Paris in September 1919, and together with an army buddy opened, at 19 rue St. Roche, a secretarial service called The Franco-American Public Stenographer. Paris was then full of American businessmen, and we made good money. The stenography I learned for the enterprise came in handy when I got the job as

*See pages 201 and 202, below. [Ed.]

interpreter on the Reparations Commission. Simultaneous translation over a transistor system was of course unknown then. Each
speaker at an international conference had his say, in shorter or
longer pieces; the interpreter took it down and gave it out in one of
the official languages. It was exhilarating work, full of rapid-fire and
tricky linguistic challenges; it was also very well paid.

But that was not why I took it on. The writing for which I had
had myself demobilized in Paris had come to a dead end. The Left
Bank, which was then assembling its expatriates of the American
"lost generation," had become tiresome. I was fed up with the blather
at the Coupole and the Café du Dôme. My experience with the Polish
Pogrom Commission had shaken me up badly; I was beginning to feel
that the Jewish problem, like many others, was not by a long way on
the point of solution: the wickedness of men in power symbolized a
far greater obstacle than I had imagined, and Lord Acton had been
only too right. My experience on the Reparations Commission
confirmed my pessimism.

The officials for whom it was my duty to interpret in French and
English were not in the front rank of the famous. I never heard again
of Sir Philip Goodenough of England, or of Dr. Zaghradnik of Czechoslovakia, or of M. Tsouderos of Greece, unless the last is the one
who became prime minister. They were intelligent men; their work
was important; but my memory and my notes do not testify to a
single exchange of views that could by a generous estimate be considered on a level either with their capacities or with the seriousness of
the time. I recall much squabbling over the allocation of loot, precedence, and credit for victory. I recall an atmosphere of excessive
nationalist sensitivity, and of an indifference to the condition of the
vanquished. And I recall a certain M. Klobukowski.

M. Klobukowski was an elderly, pink-faced, white-mustachioed
French assistant minister who came to us from Paris to discuss an
Austrian petition for a downward revision of the costs of the Reparations Commission. M. Klobukowski summed up his refusal with
Gallic charm: *"Messieurs, j'ai essayé de mal dîner à Vienne, mais je n'ai pas
réussi"*—I have tried to dine badly in Vienna, and I have failed. The
Austrian kroner had climbed to the ten-thousand-per-dollar mark
and was poised for its subsequent flight into the billions; at the
Bristol Hotel, at flashy cafés like Tonello's and Sacher's, the hangouts
of the *Schieber* (black-market profiteers) and foreign correspondents,
one did indeed fare luxuriously for next to nothing in foreign exchange; but the streets of Vienna swarmed with beggars, and a blight
of hunger and hopelessness lay on the city. M. Klobukowski had *tried*

to dine badly in Vienna and had failed. It was not the refusal of the petition that horrified me; it was the blasted wickedness of the form. I choked when I had to interpret.

The last of my significant contacts with Paris was in August 1939, not a sojourn but a five-day pause in transit. The *New York Post* had commissioned me to write, from on board, the story of one of the boats laden with Jewish refugees which were crawling over the Mediterranean, forbidden to make port in Palestine or anywhere else. I got to Paris the day the Hitler-Stalin pact was signed, and my assignment collapsed. Nobody would be interested in the story. There was barely time to run down to Basle, where the Zionist Congress was closing its sessions, and to get back to London via Paris.

In the Paris of August 1939 there were no demonstrations like those that flared up in 1914, no *hein-hein-hein! hoo! hoo!*, no madness. Even before the blackout was ordered, no evening crowds congregated in the boulevards or the Place de la Concorde. I saw only little knots of people, for the most part silent, before the offices of *Paris Soir* and *Le Matin,* scanning the bulletins. I saw scrawlings on the walls: *"Mieux vaut Hitler que Blum"*—better Hitler than Léon Blum. In London no singing of Tipperary. The year 1939 was reaping what the years since 1918 had sown.

I go back to fill a hiatus. From my Paris visit of 1914 I returned to Manchester late in August, when the Germans were at the Marne and the government was preparing to evacuate to Bordeaux. (It got there in 1940. Bordeaux! It was only a name to me then, but I was to spend the better part of a year there, 1918–1919, attached to G II.) I managed to get on one of the last trains permitted to leave Paris for the north, and during the go-stop-go-stop journey I saw the beginnings of that hideous phenomenon which has since then become a universal commonplace—a population in flight ("fleeing from the foreign faces and the foreign swords"), desperate men and women, weeping children, jammed railroad stations and carriages, and bundles, bundles, bundles, baskets, pillows, bottles, pots and pans, and kettles and toys. A dissolving world—but only a miniature of what was to be a quarter of a century later. And in Calais I saw the famous London buses being rushed to the front. Some of the buses had advertisements running along the top, *Potash and Perlmutter,* Montague Glass's play, the hit of that season; and crowds lining the streets of Calais cheered them on with: *"Vive Potash! Vive Perlmoutaire!"*

In the Paris of August 1914 I also saw the beginning of something as symptomatic of later calamity as the refugees, namely, the bigger and better queues. Oh, that waiting in loathsome *couloirs,* that going from office to office, that subjection to jack-in-offices! I learned a new law: put a man behind a desk and he'll want the world to stand in line.

Three miserable months ensued for me. It is easy to say: "I was a pacifist and refused to join up." It was not so easy to sustain the refusal. I doubt whether my "principles" were determinant; a powerful deterrent was pride, the dread of ridicule: "Look at him! The socialist-pacifist, the Norman Angellite! One drum roll and he's off!" Self-ridicule and the ridicule of others. I was therefore the more scornful of fellow socialists who defected. And all the time there was a tug at the heart to take the irrevocable step, to be done with the suspicion that I was simply a coward. And then again, on the other hand: "It'll all be over by Christmas anyhow."

And, oddly enough, I was becoming more Jewish in my feelings all the time. There was no road-to-Damascus conversion, only a steady deepening of conviction, or preconviction. I won't try to psychoanalyze myself; I only make a guess that in the big upset my fundamental values were beginning to assert themselves.

I got a clerical job. September and October passed. "Next spring" took the place of Christmas as the terminal of the war; I grew more restive, more irresolute. My mother urged me to go to America; my father said: "The sons of the noblest English families are lying in the trenches." There was discord in the house. I quarreled with my father, argued socialism with him in my pidgin Yiddish, and exchanged insults with him. My quarrels with my father had something to do with my final decision.

My father was no longer a shoemaker. He had opened a shoeshop on Bury New Road and had failed; he had opened a grocery shop on Sussex Street and had failed; now he was working as a presser in a large clothing factory in which my two older brothers were the managers. The factory was flourishing on war orders, and my father, now in his fifties, was making more money than ever before in his life, but under a terrible physical strain (all the members of my family have been addicted to overwork). He very much wanted to have a son of his in the army, a renewal of himself. When I came home on leave from France in December 1919, in my American uniform, he could not take his eyes off me. He kept repeating, dreamily: *"Der serjent, der serjent."* He would not believe that I had seen no fighting, that in France I had been transferred from the infantry to intelligence. He would have it that I was suppressing, lest it come to my mother's ears, participation in desperate melees from which—since there was no evidence of a wound—I had emerged miraculously unscathed.

Well, then, I left for America on the *S.S. Adriatic* on November 14, 1914. Incredible as it may sound today, all I had to do was buy a ticket (third class, five pounds—a little less than thirty dollars) and get on the boat; no quotas, no interviews, no forms, no consulates, no passport, no visa. I was to be in America for a few months, a year at the outset. Then I would come back and take up as if nothing had happened. I did not come back, except for visits over the years.

From *Little Did I Know* (1963)

part two

In 1924, when Maurice Samuel was twenty-nine years old, he visited Palestine for the first time. He set down his impressions of the journey in a series of articles published in the Zionist periodical *The New Palestine,* excerpts of which follow. Samuel went on to become a leading Zionist spokesman, and the selections that comprise this section reflect his abiding involvement with the Zionist cause. Drawn from such works as *On the Rim of the Wilderness, Harvest in the Desert,* and *Light on Israel,* they touch on a variety of relevant topics—relations between American Jews and Israel, problems of Arab sociology, the attitudes of Christianity and Islam toward Jews and the State of Israel. The concluding selection is taken from *The Professor and the Fossil,* Maurice Samuel's forceful rejoinder to the attack on Zionism and Jewish peoplehood by British historian Arnold Toynbee.

THE ZIONIST

4 "RETURNING" HOME — FIRST JOURNEY TO PALESTINE

On the Seas

S.S. Duilio, June 20, 1924

Hour by hour, as I stand watching the cometary furrow of the steamer moving inward from the horizon, or lie on the upper deck and see the large, quiet constellations sway left and right about the mast, the wonder of this voyage grows on me. I am "returning" to a land which I have never seen, and which my parents have not seen, nor my parents' parents. I am going "home" to a place which exists for me only by hearsay. I was born within a thousand miles of it, and though I have wandered not a little, I have never been nearer. They tell me that a long, long time ago, an incredibly long time ago, ancestors of mine were driven from the country. But so many years have passed since then, that not a single nation has survived to bear living witness to the story. The destroyer himself died hundreds and hundreds of years ago, and many another oppressor has writ his name in water between that day and ours. It is a far-off legend, an uncertain and unhappy rumor, less a story of human suffering than one of those powerful primitive fables, coming from nowhere and known everywhere, that symbolize the universal human tragedy.

And were they my ancestors that were driven from Palestine? All of them? Is there nothing in my blood that comes from darker and more obscure origins, through slaves that were welcomed into the House of Israel a thousand years ago on the northern shores of Africa, through Tartar chieftains who had been no nearer to Palestine than I have, perhaps even through blond northerners who nourished a fierce and perverse affection for the daughters of an accursed race? And before that, before the days when "we" were slavedealers and moneylenders to the whole world, and scholars only to ourselves, before that—what diverse forgotten peoples that should send down to me conflicting memories and instincts: fair Philistines from Kaphtor, swart Bedouins we picked up between the Red Sea and the Jordan, still darker animal-worshippers from round the delta of the Nile?

I say it does not matter. And this is the mystery of mysteries. There came into Palestine a horde of wanderers, half nomads, half slaves, a rebellious rabble chosen by the Life Force for the beginnings of a marvelous experiment. And there was driven out of Palestine a nation and a spirit, two in one. That spirit has invested generation after generation, has clothed itself with a changing body, has drawn in new material from a surrounding world, but has survived, clear in individuality as it was two thousand years ago.

We are told by scientists that a man's body renews itself every seven years: within that period every corporeal particle of him is shed and is replaced by alien stuff. Yet the man remains the same. How? Why? This no scientist knows. Much less does he know why the spirit which went out of Palestine, carried by that bodily nation which Rome all but destroyed, should have continued imperishably through all changes and accretions, so that I, compounded of a score of human sources, should now turn to Palestine as surely as if I had left it only yesterday.

We shall never know what alchemy transfused into the common material of our first ancestry this perdurable consciousness. Let the sophisters speak of illusions. But why do these illusions endure and give birth to the beauty which the sophisters cannot understand much less contribute to? Let grubby anthropologists measure skulls for their angles and proportions, split hairs to graph their cross sections: let them prove beyond the shadow of a doubt (as they can), that we have noses like Arabs' and teeth like Tartars'; I will go even further, and admit that we have stomachs like dogs and livers like cows, we are angry like apes and vainglorious like peacocks. Let them anatomize the inessential and obvious till there's not a fiber or a nerve that isn't accounted for: the sum total of their knowledge is that when a man's dead he is, for all but nutritive purposes, quite valueless.

Let them graph a thought, and weigh an ideal. Let them give the dimensions of beauty, and tell us whether the hunger for God is brachycephalous or dilococephalous. Let them comfort the heart of man with a chart from Linnaeus and let the laws of Mendel teach us the way and the life.

This is not their function? Then let them keep their snouts out of our councils, and when we talk of being Jewish not deafen us with their babble about craniums and statures, Tartars and Philistines and Egyptians.

I am going to visit my "home." If it was nothing else, Palestine was the alembic in which the unknowable alchemist wrought the experiment. I say, my home. For who and what am I, if not the spirit that is in me? Am I anything other than my consciousness, I, who am in all else an animal like all animals, a man like all men, of whatever race and country? "I think, therefore I am," said one philosopher. He fell short of the truth. I am my thoughts—that comes nearer. The place that gives me my thoughts, that is the place that gave birth to me. The place that gives me individuality, dreams—this is my home.

And so I am going home, and I have strange company part of the way. I am on an Italian boat: there are a thousand Italians with me here. They are going to see Rome and the Arch of Titus: I am going to see Jerusalem and the Wailing Wall. They are going to see Italy, reborn half a century ago, and struggling for a place in the sun: I am going to see Palestine, reborn yesterday, but devoid of ambitions. They are going to see a nation brought to life by the sword: I am going to see a spirit resurgent in peace.

When Moses Hess wrote *Rome and Jerusalem* more than sixty years ago he felt the same wind of liberation passing across the disrupted provinces of Italy and the scattered communities of Israel. In his mind the two were associated in rebirth, as the one was associated with the ruin of the other. But he did not see the unbridgeable difference. The Roman Empire is dead—dead forever. Young Italy, the darling of Mazzini and Garibaldi, is not the inheritor of ancient Rome. Not the same universal idea runs through both: their meaning and their spirit is not the same: what Rome was Italy can never be. Italy is a national individuality. Rome was a universal idea. Italy, a national concept, is no nearer to the Roman concept than is England or France. The ideal of Rome was the internationalization of humanity, the reduction of all national differences to one government and one form. The ideal of Italy is the ideal of every nation, the free development of its national gifts. The Roman ideal failed—and the Jewish still lives.

We are not a nation—we are an idea, a spirit. If we have most of the attributes of a nation it is only outwardly, corporeally, as men resemble animals. If we claim the rights of a nation, it is as men claim the right to food, clothing, shelter, and sleep, in common with all other forms of life; we share our nationalist attributes with other peoples: but there is something in us peculiar to ourselves.

Is there something insolent in this view? If there is, it cannot be helped. There was something insolent in our refusal to disappear: a well-behaved nation, driven from its homeland, smashed into a hundred different fragments, would not insist on surviving. It is as if a man should insist on living and speaking after he had been cut into a dozen pieces. It is not the right thing to do. It is not "form," as the English say. We are not obeying the rules.

Much worse to me than this aspect of insolence is the anxious disclaimer of the mission Jew. Ask him why we have suffered so long, he will tell you it was all on account of a little misunderstanding. The nations did not know that we were just like them. For some reason or other they got it into their heads that we were different from them —and they disliked us. It was not "dislike of the unlike." It was dislike of what they *thought* was the unlike. In reality we were the same as they.

What a pitiful diminution of our role! What? All this obstinacy and heartburning, these auto-da-fés and rackings, these mass murders and heroic suicides because of such a meaningless misunderstanding? Was it worth it? Is it still worth it? All because they *thought* we were different, whereas, all the time, we were really alike? And when they will have realized that we are really the same—will that be the end of our destiny?

Why were we picked as the heroes of such an outrageous farce? Why was no other people, resembling every other people, fastened on by the nations of the world as being *different?*

Opposite us (Aaron Glanz, the journalist and poet, and myself) there sits at table a buxom Italian lady. She is an amiable simple soul, and, like everybody else on the boat, anxious to be friendly with everybody else. The first day, at the first general meal, we introduced ourselves all round. As the meal drew to an end, she asked us, out of a clear sky, "You Jews?" "Yes," said Glanz. "Oh, Jews, Italians, alla da same," she said eagerly.

I wonder why she said it. She certainly would not have said anything like it if we had declared that we were Germans. And why did everybody else at the table as anxiously endorse her opinion? Why did they try so obviously to make us feel at home—although we were "alla da same"? I wouldn't think of telling, say, an Italian, that though he was an Italian, and I a Jew, it was really all the same. It sounds too patronizing. But this was too delicate a subject to raise with this lady—not to mention too difficult a one in view of our lack of Italian and her lack of English or Yiddish. We took her reassuring remark at its face value—an expression of kindliness which, if it conveyed more than it seemed to, did so without her consent, or even knowledge.

"Do not go to Palestine," said friends of mine, when I announced my plans. "You have wonderful illusions—why run the risk of losing them?"

I might have asked them: "How can a man keep his illusions in their freshness and strength if he is afraid to put them to the test? Men do not harbor illusions deliberately: the power of an illusion lies in its complete simulation of reality. And the moment I suspect that an illusion is nothing but an illusion it ceases to be an illusion and becomes an affectation. I *must* put it to the test, if only to keep it."

But at that I have no fears. How can Palestine disappoint me? Is not its achievement already beyond all reach of destruction? Though tomorrow some horrible inner corruption should make itself manifest in the Jewish people, foretelling its early and inevitable destruction, I should still say: "The land in which was forged an idea that so long withstood the alternate tortures and temptations of time has some mysterious quality of its own: for it has almost found the philosopher's stone of spiritual life."

I will put these illusions of mine to the test. I say that if the most odious predictions of our enemies were true, one hundred thousand Jews in Palestine for twenty years cannot undo the marvel of one hundred million Jews throughout the world for twenty centuries.

Jerusalem—The Heart of Infinity

The Holy City, July 10, 1924

"These are the mountains of Judea," I said to myself, and was afraid to believe it lest they should disappear, as dreams are said to disappear when the sleeper says to himself, "I am dreaming." They crowded on me as the train wound its laborious way from village to village, and I felt like a blind man who, given sight for the first time, is terrified because he thinks that whatever he perceives he must be touching, since he is accustomed to perceive the outside world only by touch. The rounded summits were within reach of my hand, and distances were all confounded. We seemed to be moving on the surface of a crystal, and perspective was an illusion. I saw the barren masses, alternate gray and green, now dusty in the shouting sunlight, now fresh with oases of foliage; I saw tiny donkeys galloping noiselessly along roads; I saw camels moving with graceful reptilian undulations; cacti like odd green waffles with jagged edges; huts and houses, terraces on hillsides, cultivated patches, knolls of palm trees: all of it unreal by virtue of an intenser reality than I had ever experienced. It *must* be visionary, it must be only within myself, to be so intimately near, I thought.

There is some mystic configuration in these hills, unfolding mile after mile, lifting and lowering the path of the train, till I believe we have traveled a thousand miles in an hour. There is an effect of infinity in miniature, a distillation of space. There must be, there is, a particular meaning and power in this tiny territory. Why was it that in these hidden valleys, toys, playgrounds, now shrink to the infinitesimal, now expand into the immeasurable? It is a span, it is a universe, it is a footstool, it is a palace. Against its background man looms a moment, the greatest and the Godliest of all creation's children, and the next moment all but vanishes, a thing creeping on a hillside, a grain of dust carried by the wind.

The mind plays with space, almost seizes its most mysterious quality, its essential secret. A trick of the Creator, perhaps, who, having flung across the tremendous void bridges of fire and of fiery mists, now, in tenderer mood, concentered His will in a tiny jewel and wrought the same wonder with a thimbleful of earth as with engulfing nebulae. "Read," he said: "If you will touch the heart of this miniature, you will touch the heart of infinity." And He crowded into the orbit of an atom all the marvels of the stellar circuits. All the universe is here, all of mankind, all its desires, its follies, its greatness and its pitifulness, its glory and its shame. Write in a book what you will see within this minute circle, and there is nothing to be added. And there were men who wrote, words of fury that will stir the heart forever, and forever baffle the mind.

Perhaps it is the sunlight. I stood on a hill in Jerusalem, and I saw at the foot, almost touched by the shadow of the house, a blue lake set in mountains. "Let us go down to that lake," I said. "It is only a mile or two away."

"It is twenty miles away and more," they said. "It is the Dead Sea."

"I do not believe it," I answered. "Those mountains behind the lake are not more than three or four miles distant."

"They are the mountains of Moab, fifty miles away."

"I do not believe it," I said again.

"These things are not to be believed," they told me. "They are among the lies of Palestine."

But as I came up toward Jerusalem through the mountains of Judea, I did not know this, and I could not understand the double effect of pent narrowness and oppressive amplitude. I do not understand it now, as I do not understand the miraculous elasticity of time. I have been here four days, I know. But I have been here only a moment, and I have been here forever.

But at least I do understand that only in such an illusive setting would men step closest into the mystery of reality. There is no need to run panting from one end of the universe to the other, no need to break into the fastnesses of matter, as though nature had craftily overlaid some ineffable word with veil after veil of deceitful seeming. The secret lies open before you here. It cries to you, in a language which you cannot understand, but whose syllables are not to be resolved through material implements. You will believe everything here; you will believe nothing. You will understand why here the greatest word of faith was uttered, and the last word of desperate and contemptuous disbelief, the flame-white faith of Isaiah, the ice-white negation of Koheleth. And both of them forever united, both of them one, burning heat and burning cold, negative infinity and positive infinity meeting.

What did I come to see here? The things of today only in part, and in passing. I was drawn to this place by a wonder which may be explained at the end of time. Why was it that in this place alone there were found men to write as the prophets have written? Are not Abanah and Pharpar, rivers of Damascus, better than all the waters of Israel? Are there not hills and dales in the land of the Hellenes? Is not the Nile mightier than the Jordan? The valley of the two rivers is broader and richer, and there are peaks that overtop ten times the summits of these hills. The vision and the voice were Palestine's alone. Why? Why? The question has drummed in my brain many years, and no man will ever answer it. But, drawing ever closer to Jerusalem, through the labyrinth of the hills of Judea, I felt the ancient power falling on me, and a faint flush of those dread ecstasies rushed through my blood.

The last Arab village slips backward, and I walk to and fro in the empty carriage, looking on either side of me, and feeling my heart beating faster and faster. The final stretch of the journey drops suddenly to a level, as though, before the denouement of Jerusalem, even the magic of these hills must for a moment be blotted out. I see a distant tower gliding along the summit of a hillock, the first tower of Jerusalem, and then I can see no more, because I am blinded by tears and all heaven and earth are encircled with a silver mist. Here is the city which is the world's center for ever and ever.

When the Lord returned the captivity of Zion we were as in a dream. Like one in a dream I went about that day. I did not care where I went. I met friends of mine again, and I think we spoke sensibly, of commonplace things, and asked and answered questions about each other and about friends we have in common. But I walked in another world, and only conversed with a stray part of my mind. I was not in a city that was then visible to them. I saw a mighty wall girdling the inner town; I walked under arches, up and down alleys that twisted and turned, and men and women went by me, and there were bazaars, and donkeys loaded with wares, and shouting and laughter and chaffering, cobbled roads that dipped and rose again, gateways, queer windows, old, old, old, with sharp sunlight and shadow, and here and there trees, alleys that swooped precipitously upward into immemorial courts. It was not real—or only half real. I saw them: they were there, and they were not there. There were other hosts. I was not myself, but a thousand others. Ten thousand times ten thousand men and women walked with me, all risen out of the gulf of the past, familiar and unfamiliar, my own and estranged from me. I came up to vantage points and saw the hills that surround the city, but not as they are now—as they were a thousand years ago, two thousand years ago, three thousand years ago, shadow piled on shadow, ruins risen again into their completed originals, city above city, tower clothing tower and buttress behind buttress. All that have ever passed through here, camped here, dreamed here, visioned here, their works, their achievements, all came into the sunlight again, like gray exhalations. The sensation of time departed from me, past and present were one. The scroll of the days, which leaves a narrowest margin of text open, rolling it out from the infinity of the future and into the infinity of the past, was suddenly flung open and encompassed me, thousands of years of text simultaneously visible, Jebusites and Hebrews and Greeks and Romans and Saracens and Crusaders, citadels, temples, mosques, fortresses, pagan and Jewish and Moslem and Christian, every drama that has ever played itself out, with all its setting and its scenery. Princelings and chieftains and kings, wise men and prophets and rulers, I saw. And I saw too the innumerable hosts of the humble, the children that have laughed and cried among these streets, the boys and girls that have made love, their dreams, their desires. And over all an immanent spirit which I have known nowhere else, a canopy, invisible and urgent, through which the light of sun and moon and stars shone with another luster, potent and revealing. I heard the pealing of trumpets and tocsins, the shouting of multitudes, whispers, cries of command, cries of agony, the crash and rumble of chariots, the cry of camel drivers coming in from the desert, the crack of whips, the sounds of all the days and nights of a hundred generations.

Yet not chaos, not like the vision of all the days and nights of any other great city in the world. In all, through all, there was a striving, an urging to utterance. These multitudes that have lived and died here have lived in a drama of more than secular import. These hills that surround the city have not sprung blindly out of the earth. There was a purpose, a sharp will, goading these multitudes, a tone in this life which tingled in their blood. Who has not been in Jerusalem, who has not invested it, who has not passed under the invisible canopy? Nations of the north and south, nations of the east and west, Egyptian and Assyrian and Greek and Roman and Arab and Crusader and Turk—like an inquisition chamber this was, into which God led nation after nation for the test, and the question pealed about them and their fate depended on the answer. And they were dumb! They felt the secret compulsion, but could not understand it. They stared about them, dully, and lived their day, and passed, to yield place to another. Save one alone, which, among these multitudes, strained its ears, caught its breath, and in startled exaltation stammered something in reply, cried out, half unwitting of its own words. And these words have gone ringing on and cannot die out. It was here, the constellation of circumstances for which time had waited, the spark caught, the light flashed out. The place, the moment and the men, all created for each other, come together at last! From that passionate conjuncture issued those words, the voice of Jerusalem.

At the Wailing Wall

Jerusalem, July 14, 1924
In the early morning sunlight the birds twitter cheerfully above the narrow lanes that lead to the Wailing Wall. A cool wind blows from

the east, but the dust still sleeps. There is a quiet happiness in the clear white light. The cobblestones underfoot, terraced downward toward the sacred place, the low walls on either side, topped here and there with greenery, the gateways that open sometimes and reveal ancient courtyards like gardens, the arches, the solid windows—all are steeped in peacefulness. And the place of the Wailing Wall is a clean, neat little retreat: on one side is the massive pile of stones, towering up, block by block; opposite, only fifteen feet away, is a low wall, not much higher than a man, shutting off the Arab houses. The length of this retreat is perhaps fifty, sixty yards. It is a blind alley at one end; at the other end the lane at right angles leads back, and upward, with devious turnings, into the heart of the old city.

This is not desolation or ruin. It is serenity itself. It falls on the heart with a healing kindliness. You know that the place is old, but it is gracious in age: its turbulent days are over, and there have succeeded the long years of friendly resignation. In the dark chinks, between the great stones, the grass has taken root: it is fresh in the cool of the earliest morning. It has been there a great many years— it feels at home.

Jerusalem is still asleep. It is so quiet that you can hear the patter of footsteps two or three streets away. The crowing of cocks comes to you, from every side, dreamily. Only the shrill, joyous twitter of birds sounds wakeful and live. I walk lightly back and forth, not to disturb the restfulness.

Hither, I should think, people come to dream away an hour or two, revolving in their minds the futility of earthly effort. Strangers might pause awhile, half in delight, half in thoughtful sadness, and say: "Someone built this massive wall a thousand years ago. He is forgotten, and his works are forgotten. His race has surely vanished and is become a legend among the nations. Peace to his memory and to his resting place!

"They are surely content to be left in peace now, these walls. They have seen enough in their time, heard enough. They have reflected the lights of many fires, have echoed a thousand times the blaring of trumpets, the shouts of fighters. Let the riot and the tumult of mankind find itself other places, build other towers. Conquest and submission, ambitions of kings, rebellions, famines, sieges—not for these walls. They have found the happiness that lies beyond effort: here they will stand in hoary meditation, an eternal mood. . . ."

But I saw the Wailing Wall again, when the late twilight was ushering in the Sabbath, and hundreds of worshippers were crowded into this quiet retreat. I had seen that day the sun setting, over the hills of Judea and, from the east, night coming up in glory over the Mount of Olives. I had seen the sky over the mountains take fire and burn with a slow, dying flame, while above a flotilla of light clouds, suspended in unfathomable blue, had passed from bright gold to purple, from purple to violet, and from violet to an extinguished leaden hue. I had seen the towers and roofs and domes of the city glow with the dying of day, beautiful with an unearthly beauty. And with the late twilight I found myself again in the place of the Wailing Wall, amid throngs of worshippers.

And in that hour the friendliness and tranquillity of the place of the Wailing Wall had given way to a fierce clamor and unrest. It was an incredible change. Three bright lamps, suspended on the low wall opposite, threw a hard unnatural light on the monstrous blocks. Above, the clear edge of the rim stood sharp against the luminous sky. Below, there was a riot of color and noise: Sephardim in fezes and Ashkenazim in fur *shtreimlach,* congregations in restless groups continuously renewing themselves, each with its own service and its own leader—a tumult that blended into one wild cry, and rose clear from that pit into the vaulted silence above. Like my imaginings, and yet unlike. They were come from all ends of the world, from Bukhara and from California, from the Levant, from Poland, from Babylon, every group with its own memories and its own traditions—but united here in one tradition that transcended all difference. I heard the monotonous chanting of the Sephardim, a united rhythm which prevailed in a kind of hypnotic regularity; and I heard the disjointed crying of the Polish Jews, the old Hasidic *hithlavuth* which prevailed in an inarticulate intensity. There were young boys too, from the schools of Jerusalem, and women clustering on one side, near the entrance, and praying to themselves. And those that were nearest the wall placed their hands upon the stones and cried into the dark clefts as into some immense chamber within, to an invisible and unresponsive power.

No peace now, no dreamy tranquillity and meditation: instead a lament that was laden with immemorial sorrows. I thought then that they were praying, not for the lost temple, and not for the departed glory, not for themselves and their own, but for all mankind: for all who suffer and have suffered; for the living and for the dead and for the unborn; humanity pleading with its creator for a respite from the burden of life; universal misery finding its voice at last; the perplexity that haunts us from the cradle to the grave, the bitterness of mortality, the eternal question, the unanswered and unanswerable "Why?" . . .

And late that night I wandered through the loneliness of the inner city, thinking of these strange contrasts of the place of the Wailing Wall: the peacefulness and contentment of the morning and the comfortless clamor of the evening. I had heard, that same day, a hundred hammers making merry music on Mount Scopus, where the Hebrew University is rising, and in the night the happy ringing of steel on stone mingled in my ears with the dread lamentations of the evening: the same people, the same destiny—utterly beyond my understanding.

So walking, not caring whither I walked, I fell again under the spell of my first days in Jerusalem. These labyrinths, which by day are dazzling with colors, are at night somber and mysterious. City below city lies Jerusalem, labor piled on labor, life flourishing on its own sepulcher. But to me, walking alone and in silence, the buried levels were uncovered, and from their darkness the hidden cities rose again and were alive. A ghost among ghosts I wandered, and above me the strips of the sky refashioned the labyrinth below. Only the stars were the same, and the power beyond the stars, and by the token of these immutable things we were united.

I became aware again, after I had wandered, it seemed for centuries, of night and silence. I walked in the same streets—but not the same. They were deeper, darker. Something breathed around me, a greater and more populous city. It was a more passionate pulse that beat in sleep. I was aware, dimly, of a fierce power in repose. There were watchmen about, shadowy figures whose weapons glinted in ghostly lamplight—and now and again a ghostly voice that uttered familiar but incomprehensible syllables. And suddenly there flitted by me a quick vision, something dark and radiant, something fleet and noiseless—I know not what—a flutter of robes, a whisper, a scent of spices, saffron and myrrh and aloes. I turned swiftly, and it was gone; there only lingered a sweetness in the air, and my senses were taken captive, and I cried out.

I tried to follow and I lost myself. I hastened by sleeping houses, under arches and by lofty pillars. I sped by watchmen, a ghost, unmolested by ghosts, and climbing alley after alley I came upon a level place, and all the stars were uncovered; only, on one side, a great abyss among the stars was shaped like a palace or a temple blotting out the sky, but itself invisible. Then I saw, in a faint clearness, steps and columns and towers and watchmen, and I was following someone, I knew not whom, a regal figure that walked, stately and slow, toward a battlement that overlooked a gulf. I heard challenge and answer, and something thrilled in me, though the words were strange. Who is this, walking at night in the courtyard of the Temple, before whom the guards tremble and send a message of warning, each to the other? Is not this the Valley of Jehoshaphat into which he looks, so steadily, so darkly? There is silence down there; the shepherds have returned to the fold, and no voice is heard. But far below, fronting the Temple Wall, there is a tomb—the tomb of Absalom. Is this his brother, the king himself, who, troubled by memories, comes out at night to look down on the last resting place of the impious and unsuccessful rebel? How long he looked into the darkness I cannot say; he turned and I made to follow him, but suddenly I was aware again of the vision I had lost—the lightness and radiance went by me, and the odor of many sweet spices, and a cry, a sound like a clear instrument, piercing sweet—and all was gone. The king, the Sulamite, the guards, the softness of night—gone!

In their place were multitudes of running figures, there were flames, there was shouting and weeping, a ghostly battle and the ghostly sack of the city. Far through the darkness the smoke rolled, billows of intenser blackness in the blackness of night. There was a moon risen, a bloody moon that came up like a sign over the hills of the west. And then there was silence again: the rout was gone; dark figures were strewn about the courtyard of the Temple, and the blood was doubly red under the red moon. Only below, in the city and valley, a distant wailing was heard, and a savage laughter. I stood still, life frozen in me.

A sharper coldness clove me through—for I was not alone. A figure came stumbling through the bloody and encumbered court-yard, and from him came such a cry of anguish as mortals should never hear. I could not move toward him or away, but stood and watched him as he ran, crying, from figure to figure, his tattered cloak flying behind, his hands now raised wildly to the sky, now locked together, writhing in unutterable pain. And when he was close to me he fell to the earth, and looking down I saw, in the red moonlight, the footsteps of children imprinted in the bloody soil, the footsteps of children leading outward from the court and downward, their first steps toward the land of their exile. And the mourner who had thrown himself to the earth pressed his lips into the bloody footsteps, and could cry no more. And on his knees he followed the track and passed by me, like a wounded beast. Him I did not need to ask his name. This was he who had foretold the ruin and had lived to see it, Jeremiah, the son of Hilkiah, and those whom he had cursed he was following now, to bring them hope and comfort, the dream of Zion rebuilt.

They vanished, king and shepherdess and spoilers and prophet. I stood in sunlight on the mountain overlooking their city, and the white road wound away northward, leading to Shechem and to Damascus, and round across the desert into Babylon: the road of their exile and the road of their return.

The New Palestine, July 18, 1924;
August 8, 1924; August 15, 1924

5 LIBERATING THE FELLAH

It is always difficult to trace to a recognizable beginning a movement involving living values. European nationalism is generally traced back either to the Renaissance or the Reformation: or else to the introduction of gunpowder. In the East the nationalist movements are still so close to their beginnings that we cannot get the foreshortening effect of time. Periods therefore merge into each other. We do not know whether Egyptian nationalism is a reality as yet: and whether, if it be one, it was the long reign of Mohammed Ali which should be set as its beginning; or whether that nationalism is now aborning.

If anything can be fixed today as Palestine Arab nationalism it is a phenomenon closely connected with the coming of the Jews; and if the emergence of a renewed will to life (in the group this means renewed nationalism) can be symbolized at all, that symbol will be found in the processes which have taken place in Arab settlements adjacent to Jewish colonies.

Near Rehovoth, one of the Jewish colonies, there is an Arab village called Zarnuga. Before the Jews bought the land in the vicinity, there were 80 dunams of orange groves in the village owned by the local peasantry, fellaheen. Originally Zarnuga covered 13,000 dunams of land; but in the course of time, with the growth of Rehovoth, the villagers sold 6,000 dunams to the Jews. (A dunam is about one-quarter of an acre.) The price of the land had risen to 15 and 17 pounds per dunam (the average price of the Rehovoth stretch was originally half a pound a dunam). The proximity of the rising colony of Rehovoth had three effects on the life of the Arabs. (1) It provided the seller of land with initial capital for improvements. (2) It set an example as to how this capital should be invested. (3) It provided a market for the labor of the fellah so that today (1930) several hundred Arabs are being employed in the Jewish orchards and fields.

Today, again, thirty-two fellaheen families of Zarnuga own 1,176 dunams of orange orchards, divided as follows:

2	fellaheen	own	80	dunams	each
3	"	"	60	"	"
4	"	"	50	"	"
5	"	"	40	"	"
10	"	"	30	"	"
3	"	"	25	"	"
3	"	"	15	"	"
1	"	"	10	"	"
1	"	"	6	"	"

The fellaheen of Zarnuga cultivate 300 dunams of irrigated vegetables and several hundred dunams of unirrigated vegetables, for sale in the Jewish colonies. Straw sells here at three pounds per ton, while in villages remote from the Jews it sells at half that price. There are in Zarnuga European plows, scrapers, and harrows, introduced into the country by the Jews and acquired by the fellaheen with money obtained by sales of land to the Jews. Fellaheen learn not only by observing, but by asking advice and following it. Zarnuga has three coffee-houses—an astounding achievement for an Arab village of this size.

It is an extraordinary and obvious truth that the one Jewish colony of Rehovoth has done more for the fellaheen of the district (or for that matter for the fellaheen of all Palestine) than all the Arab leadership.

Zarnuga is an instance. In the village of Sarafend-el-Harab (recently, as its name indicates, a place of ruin), thirty-three fellaheen own 1,036 dunams of orange groves. These were planted since the coming of the Jews into the neighboring areas of Nes Ziona and Rishon le-Zion. Again, the capital was acquired by sale of land to the Jews and applied to intensive cultivation of the smaller area, the example and advice coming from the Jews.

The same story is repeated in al Kubeibe, Saffrieh, Beit Dejen. Nomad Bedouins in the vicinity of this complex of Jewish settlements have settled down and become prosperous. Rantieh, Kuf Anna, Selemeh, Sakieah, Yehudieh, and B'nai B'rak have gone through the same transformation as Zarnuga.

It is obvious that intensive cultivation answers only a part of the problem of the fellah. But the impulse imparted by Jewish colonization extends along the whole line. Only a part of the soil of Palestine (about 250,000 dunams) can be used for orange growing, but there is not one aspect of agriculture which Jewish enterprise has not taken up and shown to be capable of higher development. And the examples of Petach Tikvah, Rehovoth, Nuris, Nahalal, etc., have shown clearly that many areas abandoned in the despair of indolence can be made to support large populations.

I have cited till now only the older Jewish colonies which have influenced decisively the psychology, the outlook, and therefore the capacity of the fellah. In the case of many of the new Jewish colonies something more striking has occurred. In the Arab villages quoted above, independent fellaheen sold part of their land in order to be able to develop the rest. In the case of the villages quoted below, tenants living on the land of an absentee landlord were able for the first time in their lives to lay their hands on some capital of their own. When, in 1921, the Jewish National Fund acquired the Nuris block of land from the Sursucks, it gave every tenant adequate money compensation. The tenants were now able to move. They established themselves in three villages, Mazir (in the Nuris block), Metullah (in the Beisan district), and Karata. When Nahalal was bought, the Jews leased 3,150 dunams to the former tenants—and gave them the use of the water supply which they had constructed at their own expense. Part of the former tenants, with the compensation which they received, moved to a village in the vicinity of Acre.

Basically, the solution of the problem of the fellah lies, therefore, in the introduction of intensive agriculture. This, however, means not only plantations, and not only new varieties of plantations (like bananas and the varieties of grapes introduced by the Jews). It means also the application of intensive methods to grain farming: irrigation, deep plowing, eradication of weeds, the use of fertilizers. It means, further, the development of dairy-farming, poultry-raising, beekeeping and vegetable-growing. To these ends capital must be supplied to the fellah; and here he finds himself locked in a vicious circle. Under his present method of cultivation his land is worth so little that he cannot obtain sufficient capital as a loan; and he cannot improve his method of cultivation until he has obtained sufficient capital. Basing the value on the yield, he cannot obtain more than half a pound on every dunam. With a loan of fifty pounds on one hundred dunams he cannot embark on a scheme which needs one hundred to one hundred and fifty pounds.

There is only one way out for him, and that is bound up with the entire work of Jewish colonization. An increase in immigration creates a larger demand for vegetables, eggs, poultry, etc. The capital for the introduction of these new features can be provided only by a sale of part of the land at the prices which the Jews are willing to pay for it.

But Jewish immigration is opposed by the Arab leadership on *political* grounds. And emergence of an independent fellaheen class is felt properly to be a danger to its rule. After his visit to Palestine, Ramsay MacDonald wrote:

In studying Zionism in Palestine, I found changes with which I was familiar producing reactions with which I was equally familiar. The land of Palestine is held by large owners, and the same class has concentrated in its hands the ownership of towns, the employment of labor and trade. More than that, it has ruled, collected taxes, led an obedient people. All this is threatened. Palestinian social economics has had its foundations removed by the ending of the Turkish occupation. . . . The winds of Europe are blowing in upon them and they cannot stand the cutting blast. They see the coming shadow of a cultivator protected in his labor and property, they see the end of unjust exactions, and they see their power vanishing and they are fighting for their lives. . . . The Arab leaders are in possession. They are conservative and their interests are wrapped up in their conservatism. They have power over their people, they are still leaders; they can get their people to believe foolish things and to act against common interests. . . .*

What these foolish things are we have already seen: that the Jew wishes to occupy the Moslem sanctuaries; that the Jew, disguised master of most of the world, wishes to extend his sinister sway to Palestine; that the Jew wants the land, the houses and (yes!) the wives of the fellaheen. There is nothing strange in the fact that many simple Arabs can be led to believe these and crazier things. What is exceedingly strange is that outsiders, Westerners, have also been led to accept, by and large, the stories of the Arab leadership.

For the West, of course, the accounts have been cooked a little, in both senses of the phrase. A species of argument has been employed, backed with fantastic figures, which appeals not to the mind but to the vague emotions. It is made to appear that there is a deepgoing clash of interest between the Arab and Jewish peoples; that against the Jews, with their money, initiative, ability, and acquisitiveness, the backward neglected Arab has no chance; that the Arab people is faced with a type of conquest roughly similar to that which disinherited the American Indians and the Negroes of South Africa.

*I need hardly point out that this was written before Mr. MacDonald became prime minister. [M.S.]

It is the basic assumption which is false, namely, that there is a natural clash of interest between the two peoples. There is a clash in the country: but it is between the Arab people and the Jews on the one side, and the Arab hereditary ruling class on the other. If I have been at great pains to explain the character of the Arab leadership it has not been for the purpose of discrediting its arguments by indirection: for I shall take up the arguments for what they are worth in themselves. My purpose has been to expose the sources of the conflict in Palestine, and to indicate along what lines a stable relationship between Jews and Arabs can be established.

And now let us take up the first and most serious charge of the Arab leadership against the Jewish settlers, namely, that the Jewish purchases of land have resulted not in a rearrangement of holdings, but in the mass creation of a landless *Lumpenproletariat* which has gone to swell the city mobs.

It should be noted first that of land purchased by the Zionist Organization agencies, only one-tenth came from independent fellaheen: the rest was sold by the large landowners, that is to say, by the Arab leadership. If a process of displacement of the landworkers had taken place, it would have been chargeable to the patriots who inveighed against it. I have, however, already given instances of what actually took place, namely, not displacement but readjustment.

It is a remarkable fact that when the Arab leadership laid its case before the Inquiry Commission of 1929, it failed to produce a single victim of the Jewish land policy. Equally remarkable is the fact that during the 1929 riots, among the slogans one heard among the rioters, there was not one which referred to a displaced peasantry. One heard: "The Jews want the mosque!" "The government is with us!" But if the city mobs of Jerusalem, Hebron, Jaffa, and Haifa had been swelled by enraged and landless peasants, one would have expected to hear: "Give us back our land!" No one has reported such a cry.

The financial records of the Zionist Organization give a clear list of purchases made, and of compensation paid (in addition to purchase price) to the tenants. Study of actual movements, village by village, reveals the simple fact that of the tenants who obtained money from the Jews, less than 10 percent have drifted to the cities, and this represents nothing more than the normal shift of population in a country which is developing its first industries. The rest are still working the soil: thanks, not to the Arab leadership which was ready to sell them out, but to the Jews who gave them compensation over and above the requirements of the law!

But even the general charge, that the Jews have purchased exclusively, or largely, such areas as were heavily settled and worked by Arabs, is quite without foundation. Above one-half of the land which the Jews acquired from the large landlords was utterly waste, neglected, and useless. Some of the areas I have mentioned by name, adding a brief description of the transformation that has taken place. But it should not be imagined that Jews are the only purchasers of land. Arab usurers have frequent occasion to foreclose mortgages and to oust owners, or transform them into exploited tenants. Of the land sold in the country between 1920 and 1927 only 56 percent went to Jews. The remainder (with the exception of 2 percent) went to Arabs. There is continuous speculation in land. It is only the Jew who buys not for the purpose of gambling, but for that of developing.

In the first part of this chapter I have indicated how Jewish contact with fellaheen has affected the life of the latter. Since the growth of the older Jewish colonies there has been an astounding shift in the proportions of orange groves owned by big landlords and small holders. Before the war Arab landowners possessed all the orange groves there were among Arabs, i.e., 20,000 dunams. Today, in 1930, the 45,000 dunams of orange groves owned by Arabs are divided as follows: 25,000 to the big landowners; 20,000 to fellaheen. As applied to the whole country, the change is small. As applied to one district and one industry, it is remarkable. It is perfectly clear that, but for the coming of the Jews, all orange groves would today be owned exclusively by the big landowners.

This small group of independent farmers is a symptom which troubles the Arab leadership. It is worth mentioning that during the riots of 1929 one of the districts which remained quite calm was that surrounding the richest Jewish colonies of Judea—an area which is dotted with Arab orange groves owned by the fellaheen in contact with the Jews. It is a sign of the moral decline of the Arab leadership that in this area the insane propaganda against the Jews produced its minimum effect. *A priori,* this should have been the area where the rioting should have been fiercest. Here the Jews had scored their greatest success: here the looting was more tempting than elsewhere. But there were no riots, and no attempted riots, in Petach Tikvah and Rehovoth.

I must anticipate here an observation dealing with the Jewish contribution to the country's income from taxation. The *Werko* is an annual tax levied on real estate and calculated on the basis of the last purchase price. Forming one-fifth of the population, the Jews contribute one-half of the amount realized on this form of taxation. In many neighborhoods adjacent patches of land will be found, identical in character, paying extraordinarily different rates: the Arab-owned patch, having been acquired long before the war, will be paying four or five mils (between two and three cents; the last general assessment was made in 1896) per dunam; the Jewish patch, more recently acquired, anywhere from five to ten times as much. The point is relevant here as indicating the prices which Jews pay for their land—and the opportunity which is thus afforded independent fellaheen to change extensive, unprogressive agriculture for intensive and progressive agriculture.

The process which has been set in motion foreshadows a deep-reaching restratification of the social organism of Arab life. Old forces will be ground down, new ones will emerge. The Arab people as a whole is, however, ignorant of the fact that this restratification is not a local affair, but is related to the general forward movement of the world. What the Arab leadership sees as a local catastrophe for itself is only an extension—in which the Jews happen to be the instruments—of a slow human advance which no force can turn back indefinitely. And perhaps, if it does perceive the range and inevitability of the process, it is concerned only with itself. It will fight to save itself and the next generation or two. It will employ all the old devices, make pretended concessions, line up the appeal to tradition and national honor—and perhaps even make real sacrifices in the hope of recouping later. But let it be understood that the upbuilding of Palestine and the survival of the social system of the Arabs are incompatible: if this is not understood, nothing else in the recent history of the country is intelligible.

From *On the Rim of the Wilderness* (1931)

6 THE HAUNTED LAND

I

I begin with the land, which I saw for the first time some twenty years ago. In those days Jewish colonization and settlement were—after forty years of uncertain effort—in their preliminary stages. The Jews in the country were one-sixth of their present number, the Arabs less than one-half of theirs, and the total population was less than seven hundred thousand. Since the land is still comparatively empty, the effect at that time was one of extreme desolation.

It was, above all, a haunted land. The populational density in ghosts was out of all proportion to the apparent natural resources. For you asked yourself: "Where did they all live, and on what, when they were in the flesh?" They were extraordinarily important ghosts, too, with a worldwide reputation, and they oppressed the imagination by their stature and intensity not less than by their numbers.

I stood one day on a hilltop in northern Samaria and looked down into the Valley of Jezreel and across at the hills of southern or lower Galilee. Except for a few tiny points lost in the waste, the plain was uninhabited. Once—two thousand years ago and more—the area had swarmed with life. Cities and villages had filled it to the brim, and its fields had been a famous granary. Now I saw only the beginnings of a few Jewish colonies; I saw a few Arab villages, gray adobe huts like exhalations of the exhausted earth; and I saw here and there the black, square, three-sided tents of the Bedouins—*oholei Kedar* (the tents of Kedar), which Solomon mentions in Song of Songs. Black they certainly were, but far from comely. The verses of the king were displaced in my mind by those of the prophet: "Your land is laid waste; your cities are burned with fire. Your soil, strangers consume it in your presence, and it is desolate as by the overthrow of strangers." Alas, not even strangers were now consuming the soil. The spoilers had disappeared with the spoiled, and only the desolation was left.

I was aware, however, of those great ghost presences. To the right rose Mount Gilboa, on which the first Jewish king had fallen in battle with the Philistines. Him the second king, the shepherd boy and singer, who was to be the forebear of the Messiah, lamented in unforgettable verse: "Mountains of Gilboa, let there be no rain and no dew upon you!" The curse had apparently stuck, for the head of the mountain was as barren as the palm of a man's hand, and at the foot of it the swamps stretched out, the paradise of the anopheles mosquito. To the left was the Carmel range, on which one day Elijah had conducted his bitter contest with the prophets of Baal. Before me wound a narrow ribbon of road, leading north first, and then east. Along this road Jeremiah had followed the exiles toward Babylon, and had gone down on all fours to kiss the bloody footprints of the little children.

It was so that the dead crowded out the living, and it was for the sake of the dead that thousands and tens of thousands of pilgrims came annually from all over the world. It did not matter from what point of the compass the traveler entered the country; always he was accompanied or confronted by memories which interposed a heavy veil between him and the immediate. If from the south, he would say to himself: "Across this desert wandered the rabble of slaves which Moses welded into a people." If westward from Transjordan: "Here Moses stood, forbidden to enter the land, and hereabouts he was buried in the unknown grave." Or coming down from the north: "This is the country of Elijah the Gileadite, the rebuker of kings and provider of widows." If he landed at Haifa it was under the shadow of Carmel, and if he landed at Jaffa he remembered: "From this point Jonah fled, reluctant to prophesy in Nineveh; hither he was brought back, to learn that a prophet's business is to prophesy, even if God plans to make a fool of him."

Within the country itself he could not move without constantly jostling the world's foremost immortals. In Nazareth and on the shores of Galilee he walked in the footsteps of the supreme teacher of the Western world. In Hebron he saw, under the terebinths, the patriarchs of these ghostly generations, and the natural mausoleum which holds their bones. And lesser names crowded on him, of men, places, and peoples which are fixed forever in the human mind as intense prototypes of experience, to be referred to as long as men are good and bad, weak and strong, wise and foolish—that is to say, as long as they are men. The heavy, metallic waters of the Dead Sea recall the cities they cover, eternal types of unredeemable corruption. In the eastern plain, across the hills, the Philistines labored to acquire their place in history as the representatives of the dull, the aggressive, and the unspiritual; and there Samson dramatized forever the complex of the strong body and the weak will.

And what shall be said of the heart and center of the land, Jerusalem? Its summits, valleys, and slopes could hardly accommodate the accumulation of sanctities and memories. The suggestion of first and last things, of the utmost range of human effort and hope, emanated from the scene. A thousand recollections struggled for the possession of the pilgrim's attention, and left him helpless. There is no comparable spot anywhere else on the face of the earth; nor is it likely that one like it will be created again.

Now I have not dropped into this vein of piety and sentiment simply because it is the proper thing to do in recalling a first visit to Palestine, and not even because I want to record my own emotions. I have done it because it is relevant to the story I have to tell. Palestine cannot be understood without its memories. They are as real and formative a part of it as its climate. The struggle of the Jews to rebuild the country is meaningless if those memories are eliminated; so is the world's interest in the struggle. Therefore they must be conjured up, in the appropriate mood, as a prelude. And they must be borne constantly in mind, even when we come down to the workaday, the secular, the trivial, and the comical. There is much in the story which is quite incongruous with the exalted note I have tried to sound. We shall come down to politics, unemployment, strikes, agrarian credits, investments, and chambers of commerce. We shall meet with low egotisms as well as high idealism. The story is human; it moves for the most part on an everyday plane; but it is unintelligible without the background of memories. For the people concerned is the one which stems from those former inhabitants of Palestine who are part of the world's consciousness wherever the Bible is read; and if the world at large always thinks of Palestine predominantly in connection with its ghosts, what shall be the relationship to it of the descendants of the ghosts?

It is one which cannot be described; it can only be shared, and one who does not share it cannot give a true account of the Return. A constituent element in the relationship was, for me, a great wonder and curiosity, which took the form of an apparently unanswerable question: what properties are there in this land, what features in its configuration, to account for its stupefying output of spirit presences? I made a special effort to shut out the past, and I considered only the men and women I encountered—those that were native to the country. I found no clue there. I saw ragged shepherds of lean flocks on stony hillsides; tumbledown cities given over to dirt and poverty; the picturesqueness of decay; a people sunk in listlessness and ignorance, unaware of the universal meaning of the land it inhabited. I accepted the hospitality of the tribe of the Halsa, near the Syrian border; primitive, courteous, illiterate, they might have been Afghanistans in deep Asia, or Sudanese of Omdurman, for all their awareness of great surroundings. By the melancholy wastes of the Huleh marshes, where the Jordan passes through a million reeds to the Sea of Galilee, I stayed awhile in an Arab village. A child playing in the shadow of a hut seemed to have two holes for eyes; but when I stepped closer the two holes burst into two clouds of flies, and the sick eyes were revealed. In the open square women sat weaving the swamp reeds into mats. I was taken into one of the huts: a single room, a hole in the roof to let out the smoke, an earthen floor with two levels, the upper for the family, the lower for the animals. What did these people know of the Palestine the world remembered? Nothing.

I went among the Jews of the old city settlements. *They* knew. They had a special relationship to the land. But their lives were untouched by it. They studied the sacred books, they prayed for the Messiah, not without conviction. Yet one looked among them in vain for a trace of the creative energies which the land had once possessed. Neither they, nor the shepherds, nor the tillers of the soil, nor the keepers of the bazaars, nor the smiths and potters in the booths, were in any way connected with the primordial strength of the country. A deadly inertia lay on the living; this might just as well have been a nameless territory without a record.

But when, still shutting out the past, I dwelt on the sheer physical characteristics of the land, as I saw them there and then, a hint of the unusual stole into my mind. Without a knowledge of history I could have told that the desolation I surveyed was not native to the place. The crumbled terraces on the hillsides bore witness to a time when men had found their cultivation profitable. In certain areas the rich black soil stopped abruptly, not at a natural boundary of recalcitrant rock, but to disappear under a blanket of sands which wind and drift had spread over its fertility. There were gloomy marshes, habitations of disease, avoided even by birds in their flight, bearing similar witness to human neglect rather than the harshness of nature. Lonely trees in the valleys and on hilltops testified that forests had once stood there. All this spoke of the vanished habitability of the land.

There was something else—a hint concerning the sources of that strange capacity of the country, now gone with its habitability, to raise life to a fierce intensity.

An extraordinary degree of fantasy entered into the modeling of this territory. It is a land of contrasts and tensions. The southern base is soldered into the hot, forbidding wilderness of Sinai; the wedgelike northern extremity runs into the rich crescent which arches over toward Mesopotamia. A double range of hills, irregularly molded, crossed by valleys, pitted by glens—as though a thumb had been pressed here and there into the heights before they had hardened and set—marks the length of the land. To the east it is cleft by a singular riverbed, which burrows closer to the core of our planet than any other part of it still uncovered by the sea. This is the Jordan, the little river which, starting from the slopes of Hermon, descends so precipitously that they named it *Yarden*, the Descender. The heights towering above its source are covered with eternal snow; less than two hundred miles away, the shores of the Dead Sea, where the river ends, have never been touched by snowfall. Right of the Jordan and the Dead Sea, the land rises again, and offers rich pasture to shepherds; but left of the Dead Sea, the hills are incredibly desolate, mile beyond mile of bulging shale rock, heartbreaking to look at. This is the Wilderness of Judea. No other land of comparable size experiences such a variety of climates and scenic effects. No other land offers such a multitude of exposed plateaus and isolated retreats, of loving intimacy and devastatingloneliness, within so small a compass. It is a land, then, which spurs to action and lulls to meditation, fit for extremes of willfulness and inwardness.

The sunlight is strong, and for the greater part of the year continuous. The nights are so clear that it seems as if even the air had vanished with the day. The multitudes of the stars are then as it were within reach, and the infinity of space takes hold of the human spirit. It is impossible to sojourn in this land and escape the spell of its purely physical character. A chance visitor, wholly ignorant of its history—if such could be found—but sensitive to form and space, must exclaim: "Something has happened here, or will yet happen. It is a land with a destiny."

But that something had happened, of course, and was known to all the world. This was in a sense the curse of Palestine. Those that thought of it from afar, or made the pilgrimage to see it for themselves, were incapable of contemplating it under any other aspect than that of its past. The land was burdened with a reputation which blotted out its present and denied it the possibility of a future. Its inhabitants were regarded as irrelevant apparitions among the true tenants, the ghosts. Enough for the former if they managed to exist as the attendants of the ghosts. If they served any purpose it was to accentuate by their presence the dedication of this land to the dead.

II

All travelers returning from Palestine said the same thing: the country as such, in physiognomy and atmosphere, proclaimed itself as set apart for the unusual, as if one should stumble, in a waste, across a ready-made theater, equipped with every variety of scenery, and even with lighting effects. The landscape was one which exercised a peculiar compulsion on the spirit; it was not made for commonplace occupants.

But if this was so, there was a riddle to be solved. How was it that only one people, the Jews, had responded to the compulsion? How was it that only one Bible had been written there, and that its figures, which still haunted the hills and plains, were exclusively Jewish? There were nations in Palestine before the Jews—the Amorites, the Canaanites, the Jebusites, the Girgashites, and the rest of them. There were occupying nations after the expulsion of the Jews —the Greek, the Roman, the Saracen, the Arab, the Turk. Why had they not established the compulsive affinity with the country?

Well, as to the first, we might say they never got their chance. They came too early in the history of the race. Or—this is barely possible, if somehow quite implausible—they *did* have their Isaiahs and their Elijahs, whom no one now remembers. That is hard to believe; Isaiahs and Elijahs have a knack of impressing themselves on the generations. But what shall be said of the latter inhabitants, who followed the Jews? *Their* records are copious and explicit. They lie open to our scrutiny. They are not lacking in evidence of great gifts. But they are completely devoid of the particular relationship which

Palestine calls for or leads us to expect. Only the Jews clicked with Palestine.

And if we examine the matter more closely, we begin to understand why. Palestine may be a land of destiny, but only to those who submit to it completely. The latter occupants entered the country under the wrong auspices and without the proper predisposition. To all of them Palestine was peripheral; the center of their consciousness remained in Athens, or Rome, or Mecca, or Constantinople. Palestine was an annex, an outpost, a province, not the heart of their world. And this made all the difference.

To the Jews Palestine was, from the beginning, everything. The surrender was complete, premeditated, and preordained. It became an incurable fixation. It does not matter if we challenge the historicity of the Bible in regard to the accounts of the first Jewish ascent to the country. What matters is that every surviving record tells of the belief in those accounts. We cannot find anywhere else, in legend or mythology, a people which regarded itself as having been created in order to live a certain life in a certain country by divine command. Driven from it once into the Babylonian exile, the Jews achieved the impossible: they returned and reconstituted themselves a people, in the tradition. That settled it, so to speak. Once is an accident; twice is a habit.

They never got over it. That is the all-important point of Jewish history. I do not mean to say that there were not Jews who did not liberate themselves from the connection. Within the last century or century and a half considerable numbers of them have, in effect, declared: "Enough is enough! After eighteen hundred years we are entitled to forget, and to come to terms with reality. There will be no Return." They even made a virtue of it, saying: "It was never intended that we should return," and adding: "God wants us to be scattered throughout the world, to set an example." But they were a minority. The others remembered.

Their whole life was a remembering, a vivid and tenacious remembering. On the day which commemorates the destruction of the Temple, they fasted and mourned, after the lapse of a thousand, two thousand years, as though they had been the witnesses and victims of the catastrophe, as though they had themselves escaped from the blazing ruins, leaving behind them their nearest and dearest. I have sat on the floor in stockinged feet among fellow mourners, listened to the sobbing recital of the Lamentations of Jeremiah, and, by the light of the commemorative candles, seen the tears run down the cheeks of grown men. This was no mechanical ritual. It came from the heart of a frustrated people. It was real, poignant and terrifying, a Fourth of July in reverse.

The eternal presentness of Palestine in their minds cannot be conveyed without a description of the texture of their life. Three times a day, and oftener on special occasions, they prayed for the Restoration. Even when they prayed for timely rains and abundant harvests, it was in Palestinian terms. Morning and evening, at the daily services, they exhorted themselves to be good, for then God would send the *yoreh* and *malkosh* (the former and the latter rains) in due season. They might be living in a northern country, where there are no former or latter rains; they might be living in a tropical belt, where the rains are a curse. No matter. As far as they were concerned, Palestine set the standard. Perhaps they felt that what was good for Palestine must be good for the rest of the world.

Long after they had been driven from the soil, and had become an urban people, they continued to celebrate the harvest. They did not sow, in tears or otherwise; but they pretended to reap in joy; and the symbols of the celebration had nothing to do with the locality. When the harvesting comes in Palestine, the sun is at its hottest. In ancient days the reaper used to put up a booth in the middle of the field, and there he took shelter between spells of work. Jews living in the Arctic Circle continued to put up the booth *(sukkah)* at the time of the Palestinian harvest, to protect themselves from the rays of the aurora borealis.

They refused, likewise, to relinquish the language of ancient Palestine. Moving from land to land, they acquired and used in ordinary converse, a variety of languages, Arabic, Spanish, Yiddish. Hebrew remained the language of prayer and study, of hope and scholarship. Even when it had become largely unintelligible to the unlettered, the sound and flavor of it were retained by repetition; and when they wrote Spanish or Yiddish, at least they used the Hebrew letters.

The scholar was always their highest ideal of a man; but his scholarship had to mean a mastery of the ethical and religious principles which had been formulated in Palestine, and of the legal code which had governed Jewish life there. To live mentally in Palestine was the purpose of such scholarship.

It was all a retention of the machinery of Palestinian life. Some day they would return. They would be ready to slip into the Palestinian landscape. They would have no difficulty—they thought—in adapting themselves. They would have the proper intellectual and folkloristic equipment. Thus the act of "remembering Zion" was not a single and special gesture. It was a total art. It was the constant rehearsal of the mode of Palestinian life.

They said that merely to live in Palestine was equivalent to the fulfillment of all law. To be buried in Palestine was a wise precaution. For the resurrection could take place only in Palestine, and they shuddered at the thought of their bones having to roll underground to the last assembly. It was best to be on the spot. Failing this provision, they asked that a handful of Palestinian earth be placed under their heads when they were buried in the exile.

The world changed, and Jewish life changed, too, in many ways. The peoples with whom the Jews had dealt of old passed away. The course of empire took its westward way, dominion shifted from continent to continent. The Jews settled in Babylon, in Spain, in Russia, in America. They created centers and traditions of the exile. They established dynasties of scholars and rabbis. They had their rich and poor, their aristocrats, their snobberies, their saints, their internecine quarrels. They were split into warring sects. They were driven from land to land, lived a few hundred years here, a few hundred years there. The affinity with Palestine remained undiminished. So much so that the rest of the world was compelled to acknowledge it. Mobs attacking the Jews incited themselves with the cry: *"Hep! Hep!"* The syllable, some say, is made up of the first three letters of the words: *"Hieroselyma est perdita!"*—Jerusalem is lost! My father heard that cry in Rumania, in his boyhood, seventy years ago. Why should Rumanian peasants taunt the Jews with the destruction of Jerusalem, if Jerusalem was nothing to the Jews? But the truth is that the rioters really doubted what they said. Jerusalem was not lost; only its people had been mislaid.

It was not an easy thing to maintain and transmit the technique of this discipline of remembrance. It did not have the support of the legal machinery of the state. It did not have the sympathy of the surrounding population. On the contrary, there was every worldly temptation to defection. In fact, there were defections and failures; but they only emphasized the wonder of the persistence. For if the Jews had been incapable, through a sort of fossilization, to do otherwise than they did, if they had been, as it were, deprived of choice, the phenomenon would have been without moral meaning, something like the turtle's carapace. But they were free; free, that is, in the ordinary sense that a man may choose to be true or untrue to his character. And having chosen, he must renew the choice, beginning anew each day. This they did, days and years and centuries.

From *Harvest in the Desert* (1943)

7 ZIONISM REBORN

The Beginning of the Snarl

Zionism is as old as the Jewish Exile: neo-Zionism, the notion of the Return as a non-messianic, practical mass enterprise, was born in the nineteenth century; political Zionism, which is simply neo-Zionism with a political apparatus, was founded at the close of the nineteenth century by Theodor Herzl (1860–1904).

Herzl did not at first understand Zionism otherwise than politically and sociologically. It was for him a great plan to solve the Jewish problem by lifting the Jews out of their hostile environment and resettling them in a territory of their own, not necessarily Palestine. A Westerner, brought up in Vienna and wholly steeped in Western culture, only superficially acquainted with the folk tradition, he was a stranger to the peculiar *Heimweh,* the incurable nostalgia for the Holy Land, which invested Zionism among the masses of Eastern Europe. When, in 1896, he wrote his remarkable pamphlet, *Der Judenstaat* (The Jewish State), he knew nothing about the powerful neo-Zionist sentiment agitating the Jews of Russia, Poland, Galicia, and Rumania, nothing about the literature it had produced or about the men who were preaching the Return in the cities and ghettos and *shtetlach* of the Pale. Zionism was not for him, as it was for them, a comprehensive double program for the re-creation of the Jewish homeland and the revitalization of the Jewish people everywhere. He learned with a shock of the Jewish thinker Ahad Ha-Am (1856–1927), who envisaged the rebuilt homeland—which could only be in Palestine—as a center of spiritual renewal for all Jewry; and it broke his heart, literally, when Russian Jewry, in the midst of a wave of pogroms, turned its back on Great Britain's (tentative) offer of a territory in Uganda, even though he presented it as a temporary refuge from the Czar and the Cossacks.

Political Zionism began with a search for a patron or protector. Herzl thought first of Germany, and wooed Wilhelm II. Failing there, he turned to England, which offered him Uganda. (Marvelous are the blindnesses of creative genius: Germany, which was to produce Hitlerism a generation later; Uganda, next door to the Mau Mau country.) He died in the prime of his manhood, worn out by his exertions to organize Zionism and to obtain the charter of a homeland from the then ruler of Palestine, the last sultan of Turkey, Abdul-Hamid II—Abdul the Damned. The second great leader, Chaim Weizmann (1874–1952), lived long enough to become the first president of the State of Israel. In vivid contrast to Herzl, with whom he maintained a running battle over the nature, aims, and methods of the Zionist movement, he was of the folk and the tradition, an admirer and disciple of Ahad Ha-Am. From the beginning—remarkably enough, from his early boyhood, as a letter of his written at the age of eleven attests—he believed in England as the instrument of Jewish liberation, and despite many disappointments he stood by this choice almost to the end.

Folk Zionism was wholly democratic, for among other things it was the revolt of the Jewish masses against the wealthy, self-appointed leaders who, well connected with the non-Jewish world, undertook to keep their people obedient to the ruling powers. Political Zionism, conducting as it were the foreign policy, was tinged with imperialism at its outset. Herzl would have lent the support of the movement to the German *Drang nach Osten;* and Weizmann and his circle urged upon England the usefulness of a client Jewish state in Palestine, guarding the Suez Canal and the line to India.

It was not from inclination but from life-and-death necessity that the Zionist movement went through that phase. Without a patron it could not take the first step. There were no great countries that were not imperialistic, and all liberation movements begin with the search for an interested ally, without too much squeamishness over his character (e.g., the early American alliance with France). Still, there was a difference between the two choices: Germany was imperialism on the rise, and her triumph would have thrown back for a long time the universal liberation movement; England's was an imperialism in decline, increasingly tolerant, tired, and approaching abdication. It did not take long for the contradiction between the liberationist spirit of Zionism and the imperialistic purposes of England to be revealed. A confused and complicated relationship set in between the two partners with disparate objectives, and before Weizmann was succeeded by Ben-Gurion—the third in the triad of Israel's founders—the partnership had turned into an enmity.

England's rejected offer of Uganda in 1903 was political Zionism's first victory; it marked the official recognition by a great power of the Jewish right to a homeland. Her Balfour Declaration of November 2, 1917, marked the recognition of the indissoluble tie between the Jewish people and Palestine. Issued with America's concurrence in the midst of World War I, it read:

His Majesty's Government view with favor the establishment in Palestine of a national home for the Jewish people, and will use their best endeavours to facilitate the achievement of this object, it being clearly understood that nothing shall be done which may prejudice the civil and religious rights of the existing non-Jewish communities in Palestine, or the rights and political status enjoyed by Jews in any other country.

The *quid pro quo* consisted of two parts: the aligning of Jewish sympathy everywhere on the side of the Allies, with an eye particularly on America's three million Jews and on Russia's seven million, recently liberated by the Russian Revolution, and the acquisition of a client state next door to the Suez Canal. This practical aspect of the transaction makes it easy to stamp the Balfour Declaration as devoid of any moral content; but here it happened, as it sometimes does, that selfishness coincided with a disinterested principle. The Balfour Declaration corresponded to a widespread sentiment in the Christian world in favor of the Return, and was in effect the first step toward the righting of an immemorial historic wrong.

A sharp demurrer may be entered here. It is the Arab claim that the Balfour Declaration was the first step in the infliction of a new historic wrong. Its phrasing is ambiguous or even self-contradictory. "Nothing shall be done which may prejudice the civil and religious rights of the existing non-Jewish communities in Palestine." Was it not the civil right of these communities to call Palestine their own and separate country, in which they, as the overwhelming majority —some six hundred thousand versus some seventy thousand Jews— were to set up their own government? Had they not the right to set up a Palestinian nationality, and did not the Balfour Declaration propose to deprive them of that right?

I draw attention to the phrase "set up a Palestinian nationality," for a Palestinian nationality did not exist. Palestine was not the locus of a nationalist sentiment. Professor Philip K. Hitti, probably the most widely accepted authority on Arab history and Arab affairs today, opens his *Syria: A Short History* thus:

Syria, in its geographical sense, occupies a unique place in the annals of the world. Especially because of the inclusion of Palestine and Phoenicia within its ancient boundaries, it had made a more significant contribution to the moral and spiritual progress of mankind than any other comparable land. . . . As the cradle of Judaism and the birthplace of Christianity it originated two of the great monotheistic religions and prompted the rise and development of the third and last . . . Islam. . . . Closely associated with its religious contribution was the ethical message southern Syria—Palestine—conveyed. Its people were the first to insist that man is created in the image of God and that each man is the brother of every other man under God's fatherhood.

The extinction of the Jewish people in this strange passage, and the appropriation of Moses, Isaiah, Jesus, man in the image of God, etc., to the credit of the Syrians is all very well—who would not like to claim them on the slightest pretext?—but it disarmingly, if unintentionally, makes the point that if Palestine ever had an identity it was because of what the Jews did there. And if the Jews were, after all, nothing more nor less than southern Syrians, their right to reoccupancy is strikingly reconfirmed.

Still the question will be urged: "Did not the Arabs of Palestine or southern Syria, a majority of seven or eight to one in 1917, have the right to declare themselves a distinct nationality and refuse to have their territory turned into a Jewish homeland?" It is true that a community does not become a nationality, does not acquire the emotions and specific needs of nationality, by a declaration; nevertheless, a community may decide to turn itself into a nationality. Should not such a decision be respected?

I am pushing the Arab argument to its extreme. Not only was there no Palestinian nationalism, there was not even an inclination to create it. But if there had somehow been any such inclination (and its existence would already imply an embryonic nationalism), there is a decisive difference between intention and actuality. In the actuality of a nationalism a corporate spiritual identity already exists; it is entitled to recognition; it must be treated with solicitude. Infringement of this identity is an invasion of the personality of the individual. A man who feels himself spiritually and culturally and psychologically rooted in the fact of a certain nationality must not be compelled to relinquish it. The deliberate destruction of the conditions that nurture his nationalism is a great wrong.

But is it also wrong to disturb the conditions under which a community, if left alone, *might* develop a nationalism? Let me emphasize that I am speaking of *Palestinian* and not of *Arab* nationalism, of the Palestinian Arab's right to develop an as yet nonexistent *Palestinian* nationalism, and not of his right to retain his *Arab* nationalism there, which has never been challenged. To put it otherwise, was it the right of the communities of Palestine, overwhelmingly Arab, nationalistically conscious or not, to be left alone, to do with the country whatever they liked?

If the question is so phrased, the answer must be: "Yes, unless another claim existed." And if that claim, the Jewish claim, which I have tried to establish, is disallowed, the Balfour Declaration was an unjustified act of violence committed upon the seven hundred thousand Arabs inhabiting Palestine in 1917.

Later developments may alter the perspective. The situation of the Jews of Germany after Hitler's advent to power reduced the question to elemental terms. With the rest of the world mostly closed to them, with despoilment and destruction facing them where they were, the German Jews—and later the Jews still unable to escape from territories occupied by the Germans—had to choose between Palestine and death, and they would not choose death. And after them, the hundreds of thousands who survived the death camps, only to find the world still closed to them, had to choose between reconstructing their lives in lands that had become their charnel houses and reconstructing them in a welcoming and helpful environment, and they chose the latter. The picture in the 1940s was totally different from that of 1917, and a reassessment had to be made of the relative rights of Jews and Arabs in respect of Palestine. The Arabs refused to make it, but it could be said by the Western world, including Russia, that the homeland which had its political beginning in the Balfour Declaration had justified itself.

For the Zionists the moral perspective was not altered. Their claims referred to a larger historical perspective and were concerned with more than the refugee problem. They had always seen their relationship to the Arabs in affirmative and creative terms, and at the time of the Balfour Declaration there had been Arabs who shared their views.

In March 1919, Dr. Weizmann, the leader of the World Zionist Organization, and the Emir Feisal, the leader of the Arab peoples liberated by the Allies, were both in Paris, at the heads of their respective delegations to the Peace Conference.

On March 3, Feisal addressed the following letter to Professor (later Supreme Court Justice) Felix Frankfurter, an American member of the Zionist delegation:

I want to take this opportunity of my first contact with American Zionists, to tell you what I have often been able to say to Dr. Weizmann in Arabia and Europe.

We feel that the Arabs and Jews are cousins in race, suffering similar oppression at the hands of powers stronger than themselves, and by a happy coincidence have been able to take the first step forward toward the attainment of their national ideals together.

We Arabs, especially the educated among us, look with the deepest sympathy on the Zionist movement. Our deputation here in Paris is fully acquainted with the proposals submitted by the Zionist Organization to the Peace Conference, and we regard them as moderate and proper. We will do our best, in so far as we are concerned, to help them through; we will wish the Jews a most hearty welcome home.

With the chiefs of your movement, especially Dr. Weizmann, we have had, and continued to have, the closest relations. *He has been a great helper of our cause,* and I hope the Arabs may soon be in a position to make the Jews some return for their kindness. *We are working together for a revived and reformed Near East,* and our two movements complete each other. The Jewish Movement is national and not imperialistic. Our movement is national and not imperialistic; and there is room in Syria for us both. Indeed, I think that neither can be a real success without the other.

People less informed and less responsible than our leaders, ignoring the need for cooperation between the Arabs and the Zionists, have been trying to exploit the local differences that must naturally arise in Palestine in the early stages of our movement. Some of them have, I am afraid, misrepresented your aims to the Arab peasantry, and our aims to the Jewish peasantry, with the result that interested parties have been able to make capital of what they call our differences.

I wish to give you my firm conviction that these differences are not questions of principle, but on matters of detail, such as must inevitably occur in every contact with neighboring peoples, and as are easily dissipated by mutual goodwill. Indeed, nearly all of them will disappear with fuller knowledge.

I look forward, and my people with me look forward, to a future in which we will help you and you will help us, so that the countries in which we are mutually interested may take their place in the community of civilized peoples of the world.

Yours sincerely,
Feisal

This letter (to which I have added the italics) does not stand alone. "The proposals submitted by the Zionist Organization to the Peace Conference," which the Arab deputation regarded as "moderate and proper," were also spelled out in an agreement entered into by Feisal and Weizmann two months earlier. Paragraphs three and four read:

In the establishment of the Constitution and Administration of Palestine, all such measures shall be adopted as will afford the guarantees for carrying into effect the British Government's [Balfour] Declaration of November 2, 1917.

All necessary measures shall be taken to encourage and stimulate immigration of Jews into Palestine *on a large scale* [italics added] and as quickly as possible to settle Jewish immigrants upon the land through closer settlement and intensive cultivation. In taking such measures the Arab peasant and tenant farmers shall be protected in their rights, and shall be assisted in forwarding their economic development.

The italicized words should clarify what was in the minds of the Zionist and Arab leaders; not, as some have argued, a token admission of Jews, but a solid occupation. This is also evident from the Feisal letter, which contemplated the advantages of cooperation between the Jewish and Arab national movements.

During the course of the war, and before the signing of the agreement and the letter, several conferences had taken place between Feisal and Weizmann, the first of them near Amman (now the capital of the Hashemite Kingdom of Jordan, ruled by King Hussein, the great-nephew of Feisal). Feisal was the commander-in-chief of the Arab forces assisting the Allies in ejecting the Turks from Arab countries. T. E. Lawrence ("Lawrence of Arabia"), the fiery Arab partisan, was the intermediary at the first conference and continued to serve both sides—he was an equally fiery Zionist partisan—at the Peace Conference. In his autobiography, *Trial and Error,* Weizmann justly points to the negotiations and agreement as an answer "to the critics who have accused us of beginning our work in Palestine without ever consulting the wishes or welfare of the Arab world." The accusation could be truthfully leveled at Herzl; it cannot be leveled at Weizmann. It is almost certain that if the Arab leadership had not been eager to draw a Jewish homeland into the Arab world for the mutual benefit of Jew and Arab, if it had opposed the Balfour Declaration at the Peace Conference, the Zionist movement would have collapsed, to await another occasion. The anti-Zionist elements in England would have gotten the upper hand then, instead of some years later; for the war was won, and the practical reasons for a pro-Zionist policy no longer had the same force. The Jewish claim to a homeland in Palestine would still have been valid, but it could not have been successfully pressed. There had to exist a recognized coincidence of interest between the Jews and the Arabs, and it existed.

Shortly after Feisal reached his agreement with the Zionists, he added the following condition: "If the Arabs are established as I have asked in my manifesto, I will carry out what I have written in this agreement. If changes are made, I cannot be responsible for failure to carry out this agreement."

He was stating the obvious. What he had asked in his manifesto to the Allied Powers via the British secretary of state was the establishment of a free Syria. Like Professor Hitti he understood under the term Syria the territory from the Taurus to Sinai, including Palestine and what is now called Jordan, but what was then named Transjordan, that is, the part of Palestine lying east of the Jordan River. Within this large territory there was room for populational maneuver. Palestinian Arabs could be relocated by purchase and compensation, involving no change of country. The Jewish homeland could then emerge within the framework of a Jewish-Arab federation.

Unless this is what the Zionist and Arab leaders had in mind, the agreement has no meaning. As Weizmann was to put it shortly afterwards, Zionism was striving for a Jewish homeland that was to be as Jewish as England was English. This was not to say there would be no Arabs in the Jewish homeland or no Jews in other parts of Greater Syria. England, too, has her minorities. In the frustrated dream of the Zionist and Arab leaders, the entire Middle East, equitably apportioned, was to afford room for the peaceful and cooperative development of the Jewish and Arab nationalisms, with Palestine as the area allocated for the Jewish national home.

The area of Palestine on both sides of the Jordan was 44,000 square miles. Much of it was desert, but a great part of that was, as the Jews have proved in the Negev, reclaimable. The possibilities were enormous, but possibilities are seen only by those who have the will to use them, and what the Jews have done in Israel could have been done in the rest of Palestine. Had Israel been permitted to concentrate on Transjordan—and on the Middle East generally—the skills it has scattered through Nigeria, Ghana, Mali, Liberia, Ethiopia, and a dozen other emerging Afro-Asian states, had its social forms penetrated to its Arab neighbors, had its market been open to them, as theirs to her, had the insane arms race been aborted, the Middle East would have been today a radiating center of prosperity and democracy.

And how eager the Zionists were to play that role! With what fervor we used to speak, long ago—it is like another age—of the "bridge" we would build between East and West, and of the rebirth of the ancient center of civilization. How naive it was, and how valid it still is as the only way out of the dreadful snarl.

It had the naiveté of all great visions that must travel to realization by unforeseen detours. The last and most difficult detour confronts us today; the first was already in the making before the issuance of the Balfour Declaration. The straight road was blocked when Feisal's hopes of a free and united Syria were dashed by the rivalry of the French and British for spheres of influence in the Middle East. Initially an attempt was made to harmonize this rivalry with the genuine interests of the Arab peoples. The now forgotten Sykes-Picot Agreement between France and England—negotiated but never carried out in its original spirit—anticipated a mandatory system very different from the one which was ultimately installed. It proposed the beneficent and transitional tutelage of a divided Syria—the term is used here in its proper all-inclusive sense—with France administering what are now called Syria and Lebanon, and Palestine on both sides of the Jordan assigned to England. The arrangement need not have been inconsistent with the Balfour Declaration; but the two men who negotiated it, Sir Mark Sykes for England, and Georges Picot for France, did not foresee the practical consequences of the division. The rivalry between France and England in the Middle East became so bitter (we might compare it with the episode in World War II when England was fighting in North Africa and Syria was held by the Vichy French) that the interests of the Arabs were pushed into the background, and the Balfour Declaration began to turn sour for the British.

The Weizmann-Feisal grand plan was never given a chance. When in 1920 Feisal tried to assert his claim as king of an independent Greater Syria, he was thrown out of Damascus by the French, and he wound up, with more good fortune than he might have expected, as king of Iraq, with no say in the affairs of Syria or Palestine. He learned to regret his brief and bright vision of an Arab-Jewish union and to forget the help he had received from the Zionists at a difficult time.

The second road block on the path of Zionist realization, far more formidable than the first, was created in June 1922, strangely enough, when the strongly pro-Zionist Winston Churchill was colonial secretary, and a Jew, Sir Herbert (later Lord) Samuel, was high commissioner to Palestine. Abdullah, Feisal's older brother, having invaded Transjordan with a tiny army, was confirmed as emir of that territory by the British, who had just set his brother on the throne of Iraq. The effect was calamitous for Zionism and Transjordan. The new emirate was an artificial and by itself a nonviable state, not so much because it lacked possibilities but because, withdrawn from the area of Zionist operation, it was doomed to stagnation. The Jewish homeland, which had been offered 44,000 square miles within which to find room for itself and the Arabs, now had to make do with 10,000. A great many of the difficulties and sufferings that have attended the birth of Israel are the result of that unstatesmanlike act of 1922.

The reader will notice that I have used "Jewish homeland" and "Jewish state" interchangeably. Much has been written about the difference. It has been pointed out that the Balfour Declaration speaks of a Jewish homeland, not of a Jewish state, and the Zionists have been accused of duplicity in the representations of their intentions. But it is difficult to see how there can be a Jewish homeland without Jewish self-rule, and a Jewish homeland with self-rule is a Jewish state. There were undoubtedly some Zionists who thought "homeland" a less aggressive word than "state," but they pulled the wool over nobody's eyes. Actually, "homeland" (*"Heimstätte"* in the original Zionist platform) had a particular appeal to the homeless Jewish people, and it still remains a popular designation for the Jewish state.

The Snarl Thickens

Neither the Jews nor the Arabs were ready for the Weizmann-Feisal plan. The Jewish longing for the Return was a genuine impulse; so was the surge of Arab "nationalism." Both were handicapped, each in its own way, by historic conditions and internal divisions. Both came unexpectedly into the blinding light of opportunity; both blundered and stumbled. The handicaps were further weighted by developments beyond the control of both.

Neo-Zionism took hold first among the poor and the religious, and at the center of the awakening were the millions of East European Jews. Among the religious I include the secularists who had been brought up in the tradition and had been conditioned by it, even though they were no longer observant Jews. But large numbers of the poor turned to the anti-Zionist revolutionary movements, and many of the pious repudiated a secular folk-messianism. The rich, with an exception here and there, were as shocked by the Zionists as by the revolutionaries, and where wealth went hand in hand with piety the shock was painful and vocal in the extreme.

At the time when neo-Zionism arose, as in our time, and as at all other times, large numbers of Jews—it is impossible to be statistical here—were abandoning their Jewish identity. To those who would not or could not follow their example, the action was a betrayal: of the God of Abraham, Isaac, and Jacob in the eyes of the religious; of the folk, in the eyes of the secular. However narrow this judgment may seem, it remains a fact that with every defection the position of the loyal Jews becomes more precarious. In the nineteenth century neo-Zionism was the particular reaction of the time and the circumstances to the threat of mass defection. The reborn Jewish homeland was to be the physical rescue of those who elected to go there, the spiritual rescue of all.

Those who were bent on escape—and many were escaping without making a principle of it—regarded Jewish loyalty as an anachronism, and worse. In the form of Zionism it was a perversity, and they reciprocated the contempt and resentment of the Zionists. For just as the latter saw Zionism as a re-Judaizing movement that would improve the status and inner condition of the Jew, so the assimilationists saw in it an assault on their chances for assimilation. They denounced it as offensive to the ideal of universalism, a return to the ghetto, to medievalism and obscurantism. It also compromised their patriotism, which was somehow part of their universalism. It tainted Jews with the suspicion of dual allegiance, and was therefore a weapon in the hands of anti-Semites. They put their trust in "Progress," which would soon make the Jews at home everywhere, and fifty years ago they hailed the Russian Revolution as the collapse of the last citadel of anti-Semitism.

This group has slowly lost its influence and since May–June 1967 has almost disappeared; but its survivors still come out, armed with intellectual flintlocks and fowling pieces, to do battle with the idea of the Jewish state. In the early days of Zionism, however, it was strong enough to discourage the weaker-willed. But even those Jewish masses that were unshaken in their faithfulness to the tradition of the Return did not respond at once to the Zionist call. They were like a patient long bedfast trying to recover the use of his limbs; and a man in that plight is not helped if his first steps are discouraged and derided by his relatives. Moreover, they had doubts of their own. Could it really be done by *them?* Might not this hope of self-redemption dissolve into a fata morgana? Had not these twenty centuries atrophied the faculties of hand, brain, and heart that are the hall-marks of an independent people?

The Balfour Declaration was a great lift to the hopes of Zionists, but no mass rally of action followed it. The Jewish people was less disposed than any other to put its trust in princes and rulers. Did England really mean to give Palestine to the Jews? And if it did, would not someone else take it away? But perhaps the severest blow to Zionist self-confidence was the outcome of the Russian Revolution, or rather of the Bolshevik *coup d'état* that diverted the Russian Revolution from its historic purpose. Coming almost simultaneously with the Balfour Declaration, the Revolution cut off millions of traditionalist Jews from participation in Jewish history. As it was, the contingent of Russian Jewry that got out in time laid the foundations on which most of Israel has risen; it determined the character of the structure and is only now being replaced by a new generation. Chaim Weizmann, David Ben-Gurion, Berl Katzenelson, Menachem Mendel Ussishkin, Shmarya Levin, Zalman Shazar, Golda Meir, Levi Eshkol, some living, some dead, some remembered, some forgotten, are a small part of the roster. Very few names from the Western or Oriental Jewries appear side by side with them. But half the reservoir of manpower for the Jewish homeland was frozen in its place by Communist decree.

For all these reasons, the end of World War I was not followed by a tide of Jewish immigration into Palestine. Less than two thousand Jews entered the country in 1919, and a few more than eight thousand in each subsequent year until 1923. In 1924 there was a tremendous leap to thirty-four thousand, as anti-Semitic pressures were increased in Poland. But again the figures dwindled, and in 1927 the gain of immigration over emigration was three thousand. A land as primitive as Palestine then was could not absorb newcomers easily. The populational base was small; the conditions were trying. Vast sums of money were needed, and rich Jews were ready to give for anything but Palestine. I have painful personal memories of those years, when I sometimes accompanied Dr. Weizmann on his begging expeditions to a Jewry that had not yet awakened to the needs, the possibilities, and the realities of the Jewish homeland.

So the work went forward irregularly, with maddening slowness, with pioneers ready and no funds for land to settle them on, with dissension among Zionists as to method, with fierce opposition in Palestine on the part of the old settlement of pietists, whose dreams of the Redemption were being shattered by a form of realiza-

tion that to them was blasphemy. When I look back, when I recall
what a ludicrous and piddling thing the Zionist movement was in the
eyes of the world, and how unperceptive most Jews were, I realize
again, with a sense of shock, the inevitability with which Zionism
must have been endowed to have reached its present stage.

The unreadiness of the Arabs to accept the Weizmann-Feisal
plan has now turned into a ferocious rejection of it. In those days it
was largely passive. I am speaking here of the Arabs of Palestine. As
we have seen, they outnumbered the Jews by about eight to one. Had
there been a deep folk resentment against Jewish immigration, had
a genuine national opposition to it arisen, then again the Zionist
dream would have had to wait for another occasion. But if the Weizmann-Feisal plan meant nothing to the Arab masses, the threat to
their nationalism meant little more. Wherever the contact was made,
they got along very well with the Jews. They had found an unexpected market for their fruit and vegetables and fish. Arab villages
adjacent to Jewish settlements prospered. Thousands of Arabs immi-
grated from Transjordan and Syria. Daily I saw streams of Arab
farmers and workmen pouring into Jerusalem and Tel Aviv, with a
contingent of fishermen in the latter city. Jewish shopkeepers who
had not yet learned to speak Hebrew, let alone Arabic, chaffered with
them in Yiddish, so that Yiddish-speaking Arabs were added to the
world's ethnocultural curiosities.

The Arab leaders describe the process differently: as they see it,
the simple Arab masses were being slowly and craftily robbed of
their heritage, while they, the leaders, warned and protested, staged
demonstrations and called to resistance. If many years passed before
the Jewish masses could be activated toward the creation of their
homeland, in those same years the Arabs have been activated into the
defense of their natural rights. Independently of the claim that the
Jews had the right to establish their homeland in Palestine, the merit
of the pleas entered by the Arab leaders must be examined in the
light of their relationship to the Arab masses. It will become evident
from the record that the Arab leaders in Palestine, which almost
always means the wealthy Arabs, cooperated with the Jews for the
purpose of gain as much as they opposed them for the sake of Arab
nationalism. Landowners, moneylenders, the effendi class generally,
were happy to profit from Jewish colonization, even though their
nationalist feelings were wounded. It will also become evident that
the concern of the Arab leaders for the welfare of the masses was,

outside the area of a common nationalist sentiment, of even more dubious quality.

Arab resistance to Jewish colonization—that is, the Jewish establishment of the homeland—during those early years has a double interest for us, for it tells us much about the British administration of Palestine as well as about the Arabs.

As to the second, there was actually little evidence of major hostility until 1929. If the events of 1929 perturbed us greatly at the time, in perspective they bear out the claim that the Arab masses, exploited and oppressed for centuries by Turkish rule, were simply glad to be able to breathe more easily. There were only two outbreaks that could be associated with anti-Zionist feelings, one in April 1920, the second in May 1921. (The attack on the far-north border of the colony of Tel Hai, in March 1920, in which Joseph Trumpeldor and five of his comrades were killed, was an act of banditry with no political content.)

The first was confined to Jerusalem and resulted in twelve deaths, six Jewish and six Arab. The second began in Jaffa and spread to other areas. The casualties totaled over three hundred, with forty-eight Arab and forty-seven Jewish deaths. On both occasions the preparations for the riots were open and flagrant: inflammatory sermons in the mosques, wild stories circulated of Jewish atrocities and Jewish plans to destroy shrines—this type of Arab propaganda, and the credulity of the Arab masses, have recently become familiar to the world at large. With ample warning in both instances, the preparations of the administration against the events were half-hearted, its handling of them dilatory.

Concerning the first episode Philip Graves, a British correspondent unsympathetic to the Zionist program, wrote:

> It must be admitted that, if most of the accusations brought by the Zionists against the military administration as a whole were unfounded, there were cases in which individual officers showed pro-Arab or pan-Arab sympathies. The Arabs, sometimes encouraged, perhaps unwittingly, by such officers, grew more and more petulant.

The second episode speaks for itself. It lasted for over a week when a large British garrison in Palestine could have been dispatched at once to the points of unrest. But the ambivalent attitude of the administration or of most of its officials came out with devastating clarity in the riots of 1929.

In his autobiography, published when he was already president of the State of Israel, Weizmann asks:

Why from the very word "go" did we have to face the hostility, or at least the frosty neutrality, of Britain's representatives on the spot? . . . Why was it an almost universal rule that such administrators as came out favorably inclined toward us turned against us in a few months? Why, for that matter, was it later an invariable rule that politicians who were enthusiastic for the Jewish homeland during the election forgot completely about it if they were returned to office?

The question was rhetorical. The representatives on the spot did not, with very few exceptions, have a dynamic and creative attitude toward the idea of a Jewish homeland. It was too much to expect that they would be gripped by the visionary enthusiasm of the Jews, or even to understand it. Many of them were accustomed to dealing with "natives," and to adjudicating their disputes in a decent spirit of fair play; the Arabs were "natives" to them, but the Jews—especially those now coming in—were obstreperously un-native. They were educated Westerners, and they knew their rights, which the British administrators often thought one-sided. And the truth is that a recognition of these rights, stemming from an acceptance of the great philosophy of the Return, still has to penetrate to much of the world today.

If this was not enough, there were also British imperial interests to consider. The Balfour Declaration had at its issuance seemed to coincide with them; it did so less and less as time went on. The Arabs were, after all, more important than the Jews, and until the Balfour Declaration could be gotten rid of, as it was finally, one had to manage somehow. A dual policy of fulfillment and frustration played Arabs against Jews, and Jews against Arabs in truncated Palestine. Until its open repudiation, the promise of the Balfour Declaration was often kept to the eye and broken to the heart. This was not always intentional; it simply arose from the discomforts of an unusual and unwelcome political situation.

Still, for eight years after 1921 the land had rest. This was a decisive period in the growth of the Jewish homeland. The foundations were laid of the spirit and institutions that give Israel its character: the *kibbutzim* (collective colonies), the *moshavei ovdim* (cooperative colonies), the labor movement, the educational system, the social services, the democratic framework of government under a National Council *(Va'ad Le'umi)*, which unfolded at the right moment into the

Knesset or Parliament. Between my visits of 1924 and 1929 the *Yishuv* (Jewish settlement) had undergone an inner transformation. It had clearly become the state in the making.

In the matter of learning the principles of self-government, the Arabs of Palestine were in a more favorable position than those of any other country. The leaders turned down the opportunity. In 1922 they were offered a "Legislative Council" to be composed of twelve Arabs (nine Moslem and three Christian), three Jews (all elected by popular vote), and three members of the administration. With most of the administration lukewarm, to say the least, on the question of the Jewish homeland, the Legislative Council would have been a powerful weapon in the hands of the Arabs. But they would have nothing to do with it unless the government first abrogated the Balfour Declaration. This intransigeance has been a permanent feature of the Arab leadership; the less it succeeded the more rigid it became, and it still stands in the way of a fruitful Arab-Jewish accommodation.

The Zionists disliked the idea of the Legislative Council intensely, but they accepted it. They could not bring themselves to oppose a measure so obviously consonant with the principles of democracy. Some of them hoped that if the Arab masses were given a voice they would protect the benefits they were reaping from Jewish immigration. They believed then, as they do still, that the interests of the Arab leaders and those of the Arab masses were diametrically opposed, and time would make this truth obvious to the Arab masses. It was possible that the proposed Legislative Council, with all its dangers, would finally lead to an understanding between Arabs and Jews. This may have been the very reason, certainly one of the reasons, that made the Arab leaders reject it.

There had been a fleeting moment when an overall Arab leadership had risen to a larger view of its relationship to the Arab masses. Had it survived, in the local leadership, the partition of Syria and the excision of Transjordan from Palestine, the Zionist hope could have found bloodless fulfillment even in truncated Palestine. Even within that diminished area a peaceful sifting of the Arab and Jewish populations could have taken place, with a Jewish state rising beside an Arab state. Many Zionists advocated a single binational state. Of course the Arab leadership would not hear of it. Thus what should have been a cooperative enterprise became a contest of wills, and the snarl of problems thickened until the Arab leadership felt driven to cut through it with the sword.

In the contest of wills the Jews, a minority, had the advantage because they were moved by a great ideal and, more significantly, because they were a close-knit, democratic group, with a leadership sprung from the masses and at one with them. When in 1930 I made my own extensive researches among the Arabs, I was staggered by the contrast between the self-rule implicitly practiced by the Jews, and the absence of it implicitly accepted by the Arabs. I had never come in contact with the phenomenon before. Tel Aviv, the all-Jewish city, with a population of 28,500, had an electoral roll of 12,973; in Nablus, all-Arab, the corresponding figures were 15,947 and 928; in Hebron 18,700 and 860; in Gaza 17,480 and 560; and thus throughout all the Arab towns, the proportion of voters to population ranging from one in thirty to one in eleven, with an average of one in twenty. The masses of the Arabs had no political life, and not even the illusion of it, which they got later.

On the land, the lot of the fellaheen, or peasants, who constituted the large majority of the population, was miserable in the extreme. They were for the most part sharecroppers, and the condition of the landowning fellah in the grip of the moneylender was not much better. Only in areas adjacent to Jewish settlements had life begun to rise above its ancient Asiatic level. It was upon these fellaheen and upon the equally oppressed workers in the cities that the Arab leadership called to repel the Jewish invaders.

As long as the leadership played on a mixture of motives—patriotism, self-interest, religion—it evoked, as we have seen, comparatively little response. But in 1929 it focused entirely on the religious motive, and this time it was more effective. The riots of that year call for closer attention on several grounds. They were the beginning of mass action on the part of the Arabs; they revealed an Arab capacity for wild, indiscriminate murder; they confirmed the Arab leadership in a policy of violence as the only solution of the Arab-Jewish problem; they alerted the Jews to the greater need for military preparedness; and they brought into clearer view the indecisions and ambivalences of the British administration.

The focus of attention was the Wailing Wall (or, as the Jews call it, the Western Wall) in Jerusalem, the last vestige of the Second Temple, destroyed by the Romans in the year 70 c.e. Occupying the same site as the First Temple, Solomon's, it was to religious Jews the most sacred spot in the world, to secular Jews, a deeply moving reminder of one-time national liberty. On this spot fervent services were held on the Jewish High Holy Days, the New Year and the Day of Atonement, and as long as the British Mandate lasted the Jews had free access to it. But the spot was also sacred to the Moslems, for from here Mahomet had made his ascent to heaven on his horse, el-Burak.

Until 1922 or 1923 it had been the custom of pious Jews to bring into the narrow alley before the Wall a portable screen to divide the male from the female worshippers on the High Holy Days. For some reason the custom lapsed until 1928, when it was revived, and the incident was seized by the Arabs as evidence of Jewish intention to take over the area.

The agitation simmered for a year, then, some weeks before the New Year, 1929, Arabs turned the cul-de-sac before the Wall into a public thoroughfare by breaking a door into one of the houses at the dead end of the alley, so that Arabs were continually passing through, disrupting the services. Protest and counterprotest, incident and counterincident followed, until a tremendous uproar had been created in the country. The Arab leadership kept hammering away at the "Jewish plan to capture the Mosque," and when the Ninth of Av (the day of mourning for the Destructions) came round, and Jews again gathered before the Wall for traditional prayers, the agitation rose toward its climax. An Arab proclamation was issued, which read in part:

On the day of remembrance of destruction of the Temple, Jews gathered to march in a big demonstration with a Zionist banner. . . . They arrived at el-Burak and held there speeches which offended Moslem honor. In the markets and el-Burak they cursed the Prophet and the Moslem religion . . . the Moslems therefore gathered . . . after prayer . . . and swore unanimously in the name of Allah to defend the honor of the holy places to the last drop of blood.

All over the country groups sprang up pledged to the defense of the Mosque. In one city a committee was founded called "The Knights of el-Burak." Tens of thousands of Arabs were thrown into the frenzied belief that a Jewish armed assault on the Mosque was about to take place. When it did not take place the Arab leaders claimed credit for having averted it. The Arab Executive, the then central Arab authority, proudly announced: "El-Burak is with God's help intact and will remain forever in Moslem hands"—an anticipation of the many announcements more recently issued by Nasser.

The riots which "averted" the taking over of el-Burak cost the Jews one hundred thirty-three lives and several hundred wounded. Most, if not all, of this could have been prevented if the government had shown a modicum of alertness. The warnings were unmistakable, their duration gave ample time for preparation. Only when the killings were over did the government bring in extra troops from Egypt, where they were within a day's call, and naval ratings from Malta, two days away. Most of the murders were perpetrated far from Jerusalem and the "threatened" Mosque. In Safad and Hebron completely defenseless men, women, and children were slaughtered under the most revolting circumstances. In these cities there happened to be no Zionists; Hebron was the center of a yeshiva, or talmudic college, twenty of whose members were among the victims. Safad, like Hebron, was populated by other-worldly pietists, precisely the kind of Jews the Arabs declared "acceptable."

The conduct of the administration before, during, and after the riots led some Jews to think that it was not altogether sorry to have the Zionists taught a lesson. This is unjust. But there was complete justice in the accusation that its conduct was such that the Arabs could draw that conclusion. One of the mob cries heard frequently those murderous days was: "The government is with us!" Except for a first condemnatory statement issued by the British commissioner, Sir John Chancellor, when he returned from abroad (he was absent during the riots), the administration adopted the attitude that these were not bloodthirsty attacks by Arabs on Jews; they were "disturbances," in which no culprits were named. And this, although of the one hundred sixteen Arab deaths all but six were due to belated police action—which is perhaps not altogether creditable to the Jews. The Hebrew press raged over the difference between *hitnaplut* (assault) and *hitnagshut* (clash)—the similarity of the Hebrew words giving bitter point to the differences in meaning.

The riots of 1929 were far from what the Arab leadership hoped they would be—a general uprising. Had a solid proportion of the eight hundred thousand Arabs risen against the one hundred sixty thousand Jews the casualties would have run into the thousands. The concentrated appeal to the Arabs' most susceptible emotions, the religious, was planted with vicious cleverness; but only a minority rose to it. What went on in the mind of the majority is hard to say; it was not indifferent to religion; the only reasonable conclusion we can draw is that it simply did not believe its leaders, and it did not believe in a Jewish danger.

Such was the first concerted attempt to destroy the Jewish homeland. It was a failure in the short run as well as in the long. Jewish-Arab relations were soon re-established; buying and selling went on, Arab farmers and fruit growers continued to prosper around Jewish settlements, young Arabs from Jaffa resumed, after a pause, their evening visits to Tel Aviv to get a taste of "European" life. But it was never the same again. The Arab leadership had, in the literal sense, tasted blood; and it had become too keenly conscious that its aspirations were not wholly repugnant to the administration. It had also become convinced that it had found the right method: violence.

During the several months I spent in Palestine before, during, and after the riots of 1929 I found little hatred of the Arabs among the Jews. But there was a growing hatred of the British administration. I believe that the general attitude was best described by the weekly *Ha-poel Ha-tzair,* in its issue of August 30, when the riots were barely over:

Since the days of the Crusades no such massacre of Jews in Palestine has occurred. Under barbaric and semibarbaric regimes, during many centuries and changes of rulership, during periods of political anarchy, no events took place like these, which have taken place under modern, enlightened British rule. . . .

We have no dispute with the Arab nation. It was blindly misled by political agitators, and by agents who circulated lies among the Arabs and stirred up the instincts of robbery and murder. But we have a case against the British government. Its duty was to prevent the disaster, which it could have done if it had not refrained from action. . . . The cynical behavior of some of the Palestinian officials raises the suspicion that there were those who wanted the disturbances and had secret motives in desiring them.

Our forefathers wrote elegies on massacres like those of Hebron, Safad, and Motza, and preserved their memory in the tears of the Jewish exile. We will not mourn with broken hearts. We will not be discouraged. On the contrary, our connection with the country will be strengthened and our constructive work stimulated. . . . Our return to this country, and the reconstruction of our national life here, constitute a historic destiny which cannot be undone by cunning officials, malefactors, and rioters. . . . We mourn for the Arab blood which was shed; it was not the blood of the instigators, but of those who followed blindly. We do not desire and we do not seek revenge. But we will not abandon our positions. We shall not give up any part of our right to return in masses to Palestine, to build this country, and to live here our free national life. Let this be known to our Arab neighbors, and let it be known to those who advise them evilly to shed our blood in order that they may, in turn, afterwards shed Arab blood.

From *Light on Israel* (1968)

8 CONTRA TOYNBEE

Suppressio Veri

I

The *Survey of International Affairs* is a publication issued, like Professor Arnold J. Toynbee's *A Study of History*, under the auspices of the Royal Institute for International Affairs. This body was "founded in 1920 to encourage and facilitate the scientific study of international questions." Its director of studies is Professor Toynbee himself; he is also the editor of the *Surveys*, in one of which a Mr. George Kirk gives his version of the events attending Israel's achievement of independence. It is in my opinion a biased version. I did not expect anything else. It did not surprise me that, in an earlier account, Mr. Kirk had written:

> Zionists were apt to compare the discrimination against Jews in the Diaspora with that against "colored" people; but once in their "ancient homeland" they themselves behaved as a *Herrenvolk* [*Survey for 1939–46*, Vol. II, *The Middle East and the War*, 1952, p. 250, n.].

It did not surprise me because I had learned to regard the *Surveys* not as "scientific" studies, but as slanted pronouncements with a general conformity to the group view of the "Chatham House" (the Royal Institute) membership or following. I have therefore chosen Mr. Kirk's account as being the least open to the suspicion of pro-Jewish or pro-Zionist bias; and in giving below a resume (almost entirely in quotations) of this account of the events under discussion, I am willing to accept it at face value as the basis of my charges against

A Study of History. (The account is entitled *The Middle East 1945–50,* and was published in a 1954 volume. Mr. Kirk refers throughout to "the Zionists," for which read "the Jews of Palestine.")

I begin with an observation that occurs in the middle of the account. The rest, except for the closing excerpt, is in chronological order.

The Secretary General of the United Nations had optimistically told the Palestine Commission [UNSCOP—United Nations Special Commission on Palestine] at its first meeting on 9 January [1947]: "You are entitled to be confident that, in the event it should prove necessary, the Security Council will assume the full measure of responsibility in implementation of the Assembly's resolution" [p. 257].

The resolution that later had to be implemented was that of November 29, 1947, which, by a vote of 33 to 13, called for the partition of Palestine and the setting up of a Jewish state.

During the four months that had elapsed since the departure of the United Nations Committee from Palestine, there had been sporadic attacks by Arabs on Jews which had been checked by Haganah reprisals . . . [p. 251].

The Haganah was mobilized for self-defense, the Zionists complaining that the British security forces were not doing enough to protect Jewish lives and property. Almost certainly they were now doing less than their strict duty in the matter, for the temper of the British soldiers in Palestine had been affected by the fact that they had lost 127 killed and 331 wounded at the hands of Jewish terrorists between the end of the Second World War and 20 October 1947 . . . [p. 252].

The general fighting increased:

Both sides committed shocking outrages in Haifa and Jerusalem as the new year [1948] came in . . . [p. 253].

Frontal attacks upon Jewish settlements were almost invariably costly failures for the Arabs, but they evolved a more effective, if more protracted strategy of reducing the outlying settlements by attacks upon the road communications by which they were supplied with provisions and munitions; these attacks were bloody affairs in which neither side was accustomed to give quarter or return prisoners . . . [p. 254].

At the beginning of April the Zionists were still seriously challenged by the "Arab Liberation Army," which had by this time publicly received the blessing of the Governments of the Arab states and had been reinforced to a strength of between 6,000 and 7,500 men, preponderantly Syrians and Iraqis, with an Egyptian contingent at Gaza. The Arab forces were based, with a large measure of British tolerance, on localities within the territory assigned to the Arab State by the resolution on partition . . . [p. 260].

[On April 9] . . . an I.Z.L. (Irgun Zvai Leumi, Revisionist) and Stern Group force about 200 strong attacked the Arab village of Dayr Yasin. . . . The I.Z.L. afterwards claimed to have suffered appreciable casualties in the house-to-house fighting that followed; but of Arabs some 250 were killed, about half of them women and children. . . . The Arabs retaliated in their turn by intercepting on the outskirts of Jerusalem a Jewish convoy bound for the isolated Hadassah Hospital and the Hebrew University on the strategic Mount Scopus ridge, and killed some seventy-seven doctors, nurses, and university teachers and students . . . [pp. 260 f.].

[The Arab Legion of Transjordan] . . . after taking part in the occupation of the Kfar Etzion group of Jewish settlements isolated in Arab territory 12 miles south-west of Jerusalem, intervened to defend what remained of Arab Jerusalem, and began shelling the Jewish New City. In the first fortnight of fighting they inflicted upon its 100,000 civilians some 1,200 casualties, of whom 450 were killed, and slow paralysis was threatened by the cutting of supplies and reinforcements . . . [pp. 271 f.].

On 17 May, three days after the open intervention of the Arab states, the United States delegation had submitted to the Security Council a resolution, under Article 39 of the Charter, ordering the belligerents to cease fire within thirty-six hours. However, the chief British delegate, Sir Alexander Cadogan, questioned both the desirability of invoking Article 39 (with its attempt to define an aggressor against whom sanctions might be taken) and the practicability of applying a stand-still order in the present fluid situation . . . [p. 272].

I have left for the end of my quotations from the Kirk Report a passage that occurs in the middle, in order that the reader may be able to contrast it more easily with Professor Toynbee's statement on the "expulsion."

The beginnings of the Arab mass flight went back to an early stage in the Arab-Jewish fighting. As early as 27 January the High Commissioner had confirmed a "steady exodus" of Arab middle-class families who could afford to leave the country, taking with them cars and considerable quantities of household goods. In March Zionist sources estimated that 20,000–25,000 Arabs had already left Haifa and 15,000–20,000 Jaffa; and the Arab irregulars' use of conveniently situated Arab villages as bases for attacks on Jewish localities, and the consequent Jewish reprisals against such villages, had caused a substantial flight of Arabs from villages on the fringes of Jewish territories to safer places. A subsequent Zionist assertion that "many weeks" before the Dayr Yasin massacre the Arab Higher Committee had "called on the Arab population to leave the country en masse" should be treated with reserve in the absence of positive evidence to corroborate it; but there can be no question that the publicity which the Arab press and radio gave to the massacre at Dayr Yasin for the purpose of attracting sympathy greatly accelerated the demoralization and flight of non-combatant Arabs. At this stage of the fighting the Jewish attitude to the Arab flight was ambiguous, since, while there is clear evidence that the civil authorities at Haifa tried to tranquillize the Arab population, the Jewish combatants there and elsewhere made skillful use of psychological warfare to break their opponents' morale, and the effect upon the civilians was only what was to be expected. At a later stage, the Israeli armed forces did not confine their pressure on the Arab civilian population to playing upon their fears. They forcibly expelled them: for example, the population of Akka (including refugees from Haifa) in May [1948]; the population of Lydda and Ramla (including refugees from Jaffa) in July; and the population of Beersheba and western Galilee in October [pp. 263 f.].

II

Such is the account prepared by Mr. George Kirk for the *Survey of International Affairs* and published under the auspices of the Royal Institute for International Affairs and *under the editorship of Professor Toynbee*. I accept it, as I have said, at its face value for the purpose of the present discussion.

How does it compare with Professor Toynbee's observation in *A Study of History* on the relations between Jews and Arabs during the relevant period? What I am about to say will leave the reader incredulous. A comparison is difficult because, as far as *A Study of History* is concerned, no assurance had been issued by the permanent official of the United Nations that the Security Council would "assume the full measure of responsibility in the implementation of the Assembly's resolution"; there had not been, "during the four months which had elapsed since the departure of the United Nations Commission from Palestine," any "sporadic attacks by the Arabs which had been checked by Haganah reprisals"; there had not been any Zionist complaints "that the British security forces were not doing enough to protect Jewish lives and property"; nor could it be said that "almost certainly they were now doing less than their strict duty in the matter"; there had not been "shocking outrages" on both sides as the new year came in; there had not been unsuccessful frontal attacks by the Arabs on Jewish settlements, followed by "a more effective if more protracted strategy of reducing the outlying settlements by attacks upon the road communications by which they were supplied with provisions and munitions"; there had not been an invasion by the "Arab Liberation Army," based, "with a large measure of British tolerance, on localities within the territory assigned to the Arab States by the resolution of partition . . ." (that is, within the borders of territory subject to British administration under Britain's still unexpired mandate); there had been no intervention by the British-subsidized Arab Legion; there had been no shelling by the Arab Legion of the open city of Jerusalem, there had not been 1,200 casualties—including 450 deaths—among its 100,000 civilians; there had not been a threat of "slow paralysis . . . by the cutting of supplies and reinforcements" (that is, there had been no attempt to deprive the civilian population of Jerusalem of food and, what is worse, water, in an effort to reduce the city). *None of these things are mentioned in Professor Toynbee's account.* The reader is, I suggest, incredulous, perhaps even aghast. "But that is impossible," he exclaims. "Such things are not done even by propagandists of a hired press, let alone by the director of studies of a British institute for scientific study operating under royal patronage. He cannot wholly have ignored the report of his subordinate or colleague!" And as it happens the reader is right! Professor Toynbee has not wholly ignored Mr. Kirk's report: he has taken from it the single item of the massacre of Dayr Yasin—and has linked it to his version of the "expulsion" of the Arabs in a manner unwarranted by Mr. Kirk's account. (Of this, more below.) Thus, from a reading of Professor Toynbee's observations, one obtains the impression of an utterly unprovoked universal uprising of the Jews against the defenseless and peaceable Arabs, an outburst of murderous cruelty in the worst traditions of savage peoples. This impression he deepens by his comments. He writes in *A Study of History*:

On the morrow of a persecution in Europe in which they had been the victims of the worst atrocities ever known to have been suffered by Jews or indeed by any other human beings, the Jews' immediate reaction to their own experience was to become persecutors in their turn for the first time since A.D. 135—and this at the first opportunity that had since arisen for them to inflict on other human beings *who had done the Jews no injury,* but who happened to be weaker than they were, some of the wrongs and sufferings that had been inflicted on the Jews by their many successive Western Gentile persecutors during the intervening seventeen centuries. In A.D. 1948 some 684,000 out of some 859,000 Arab inhabitants of the territory in Palestine which the Zionist Jews conquered by force of arms in that year lost their homes and property and became destitute "displaced persons" [VIII, pp. 289 f.].

The Jews in Europe in A.D. 1933–45 had been the vicarious victims of the Germans' resentment over their military defeat at the hands of their Western fellow Gentiles in the war of A.D. 1914–18; the Arabs in Palestine in A.D. 1948 became in their turn the vicarious victims of the European Jews' indignation over the "genocide" committed upon them by their Gentile fellow Westerners in A.D. 1933–45. This impulse to become a party to the guilt of a stronger neighbor by inflicting on an innocent weaker neighbor *the very sufferings* that the original victim had experienced at his stronger neighbor's hands was perhaps *the most perverse* of all the base propensities of Human Nature; for it was a *wanton* endeavor to keep in perpetual motion the sorrowful wheel of *Karma* to which Adam-Ixion was bound and from which only Love and Mercy could ever release him [VIII, p. 291].

It would be an affectation, and it is perhaps impossible, to comment with moderation on this sanctimonious pretense at historical (and, indeed, cosmic) objectivity by the Director of Studies of the Royal Institute for International Affairs. There is not a sentence in the quoted passages which does not affront the intelligence and outrage the moral susceptibilities of an informed reader.

Sentence No. 1: To speak of the fierce struggle between the Jews and Arabs as a persecutory reaction of the former to the Nazi extermination of Jews in Europe is not merely mendacious, and not merely intellectually contemptible; it is a calculated effort to divert attention from British responsibility, which the writer elsewhere admits in uneasy mitigation. That the Arabs had done the Jews "no injury" is an impression that Professor Toynbee can only have derived by forgetting large parts of this and of other reports that he had edited; and I will not speak of the history of Arab assaults on Jews in 1921, 1922, 1929, 1932–33, 1936–39. It is, to say the least, extraordinarily disingenuous to use the phrase "who happened to be weaker than they" as contrasting the Arabs with the Jews. Such was not the belief and hope of the attacking Arabs in those days; it was hardly the belief of the desperate Jews; it was undoubtedly not the belief of the British and of the British delegation to the United Nations when Sir Alexander Cadogan, opposing the American resolution "three days after the open intervention of the Arab States . . . questioned both the desirability of invoking Article 39 (with its attempt to define an aggressor against whom sanctions might be taken) and the practicability of applying a stand-still order *in the present fluid situation."* We may be quite sure that if Sir Alexander Cadogan (or his chief in London, Foreign Secretary Ernest Bevin) had foreseen the pattern in which the fluid situation was ultimately going to congeal he would not have questioned "the desirability," etc. It was, again, fear of the outcome which prompted the American proposal.

No. 2: ". . . of the territory in Palestine which the Zionist Jews had conquered by force of arms. . . ." Of the territory that the Jews had conquered by the sweat of their brow and by means of the contributions of world Jewry, of the territory that had been converted from noisome swamp and uninhabitable desert into fertile orchards and grainfields, and of the cities they had built, not a word; of the threat to those hard-won possessions—as well as to the lives of the Jews—posed by the invading armies, which were advancing with the avowed intention of "pushing Israel into the sea," not a word; of the complicity of the Palestine Arab population, whether intermingled with the Jews or living apart, in the plan of invasion and conquest, not a word; of those Arab populations within Mandated Palestine which lent themselves ("with a large measure of British tolerance") to the plan, not a word. And I have yet to deal with Professor Toynbee's other references to the "expulsion" of the Arabs.

No. 3: What took place in Palestine in "A.D. 1948" was not an outburst of indignation over the genocide committed upon the Jews of Europe, deflected against the Arabs; it was a passionate outburst of longing to bring into Palestine the survivors of the genocide and an upwelling of determination to see that by additional immigration the homeland into which they were welcomed should be a place secured for the future by numbers and stability against such attacks as were now being launched on it.

No. 4: That the Jews inflicted upon the Arabs *"the very sufferings"* which they [the Jews] had experienced at the hands of the Germans is a monstrous and unforgivable untruth. With this too I shall deal later. And that the furious reaction of the Jews to the Arab attacks was *"wanton"* is of a piece with the shameless perversity of Sentence No. 1.

III

I must preface my remarks on Professor Toynbee's treatment of the "expulsion" of the Arabs from Israeli-held Palestine territory with renewed reference to what I call the Blurring Effect. Its purpose is to create the impression of an affirmation out of a number of statements that cancel out logically but not psychologically. The thesis is stated, then modified out of validity, then mentioned again without the modification, then referred to tangentially as *chose connue. . . .* In writing on the "expulsion" of the Arabs, Professor Toynbee interweaves semi-retractions and modifications in respect to both this subject and that of the resemblance between Jewish treatment of the Arabs and the Nazi treatment of the Jews. We have just heard him refer to *"the very sufferings."* We shall now hear him retract. We shall then, in the same passage, see him introduce a sort of "nevertheless"; and in the end there remains only the association: *"Jew is to Arab what Nazi is to Jew."* In a footnote to page 290, volume VIII, we read:

The cold-blooded systematic "genocide" of several millions of human beings in extermination camps, which had been the worst of the Nazis' crimes against the Jews, had no parallel at all in the Jews' ill-treatment of the Palestinian Arabs. The evil deeds committed by the Zionist Jews against the Palestinian Arabs that were comparable to crimes committed against the Jews by the Nazis were the massacre of men, women, and children at Dayr Yasin on the 9th April, 1948, which precipitated a flight of the Arab population, in large numbers, from districts within range of the Jewish armed forces, and the subsequent deliberate expulsion of the Arab population from districts conquered by the Jewish armed forces between the 15th May, 1948, and the end of that year—e.g., from Akka in May, from Lydda and Ramla in July, and from Beersheba and western Galilee in October. When Nazareth was captured in July, most of the population seems to have been allowed to stay. On the other hand, the Arabs who were expelled from Akka in May included refugees from Haifa, and those who were expelled from Lydda and Ramla in July included refugees from Jaffa, in addition to the local Arab population. The massacre and expulsions, between them, were responsible for the exile of all those Palestinian Arab "displaced persons" (to use the current euphemism), from the territory conquered by the Israelis, who fled from or were driven from this territory after the 9th April, 1948. The expulsions seem to have accounted for about 284,000 out of the total of about 684,000 Palestinian Arabs who became "displaced persons" from first to last, including those who had already been evacuated by the British mandatory authorities or had already fled on their own initiative or had already lost their homes as a result of military operations between the outbreak of hostilities in Palestine in December 1947 and the massacre on the 9th April, 1948.

The Arab blood shed on the 9th April, 1948, at Dayr Yasin was on the heads of the Irgun; the expulsions after the 15th May, 1949, were on the heads of all Israel.

If, on behalf of Israel, it were to be pleaded that these Jewish outrages in A.D. 1948, even reckoned *pro rata*, were dwarfed in quantity as well as in heinousness, by the Nazi atrocities in A.D. 1933–45, it would have to be taken into account, on the other side, that the Jews had had much more experience than the Germans had had of the sufferings that they were inflicting. If the Nazis were debarred from filing the plea that they knew not what they did, the Jews were debarred *a fortiori.*

That last sentence is a gratuitous piece of cant; the Jews did not file, never suggested filing, a plea that they knew not what they did. They were driven by an agony of necessity, and upon this agony there came into play the rages and brutalities that all wars engender. This pious snuffle of Professor Toynbee's is one of the repetitions that fasten into the reader's mind the suggested, withdrawn, resuggested formula: "Jew is to Arab what Nazi is to Jew."

But we return to Mr. Kirk's report, which, on the subject of the expulsions, opens as follows:

The beginnings of the Arab mass flight went back to an early stage in the Arab-Jewish fighting. As early as 27 January [1948] the High Commissioner had confirmed a "steady exodus" of Arab middle-class families who could afford to leave the country, taking with them cars and considerable quantities of household goods. . . .

Who were these "middle-class families" who began to move out of Palestine in large numbers shortly after the passing of the Partition

Resolution by the United Nations? They were the Arab leaders—
merchants, professionals, landowners, moneylenders—who had been
the main support of the Mufti and the Arab Higher Committee
during all the years of Britain's Mandate over Palestine. Some of
them had incited the Arab workers and peasants to murder and
pillage since the time of the Balfour Declaration. Now they packed
up and moved, and the Arabs of the villages and the countryside
watched the processions of laden automobiles streaming toward the
Egyptian and Syrian frontiers. Mr. Kirk accuses the Jewish combatants of making "skillful use of psychological warfare to break
their opponents' morale" (an unheard-of crime!). He adds: "The
effect upon the civilians was only what was to be expected." What
effect does he think was produced upon the civilians by the sight of
the thousands of leaders getting away from the scenes of the troubles
they had helped to precipitate, taking their movables with them? Of
course these leaders had every hope and intention of returning later,
when the "Arab Army of Liberation" should have done its work and
obliterated the Jewish cities and settlements; and, as during the days
of the war, when Rommel was nearing Alexandria, and Palestine was
the next step, they could look forward to a sharing of the booty
according to prearranged schedules. Mr. Kirk's grave warning that
one must take with reserve the "subsequent Zionist assertion that
many weeks before the Dayr Yasin massacre the Arab Higher Committee had 'called on the Arab population to leave the country en
masse' " has more than a touch of driveling pseudo-importance. I do
not know whether the Arab Higher Committee ever issued such a
call, and I do not put it past Zionist propagandists to have invented
it and fathered it on the Arabs. What puzzles me here is the question
of what the members of the Arab Higher Committee and the other
Arab leaders said to the Arab villagers and fellaheen among whom
they may have stopped here and there outward bound; and what
they said to their hosts in Alexandria and Cairo and Damascus and
Beirut; and what they sent by way of answer to any messages that
may have reached them from their followers in Palestine. The more
I ponder the question, the more it seems to me that the only thing
they *could* have said was: "Let us vacate the battlefield so as to give
our brave liberators from the Arab lands a free hand. When it's over
we will return. . . ." But this is a digression. I return to Professor
Toynbee.

Throughout he ignores the Arab uprising against the Jews; and he begins his note on the massacre and expulsions by ignoring Mr. Kirk's account of the sequence of events. Farther down he refers vaguely to those Arabs "who had already fled on their own initiative," without even hinting that at the outset these consisted of the well-to-do classes to which the Arabs looked for leadership, and that their flight occurred long before the Dayr Yasin massacre—and if Mr. Kirk does not choose to draw the inevitable inference from the fact, Professor Toynbee is unable to do so, because for him it does not exist. He seems to place the number of Arabs actually expelled by the Jews at less than half of the total number of refugees (284,000 out of 684,000), but there is not even a hint of the direct and indirect responsibility of the Arab leadership. There is not a word of condemnation for the men who, whether they proclaimed it or not, whether they planned it or not, executed a strategic military withdrawal in which a considerable part of the population was involved when it followed suit. Every disaster that came upon the Arabs is made the consequence of Jewish malevolence.

It is not a question of clearing the Jews of their share of the blame. Once war is unleashed and human beings begin to kill one another systematically, crimes will be committed, injustices inflicted, for which the miserable tradition of history provides a certain latitude. No one can say how much of the Jewish expulsion of the Arabs from Palestine falls within it. When one reflects on the intentions of the Palestinian Arabs toward the Jews, on their cooperation with the Arabs of the invading countries, on their readiness to act as a massive fifth column against the emerging Jewish state sanctioned by the United Nations, one must hesitate before pronouncing judgment. The massacre of Dayr Yasin certainly does not fall within the latitude mentioned; but even this abomination—an isolated incident—had a setting that Professor Toynbee withholds from the reader in what he calls *A Study of History*; and his use of it in the continuous bracketing of Jews and Nazis disqualifies him from pleading in any court the cause of the wronged Arabs. Only this remains to be added—the most tragic sentence in all of Proust: "It is necessary that even those who are right should be wrong also, so that justice may be made an impossible thing."

Suggestio Falsi

I

In the preceding chapter we have seen how, in dealing with the struggle over the birth of Israel, *A Study of History* made use of the device of *suppressio veri* in the service of *suggestio falsi*. In the persistent bracketing of Nazi-Jew and Jew-Arab relationships it is *suggestio falsi* that takes the lead; but here, as there, the Blurring Effect is heavily employed as it rises, in its anti-Jewish prejudice, to a climax of poisonous innuendo mingled with pseudo-prophetic indignation.

In Volume VIII, pages 272–312, Professor Toynbee gives us in a section entitled "The Modern West and the Jews," a rapid survey of the development of relationships between the Jews and the Western world, leading up to what he calls the fourth act, which is the Nazi attempt at the extermination of Jewry. He then begins the subsection "The Fate of the European Jews and the Palestinian Arabs, A.D. 1933–48," with the following words:

The peculiar horror of this fourth act lay in the unprecedented wickedness of the malefactors and unprecedented sufferings of both innocent Jewish victims and an innocent Arab third party [VIII, p. 288].

Let us note carefully the implication of this opening. "Unprecedented sufferings" is made to apply equally to what happened to the Arabs of Palestine and to the Jews of Europe. This is *suggestio falsi* at its slyest. Only the heartless will make light of the sufferings that have come upon the Arabs of Palestine—in no small part through the folly and cruelty of their kinsmen in the neighboring states; but only a reckless partisan will talk, here, of "unprecedented" after the word has been used to characterize the experiences of the Jews under the Nazis. The effect is, of course, the Blur; for thus the impression is left that what the Jews suffered was the killing of a certain comparatively small number, and the expulsion of the rest; or else that the vast majority of the Arabs were exterminated and a minority permitted to escape. Yet this was not all that the Jews suffered, as we shall observe below in touching on the Nazi action against them; and I must add the miserable reflection that as far as the Jews are concerned the murder of a certain number of them in a given territory, and the expulsion of the rest, are far from unprecedented; these have, indeed, been regular occupational hazards for many, many centuries.

After a comparison with the persecutions suffered by the Jews in fourteenth- and fifteenth-century Spain and Portugal, Professor Toynbee continues:

The full measure of the Nazis' depravity is not given in the bare statistical statement—appalling though these figures are—that, within a period of no more than twelve years, they reduced the Jewish population of Continental Europe, west of the Soviet Union, from about 6½ million to about 1½ million by a process of mass-extermination which was so unprecedentedly systematic and cold-blooded that the new word "genocide" had to be coined to describe what was in effect a new crime. In the operation of the destructor-plants in which the Nazis' victims were asphyxiated, the maniacal sadism of the men and women in command was less appalling than the criminal docility of the hundreds and thousands of subordinates who duly carried out their monstrous instructions, and the moral cowardice of the German public, who took good care to avoid acquainting themselves with the atrocities that their husbands, sons, brothers, and even their sisters, wives, and daughters, were committing in their name. . . . *But the Nazi Gentiles' fall was less tragic than the Zionist Jews'.* On the morrow of a persecution in Europe . . . the Jews' immediate reaction to their own experience was to become persecutors in their turn [VIII, pp. 288 f.; rest of passage quoted above, p. 106].

The sentence I have italicized is one of the most remarkable utterances on the Jewish tragedy to come from the pen of a public figure in a democratic country; and as this particular public figure presents himself in the double role of scientific historian and moralist, one is inclined to call it, like the crimes of the Nazis, unprecedented. Unprecedented—but not quite unequaled, for a little farther on Professor Toynbee does even better when he writes:

On the Day of Judgment the gravest crime standing to the German National Socialists' account might be, not that they had exterminated a majority of the Western Jews, but that they had caused the surviving remnant of Jewry to stumble [VIII, pp. 290 f.].

Now what is the man driving at? The one charitable interpretation that can be put on these last words—charitable, that is, to Professor Toynbee's idealism, if not to his intelligence—is that before 1933 Zionist Jews and Jews at large had been following the path of rectitude, and here, under the Nazi assault, they had turned aside from the path; and this impairment of the character of the Jews was a graver crime on the part of the Nazis than the extermination of a

majority of the Western Jews. If such is Professor Toynbee's sentiment, we must admit that it is one of almost stupefying nobility, even
though he entertains it at someone else's expense. But such cannot
be his sentiment, for his opinion of Jewry in the Diaspora is predominantly negative. The alternative interpretation to which we are
driven by elimination is that if the Nazis committed a grave crime in
exterminating five million (the number is actually six million) Jews,
they committed an even graver one in having caused the Palestinian
Arabs to suffer what they did at the hands of the Jews. To this
alternative interpretation we are also directed over and over again by
Professor Toynbee's opinion of that Zionist movement which had
been at work in Palestine for many decades before Hitler had been
heard of; and as if to make sure that we shall not give him the benefit
of the more charitable interpretation, he once more summarizes his
evaluation of the Zionist movement a little farther on:

> The Zionists' audacious aim was to invert, in a new life of their own making,
> all the distinctively Jewish characteristics enshrined in the Diaspora's tradi-
> tional life. They set out defiantly and enthusiastically to turn themselves into
> manual laborers instead of brain workers, country-folk instead of city-
> dwellers, producers instead of middlemen, agriculturists instead of finan-
> ciers, warriors instead of shopkeepers, terrorists instead of martyrs, aggres-
> sively spirited Semites instead of peaceably abject non-Aryans; and this
> Nietzschean revaluation of all traditional Jewish values, for destruction as
> well as for construction, for evil as well as for good, was directed toward the
> horizon-filling narrow-hearted aim of making themselves sons of a latter-
> day *Eretz Israel* in Palestine that was to be "as Jewish as" England "was
> English," instead of remaining the stepsons of a New York, London, Man-
> chester, and Frankfort that were not more Jewish than Bombay was Parsee
> or Ispahan Armenian [VIII, pp. 310 f.].

"For evil as well as for good": but it is not easy, from the tone
of this passage, to discover where Professor Toynbee sees good,
especially as all these revaluations move toward a "horizon-filling
narrow-hearted aim" to become terrorists instead of martyrs, de-
fiantly, deliberately! We suspect that even in becoming "aggressively
spirited Semites instead of peaceably abject non-Aryans" the Jews
have offended him. But it was certainly an error on his part to have
included Frankfurt in the list of places where Jews could have remained as stepsons; for most of the Jews of Frankfurt, and Berlin, and
Warsaw, and Lodz, and Cracow, and a hundred other places did not
remain there, and did not become stepsons anywhere else; they became charred remnants, and gaseous exhalations, and soap.

In one of those tortuous semiconcessions which on the surface
create an impression of overall objectivity, Professor Toynbee writes:

There was neither justice nor expediency in the exaction from Palestinian Arabs of compensation due to European Jews for crimes committed against them by Western Gentiles. Justice required that the debt to Continental European Jewry which the Western World had incurred through the criminality of a Western nation should be assumed by a defeated Germany's victorious Western adversaries; and expediency pointed in the same direction as justice; for the victorious Western countries between them did possess the capacity—for which Palestine's resources were quite inadequate—of absorbing the European Jewish survivors of the *Furor Teutonicus* without seriously deranging their own domestic social equilibrium [VIII, p. 307].

It is obvious, indeed, that the victors in the war against Germany could have absorbed the Jewish survivors of the *Furor Teutonicus* without undue internal derangement; and Professor Toynbee knows as well as we do that there was never any prospect of their doing so. When, however, he prefaces his statement with the irrelevant and nasty aside that the long-deferred fulfillment of the promises of a Jewish National Home by the very nations he is talking about was devoid of justice and expediency, and was an exaction from the Arabs of compensation for Germany's crimes, he falls into a tangle of misunderstanding from which no human intelligence can extricate him. It is enough to point out that he regards the promise made under the League of Nations Mandate, with the authority of the nations he is referring to, as null and void; and while thus encouraging them to dishonor their pledges in one enterprise, he expects them to display their honorable intentions in another. If, moreover, the gravest crime standing to the Nazis' account, graver than their extermination of a majority of the Western Jews, is that they caused surviving Jewry to stumble in the matter of the Palestinian Arabs, what crime stands to the account of the victorious Western nations which did not open their doors to this surviving Jewry, but left it heartlessly to its own devices?

Professor Toynbee speaks with high indignation of the "moral cowardice of the German public, who took good care to avoid acquainting themselves with the atrocities" being committed against the Jews. The Germans were not the only ones to avert their eyes. The trick of pretending that nothing too dreadful was going to happen to the Jews was already being practiced outside of Germany on the eve of the Second World War. Writing of the St. James Conference of February–March 1939, Chaim Weizmann has this to say:

Lord Halifax was strangely ignorant of what was happening to the Jews of Germany. During the St. James Conference he came up to me and said: "I have just received a letter from a friend in Germany, who describes some terrible things perpetrated by the Nazis in a concentration camp the name of which is not familiar to me," and when he began to grope for the name I realized it was Dachau he was talking about. He said the stories were entirely unbelievable, and if the letter had not been written by a man in whom he had full confidence he would not attach the slightest credence to it. For five or six years now the world had known of the infamous Dachau concentration camp, in which thousands of people had been maimed and tortured and done to death, and the British Foreign Secretary had never heard of the place. . . . It is difficult to say whether this profound ignorance was typical for the British ruling class, but judging from its behavior at that time, it either did not know, or else it did not wish to know because the knowledge was inconvenient, disturbing, and dangerous [*Trial and Error*, pp. 404 f.].

If a knowledge of Dachau before the time of the gas chambers and crematoria was unwelcome because it was inconvenient, disturbing, and dangerous, a knowledge of Auschwitz, Bergen-Belsen, Treblinka, and others in 1941–44 was even more so. For those were the days when it was considered essential to the victory over Germany that boatloads of refugees should at all costs be prevented from reaching the shores of Palestine.

Even more disheartening than this motivated ignorance in a time of admitted stress is the unwillingness of the world to know and consider, now that we have the opportunity to study the past, what took place between the Nazis and the Jews. Decent human beings shrink from the notion that they belong to the same species as a Hitler, a Himmler, a Frank, a Streicher, and their thousands and tens of thousands of underlings. We want to forget; and it is only because of this willingness that Professor Toynbee could permit himself the unheard-of vilification of lumping the Jews of Israel in their actions against the Arabs with the Nazis in their actions against the Jews.

However distasteful it may be, I find it necessary in the face of such a wild and monstrous charge to say something of the Nazi-Jewish *physical* actualities before I touch upon the equally revolting, almost unbalancing record on the psychological and sociological side. I quote from *Harvest of Hate* by Léon Poliakov, based on the official documents of the Nuremberg and other trials of Nazi war criminals (Jewish Publication Society of America, Philadelphia, 1954). I begin with the occupation of Poland in 1939, before the German adoption of a policy of extermination.

The SS set the example, though they were far from holding a monopoly. There were certain classic procedures. Cutting off the beards and earlocks of Jews was a widespread entertainment; it was also the thing to be pulled about in a cart by a victim. How many Germans sent their families photographs preserving these deeds for posterity! Another amusement consisted of breaking into a Jewish apartment or house and forcing young and old to undress and dance, arm in arm, to the sound of a phonograph. Following this with rape was optional, as one risked being tried for the "crime of race defile-ment." Staider spirits, combining business and pleasure, seized pedestrian Jewesses in the streets in order to make them clean their quarters or barracks (business) with the victims' underwear (pleasure) [p. 41].

Between the adoption of a policy of extermination and its scien-tific implementation the mass killings were crude and unsystema-tized. Poliakov writes:

Most of the time the extermination squads worked as follows: After going into a place, they would have the leading Jews pointed out to them, in particular the rabbi. These Jews they would charge with organizing a Jewish council. A day or so later the council would be notified that the Jewish population was to be registered for transfer to a "Jewish territory" being organized in the Ukraine or some other region. The council would then be ordered to call the Jews together; in the larger localities this was also done by posting notices. Given the haste of the operation, the order was on the whole pretty well obeyed by the inhabitants, who were still ignorant of German methods. (Later, when the last ghettos in White Russia and the Baltic countries were being closed down, the victims had to be rounded up by force in indescribable manhunts.) The Jews were crowded into trucks, or freight cars, and taken a few kilometers out of town to some ravine or anti-tank ditch. There, after being stripped of their money, valuables, and often even their clothing, men, women, and children were shot on the spot.
    This was the usual procedure, though every action group and squad had its preferred methods. Certain squads forced their victims to lie down and fired a pistol point blank into the back of their necks. Others made the Jews climb down into the ditch and lie on top of the bodies of those already shot so that the pile of corpses steadily mounted. Still others lined the victims up along the edge of the ditch and shot them down in successive salvos; this was considered the "most humane" and the "most military." . . . Sometimes only a few hours elapsed between the time the notices were posted and the execution.
    The Germans preferred warmer seasons for carrying out the executions. A report from Group A complained about the difficulties of the work. "The cold has made the executions more difficult. Another difficulty is the fact that the Jews are scattered all over the territory. The long distances, bad roads, lack of trucks and gasoline, and inadequate numbers of men strain our forces to the limit." Later the author of the report promised to finish with the Jews of the region within two months "if weather conditions permit" [pp. 122 f.].

The transition from primitive to scientific slaughter was made piece-meal, the old continuing side by side with the new for some time.

Shooting was not the only method the commandos used. On the shores of the Black Sea there were mass drownings; at Bachtchissarai . . . the drowning of 1,029 Jews during the period July 1–15, 1942, was reported. There were cases of Jews being burned alive, especially at Minsk, in White Russia. Finally, in the Spring of 1942, mobile gas chambers, designed and manufac-tured in Berlin and disguised as gas trucks, made their appearance all over Russia. A complaint from SS Lieutenant Becker on May 16 reads: "The gas is generally not used in the right way. To get things over with as soon as possible, the driver presses the accelerator to the floor. This kills people by suffocation instead of making them gradually doze off. My directives have proved that, with the correct adjustment of the lever, death comes quicker and the prisoners sleep peacefully. There are no more of the contorted faces or defecations there used to be" [p. 124].

It became apparent that the extermination of six million human beings was not a task to be left to the haphazard ingenuities of squad leaders.

Techniques had to be discovered, and these . . . proved very difficult to perfect. . . . An industry for the slaughter of human beings had to be organized in detail. Added to the problems of exterminating so many people were the problems of deportation [p. 113]. [But] German technical genius made it possible to set up an efficient and rationalized industry of death within a few months. Like other industries it had its department of research, improvement, administrative services, a business office, and archives. . . .
    . . . we shall consider only the chief establishment where extermination was systematically carried out, and pass by those other murder methods which were used almost everywhere, of which mass shooting was always the leading one. The morbid ingenuity of the Nazis devised dozens of different individual and collective techniques: the quicklime method . . . used particularly in Poland; injections of carbolic acid into the heart, used in most concentration camps; or the one which made the Mauthausen camp infamous, which consisted of throwing the victims from the top of a quarry. But these represented an exercise of local initiative, the refinements of individual sadism. What concerns us here is the more or less official method commanded from Berlin by the officials charged with the job of genocide. This method, employed in specially prepared places, resulted in the death of the overwhelming majority of the victims of Nazism; the exact figures can never be finally established. The method chosen was asphyxiation; by carbon monoxide in the four large Polish camps (Chelmno, Belzec, Sobidor, Treblinka), and by prussic-acid fumes at Maidanek and in the huge Auschwitz installations in Upper Silesia [pp. 182 f.].

Finally, as to the personality of the participants in this work:

The men of the action groups sought to distinguish themselves in the service of Greater Germany; they aspired to be "hard," and competition in savagery played a considerable role. "Paper soldier" was the scornful nickname with which Commando 6 of Group C dubbed Corporal Matthias Graf, who was in charge of the intelligence section of his group, and never had—and never sought—an occasion to take part in the massacres. . . . Such a milieu bred complete monsters, real legendary ogres. There was, for example, the police constable who afterwards at Lwow used to kill Jewish children to amuse his own children; or another who used to bet that he could cut off the head of a ten-year-old boy with a single saber stroke [p. 131].
    The attitude displayed by the leading members of the action groups in the course of their trial at Nuremberg several years later, throws light on the

astonishing confusion that reigned in the Nazi mind. Among the twenty-two accused were a university professor, eight lawyers, a dental surgeon, an architect, an art expert, and even a theologian, a former pastor. All pleaded guilty; not one expressed the least regret; at most they mentioned the harsh necessities of war and the fact that they were acting under orders. And yet in their defense they referred to the same values of Western civilization that they had trampled underfoot for years. Their witnesses and lawyers praised their honesty, their familial virtues, their Christian feelings, and even their gentleness of character [p. 132].

It is with this inferno of human degradation, the stark realities of which outrun the maddest imaginings of Dante, that Professor Toynbee classes the actions of the Jews of Israel against the Arabs who had engaged them in war. And still the iniquity of the identification is not revealed in its fullness until we have taken in the larger canvas of the Nazi policy on the Jews.

II

The war that the Nazis declared on the Jewish people is undoubtedly the only one of its kind in human history. Various attempts have been made to analyze Nazi anti-Semitism in more or less "reasonable" and familiar terms; it has been described as prejudice exploited in a bid for domestic political power by demagogues who may or may not have shared it; as a deflection of frustrated rage upon an innocent and easily available victim (suggested by Professor Toynbee); as a concealed rebellion born of a secret hatred of Christianity and Jesus the Jew; as a cunning maneuver in the international field, aimed at the demoralization of the democracies. All of these elements were certainly to be found in it, but no combination of them suffices to explain the convulsive seizure of horror, loathing, and fury which the mention of Jews or Judaism precipitated among a considerable number of Germans. The word "pathological" has been used. It is an escape word. It classifies and dismisses without explaining or even describing. The paroxysm was not directed toward an "understandable" goal—even in the sense that lunatics may be regarded as having such goals. It was not a question of getting rid of all the Jews in Germany or in Hitler-conquered territories, whether by expulsion or extermination. There was no limitation of objective, no point at which the spasm could be expected to be spent—one reason being that the furious urges were in some ways contradictory.

They wanted to make the entire earth uninhabitable for Jews; they wanted to make the name of the Jew such a by-word for infamy and repulsiveness that no people would harbor him. They wanted also to reach back into the history of the Jew and to expose his past as a prolonged calamity for the human species. At the same time they wanted to permit some Jews to remain alive, but in a condition of degradation so hideous and at the same time so indecently comical to look upon that their hatred could continue to feed upon the spectacle and find therein its justification.

The pronouncements of the German leaders on the Jews read like the incoherent ravings of the demented. The head of the great and civilized German state delivered himself as follows:

If the Jews were alone in this world, they would suffocate as much in dirt and filth, as they would carry on a detestable struggle to cheat and ruin each other, although the complete lack of will to sacrifice, expressed in their cowardice, would also in this instance make the fight a comedy [*Mein Kampf*].

But, astoundingly enough, this wretched, subhuman species is a power against which the whole world must arm.

If, with the help of the Marxian creed, the Jew conquers the nations of this world, his crown will become the funeral wreath of humanity, and once again this planet, empty of mankind, will move through the ether as it did thousands of years ago [ibid.].

And, in connection with the First World War:

If, at the beginning of, or during the war, 12,000 or 15,000 of these Jewish corruptors of the people had been plunged into an asphyxiating gas . . . the sacrifice of millions of soldiers would not have been in vain [ibid.].

These ravings, and scores of others like them, appear in the source-book of the Nazi movement, written at the beginning of Hitler's career, and issued in some millions of copies and made compulsory reading in Germany after his accession to power. I wonder if anything like them can be found in the considered statements of any other head of a government since such statements were made permanent in writing. I wonder if any other civilized people has voted into power, or permitted to come into power, a character so obviously and criminally deranged. It cannot be pleaded, on behalf of the Germans, that they did not know the man before his book had become a part of the educational system of the country, which was after his accession. It sold well between 1924, when it was written, and 1933; and Hitler's campaign speeches were shot through with the same obsessive and delirious preoccupation with the Jewish subject. (It is well to observe, in passing, that the gas chambers were in his mind as early as 1924.) I repeat here carefully what may sound like a piece of rhetoric: namely, that Hitler's investiture with the chancellorship "was proof enough that the German people had passed into a maniacal condition uncontrollable from within" and should have been the moment for international intervention. This time it will be pleaded that the foreign powers, at least, could not have known the man. How ironical that millions of dollars and pounds are spent to spy out the secrets of the atom bomb of the physicists while the placing of a human atom bomb at the heart of civilization, in the form of a maniac lifted to power by maniacs in the open light of day, is ignored by the gatherers and sifters of "intelligence." Some of this "ignoring," we know, was motivated by a low cunning that found its ghastly and bloody nemesis. The world was not big enough for the spoon one needed to sup with this devil.

To what extent did Hitler succeed in infecting parts of the democratic world with his diseased condition or in reinfecting it with a sickness already virulent enough long before his coming? There can be no scientific answer to that question. One only remembers the desperation of those Jews who, let us say in sheer self-defense, tried to warn the world of the larger meaning of the phenomenon of Nazi anti-Semitism, and the counter-warnings with which they were answered; one remembers also the timidity of many prominent Jews, who trembled to hear the protests of other Jews, and agreed with the cunning ones that it was impolitic to irritate the alligator while he was devouring his victims; and I personally remember overhearing in a club car a conversation in which reference was made to a speech on Hitlerism by the late Stephen S. Wise, and a curt, irritated dismissal of the subject in a phrase that sums up a popular attitude of those days: "It's only the Jews squawking again." It sticks in my mind together with the phrase I saw chalked on walls in Paris in August 1939: *"Mieux vaut Hitler que Blum*—better Hitler than Blum." I was sure Professor Toynbee would not agree with that preference. But today, in the light of his opinion of the Jews of Israel, and recalling that Léon Blum was favorably disposed toward the creation of the Jewish state, Professor Toynbee might be inclined to substitute: *"C'est plus ou moins la même chose*—it's six of one and half a dozen of the other."

The soul of the Western world was redeemed by groups of men and women who did understand what was afoot. Before and during the Second World War there were thousands—and some among them were Germans—who risked at first their standing, then their freedom, and later, in many cases, their lives, in protest and counteraction; and if ever there was in this world atonement for blindness or indifference on the part of hundreds of millions, it was made by the Western nations between 1939 and 1945. Still, we must make the sorrowful observation that the immense expiation has not been followed by a proportionate clarification. The Jewish Question still remains the touchstone of the condition of the Western world—and who can assert that the response is satisfactory today? How can it be when molders of public opinion equate these two relationships: "Nazi-Jewish" and "Jewish-Arab"?

To what curious conclusions Professor Toynbee perverts the moral damage done to the Jewish people by Nazi anti-Semitism when he writes:

On the Day of Judgment the gravest crime standing to the German National Socialists' account might be, not that they had exterminated a majority of the Western Jews, but that they had caused the surviving remnant of Jewry to stumble [above, p. 113].

He is in effect implying that the Nazi program for the demoralization and debasement of surviving Jewry was largely successful, for he tells us that an enraged Jewry after World War II took it out on the Arabs as an enraged Germany had taken it out on the Jews after World War I. For him, it seems, the dominant Jewish emotion was hatred, and a ferocious demand for vicarious revenge. Actually the most serious moral damage done to the Jewish people, especially in its relationship to the Jewish homeland, resulted from a panic of compassion.

I have described the struggle that has always gone on within the Zionist movement between the creative and the destructive elements —that is, according to my interpretation of Jewish values. From the beginning the Ahad Ha-Amists and the Weizmannists were the cautious builders, insistent upon quality; from the beginning they were opposed by the maximalists of quantity and speed, who were prepared to defer the qualitative achievement until later. This struggle was conducted both in the Jewish homeland and throughout that part of the Jewish people everywhere that constituted the Zionist movement. With the rise of Nazi anti-Semitism the ideological pressure for quantitative achievement was reinforced by the cry for help from European Jewry and by the emotional response of fellow

Jewries throughout the world. This was not a time for social idealism, for the higher moral statesmanship of the Jewish Restoration, for picking and choosing men and forms; it was a time for unreflecting rescue of fellow Jews; they had to be got out of the threatened area; and with the doors of other lands all but closed, there was only Palestine to look to—and the doors of Palestine had been closed by Great Britain.

Professor Toynbee is at pains to rebuke the victorious Western nations for not having admitted into their lands the Jewish survivors of the Nazi mass-murderers, thus preventing by anticipation the pressure upon Palestine. But what of the failure of the democracies to open their doors *before* the outbreak of the war, when all but the willfully blind could see what was coming? He has not a word to say about the pitiful and ignominious spectacle of the proud Royal Navy chasing boatloads of refugees in the Mediterranean before and during the war. He does not seem so much as to glimpse the madness of frustration which came upon millions of Jews who had to stand by and watch the consignment of their kin to destruction and worse than destruction in what seemed to be a worldwide conspiracy. What a good thing it would be if we could forget that the democracies had their part in creating the circumstances that caused surviving Jewry "to stumble"! But Professor Toynbee will not let us forget; he compels us to exhume the memory as testimony against his aspersions.

When, after the Second World War, it was a question of getting out of Europe those survivors who, even according to Professor Toynbee's view, could no longer remain there, the international pre-war situation reproduced itself and remained in force until the State of Israel was proclaimed on paper by the United Nations and established in fact by the Jews of Palestine. Surely the man who wrote—perhaps in an uncaught moment of absent-mindedness—of the "splendid failure" of the Bar Kochbas could have "stumbled" into a phrase of commendation for the splendid success of Ben-Gurion. What the United Nations gave Palestine was the right to risk everything in a last desperate gamble. Simultaneously with the acceptance of the challenge, the Jews of Palestine, now the Israelis, opened wide the gates and called upon every Jew who felt the need to join them without delay. Two things then happened—one of them unbelievable, the other inevitable. The Israelis threw back the invading Arab nations; and the onrush of immigrants placed an intolerable strain on the economic, social, and organizational structure of the community. It is my personal opinion that in the joy, relief, and triumph of the moment the Israelis overextended themselves; despite all pressures, they could and should have limited immigration to a maximum of one hundred thousand a year instead of admitting nearly three quarters of a million in three years. They not only invited, they also cajoled; and in the wake of the systemless wild welcome there followed a deterioration of standards and ideals and forms from which it will take the country a generation or more to recover.

This is not the place for a detailed examination of both sides of the case: the one pleading that speed was of the essence because only numbers could ensure safety; the other countering that quality too was of the essence even from the strictly utilitarian and security point of view. In place here is the observation that the stampede that had been precipitated by the long agony of martyrdom in Europe and by the long agony of helpless watching everywhere else gave an immense forward thrust to the physical being of the Jewish state and a backward thrust to its moral and social being. Had there been no Hitlerism, had the pace of growth maintained a slowly mounting rate, the ideal that permeated the classical chalutzic urge would have had a longer span in which to operate. Is there a Jew anywhere who would not have the six million of Europe still alive though it might mean that the Jewish state would still be in the making?

We have no record—there is no system for the compilation of such data—of the psychic damage that had been wrought on those Jewish survivors from Europe who poured into Israel by the hundreds of thousands from 1948 on. There is no way of computing the cost—in money, effort, discouragement, retreat from early standards —of integrating with the Israeli society the young and old whose first need was moral and psychological therapy. And I still believe that, looked on as a whole, this Israeli society is an astounding achievement. Its problems were superhuman; its failures are human; its successes have been creditable in the highest degree.

One can easily understand the readiness of an unsympathetic observer to stigmatize as revengeful rancor the leading motive in this enormous effort. To some degree this sort of imputation is natural in those who will not frankly admit the degree of their own guilt. It is incomprehensible to them that the Jews should not have emerged from this unparalleled ordeal contemptuous of a world that had betrayed them, and cynical of all moral values. And it is true that a corroding cynicism appeared here and there, and that here and there the Nazis produced the kind of Jewish individual who would justify their scurrility. The poet Segalovitch wrote in moral, not cynical, despair:

My stomach turns when I reflect on Man,
His vileness and the vileness of his deeds:
And not alone the Prussian torturer,
The manufacturer of human soap,

But the two billions of the globe entire,
Who looked on at the greatest of all murders.
My stomach turns, my mind and body fail me;
My words stick in my throat.

How many fell into such a mood at times? We do not know. Their number cannot have been great or the seizures enduring; it is not in this mood that an enormous constructive enterprise is furthered. How many were there whom the Nazis turned, by ingenious manipulation of deferred hopes, delegation of power, hierarchies of Jewish councils, and the rest, into monstrosities like themselves? There were some—and they too cannot have been many. They represent that quota of weaklings, cowards, criminals, and just ordinary people driven below the human level, who, whether as American prisoners in Korea or British prisoners under the Nazis, bring into sharper relief the stronger natures that endured until death without surrendering their souls. In suggesting this analogy, I should like to remind the reader that the volume and the depth of the villainies employed for more than a decade by the Nazis against the Jews have no parallel in what was inflicted on prisoners of war for much shorter periods. The survival of a sound Jewish people is perhaps in itself that people's greatest achievement in these last two decades.

And as we are talking of the failures and defects of the State of Israel, what has become of the historic "sweep" in Time and Space? At this writing less than eight years have passed since Israel was created in the midst of almost unimaginable discouragements and difficulties. At this writing the Arab states still consider themselves at war with Israel; an economic blockade surrounds Israel from all sides but the sea; the Suez Canal is closed to it; on the borders a continuous guerrilla warfare flickers; the Arab states still refuse to consider the resettlement of their refugee kinsmen within their underpopulated territories, and openly proclaim that nothing will satisfy them but the erasure of the State of Israel from the map—to King Saud of Saudi Arabia the removal of this "cancer" is worth ten million Arab lives;* as they once used the Arabs of Palestine in a military maneuver to facilitate—as they hoped—the destruction of Jewish Palestine, they now wish to use them for the destruction of

*Address to Arab journalists at Riyadh, Saudi Arabia, January 9, 1954, reported in the *New York Times*, January 10, 1954. [M.S.]

the State of Israel. The constellation of international forces which made possible the creation of the state in 1948 has disappeared; in its place we have the constellation of the Cold War, and within it the Arab states occupy the same advantageous position as they did in the constellation of the War of Nerves before 1939; and Israel is at the same disadvantage now as Jewish Palestine was then.

Is this the exact moment to pass judgment on the meaning and value of the State of Israel? How long should it take for a people to recover from the effects of such calamities as have been visited upon the Jews in the last twenty-odd years? How long should it take a people that has not practiced statehood for eighteen hundred years to set up the machinery of a state while coping with problems that would baffle governments with centuries of tradition and practice? How long should it take to create out of nothing, or almost nothing, a postal system, a tax system, a police service, a diplomatic service, a foreign policy, a democratic system of elections, an army, and, above all, a tradition of governmental forms?

At one point in *A Study of History* Professor Toynbee, while crying down the narrowness and mundaneness of a Zerubbabel, concedes that the state which he founded lived for more than three hundred years in the Way of Gentleness. Nearly ten times eight years had to pass before Zerubbabel's second Jewish state began to find itself with the help of Ezra and Nehemiah, and perhaps the second state did not have to face such formidable obstacles—physical, political, and psychological—as the third faces. Again, this is not an attempted justification of the means by the hoped-for ends. Given the Jewish situation as it was in the middle decades of the twentieth century, considering what the Jews of Europe and Palestine have gone through and what the Jews of Israel are now going through, the performance, with all its imperfections, is from the moral point of view a creditable one. If it could have been better, it could also have been expected to be much worse; the behavior of Israel in the unique, complicated, multisided war it has had to fight for survival stands comparison with that of the best of peoples at war. It is admittedly a miserable standard; an objective historian ought to have waited until he was in position to apply the standards of peace. That is what the Israelis are waiting for.

From *The Professor and the Fossil* (1956)

9 DIGRESSION ON AN ASTRONOMER

For many years I was puzzled by some of the arguments which the opponents of the Uganda proposal had urged against its feasibility. I could understand them when they said: "The Jewish people won't put its heart into the project. It isn't enough that need should drive them. The creative power of need is limited. It does not tap the same deep sources as affirmation. Men and women don't do their best under compulsion; they must have the encouragement of a free ideal. A homeland will blossom only where Jews experience, in addition to need, an opening up of the play impulses." I could understand them, but I could not get a picture of what they meant. And when I asked them to paint it for me, as part of their concept of the future, they said:

"That's just the point. You can't paint it. Its details are unpredictable. In colonizing Palestine we shall have plans in many ways identical with plans for the colonizing of Uganda, or of the Argentine. We shall foresee so much and so much of the growth, no doubt inaccurately, but at least on the basis of calculable factors. The essential feature in the release of a national movement is the emergence of incalculable creative factors; of personalities and enthusiasms which cannot be hired, contracted for, or organized. It's like dealing with a genius. You can encourage him by providing him with a favorable environment of freedom; but you can't tie him to a schedule. One of the differences between Uganda, or Baron de Hirsch's Argentine, and Palestine is this: the former will be the point toward which oppression will *thrust* Jews; the latter will be the point toward which sentiment will also *attract* Jews. The former will be only an expression of frustration; the latter will also express liberation. Only those Jews will go to Uganda who can't go anywhere else; many will go to Palestine who could go elsewhere, but who choose Palestine because it sets off in them a certain excitement, with deep reverberations in the folkways, and with constructive values which cannot be tapped otherwise. You'll see!"

A time came when I began to see, and now I must try to convey to others, who may be as puzzled on this point as I was, exactly what I saw. I have chosen, out of my notes and recollections, one central incident, a rather odd and even trivial one, as symbol and illustration.

On one of my early visits to Palestine, a long, long time ago, I got into a public conveyance to take the trip from Tel Aviv to Jerusalem. I had been by that road before, the winding, ascending road which follows more or less the route of the camel-drivers, from the plain to the mountain heights. But neither on my tenth nor my fiftieth trip had I lost my delight in the journey, and I look forward still to watching the levels drop away behind me, and the rugged hills come sailing to meet me in swinging semicircular motion as we take the hairpin bends to left and right. The ancient terraces on the slopes, the gray villages in the valleys or on the summits, the clusters of cacti, the alternations of the desert and the sown—they are much the same now as they were thousands of years ago. The scenery is wild and exhilarating, the air lucid. I sat on that trip, as I almost always do, in a trance of astonishment—astonishment that the journey is really lovelier than my recollection of it. On this occasion, however, we had barely traversed the foothills when I was brought to by a slap on the knee and a joyous exclamation. A book was thrust under my nose, and a voice exclaimed: *"Re'ei et zeh*—look at this!"

The man who had broken into my enchanted mood was a little, middle-aged, bespectacled fellow, with a wizened face, a bald head and childlike eyes which, as I saw in the brief glance I gave him, were flooded at the moment with something like ecstasy. I turned my attention to the book. It was a Hebrew geography; not of the kind already in use in the Palestinian schools, but a hundred years old, written by one of the *maskilim* whose name I have forgotten. A curious work, certainly, but not one to warrant the violent demonstration of which I had been the victim. The first thirty pages or so consisted of letters of commendation, from scholars, rabbis, philanthropists, men of affairs, communal leaders, poets, biblical commentators, and educators, addressed to the writer, apparently in response to the prospectus on the work sent out before it was begun. All of them were moved, edified, and delighted that he should have undertaken the enterprise. The last thirty pages consisted of letters of congratulation from the same rabbis, philanthropists, scholars, biblical commentators, etc., addressed to the writer on the occasion of the completion of the work. Once again they were moved, edified, and delighted; this time that he should have carried the enterprise to a successful conclusion. In between the layers of commendation and congratulation was sandwiched the geography.

A hasty examination revealed that the writer had drawn his information largely from Marco Polo, Benjamin of Tudela, and other "recent" medieval explorers. An astronomical addendum seemed to have been taken from the *Almagest* or from Maimonides. But not these had caused my companion to jump almost out of his skin. He directed my attention once more to the page he had first shown me. It contained, in one column, a table of latitude and longitude for the principal cities of the world. In the second column it gave the comparative times of day. But this man, who had written in Russia, had not used, as the Russian geographies did, the city of Poltava as the zero point, saying: "When it is midday in Poltava, it is eleven A.M. in Berlin, ten A.M. in London, five A.M. in New York, four P.M. in Bombay." He had not used Greenwich, as the British did, or Paris, like the French. Instead he had made the city of Jerusalem his zero point. "When it is midday in Jerusalem it is this and this hour in the other cities of the world."

I smiled, and said: "The funny things Jews do!"

"No, no," exclaimed my companion. "That isn't the point. Don't you understand that this man was anticipating the time when Jewish children would be going to a modern school in a rebuilt Palestine, and would have to orientate themselves geographically by Jerusalem?"

"He might at least have put in a word for Vasco da Gama and Copernicus," I objected.

"He did the best he could," said my companion. "There's no satisfying some people. Don't you think it's enough that he at least tried to contribute something to our school system? And that he foresaw, even if he couldn't properly meet, one of our requirements?"

I felt a pang of remorse for my seeming coolness, and it suddenly occurred to me that no one had ever prepared, for a future generation of Jewish schoolchildren, a list of comparative times of day with Juba, the capital of Uganda, as the zero point. I warmed up to my companion (I have forgotten his name; it was something like Hillel, and I will use that), and we spent the rest of the trip in friendly conversation. He told me that he was a secretary in some institution, but that his avocation was astronomy. Moreover, he was at work compiling and creating a modern Hebrew astronomical terminology, inasmuch as the classic language came into existence when things like binaries, nebulae, spectroscopic analysis, lunar librations, asteroids, solar coronas, stellar parallaxes, and solar transits were unknown. He grew understandably excited when he discovered that, having a smattering of astronomy in addition to a smattering of Hebrew, I could appreciate some of his etymological ingenuities. In those days Hebrew was receiving all sorts of extensions: for of old there had been (for instance) no automobiles, therefore no clutches, differentials, spark plugs, gear shifts, and the like; nor telephones, nor telegraphs, nor any of the modern appliances. Though, to be sure, for some of these, Hebrew adaptations had been devised before my friend Hillel came to Palestine.

I parted from him in Jerusalem, promising him, as I promised hundreds of interesting people I met, to look him up again. I never did. But this is not the whole of the story, not the complete symbol which I promised the reader. The rounding off came years later.

I was in Tel Aviv again, after a tour of the colonies of the Valley of Jezreel (always called, in Palestine, "the Emek," *the* Valley), of Galilee, and of the Sharon plain. An immense gulf of time separated the land from its early struggles, immense not by the count of days, but by the volume of change. Tel Aviv itself was as good an instance as any of this relativity of time. In less than thirty years the tumultuous city on the sand dunes already had its periods, in architectural styles, in economic tendencies, and in types of immigrational problems: the crenellated—and somewhat dilapidated—high school, or *Gymnasium,* at the foot of Herzl Street, belonged to the early, silly, functionless romantic of the (first) prewar period; the older houses on the Ahad Ha-Am Street were taken over from the Arab-city style; the jerry-built homes on the side streets of the Allenby Road belonged to the feverish Fourth Wave episode; the well-to-do section called Lev Tel Aviv (Heart of Tel Aviv) was reminiscent of Brownsville; and in the newer sections German architecture suggested little annexes to provincial world fairs. Economically the first residential period (now practically forgotten) had been succeeded by the mixed commercial and industrial; there had been the dangerous boom of the Fourth Wave; there had followed the stabilization, the expansion of labor, the building of the fair, the creation of the harbor. The streets of Tel Aviv had received and had swallowed the predominance of Yiddish and of Russian. They were now slowly engulfing German, and digesting it, as they had digested the others, into Hebrew. You had to forget fast, and learn fast, in Tel Aviv.

On the evening of my return from the Emek I went to see a performance of Stefan Zweig's *Jeremiah* by the Habimah players. Surely Stefan Zweig, the uprooted Jew who was to take his own life in exile when the world to which he had given himself crumbled about him, never dreamed, when he wrote this play, that some day it would be given, in the original language of the prophet he portrayed, in the land where the prophet had lived, by and for the returned descendants of the prophet and his contemporaries. I might perhaps have made this circumstance—and for that matter many others—the illustration of the unpredictable, creative evocations which distinguish a national from a sociological movement. For who could have foreseen a Stanislavsky and a Zemach in Moscow preparing a dramatic troupe of the first order which would prove to be one of the spiritual constituents of a Jewish homeland? But I have not yet reached the point of this chapter.

I went out of the theater, along streets thronged with Tel Avivians, among crowds of gay young people, past cafés jammed with customers. The movie houses and meeting halls were emptying. At the corner of Allenby Road and the seafront I ran into an American journalist, fresh from the west, and we walked to and fro along the beach while the crowds dwindled and the lights in Jaffa across the bay were extinguished one by one. In a pause of the conversation I happened to stop and look up at the sky, which was, as always between the rainy seasons, marvelously clear. I noticed then that an astronomical event, of minor significance but of great beauty, was in preparation. The gibbous and brilliant moon was close to Spica, a star of the first magnitude in the constellation of Virgo. The whole sky was revolving, against the diurnal motion of the earth, to the right; but the moon, in her slower motion about the earth, was crawling leftward through the constellations. The illumined half of the moon pointed right, toward the long-vanished sun, the unillumined and invisible half, or rather less than half, pointed left. Some time that night an occultation would take place; this is to say, the invisible bulk of the moon would blot out, at a given instant, and with startling, instantaneous effect, the star Spica. Now that, as every amateur astronomer will attest, is something to be seen, especially through a telescope.

I explained all this to my friend, and told him that I had a telescope at home; and if I only knew what time the occultation would take place, I would treat him to the celestial spectacle at my expense. Very much at my expense, since only one of us could have his eye glued to the telescope at the climactic moment. Such are the enthusiasms of Zionists and amateur astronomers. But how was I to know when the occultation would take place? And where, in God's name, was I to find out? Now if this were only New York, I would surely be able to ring up someone with a nautical almanac. And failing that, there was always some newspaper information service. But we were in Tel Aviv, a great city no doubt, but after all . . .

My friend said: "The other day, walking through the *Shechunat ha-Po'alim* (the Workers' Quarter at the seaward end of Rothschild Boulevard) I saw a telescope mounted on a roof. If you're so set on the occultation, let's go there. The owner of the telescope may know."

"At this hour of the night?" I answered, dubiously.

"If he's as hipped on the subject as you are, he'll be up right enough."

So we set out along the Yarkon Street, parallel with the beach, and came to the Workers' Quarter. There, sure enough, on the flat roof of one of the single-storied houses, a telescope was mounted on a tripod. No one was standing beside it, but a light was shining in one of the windows below.

"Vive Tel Aviv!" I exclaimed. But the best was yet to come.

We knocked timidly at the door, and a woman came out. I asked whether the *ba'al ha-bayit* (the man of the house), or whoever else it was owned the telescope, was in. She shook her head. The *ba'al ha-bayit,* her husband, was the owner of the telescope. But he was a night worker and was away till morning.

What a pity! I was about to apologize and withdraw, when the woman said:

"Before he went out, an hour ago, he left a message with me. He said: 'It may be, it *may* be, though it is not at all likely—and still one can't tell—it may be, and one must always be prepared, that someone will come to the house because there's a telescope on the roof, and ask you what time a certain event will take place."

She produced from her pocket a slip of paper, and continued:

"What that event is, he did not tell me, as I know nothing about the stars. But whatever it is, I was to advise anyone who asked about it, that it will take place"—she looked closely at the paper in the light streaming out from the kitchen—"it will take place at eleven seconds and fifty-three minutes after one o'clock. If anyone wanted to use the telescope at that time, he was welcome to it."

When I was able to catch my breath, I thanked her. No, we did not want to use the telescope. I had one at home. I only wanted the information. I asked her also to convey our thanks to her husband —to *Adon* (Mister) . . .

"Hillel," she said.

It was my man of the geography book.

But by now the excitement of the occultation had been displaced in me by another excitement.

"The absurdity of it!" I said, exultantly, as we walked back. "The utter, delicious, and heartening absurdity of it! That's what makes a homeland. Not just land, agriculture, funds, factories, experts, administrators, and blueprints, but cranks, mystics, vegetarians, bibliophiles, poets—and amateur astronomers who remember that someone might want to know the minute and split second of an occultation. A thing like this couldn't have happened in Uganda."

"No, it couldn't," said my astonished friend. "Why should it?"

From *Harvest in the Desert* (1943)

part three

Maurice Samuel lived in a century which saw the historic encounter between Gentile and Jew erupt into unprecedented tragedy and horror. As a profoundly engaged Jew with a talent for expression to match the integrity of his thought—"probably the ablest Jewish intellectual of his time," Ludwig Lewisohn called him—he addressed himself to an examination of the particularity of the Jewish ethos. This effort produced a series of polemical works that were in effect variations on a thesis first set forth in *You Gentiles* in 1924: "the conviction that an understanding of the Jewish episode in civilization is the key to the Western world's intellectual and spiritual difficulties." The Gentile world, Samuel stressed, was not "Christian"; it rejected the Jew as it rejected the God the Jew had foisted on it. To the Gentile—a theme Samuel elaborated in *The Gentleman and the Jew* —life is a "game and a gallant adventure"; to the Jew it is "a sober duty." An exploration of the antithesis between Jewish and non-Jewish modes, as well as the affinities, came, as Samuel observed, "to occupy most of my life and provide the substance of many of my books." The selections in this section are extracted from that considerable substance.

JEWS AMONG
THE NATIONS

10 THE GREAT HATRED

The Evasion

What brought you to this pass, you Western Christian peoples? What crimes and what follies have you begun to expiate in bloodshed and in expectation of bloodshed, in suffering and in an expectation of suffering almost as difficult to bear? For these are man-made calamities, not visitations of nature; their sources are men's ill will and blindness; their alleviation lies not in the fulfillment of vast impersonal processes, but in the application of a rightly motivated human intelligence.

To this riddle of death I attempt here a partial answer, or a pointer to the answer, by examining a single question on which have been concentrated more blindness, more willful evasions of heart and head, than on any other—and that because it is a key question, or the key question. You would not think it through in time of peace; now you will have to think it through in the midst of your agony, and endure a revolution even while you struggle to keep alive. Without such a revolution—a convulsion of the spirit comparable to the physical convulsions you must endure—you will not come out alive.

Your reluctance to see clearly on this focal issue springs more from a moral than an intellectual obtuseness. The inertia of the mind is weighted with the fear of self-understanding, fear of the confession which must accompany self-understanding and of the purgation which must accompany confession.

The issue of which I speak is anti-Semitism.

Let me anticipate the first probable misunderstanding. I am writing neither in defense of the Jews nor in the hope of provoking a change of outlook in anti-Semites. The futility of such a head-on approach will be demonstrated in its place. Here it is enough to note that for the anti-Semite my very point of departure is the lie of lies, the Jewish lie. Yet no other point of departure is possible. For I must open by asking:

"How shall we begin to account for the mad disparity between the actual proportion of Jewish participation in contemporaneous Western life and the extent of the world's preoccupation with the Jews? And how shall we explain the related phenomenon, the obsessional exaggeration of Jewish numbers, Jewish financial and political power, and Jewish unity of purpose, which seeks to justify this preoccupation?"

For the anti-Semite the question is unreal, and the asking of it the central offense. For him there is no such disparity, and what I have called "obsessional exaggeration" he regards as objective evaluation. He knows—I do not say he believes, or is convinced, or is quite certain—he *knows,* in the sense of "I know that my Redeemer liveth," that the Jews play so enormous and so malignant a role in the affairs of nations that Christians must tremble at the prospect (or fact) of Jewish world domination, and that Christians not thus alarmed are blind to the one significant danger of modern times. Therefore, in putting my opening question, in using the insolent words "mad disparity," I have, for the anti-Semite, placed myself automatically outside the pale of discussion. Whatever I add now will interest him, if at all, only as a continuous demonstration of the Jewish and pro-Jewish technique of world deception.

I address myself, then, not to the anti-Semite, but to the liberal, or the objective reader. But in seeking for him an approach to my opening question, I encounter another obstacle, a fundamental block or resistance as characteristic as the hallucinations of the anti-Semite, and perhaps less defensible. It exists among Jews, too, who in this matter have shown the same cowardice as Christians, but for different reasons, and with different results. These remarks, however, are directed chiefly at the Christian world. It is its condition that I am studying primarily, that of the Jews incidentally. When I use the vocative you, as I do occasionally, the purpose is to emphasize the terrain of the problem, and not to exonerate the Jew from the moral and intellectual deficiencies which he shares with the rest of the world.

The immense majority of objective Christians or Gentiles have made up their minds that anti-Semitism is merely one among the countless cases of group hostility with which the world is distracted.

For them it is an ordinary "minority problem," aggravated perhaps by the double irritant of race and religion, but in no fundamental sense differing from a hundred other problems in group relationships. It is a case of intolerance, of prejudice, of the usual inability of human beings to bear graciously with the proximity of the unlike. Across it runs the familiar theme of economic motivation, and behind it stands the treacherous figure of the demagogue, quick to discover human discords and make their exploitation his career.

Now this attitude too leaves utterly untouched the riddle of the mad disparity. If anti-Semitism is indeed an ordinary intolerance somewhat exacerbated by special circumstances, why has it become a world cult of such extraordinary power? And—equally baffling— whence does it derive its characteristic tone, a terrified and driveling diabolism, absent from all other instances of group intolerance, and inaccessible to ordinary modes of discourse?

"I refuse to be intelligent about the Jewish question," writes H. G. Wells, a typical liberal. *"For me it does not exist."*

An extraordinary statement indeed. One of the most tangled, poignant, and fateful human problems does not exist for Mr. Wells! What he means of course is that anti-Semitism is for him not a special and peculiar problem. And certainly it is simpler and easier to dwell on those features of anti-Semitism which it possesses in common with all other group hatreds—the herd's distrust of the dissimilar, the religious paradox of extorted love, the sublimation of economic rivalry into ideological delusions, the manipulation of confused masses by careerist mobsters. But just because these features also exist everywhere else they fail to explain the peculiar and identifying spirit of anti-Semitism, from which alone we can deduce its special law.

Or perhaps liberals and objective Christians will even deny that there is in anti-Semitism a peculiar and identifying spirit. Perhaps it is necessary for me to quote for their special benefit from the anti-Semitic literature which has flooded the Western world. In doing so I ask you first to observe not only the stupefying disassociation from all reality, but the tacit presentation of "fact" without explanation or preparation. The statements about the Jews occur offhandedly like references to an accepted folklore. They are reminders, not revelations; they are allusions to *choses bien connues,* not to be discussed. And they appear in books, pamphlets, and periodicals in every modern language. I do not have to go in search of them. One has only to travel and be literate.

In Johannesburg I glance at a local paper and find a complaint against the political power of British Jewry, symbolized by "The London *Jewish Chronicle,* with a circulation of 500,000." It happens that the total Jewish population of England is 300,000, and the circulation of the *Jewish Chronicle* less than a fifteenth of that figure.

In New York I pick up a book by a travelogue journalist, Peter Fleming, and find among light reflections on Russian and Chinese customs the offhand reminder that of course most of Russia's Bolshevik leaders have Jewish blood in them. The writer does not make a point of it. It is not something that one argues about.

I am in Las Palmas on September 6, 1937. The local daily *Falange* has on page four a full-spread article on General Quiepo de Llano. The subheading reads: *"Nuestra Guerra es una Guerra contra el Judaismo—* Our war is a war against Judaism." We are given the figure for "the worldwide Jewish collections gathered in the last eighteen years by the head of the Jewish world government" *(el Hasal del Gobierno Judico).* It is 4,181,399,353,000 (four trillion one hundred and eighty-one billion, three hundred and ninety-nine million, three hundred and fifty-three thousand) pesetas. In American currency over one hundred billion (not million) dollars. With a disconcerting touch of sanity the writer sets the number of Jews in the world more or less accurately at 16,000,000. From this it would appear that for the last eighteen years every Jewish man, woman and child—including the nine or ten million Jews in Russia, Poland, Germany, Rumania, and Hungary—has been making a voluntary annual contribution of three hundred and fifty dollars to "the head of the Jewish government."

What is the essential character of such utterances? That they are inaccurate? That they proceed from malice or ignorance? That they are the product of race prejudice and religious bigotry? Of course they are inaccurate, and of course they are accompanied by emotions of hostility. But what is that to the point?

Let us consider a statement on the Jew by Joseph Goebbels: "This is the world enemy, the destroyer of civilization, the parasite among the nations, the son of chaos, the incarnation of evil, the germ of decomposition, the plastic demon of the decay of humanity." Does it help us in any way to classify this with all other expressions of interracial or interreligious hatred, like the Franco-German, the Germano-Polish, the Japanese-American? Do we not stultify ourselves by refusing to perceive that we have left the "normal" field of human enmity, and entered the realm of the primitive demonological?

In every liberal discussion of anti-Semitism which has come to my notice, I have encountered the same obstinate refusal to distinguish between anti-Jewish sentiment and anti-Semitic hallucination. Anti-Jewish sentiment (a dislike of Jews based on contact, direct or indirect, with some Jews) is in fact the ordinary variety of racial, religious, and economic bitterness, overflowing in ordinary human abuse. Anti-Semitic hallucination is a unique phenomenon (the word unique must be taken quite literally here) in modern group relations. No other people precipitates such a reversion to primitive terror and folkloristic mental helplessness among civilized nations. Regarding no other people could such "inaccuracies" and "exaggerations" be given currency. And this amazing distinction is systematically ignored by liberal writers on anti-Semitism, so that the only approach to the right analysis of the phenomenon remains permanently closed as by a conspiracy.

It is again with the strictest attention to the meaning of words that we must speak of the "myth" of Jewish unity. (Myth: a purely fictitious narrative usually involving *supernatural* persons, actions or events, and *embodying some popular idea concerning natural or historical phenomena.* Oxford Dictionary. Italics mine.) Here the historical phenomenon is the millennial persistence of a group of people called the Jewish: the myth is the universal folk notion that there is among the Jews an inner unity of which no other people in the world is capable, a unity directed in programmatic destructiveness at the outside world.

This mythological attitude expresses itself in the belief that Jewish Communists and Jewish capitalists work hand in glove for the destruction of Western civilization. Liberal writers and well-meaning people generally conceive that they have done their full intellectual duty when they have pointed out the absurdity of the belief. They make no attempt to explain the crucial and baffling fact—they do not even acknowledge it!—that no other racial or religious struggle is accompanied by a similar accusation. There is a vast enough literature of international hatred, but the French have never accused the Germans, or the Germans the Poles, or the Americans the Japanese, of concealing a unified plan of campaign behind the ostensible division into capitalists and Communists.

What is the sense of just saying, indignantly, "Absurd!" when the point is *"credunt quia absurdum"?*

Here we have the detailed exposé by Hitler himself:

"Jewry has tried a ruse which, from the political point of view, is really very clever. This capitalistic people which was the first on this earth to introduce the enslavement of man, has managed to take the leadership of the Fourth Estate into its hands. In so doing it has adopted two kinds of tactics, one of the Right and one of the Left, since it has apostles in both camps. . . . Through clever management of the press, he [the Jew] so influenced the masses that the Right looked upon the mistakes of the Left as the mistakes of the German workers, while mistakes made on the Right in their turn seemed to the German worker the mistakes of the so-called *bourgeois.* And neither of the two noticed that the mistakes on both sides were the objectives sought by those devilish agitators. Thus did there come to pass the ghastliest joke in history—Jewish speculators became Jewish labor leaders . . . The [German] people is to destroy the backbone of its independence—its own industry—in order that it may sink into the golden chains of the slavery of interest imposed by this people."

What are the implications of this analysis? That the laws of economics, operative everywhere else, have been suspended for the Jewish people; that either class distinctions among Jews are a *blague* to gull the Gentiles, or that poor Jews are content to be poor as long as the gentile world can be enslaved for the benefit of the Jewish rich; that the revolting Jewish slums of London's Whitechapel, New York's East Side and the Baluta of Lodz either conceal great possessions or harbor great masses of voluntary slaves whose lives are dedicated to the aggrandizement of their masters at the expense of the Gentiles; that Kuhn, Loeb, and Company of Wall Street and the *Yevsektzia* (the Jewish branch of the Russian Communist Party) are the right and left wings of a single army executing a pincer movement about the gentile world. Fantastic? Yes or no, according to whether the point of view is on the plane of experience or on the plane of the mythological. But to pour derision on the theory with a view to shaming its proponents into common sense is as sensible as trying to cure a lunatic by laughing at him.

But what is involved here is a question of a moral order, to wit:

"Why are you laughing at the lunatic? Why do you spend your time 'disproving' his hallucinations, instead of making an effort to penetrate to the nature of his derangement? Are you afraid that in understanding him completely you will also understand yourselves too well? Are you, in short, afraid of a backfire of revelation?"

Fury and Fable

Let us dig deeper into the confusion which covers the access to the source of your calamities. And do not start away with the cry: "Oh, the Jewish question again! But we know all about that! We understand it thoroughly, we intelligent liberals, we kindly Christians. Let him talk to the others!" Do not exclaim, either: "Here is another Jew, unbalanced by the disasters which have overtaken his people, forgetting that these have now been caught up and obliterated in a universal tide."

I repeat: It is not of my people that I am thinking primarily. The perceptions toward which I seek to guide you are related to your great Christian world. They deal with matters which would be relevant to your fate even if the Jews were to disappear from the earth tomorrow.

Let us return to the distinction between anti-Jewish sentiment and the anti-Semitic outlook, a distinction of crucial importance in the discussion. However closely the two may intertwine in any person's mind, they are in origin and character as distinct as a personal antipathy and a folkloristic tradition.

Dislike of Jews may not have anything to do with anti-Semitism. It may be a psychological fixation, quite unrelated to "some popular idea concerning a natural or historical phenomenon." In that case it is one form of a common human weakness. Perhaps it is the extension of an unpleasant personal experience. Perhaps it is connected with a group rivalry of one sort or another. Perhaps it arises from what is generally defended as "an ingrained antipathy"—which is only a highfalutin name for a bad habit acquired in childhood. Then it has nothing to teach us that cannot be learned from the study of other intolerances.

An initial dislike of Jews may predispose a suggestible person to anti-Semitism, as weak lungs predispose a person to tuberculosis; but tuberculosis is not caused by weak lungs. Anti-Semitism, in turn, will almost always result in a pathological aversion to Jews, just as tuberculosis will aggravate the unsoundness of the lungs. But there is a fateful difference between the emotions which accompany simple anti-Jewishness, and those which characterize a ripened anti-Semitism.

Anti-Jewishness manifests itself in the readiness to think badly of Jews at large, to believe evil of them, even extreme forms of evil, but always conceivable and, as it were, reasonable evil. Anti-Semitism manifests itself in unmistakable symptoms of hallucination. Anti-Jewishness is marked by feelings of distaste, distrust, and perhaps contempt; anti-Semitism by fear, convulsive horror ("the horrors," in fact) and vast delusions of persecution. Anti-Jewishness goes hand in hand with self-assurance and an at least ostensible conviction of superiority; anti-Semitism betrays a cringing inferiority complex and a haunting, unremitting fear.

The cue words for anti-Jewishness are "kike," "sheeny," "swindler," "Ikey-Mo," "old clo' man," etc. For anti-Semitism they are: "world corruptor," "international plotter," "enemy of civilization."

The blend of common dislike or intolerance with fantastic fear may best be studied in *Mein Kampf*, though the anti-Jewishness is heavily overborne by anti-Semitism. It is not always easy to say where the one passes into the other, but once the mind has been opened it cannot fail to perceive that two distinct elements are at play.

Consider the following passage:

"The moral and physical cleanliness of the race [the Jews] was a point in itself. It was externally apparent that these were not water-loving people, and unfortunately one could frequently tell that even with eyes closed. Later the smell of these caftan-wearers often made me ill. Added to this were their dirty clothes and their none too heroic appearance. Perhaps all this was not very attractive; aside from the physical uncleanliness, it was repelling suddenly to discover the moral blemishes of the chosen people."

There is nothing unusual about this kind of writing; it is the familiar literature of personal intolerance. It represents a transference from a few experiences to some millions of untested cases, the translation of a private resentment into a general mental revenge. For a weakminded man all Frenchmen are degenerate, all Scotsmen stingy, all Jews dirty, all Germans Huns, all Americans braggarts, according to his case history. As writing and as mental attitude this is not only distinct from the following passage (occurring a few pages further on in *Mein Kampf*) but is actually incommensurable with it:

"While thus examining the working of the Jewish race over long periods of history, the anxious question suddenly occurred to me whether perhaps inscrutable Destiny, for reasons unknown to us poor mortals, had not unalterably decreed the final victory for this little race. Had this race, which had lived only for this world, been promised the world as a reward? . . . If with the help of the Marxian creed, the Jew conquers the nations of this world, his crown will become the funeral wreath of humanity, and once again this planet, empty of mankind, will move through the ether as it did thousands of years ago."

Now this is not anti-Jewishness at all! It moves on a wholly different level. It is primordial bogey-man stuff; it is the "mad disparity" which occurs in no other instance of group intolerance. What does it mean? What are its sources? *This* is the question we shall have to answer.

Very seldom are the two attitudes precipitated out so clearly. They almost always overlap, so that there is inconsistency within inconsistency. Would you not expect to find a certain dignity and grandeur attaching to a little people which may be destined to don as a crown the funeral wreath of mankind? No; the mixture of anti-Jewishness and anti-Semitism struggles to represent the Jew as both elemental and ignominious, sublime and verminous. Sometimes, however, the verminous achieves a perverse sublimity of its own by sheer intensity, as in this passage, still from *Mein Kampf*:

"If the Jews were alone in the world, they would suffocate as much in dirt and filth as they would carry on a detestable struggle to cheat and ruin each other, although the complete lack of the will to sacrifice, expressed in their cowardice, would also in this instance make the fight a comedy."

Only a little further on, this subhuman species is apparently capable of the most daring visions of conquest. We are told:

"Corresponding to the final aims of the Jewish fight which limit themselves not only to the economic conquest of the world, but also demand the political subjugation of the latter, the Jew divides the organization of his Marxist world into two parts, which, apparently separated from each other, nevertheless in truth form one inseparable whole, the political and the trade union movement.

"Slowly the fear of the Marxist weapon of Jewry sinks into the brains and souls of decent people like a nightmare. One begins to tremble before the terrible enemy, and thus one has become his final victim."

Terrible, indeed, but at the same time undersized, unwashed, malodorous and ludicrous.

A thorough mixture of both attitudes, the personally nasty and the massively folkloristic, is contained in the following summary:

"For a racially pure people, conscious of its blood, can never be enslaved by the Jew. It will forever be only the master of bastards in this world. Thus he systematically tries to lower the racial level by permanent poisoning of the individual. In the political sphere, however, he begins to replace the idea of democracy by that of the dictatorship of the proletariat. In the organized mass of Marxism he has found the weapon which makes him now dispense with democracy and which allows him, instead, to enslave and to 'rule' the people dictatorially with the brutal fist. He now works methodically toward the revolution in a twofold direction: economically and politically. Thanks to his international influence he ensnares with a net of enemies those peoples which put up too violent a resistance from within, he drives them into war, and finally, if necessary, he plants the flag of revolution on the battlefield. . . . In the domain of culture he infects art, literature, theater, smites natural feeling, overthrows all conceptions of beauty and sublimity, of nobility and quality, and in turn he pulls the people down into the confines of his own swinish nature. . . .

"Now begins the great, final revolution. The Jew, by gaining the political power, casts off the few cloaks which he still wears. The democratic national Jew becomes the blood Jew and the people's tyrant. In the course of a few years he tries to eradicate the national supporters of intelligence, and, while he thus deprives the people of their natural spiritual leaders, he makes them ripe for the slave's destiny of perpetual subjugation. The most terrible example of this kind is offered by Russia, where he killed or starved thirty million people with a truly diabolical ferocity, under inhuman tortures, in order to secure to a crowd of Jewish scribblers and stockbrokers the rulership over a great people."

And finally, once more in the pure anti-Semitic style:

"Is it conceivable that the representatives of the real interests of the nations which might enter into an alliance could realize their plans against the will of the mortal Jewish enemy of free folk states and national states? Can the forces—for example, traditional British statecraft—still break the destructive Jewish influence or not? This question, as we have already said, is very hard to answer."

If you have been tempted to skip or skim the foregoing quotations, I ask you to return to a very careful reading. It is crucial case material. Do not be impatient with it for its intrinsic content; on the contrary, listen as closely as the doctor to the ravings of his patient.

Ask yourselves, also, why you have not recognized that such ravings are unique in the modern history of group relations. Your reluctance in this regard is part of the world picture; your evasion of the problem, your repression of it to the level of all other group problems, has been your contribution to the catastrophe of our time. Your sickness and the patient's are intertwined.

But I am not done yet with the diagnosis. The symptoms must be hammered unforgettably into your mind.

The Birth of Bugaboo

In the city of Prague there is an ancient Jewish cemetery, set in the midst of the Jewish quarter. "The dwellers in the dirty and dilapidated houses of this quarter are engaged in petty trading and profiteering in their own as well as in other parts of the city. . . . How poor, dirty and dark these little houses looked from the outside. But it was quite different within! In the rear rooms of many of these houses the bright light of numerous wax candles was reflected in the splendid high mirrors, in expensive dishes and precious rugs. Girls and women, who in the morning perhaps walked with trays in their hands, now were seated at table in heavy silk gowns with golden chains and bracelets; their ornaments and diamonds were glittering."

One night, when the hour of eleven struck from the tower clock of the town hall, and mysterious silence reigned in that terrible place, a meeting was being held in the Jewish cemetery of Prague. There were assembled, in response to the call which came to Jewry once every hundred years, the princes of the Tribes of Israel. Judah had sent its head from Amsterdam, Benjamin from Toledo, Levi from Worms, Manasseh from Budapest, Gad from Cracow, Simeon from Rome, Zebulun from Paris, Dan from Constantinople, Asher from London, Issachar from a place not mentioned in the record, Naphthali from Prague; and two tribes were not represented, for reasons not noted.

What were the purposes of this meeting? To renew the conspiracy for the destruction of the non-Jewish world, and to formulate plans in keeping with modern industrial and financial conditions.

"Brethren," said the head of the Tribe of Levi, "the time has come when, in accordance with the laws of the founder of our union, we must determine ways and means by which the Jews shall attain their goal as soon as possible. We, who know, must direct and guide the masses, which are blind."

"It is not in vain," rejoined another tribal prince, "that Adonai our God gave His chosen people the tenacity of a snake, the cunning of a fox, the look of a falcon, the memory of a dog, the diligence of an ant, and the sociability of a beaver. We were in captivity on the rivers of Babylon, and have become powerful. For eighteen centuries we were slaves, now we have grown head and shoulders above all other nations."

A third voice was heard: "All the princes and the lands of Europe are at present in debt. The stock exchange regulates these debts. Therefore all the liquid capital must go over to the hands of the Jews. The foundations for this are already laid, judging from what we have heard here. If we will be supreme in the stock exchange, we will attain the supremacy in the government. Therefore it is necessary to facilitate loans in order to get them into our hands all the more. Wherever possible we must take in exchange for capital, mortgages, taxes, mines, jewels, and domains. Furthermore, the stock exchange is a means for the transfer of the belongings of the small people to the hands of the capitalists, by drawing them into stock gambling."

The head of the Tribe of Judah spoke: "Industry, the power of the burgher, which hinders the Jewish nation, must be paralyzed even as was agriculture. The manufacturer should be no better than an ordinary worker. The children of Israel can adapt themselves to all branches of work. Transforming the artisans into our factory workers, we will be in a position to direct the masses for our political purposes. Whoever resists the system will be destroyed by competition."

After applause from the new Sanhedrin, the representative of the Tribe of Levi contributed the following piece of counsel. "The natural enemy of the Jews is the Christian church. Therefore we must try to humiliate it, we must introduce into it free thinking, skepticism, and conflicts. Under the guise of progress and the equal rights of all religions we will destroy the study of religion in Christian schools."

Now an old, trembling voice was lifted: "Let our brethren strive for the abolition of armed force. Not the sword, but reason and money must reign. Therefore at every opportunity it is necessary to help the downfall of the military class."

Then followed "a dull voice, like a storm in the distance." It was the voice of the head of Zebulun: "It is indisputable that ours is a time of many reforms, whose main purpose is the amelioration of the material condition of the needy classes. Therefore the Jews must outwardly take a part in the movement and try to divert it from social and political reforms. The masses themselves are blind and foolish, and permit the loudest shouters to rule over them. Who shouts more loudly and more shrewdly than the Jew? The support of every kind of disaffection, every revolution, increases our capital and brings us nearer to our goal."

This frightful *mot d'ordre,* it is recorded, was followed by a long silence. Then came the turn of the Prince of Dan, who recommended that the Jews obtain control of the traffic in liquor, butter, wool, and bread. Naphthali urged that all governmental positions be made accessible to Jews. "But," he added, "I am speaking only of those posts which bring honor, power and preeminence. Positions which require work and knowledge may remain for the Christians." Benjamin warned the assembled Sanhedrin not to neglect the arts and sciences. "We can become good actors and philosophers. In science we will take up medicine and philosophy. A physician penetrates the secrets of families and holds their lives in his hands." Asher advocated a policy of intermarriage. "The Christian relationship," he pointed out, "cannot have a bad influence on us, while we can cast a strong influence over them. A Jew must never make a daughter of his own race his mistress. If he should desire to sin against the Seventh Commandment, he should content himself with Christian girls."

To this another added subtle counsel: "Substitute a contract for sacrament in the marriage of Christians, and their wives and daughters will come to you more readily."

"The terrible cynicism of these words," it is recorded, "touching so delicate a subject, must have produced a profound impression."

The Tribe of Manasseh spoke last: "His voice was hoarse and unpleasant, but he spoke skilfully and with assurance." He said: "We will attain our aim only when the press is in our hands. Our people must direct the daily publications. We need great political newspapers which mold public opinion. In this way we will crowd out the Christians step by step, and will dictate to the world what it would believe in. We will repeat the sorrowful cry of Israel and the complaint against the persecutions which are directed against us."

The foregoing is a digest, consisting mostly of direct quotations, of a chapter from a novel *To Sedan,* by a forgotten German novelist, Hermann Goedsche, who wrote under the pseudonym of Sir John Retcliffe. It is also a very accurate reproduction of the contents of the

famous *Protocols of the Elders of Zion,* that remarkable folkloristic phenomenon of the twentieth century, which has become part of the
culture-structure of millions of people. The "record" might also pass,
as the reader will have noticed, for a transcript of Hitler's political
views on the role of world Jewry.

The history of the *Protocols of the Elders of Zion* should be of special
interest to students of anthropology, for it is a demonstration, under
our own eyes, of the manufacture of a piece of folklore. Goedsche
lifted the material, which he published in 1868, from a satire by the
Frenchman Alfred Joly, written in 1864 under the title of *Dialogues in
Hell* (between Machiavelli and Montesquieu) and directed against
Napoleon III. Joly does not mention the Jews at all. Some time later
Goedsche recast the Prague cemetery scene in *To Sedan* in the form of
a factual narrative, asserting that he had obtained the details of the
Jewish world plot direct from a rabbi of Prague.

Meanwhile a Russian by the name of Nikolai S. Lvoff had
republished the cemetery scene as a work of fiction. But that did not
prevent another Russian, G. Butmi, from republishing *The Rabbi's
Speech* in 1905, as a serious sociological work by an Englishman called
Sir John Retcliffe, Goedsche's real name being omitted.

Thereafter a whole series of publications, under titles like *The
Wise Men of Zion, Protocols of the Elders of Zion,* etc., began to appear
throughout the world, all of them translations and adaptations of the
Russian "original." The material was now represented as "Protocols
taken from the secret depositories of the Main Office of Zion," generally located in France. Sometimes the Freemasons were implicated. In
1907 Butmi issued another edition, with the following explanation:

These secret Protocols were secured with great difficulty in fragmentary
form, and were translated into Russian in December, 1901. It is almost
impossible to get at the secret depositories again where they are hidden, and
therefore they cannot be reinforced by definite information as to the place,
day, month, year, where they were composed. The reader who is more or less
familiar with the secrets of Freemasonry will draw from the general character
of the criminal plot, outlined in the Protocols, and from several details which
he will suppose with great certainty, that the mentioned Protocols were
taken from the documents of the Masonic Lodge of Egyptian ritual, or
Mizraim, which is joined mostly by Jews.

However, a great many of the republications state definitely that
the meeting of the "Elders of Zion" was nothing other than the first
Zionist Congress of 1897.

The subsequent history of the *Protocols* is equally fascinating and instructive. They were presented to President Wilson and high officers of the American intelligence department in 1919. They were published in England under the name of *The Jewish Peril.* Two versions appeared in 1920 in the United States; later on they were widely broadcast in the *Dearborn Independent* and more recently in Father Coughlin's *Social Justice.* They appeared in French, Danish, Swedish, Finnish, Hungarian, Arabic, Chinese, and Japanese translations. The English *Times* and *Spectator* seriously discussed the authenticity of the document. So did *L'Opinion,* in France. Italian newspapers, beginning in 1920, followed suit. The *Philadelphia Ledger* published long articles on the *Protocols* as "The Red Bible" of the Bolshevists. It is safe to say that tens of millions of readers of books and periodicals throughout the world have become familiar with the *Protocols*. In Germany, of course, their success was assured, and of late they have become standard political equipment for millions. It need hardly be added that Hitler mentions them with approval in *Mein Kampf;* though even without him there were public educators enough to obtain the right hearing for them.

Extraordinary efforts have been made to expose and discredit the *Protocols*, but naturally without success. A mind capable of taking such material seriously cannot be affected in its outlook by a scholarly history of its origin, such as was written by the late Herman Bernstein. And a mind which instinctively recoils from this gibberish does not need the reassurance of a scholar.

The most prominent public figures denounced the *Protocols*. Ninety-three leading Americans, beginning with President Wilson, issued a joint warning against them. Henry Ford retracted his endorsement of them. American and English newspapers published their history. Courts of law in Switzerland and South Africa pronounced them gross forgeries. With what result? Today the *Protocols of the Elders of Zion* are imbedded in the minds of millions as genuine revelations. The very hullabaloo they provoked, the magnitude of the "conspiracy" to "repress" them, is cited as proof of their incontrovertibility. How could they have achieved such importance if they were nothing but silly inventions?

But in all the appeals to reason, common sense, tolerance, good neighborliness, and the rest of it, no one paused to reflect on the characteristic of the situation, and to ask the right questions, namely: "What has all this got to do with ordinary 'prejudice' and 'intolerance'? What other people has ever been confronted with such an astounding rigmarole and asked to defend itself?"

Objective writers on anti-Semitism have concentrated their attention on the shady origin of the *Protocols,* and on the absurdity of their contents. They have refused to consider the one fact pointing to the nature of the disease which grips the mind of the Western world; and of course they cannot know that their refusal is a feature of the disease.

It is precisely the fabulous element in the Protocols, *the bloodcurdling allusions to world plots, to terrific and sinister meetings, to hierarchies of doom and cosmic monstrosities of cruelty, it is precisely this element, which would have made it impossible to fasten the document on any other people, which made it possible to fasten it on the Jews.*

Why?

The Collusion of Your Churchmen

We must identify anti-Semitism in terms commensurate with its symptoms. These terms must explain its unique demonological character among group hostilities, its mad disparity with the numbers and influence of present-day Jewry as sufficient cause, and its universality throughout the Western world. They must also explain the evasiveness—amounting to collusion—of your non-anti-Semitic churchmen, and the willful blindness of your liberals. And if these terms, "collusion" and "willful blindness," seem at this point to be recriminatory and self-righteous, I ask you to suspend judgment till all the evidence is in.

The only identification which answers all the purposes set forth above is the following:

Anti-Semitism is the expression of the concealed hatred of Christ and Christianity, rising to a new and catastrophic level in the Western world.

I deal further on with the reasons for this unprecedented explosion. Here I am concerned with the attitude of your non-anti-Semitic churchmen.

The large majority of these—I allow for exceptions which have not come to my attention—think it sufficient to state that anti-Semitism is inconsistent with the teachings of Christ, i.e., that it is anti-Christian. They proceed on the assumption that anti-Semitism is the result of an inner confusion of prejudices, bigotries, and intolerances.

This is a dangerous inaccuracy, the head and front of their offense. Whatever roles prejudice, bigotry, and intolerance play in the make up of the anti-Semite, the recourse to anti-Semitism is in one sense not a confusion at all, but the right mental strategy of those who hate—and fear—Christ, and dare not be open about it even to themselves. The real confusion is in the minds of your churchmen who refer anti-Semitism to the common run of bigotries and intolerances.

The following typical quotations, in which I have italicized the collusive confusion, must carry my point.

The Reverend Harry Emerson Fosdick writes: "Anti-Semitism, *like all cruel racial prejudice,* is a denial of the basic affirmation of high religion. . . . In the sight of Christian teaching, therefore, Hitlerism, returning to the supremacy of 'blood and soil,' is sheer paganism, a primitive and barbarous faith carrying us back, as far as its basic theory is concerned, to ideas which prevailed thousands of years ago, and from which it is the glory of mankind to have escaped. Christians with an understanding of their faith, therefore, are as much outraged as Jews at what is happening in Germany, and they face with shame the prejudices which in milder form constitute *anti-Semitism in particular and racial discrimination in general* in our own country."

A meeting of bishops of the Administrative Board of the National Catholic Welfare Council, held recently in Washington, issued a statement which read in part:

"We regret and deplore the widespread propaganda in the interests of systems and theories antagonistic to the principles of democracy and the teachings of Christianity. A Christian people will oppose these dangerous aberrations with all the might of Christian charity. For that very reason our people will be on their guard against *all forms of racial bigotry,* of which Pope Pius XI, speaking of a pertinent instance, said: 'It is not possible for Christians to take part in anti-Semitism.' "

Father Cox, of Pittsburgh: "As a Catholic I feel the consequence to my fellow-Catholics in America from stirring up bigotry *whether it be Protestant, Catholic, Jew, or colored—whether it be religious, racial, economic, or political."*

Sixty-five Catholic clergymen meeting recently in New York formed a committee to combat anti-Semitism, and issued this statement:

"Recognizing that the growing *anti-Semitism in the United States is a serious threat to the principles of democracy and Christianity,* and that some

Catholics, too, have been deceived into taking part in this campaign of hate, a group of Catholics in New York has organized the 'Committee of Catholics to fight anti-Semitism.' The purpose of the Committee, as outlined in the call, is in the light of the recent bishops' condemnation of anti-Semitism 'to oppose the dangerous aberration of anti-Semitism in the fullness of Christian charity' and to popularize genuine teaching among our Catholic people. . . ."

I quote now from the record of the fight within Germany itself. It will be seen that in the hottest part of the battlefield the heroic men who have opposed the anti-Semitic front of Nazism-Fascism have not identified the enemy! In 1937 a group of ministers of the Evangelical Church (the signatories are said to be, among others, Niemöller, Barth, Assmussen, Vogel, Dibellius, Jakobi) dared to submit to Hitler a memorandum which reads in part:

"When blood, race, nationhood, and honor are raised to the rank of eternal values, the Evangelical Church is compelled by the First Commandment to reject this evaluation. If Aryan man is glorified, God's word testifies to the sinfulness of all men. *If anti-Semitism is imposed on the Christians in the framework of the National Socialist philosophy, there stands against this the Christian commandment of brotherly love."*

In all these utterances, and in hundreds more like them, anti-Semitism is called anti-Christian in the sense that it is repugnant to the spirit of Christianity, that it is, like every other kind of race prejudice, offensive to the first principles of Christian faith. And of course it is true that all hatreds, bigotries, and oppressions are a rejection of Christian law. But in connection with anti-Semitism the observation is actually pointless. For anti-Semitism is not anti-Christian in the sense that it is un-Christian. *It is the expression of the movement to put an end to the Christian episode in human history.* While all other forms of hatred are lapses from Christian practice, anti-Semitism is the conspiratorial, implacable campaign against Christ the Jew.

The classification of anti-Semitism with all other forms of racial and religious prejudice plays into the hands of the haters of Christ. For while one may intelligibly say to a criminal: "It is illegal to commit murder," or "it is illegal to steal," one cannot intelligibly say to him: "It is illegal to destroy the law."

All lapses from law are an attack on law and must be corrected. But the correction presupposes in the criminal some sort of acceptance of the idea of law. He may lie with regard to any particular crime, and say he did not break the law. He may seek to pervert the law by interpretation. The method of correction or retraining will vary but will always be based on the assumption that the existence of law is acknowledged by the criminal. No such method can be applied when the crime consists of a rejection of law as a principle in human affairs. The super-anarchist is not just a criminal; he is infinitely more significant and powerful. And to treat him merely as a criminal is a form of collusion.

Now and again a religious leader has apprehended vaguely the specific Christ-hating character of anti-Semitism, and has shied away from the implications. A speech by Father Hanley Furfey of the Catholic University of America is reported thus:

"If your mother were a Jew you would not tolerate the wholesale crimes of speech and violence being committed today against the Jewish race. Well, your mother was a Jew. Mary, the mother of all mankind, was a Jew; and when insults and epithets are hurled and crimes committed against the Jews, they are committed against your mother."

It is here that the whole shocking misunderstanding comes to a head. It is precisely *because* Christ was a Jew that Christians tolerate the "wholesale crimes of speech and violence" against the Jews. It is precisely because Christ-hatred is afraid to name itself, and afraid to make the direct attack, that it must find vent in the folk pathology which is anti-Semitism. It is at the very least an intellectual perversity to plead with anti-Semites for special kindness to Jews on the grounds of Christ's Jewishness; and every such reminder, so made without insight and explanation, produces the contrary of the effect intended.

But in truth neither Father Furfey, nor any other religious teacher, will escape the sin of complicity unless he speaks as follows:

"In all the other group hatreds which you practice or tolerate, your victims are slandered or misrepresented on the human level; but I notice that when it comes to the Jews you invoke a proliferating diabolism which testifies to a kind of insanity. When you lose your tempers with others than Jews, you resort to ordinary statistical inaccuracies and lies; but when it comes to the Jew you make him the subject of a new and horrible mythology. Therefore, while reminding you that it is sinful and anti-Christian to hate anyone, I charge you to look into the disintegration of the mind which is part of your anti-Semitism and of your anti-Semitism alone, and to discover, if it is not too late, what special spiritual disaster it indicates."

Why have your churchmen not spoken thus? Why have they not perceived that anti-Semitism transcends the so-called Jewish question, even as it transcends in function all the familiar hatreds of our time? Or, if perceiving this truth, why have they not proclaimed it?

Prudence is the first thought. If the Church were to proclaim that anti-Semitic Christians have a mad fear of the Jew because they have a mad fear of Christ the Jew, if the issue were pushed to this show-down, the anti-Semites might drop *not* their anti-Semitism but their ostensible allegiance to Christianity. Such a primal schism, such a rending of their ecclesiastical structure, the churchmen dare not face. Hence I have spoken of the cowardice of the Christian religious leaders, as I have spoken, for reasons still to be given, of the coward-ice of Jewish religious leaders.

But this prudence, which is a partnership in guilt, is backed by an antecedent collusion. Such a thoroughgoing analysis as I demand cannot be made without a self-purgation, in which most Christians, and not just the anti-Semites, would discover a sympathetic, super-stitious dread of Christ, lying concealed within the heart of Christi-anity itself. It is the secret sympathy felt by the man of imperfect morality for the man who denies all morality. It is the twinge of relief that someone has dared to defy the intransigeant Taskmaster. It is the wild moment of covert liberation which is the safety-valve of the good.

In *The Jew and the Universe* Solomon Goldman makes the penetrat-ing observation that the economic explanation of anti-Semitism is itself anti-Semitic. We must go further and insist that the reluctance to see anti-Semitism under the aspect of the revolt against Christ is part of the strategy of that revolt. It is the universal foundation for the undervaluation of the anti-Semitic problem.

From *The Great Hatred* (1940)

11 THE PEOPLE AND THE LAND

The Claim

I

To get at the substance of the Israel-Arab complex we must go back to fundamentals and beginnings. We must not try to assess the realities only on the basis of recent developments. New facts have obscured old facts that have not lost their validity, and forces that are still operative are being ignored.

Thus the relationship of the Jewish people to Israel, and the existence of Israel itself, are being discussed almost exclusively in terms of the past twenty or thirty years, as though the long past that gave birth to the present were not still at work in it. The claim of the Jewish people to its ancient homeland is made to rest on Hitlerite anti-Semitism, or at most on the neo-Zionism born in the nineteenth century. This restricted view robs the claim of its millennial weightiness, and turns Israel into an *ad hoc* enterprise more or less improvised, without reference to historical realities, to meet a special and unforeseen situation. . . .

There was never a time when there were not Jews in the land called Palestine, and now Israel, representatives of the legitimate owner, whoever might for the moment be in possession. To live in the Holy Land was always one of the highest *mitzvot*—commandments or good deeds—even though mass reimmigration waited on the appearance of the Messiah. There were even periods of substantial immigration, settlements of pietists and mystics, whose prayers and speculations and conjurations were meant to hasten the advent of the Messiah. The popular notion that with the crushing of the Bar Kochba revolt in the year 135 Palestine was emptied of its Jews is quite erroneous. The Temple had been destroyed nearly seventy years earlier, now the harrow was drawn through the sacred city, and on the ruins a new city was founded, Aelia Capitolina, in honor of Hadrian the conqueror. But there was still a Jewish community in Palestine, scholarship flourished, a measure of recognition was accorded to the remnants of the conquered; the Patriarchate, headed by a succession of great scholars, still sent out legal and religious decisions to Jewry in exile and retained the spiritual leadership until the rise in the fourth century of the Babylonian schools, founded by scholars trained in the schools of Palestine.

Throughout the long darkness of the Middle Ages flashes of light reach us from Jewish communities in Palestine. Toward the close of Byzantine rule, an attempt was made to convert the Jews forcibly to Christianity, and twenty-six thousand of them joined the Persian invader in protest. A century and a half later, under Moslem rule, a brief messianic fervor seized the Jewish community with the discovery of a sacred manuscript purportedly the work of the great second-century sage Rabbi Simeon ben Yohai. In the tenth century, according to an Arab historian, the Christians and the Jews had the upper hand in Jerusalem, and a Jew, Manasseh ibn Ibrahim al-Kzaz, was governor of Palestine. More than a hundred years later the city was stormed by the Crusaders in 1099; the Jewish community took shelter in the synagogue and perished in the flames when the building was set on fire. But Benjamin of Tudela, the famous twelfth-century traveler, records the existence of Jewish communities in Palestine in his day, and the Jerusalem community was rebuilt by pilgrims from the West. By the middle of the fourteenth century there was a considerable Jewish population in Palestine. In the sixteenth century Safad, with two thousand Jewish inhabitants, was a great center of learning. It was there that Joseph ben Ephraim Karo compiled the *Shulchan Aruch,* the code of laws which is still valid for Orthodox Jews throughout the world. The Palestine community was the springboard from which Sabbatai Zevi, the pseudo-Messiah, was launched on his brief and tragic career in 1666.

A new immigration of Jews began with the nineteenth century, preceding by more than half a century the neo-Zionist movement, and today's strictly Orthodox community of Jerusalem is their direct descendant. In the minds of these Jews, as in those of all immigrant groups since the Destruction, there was no thought of instituting the great Return. They were drawn irresistibly to the land by its sacred associations; but whatever their conscious motivation, they were constant reminders, reregistrations of the Jewish claim, appeals against any suggestion of a statute of limitations.

They represented the tenacity of the relationship between the entire Jewish people and the land. No Jewish community anywhere in the world, however dominant it became, ever spoke to exiled Jewry with the tenderness and intimacy of *Eretz Yisrael* (the Land of Israel). A messenger from one of the four holy cities—Jerusalem, Hebron, Tiberias, Safad—was always received with love and wonder; and I remember out of my childhood the stir that was created in our poverty-stricken North England ghetto when the word went out: "A Jew from *Eretz Yisrael* will be at the synagogue this coming Sabbath."

How could it be otherwise when every Jewish child was taught the word Jerusalem almost as soon as it could lisp? The heroes of the Bible were the subject of daily conversation; they were referred to with casualness as well as with reverence; their deeds were discussed like those of contemporaries, except that contemporaries were never quite so real, for contemporaries might die, or might do unexpected things, but those heroes would always be with us, and would never let us down.

The landscape of Palestine, or *Eretz Yisrael,* dominated the earliest visual imagination of Jewish children. Long before they had taken their local topographical bearings they were familiar with Mount Moriah, where Abraham had been ready to sacrifice young Isaac, and where Jerusalem rose later; with Carmel, where Elijah discomfitted the prophets of Baal; with the valley of Sharon, whose roses were like King Solomon's Sulamite; with Hebron, where the three patriarchs were buried; and with the tomb by Ephrath near Bethlehem whence the fourth matriarch, the universally beloved Rachel, issued nightly to weep for her children because they were not. They had wandered through the desert and stood at the foot of Sinai, they had rested in the oasis of Kadesh-barnea, they had heard the tremendous valedictory of Moses on the plain of Moab, and dry-footed they had crossed the Jordan with Joshua to begin the conquest.

And still the power of these vision-realities cannot be grasped without their ever-present cosmic obbligato. These are the archetypal experiences of man, whose search for God gives us the only acceptable meaning to the creation of the universe. The poignant and indestructible longing of the Jews for the Holy Land was far more than an extraordinary vitality of nostalgia, more also than an equally indestructible hope of escape from physical vagabondage, insecurity, and humiliation. It was the will to continue the search first incorporated in the land, in its heroes and topography. Through those men, among those scenes, the attempt had begun to create a moral standard for all mankind, and the history of that attempt is the essential history of the Jewish people. All its other achievements, however impressive they may be, are incidental. And wherever else Jews might settle, even in large numbers, and perhaps permanently, the land was an indispensable instrument for the continuation of the attempt.

For the land was the basic expression of social law. Man did not own it; he was a lessee under God. Its produce was not exclusively his own; part of it belonged, as of right, not as an act of charity, to the widow, the orphan, and the stranger. This was the law, the only one of its kind in the ancient world, and in an extended sense a model for the Western world. It was also the law that no lessee might be permanently dispossessed—however he had lost the tenure, through misfortune or neglect, it was restored to him in the jubilee year. None of these provisions were touched with the repellent aspects of "philanthropy." They were commandments.

The study of the commandments, side by side with their practical application, was in itself the supreme commandment. The Jew did not accept the principle of moral intuitiveness, and purity of heart was not regarded as the sufficient guide to right conduct. He was bidden to meditate on the Law day and night, for "the ways of the heart are dark, who shall know it?" and without the trained and well-informed mind goodness is easily perverted. If the Bible assures us that it is enough for man "to do justly and love mercy and walk humbly with his God," it also warns us repeatedly that without intellectual discipline man is incomplete and therefore morally defective. In no other people has the study of the Law been made a religious obligation for the ordinary citizen, and a cultivated mind a prerequisite for perfect worship. In one biblical passage we are admonished to be a kingdom of priests, but the overall directives point rather to a republic of saintly, subtle, and learned jurists.

"Israel, the Torah, and God are one" is the great summation offered by the Zohar, the mystical book of the Middle Ages, which also affirms that as long as there is no Jewish homeland, the Divine Essence, or *Shechinah,* is itself in exile. These are extraordinary statements for a people that first proclaimed and has most obstinately maintained the oneness and ubiquity of God. They must be read as hyperbolic expressions of frustration that say in effect, "As long as we have not rebuilt our homeland we are not ourselves."

II

A sympathetic outsider with a liberal turn of mind, surveying this picture, may be moved to say, "This is indeed a phenomenon without a parallel, and in its way touching. But in this world of ours, which is what it is, what does it all lead to? You cannot have peoples refusing to accept the verdict of history and clamoring for two thousand years, which is practically forever, against a fait accompli. Fifty or a hundred or two hundred years is as long as any people may reasonably demand a restoration such as you claim. It's different with the Greeks, for example, who have remained on their own soil and constitute a majority there. But when a people has been pushed out into distant places, or has been completely overrun and submerged, the thing is unmanageable. One might as well talk of returning America to the Redskins, India to its Dravidians, Egypt to its Coptic (i.e., Gyptios—Aegyptios—Egyptian) minority, England to the Welsh—the list is endless. If the Jews have chosen not to forget, or are somehow incapable of forgetting, it is their misfortune, not the world's responsibility. We are ready to acknowledge what has not always been acknowledged, and even today is not acknowledged everywhere, and that is the right of the Jews to maintain their religious and cultural identity wherever they may live, and we shall protest vigorously against any infringement of this right. But as to your right to build a homeland in Palestine, that is an entirely different matter. As it happens, you've done it somehow, and we can't deny that it is in itself a rather fine thing. To be sure, when you first set out to do it we liberals thought it quite ridiculous as well as reactionary—not to mention impossible. For that matter, we didn't see any point in this business of Jewish survival, and some of us still don't. But we, unlike you, are willing to accept a fait accompli, and we must admit that Israel has been a godsend to the Jewish refugees. We also admit that you are owed some kind of restitution after that horrible Hitler episode. We didn't come out of it well—I mean we, the democracies; and that inclines us all the more to support your Jewish state—within reasonable limits, naturally. Why aren't you content to talk of Israel in realistic terms as the product of a contemporaneous situation? Why do you brood over the irrelevancies of two thousand years, and stake out a claim on the basis of your folk fantasies, which are none of our business?"

It all sounds quite decent, if a trifle sheepish, but consciously or not, it is dishonest through and through. "Your folk fantasies, which are none of our business . . ." I do not say that if Christendom had behaved differently toward the Jews they would have vanished, or at least overcome their haunting sense of loss. But when the Western nations took over the Jewish Bible—which is, among other things, the Jewish national record—as an essential and by far the more voluminous part of their sacred writings, they undertook to keep alive, as an article of faith, the association of the Jews with the Holy Land. And how insistent they have been about it! The Jews simply have not been permitted to forget. Not only was it dinned into their ears century after century after century that by their refusal to acknowledge the Messiahship and Divine Sonship of Jesus they had forfeited their homeland, not to mention their right to remain Jews; they were forcibly reminded that they had even forfeited the right to their own interpretation of their Bible! From the time of Justin Martyr, the first patristic theologian, who was a contemporary of the final destruction under Hadrian, down to this day, the taunting has gone on, emphasized periodically by expropriations, expulsions, proscriptions, pogroms, and baptism under duress. If the Jews protested that they did not want to listen, they were sometimes herded into churches and made to listen, for their souls' good; if they said, "We'd rather not talk about it," they were told, "By God and His Son, you will," and with infinite reluctance they entered into compulsory debates in which their opponents were the judges.

"O fair hill of Zion!" "O excellency of Carmel!" "Balm of Gilead." "Sweet vale of Sharon!" The Christians could not get over the beauties and benedictions of the land. To be sure, they were speaking symbolically most of the time, but with a fervor that could not but mislead a non-Christian. If the Jews had not themselves been familiar —much more familiar than the Christians—with these and a hundred other haunting phrases, they would still have been goaded by such wistful repetitions into torments of regret. "Your land was destroyed and you have been made homeless because you crucified Jesus" was the everlasting refrain, begun by Justin Martyr. "See what would still have been yours if you had not rejected Him."

Not less galling, if less effective, was the attempt to expel the Jews from possession of the Bible itself. "It is not your Bible, because you do not understand it. Degenerate sons of glorious fathers, you have no portion in it. For you perversely refuse to see that the whole purpose of your, or rather your fathers' Bible, now ours, was to prepare the coming of the Christ. It was of Him that your prophets and singers spoke and sang. It is because you are willfully blind in all your generations that you will not recognize the obvious allusions to Him in Isaiah 4, 7, 11, 28, 31; in Ezekiel 36, 37; in Micah 4, 5, 7; in Zechariah 6, 9, 14; in Canticles everywhere—and these are only a few instances."

If the visions of the prophets and the consolations of the Psalmist spoke as intimately and comfortingly to the Jews as to the Christians, that was by a pure delusion, and a kind of intellectual misappropriation, a fraud committed on the sacred text by the descendants, according to the flesh, of those who had composed it, and an affront to the heirs according to the spirit, for whom it had been composed.

For these reasons it is improper for Christians to dismiss the claim of the Jewish people to its ancient homeland as a private fantasy for which *they* have no responsibility. Nor can they speak of it as a thing of the remote past, a historical curiosity. It is a historical thing in the most living sense, an effective element in the thinking of the Western world, and its presence can be denied only by an act of evasion.

I dwell on this point because if it cannot be established, the State of Israel is trivialized into an accident. I dwell on the continuity of the claim from ancient times because it is a permanent feature of the history of *Christendom*. When Saul of Tarsus opened up the division between Judaism and Christianity, he could not have foreseen what it would do to the Jewish people, for he was willing to let the Jews retain all that was Jewish—circumcision, the Sabbath, the festivals, the entire national ritual and culture—and all he asked of them, as of the rest of mankind, was to accept Jesus as Savior, Soter, Messiah, and Son of God. For some centuries there existed a Jewish sect, a branch of the Ebionites, which did in fact conform to this view. It hovered between the total disapproval of the Jews and the uneasy and diminishing tolerance of the Church. But by the time of the prepatristic fathers, it was already being denounced as a dangerous "Judaizing" element, and in the second century Justin declared that the Sabbath and circumcision had been imposed by God on the Jews as a mark of His displeasure, so that they might be singled out for the execration of mankind. Two centuries later the sect was denounced by the Church as heretical, and it disappeared.

The compromise was natural to Saul, who sought to be all things to all men. When he declared that there was no longer Jew or Greek or barbarian, he certainly did not mean that the nations would lose their identities, their languages and literatures. Certainly he did not demand that the Jews give up their language and literature and cult. Certainly he did not demand that they cease to be a people. This was what the Church demanded, seeing in the peoplehood of the Jews the matrix of their blasphemous religion. And when the Jewish state was destroyed the Church rejoiced, nor has it to this day become reconciled to its reconstitution.

As for the people itself, the Church, too, entered into a compromise, but one very different from Saul's. The Jewish people was accursed; not only had it been guilty of the Crucifixion, but it was the obstacle, if only by its very existence, to the total conversion and salvation of mankind. Yet though the Church was bitterly hostile to the Jews, it did not want them to disappear entirely, not even by voluntary mass conversion. For a double role was assigned to the Jew: he was at once a welcome and corroborating witness and a hateful and horrible example. He vouched for the authenticity of the Old Testament, the underpinning of the New, and he demonstrated the dire consequences of rejecting the Christ. He was the brother of the Christ and the embodiment of Satan. As a Jew he did not deserve to live, but as a Jew he had to stay alive for the apotheosis of the Second Coming. Buffeted between these opposing attitudes, the Jew survived, building himself local habitations the duration of which depended on his usefulness to the laity and the mood of the Church.

It remained for the twentieth century to produce a segment of Christendom which found the ambiguities of the double policy intolerable, and in a characteristic fit of thoroughness adopted a program of total annihilation with no escape through conversion. Germany may have had special reasons, not only of character but of circumstance, for reaching this frightful decision; but we cannot absolve the Church, as it acted throughout the ages, from a great share in the responsibility. Sooner or later the millennial cat-and-mouse game was bound to get on someone's nerves, and the cry would go up, "For God's sake, let's get rid of this Jewish problem once and for all. No more paltering with concessions and half measures. *Die entgültige Lösung*—the Final Solution! Wipe them out—all of them, men and women and children, and let the world at last be *Judenrein.*"

The word genocide was coined to express the uniqueness of Germany's crime against the Jews, and much has been written concerning the beastliness with which it was carried out. But genocide is not a new thing. Peoples have been destroyed before so that their territories might be occupied, and the Jews were not the only ones toward whom the Germans harbored genocidal intentions. Revolting cruelties, too, are a familiar feature of human history. The peculiarity of Germany's superbly organized extermination of the Jews was its idealism, its practical pointlessness. A complicated and exacting industry of death was created and maintained at a high cost to the war effort. Large numbers of men—planners, executives, workers—vast quantities of building material and rolling stock, not to speak of much inventive ingenuity, were placed at the service of the enterprise when they could have been used to great advantage elsewhere. To round up and butcher six million hogs calls for considerable investment of funds, labor, and equipment; to do that with six million human beings is far more complex and costly. We simply cannot understand it unless we realize that the German leaders and the tens of thousands who worked with such a will at the unnatural business were convinced that the destruction of the Jews served a high principle, which for some transcended the welfare of the *Vaterland* itself. Certainly there was a sadistic thrill that spurred the diligence of the executions; but, dimly or clearly, the killers could hear the applause of their country and of humanity, and this, with the consciousness, dim or clear, of God's or history's approval, added the last touch of ecstasy to their sadism.

If I repeat that this unique aberration owed as much to the cumulative effect of Christian ambivalence toward the Jew as it did to a special set of circumstances, it is for the purpose of assigning responsibility rather than guilt. The Holocaust came—and this has a profound significance—at a time when the Jews had demonstrated on the soil of their forefathers the vitalistic quality of their attachment to it. During one of the breathing spells of partial permissiveness, they had done to the land what no one else had succeeded in doing since their expulsion: they had brought it to life and reendowed it with contemporaneous significance for the world. They had proved that what they had not wanted to forget, and what the world had insisted on their remembering, had been waiting for its hour, and that the hour had struck. But even as the hour of redemption struck, the hatred of the ages gathered itself together to deny it fulfillment in the total extinction of Jewish life.

The Jewish people had stopped supplicating. Defying the tradition which bade it wait for a Messiah, it had taken its destiny into its own hands. It had resolved to become its own Messiah, announcing to the world that it could no longer tolerate the ambivalent status imposed upon it—the very resolution reached by Germany but with a diametrically opposed objective.

A German victory in World War II might not have meant the literal, total obliteration of the Jewish people; but it would have meant something hardly less appalling. With Nazi collaborationist governments in Europe, the work of the death camps would have gone forward to completion. Here and there handfuls of Jews would have lived out underground lives of terror and starvation. The Jewish homeland in the making would have been uprooted. What would have happened in an isolated and embattled America is harder to imagine, but most certainly the forward democratic surge of the previous years would have been violently reversed. Darkness in Europe, twilight in America, and everywhere the theme resounding: "It was the Jews who brought this calamity upon the world," resounding so insistently that the Jews in their hiding places would begin to repeat it, adding, "Better if we had never been born."

The Nazi attempt on the life of Jewry was not the justification of the Jewish homeland. That can be the view only of those for whom history begins with themselves. The farther-sighted know that this *Attentat* was only the latest—though the most shocking—assertion of a thesis established by the Church many centuries ago and maintained into our own times.

The Occupants

When the Arabs adopted Mohammedanism they did not, like the Christians, take over the Jewish Bible in toto; nor did it become for them a peripherally sacred book. They did, however, take over many of the principal and some of the minor heroes of both Testaments, to such an extent that without them the Koran, which is of about the same length as the New Testament, would be practically devoid of human characters and would hang in a void of doctrinal exposition. Abraham and Moses appear with great frequency throughout, and Noah is accorded an importance, or at least a degree of attention, which quite overtops his role in the Bible. The story of Joseph is told with much circumstantiality, and in his case even more than the others, many details are added from Jewish extrabiblical tradition. There are fewer references to Jesus, and his Divine Sonship is rejected as blasphemy. David slays Goliath, just as in the Bible; Pharaoh is frustrated, so is his minister Haman, transferred to his reign in Egypt from that of Ahasuerus in Persia; the great literary prophets are nowhere quoted, and of the others only Elijah and Elisha come in for mention. But the prophets are spoken of in general terms, and they, like the other protagonists of both Testaments, are praised for the purity of the messages they brought to mankind—messages that the Jews and Christians alike have perverted in their own lives, and that would have been lost if Mahomet (to use the more familiar form of Mohammed) had not appeared with the true and final restatement.

But what Mahomet got—and this chiefly from the Old Testament—besides the flesh and blood embodiment of his dissertation, was his blazing monotheism and that immediacy of rapport with God which, as in Jewish doctrine, makes inconceivable the notion of an intermediary, much less, then, a "Son of God." Mahomet proclaims himself a human being, born as all human beings are born, subject to death like all human beings, destined like all true believers for resurrection on the Judgment Day. He is a participant in the common life, he marries and begets; like Abraham he has concubines as well as the "true wife"; like Abraham he has business dealings with his fellow men. What lifts him above all human beings is the unique and final revelation or series of revelations brought to him by the archangel Gabriel, and written down or dictated by him (the tradition is not clear on this point) over the years.

Theologically, Mohammedanism is much nearer than Christianity to the spirit of the Jewish Bible. A religion proclaiming an Emanation or Son of God clothed in human form for the salvation of mankind does not need the Jewish Bible for its corroboration; and to the Jew it seems that the insistence on this corroboration does violence to the biblical text. In other words, doctrinal, if not ethical Christianity could have been born without the Jewish Bible; in fact, it existed in other forms outside the Jewish world. But Mohammedanism without the Jewish Bible is inconceivable. Still speaking doctrinally, Christianity's debt to Judaism is fortuitous, that of Mohammedanism is organic and total.

This may explain why ancient Palestine did not become the "Holy Land" for Moslems as it did for Christians. The identity of Mohammedanism would have been lost. Jerusalem is only one of its three sacred cities, ranking after Mecca and perhaps Medina. It is called in Arabic *el Kuds* (the holy), the word being akin to the Hebrew *kadosh*. It was from Mount Moriah in Jerusalem, the site of Isaac's sacrifice and Solomon's temple, that Mahomet ascended to heaven on his steed el-Burak to confer with God. The rest of Palestine is no more sacred to Moslems than Italy is to Christianity in spite of the sanctity of Rome, where Peter and Paul suffered martyrdom by fire and Ignatius was thrown to the lions. And here again the special debt of Mohammedanism to Judaism stands out. Mecca and Medina are sacred to the Moslems because in those cities Mahomet lived and labored. But Jerusalem had been sacred to the Jews for fifteen centuries before Mahomet was born. It could not be left out, and so it was appropriated by the device of a single visit.

The Koran lumps Jews and Christians together under the name of "the people of the Book," that is, the Bible, but makes a clear distinction in the matter of blood relationship. Jews and Arabs were kinsmen. They were both descended from Abraham, through his sons Isaac and Ishmael. Their languages were as close to each other as, say, French and Italian. They had been in contact for thousands of years—Arabia and the Arabs are mentioned seventeen times in the Jewish Bible. No such ethnic bonds existed between Arabs and Christians, except insofar as Christianity had spread among a small number of Arabs. To the Arabs "Christian" meant the outside world, Rome (actually it was Byzantium, later Constantinople, "Rome on the Bosphorus") which first represented the Western world to the Moslems. The Jews were "our own people," and their unresponsiveness to his message must have produced in Mahomet a baffled incomprehension, perhaps sharper than that produced in the early Christians by Jewish unresponsiveness to the message of the Christ.

In Medina, where Mahomet established himself after his flight from Mecca (the Hegira, in 622 C.E., the first year of the Mohammedan calendar), there were many Jews. They should have been his natural disciples, much more so than his pagan fellow Arabs. They had not been infected by what in his eyes was the disabling superstition of a Son of God. What was he, who claimed to be only a mortal man, saying that offended their faith? Nothing that he could see, but they saw an impiety that horrified them. At one stroke he had wiped away the vast literature and tradition of Mishnah, Talmud, and Midrash, a whole civilization which had resisted Egyptian and Assyrian, Greek and Roman. He was seeking to dispossess them of a heritage of learning and of ethical speculation that, outside of the Bible, had been developed during twenty generations in the schools of Palestine and Babylonia. To be sure, he respected the Bible and its heroes, but he demanded that his version of it replace the original, which was to sink into the obscurity of an outside text.

For the second time, then, a religion rising on Jewish foundations invited or rather commanded the Jews to vacate their place in history, and finding them recalcitrant denounced them for contumacy, blindness, and blasphemy. And like Christianity, Mohammedanism, a continuing force to this day, has made of its indebtedness an occasion for hostility.

Something must be said here about the difference between "Mohammedan" or "Moslem" and "Arab." When the Arabs burst out of their peninsula and within a century created an empire stretching from northern Spain to the confines of China—its area exceeded that of the Roman Empire at its greatest extent—they brought under their rule an immense variety of peoples, Iberian, Berber, Negro, Coptic, Jewish, Iranian, Indian. In the West the religion was predominantly Christian; in the East it was divided between Zoroastrianism and Hinduism. Though Mohammedanism spread almost as rapidly as territorial occupation, the majority of the Jews and some of the Christians held out: the other religions have practically disappeared in the lands held for any time by "Arab" rulers. But the ethnic strains were little affected. The original Arabs were not numerous enough and did not stay long enough to diffuse their racial characteristics—not always homogeneous in any case—through the conquered peoples. We speak today of the "Arabs" of Algeria, Morocco, Libya, Tunisia, Egypt, Syria, Iraq, Saudi Arabia, and I shall continue to use the term, but ethnically it is as meaningless as "Americans." "Moslems" is of course a much wider term, for it includes Persians, Pakistanis, Indonesians, and others; but if the Moslems of the first group of countries all wish to be designated as "Arabs," that is their right, as long as we remember that it is now a political and linguistic, and not an ethnic, designation.

Palestine, at that time held by Christian Constantinople, and itself Christian but for the Jewish minority, was among the earliest of the Arab conquests (634–40 C.E.). North Africa, from Egypt to the Straits of Gilbraltar, was predominantly Christian, with pockets of ancient paganisms. Spain was wholly Christian. At one moment it looked as if the Arab tide was everywhere irresistible. Had it not been turned back at Tours in 732, European history would have taken a very different course, and Gibbon would not have been able to observe (with such obvious relish) that "the interpretation of the Koran would now be taught in the schools of Oxford, and her pulpits might demonstrate to a circumcised people the sanctity and the truth of the revelation of Mahomet."

Actually the Arab thrust had spent itself in France, just as the Mongol thrust had spent itself, on the very same territory, three hundred years earlier. There was, however, an immense difference between these two threats to the development of a native European civilization. The irruption of the Huns left behind (in a later and more limited episode) an isolated memento in the gifted Hungarian people, which was absorbed into Europe while retaining its own language. The Arabs (the reader must bear in mind the quotation marks) learning from and surpassing the peoples they conquered, created together with them a brilliant civilization that has woven itself permanently into the fabric of the Western world. No one challenges the statement that if the Arab world had not kept alive, reinterpreted, and developed the wisdom of the ancient world while Europe was struggling out of the Dark Ages, the emergence of the modern world would have been long delayed and it might have lacked some of its most valuable elements.

This rapid excursus into Arab history is necessary in the approach to contemporary Arab problems. The awakening of Arab self-consciousness, miscalled "nationalism" (but again I shall be compelled to use an inaccurate term) by a false analogy with European history, is not like the awakening of primitive African peoples. It is stimulated and exacerbated by the memory of a magnificent past. It would serve no purpose here to go burrowing into details and to ask each group of "Arabs" what share *its* ancestors had in that vanished glory. It suffices that there was indeed a great civilization carried by the Arab language, which all the Arab groups speak. But superb in conquest, the Arabs are dispirited in subjugation. They could transmit their religion (though not their language) to the conquering Turk, but under his rapacious and increasingly corrupt rule they lapsed into apathy and shiftlessness. For a little more than four centuries they were the masters in Palestine and the rest of Asia Minor. From the end of the eleventh century on they lost position after position until by the beginning of the twentieth century most of them had scarcely more control over their own destinies than the Negro tribes of Africa.

The Arab record in respect of its Jewish minorities compares favorably with the Christian, which is not saying very much, and it is no consolation to add that the Christian minorities fared no better.

Arab or Moslem masses were never interpenetrated by a demonological horror of the Jew as the accursed slayer of the Son of God. The
story of the Jewess accused of trying to poison Mahomet in his later
years is incidental in the Moslem tradition. The Jew was despised and
discriminated against as an infidel. Nevertheless there were great
episodes of Arab-Jewish symbiosis, notably in the early centuries. In
Spain Jews held high positions at the court and in society; Jewish
scholars worked with Arab scholars to the enhancement of their
common civilization.

But the situation may, within limits, be compared with that of
the Jews of Germany at the beginning of the twentieth century. The
success of Jewish writers, artists, merchants, and professionals was
not inconsistent with the spread of anti-Semitism, manifesting itself
in the social world, in the aristocracy, and the army. But it would be
an outrageous injustice to make too much of the parallel. On the
other hand, the rejection of the Jew, or of Judaism, by Moslem
civilization was deep-rooted. As the fortunes of the Islamic world
declined, outright and consistent persecution eclipsed the large areas
of tolerance. There was no particular season of the year, like Easter
among the Christians, when religious teachers whipped up hatred
against the Jews, and there were no spectacular massacres of the Jews,
like those of the Crusades, of Chmielnicki in the seventeenth century, Petlura in the twentieth—and of course nothing like the transcendental wickedness of Hitlerism. There was only a relentless
denial of human rights, restrictions in the economic field, mulcting
by special taxes (also applicable to Christians), humiliations, enforced conversions, and of course sporadic pogroms. One naturally
did not hear among Arabs the ever-recurrent cry, "Jews, go back to
your own country," since the Arabs ruled it or were in occupancy.
But when Arabs protest that they are being forced, through the
acceptance of the State of Israel, to pay for the sins of Christian
Europe, they ignore a heavy account of their own. They too, even
when they were looking down on the Jew as an inferior, and embodying their contempt in laws and acts, consistently kept alive in
the Jew his bonds with the homeland he had lost.

They did not, as I have pointed out, make Palestine itself the
idealized cradle of their faith. They did not study the geography of
Palestine, as the Christians did, and make knowledge of it a piety.
What they did, what they still do, insofar as the Koran is one of their
unifiers, has been hardly less effective in keeping alive the Jewish
feeling of displacement, exile, and loss. "Why," the Jew could ask,

"must you keep reminding us of Abraham and Isaac and Jacob and Joseph and David and Solomon, and of our onetime happiness? You tell us, like the Christians, albeit in other terms, that by our behavior we have betrayed our forefathers and do not deserve to claim them. Thereby you only make them more precious in our eyes and strengthen our resolution to maintain the bond and to honor our covenant with them, according to which the land from which we have been driven still remains ours."

The Jews have been severely chided for calling themselves the Chosen People and thinking of themselves as a unicum. The rebuke comes with poor grace from the Christian and Moslem worlds. It is Christian doctrine that they were indeed chosen, and that in a cosmic sense, to produce the Savior of all humanity; and both Moslems and Christians make of them the peculiar people, small in number, negligible in power, without which neither of them could have acquired their religions. It is not sufficient for the New Testament to imbed Jesus in Jewish life; it uses an extraordinary argument to associate him with the richest of the Jewish traditions, tracing the descent of the father who did *not* beget him to King David of blessed memory. It is not sufficient for the Koran to announce that Mahomet found everlasting truth; it must also maintain that the Jews found it before him, if not in as clear a form, and it must bring forth in array all the figures that Jews revere.

One would have thought that the most elementary sense of gratitude would have dictated an act of restitution to the Christian and Moslem worlds, especially when it was so tiny a corner that the Jews longed for; and if not gratitude, then simple justice, after so long a history of harassment and taunting. But when restitution began, gratitude had nothing to do with it, and though a feeling of justice was not absent from the Christian world, the Moslem world, after some hesitation, raised a loud cry of *injustice*. "It is we who are being made to pay, and we don't want to pay for history. We want a fresh start." But sometimes—alas, not always—history has to be paid for. America is paying for the crimes she committed against the Negroes, as England paid for her crimes against Ireland. But let us not think here of history as record, tucked away in books. Wherever Jews are disadvantaged because they are Jewish—that is, wish to identify themselves as Jews, whether religiously or culturally or ethnically or in any other fashion—wherever the Jew finds the struggle for life harder because he is a Jew, wherever he must be better than his non-Jewish opposite to achieve the same recognition, history is today and not simply in books. Christian and Moslem, Westerner and Arab will answer, "Restitution and justice do not call for the reconstitution of the Jewish state, but for a cleansing away of all manifestations of anti-Semitism." This familiar answer, on the surface so complete, raises fundamental problems that I shall only enumerate. A cleansing away of anti-Semitism so thorough as to foreclose the possibility of reinfection is a far-off prospect. But the creation of a Jewish home-land is infinitely more than an answer to anti-Semitism, and the paradox of it is that if there were no anti-Semitism there would be no opposition to the creation of a Jewish homeland, at least ideologi-cally. More than that, the nonexistence of a Jewish homeland is itself a cause of anti-Semitism, for it is an abnormality, reflecting on the status of the Jewish people and therefore on the status of the individ-ual Jew who elects to remain Jewish. It is further a confirmation of the ancient superstition that the Jewish people forfeited the right to a homeland by an act of deicide.

But what a pity it is that we speak of "paying for history" when we rectify its wrongs. It is as though a man begrudges the money he spends on curing himself of a sickness. All the resentment would disappear if we could see the effort as a voluntary contribution toward our self-improvement.

From *Light on Israel* (1968)

12 THE DIASPORA OF THE WEST

Visibly and vocally anti-Semitism is at a low ebb in the Western democracies and semi-democracies. Hitler has made it so disreputable that all but the extremest reactionaries, who have no reputation to lose, shy away from open association with it. Only the extreme Negro left is vociferously anti-Semitic and anti-Israel, and here Arab propaganda has scored its greatest success. It is a dangerous success. Exploited further it will lead to a new Christian-Arab hostile confrontation like that of centuries ago. The Negro adoption of "Moslemism" is, in passing, one of the marvels of history. The Moslem record in the Negro slave trade is as bad as the Christian, and longer; the recent massacre of Negroes in the Sudan by the ruling Moslems put a ghastly climax on the record; and the American Negro in revolt marches against his brutal Christian oppressors under the banner of his more brutal Moslem oppressors. On the banner is inscribed the device: "Down with the Jews."

As a revolutionary appeal the device is extraordinarily clumsy; the revolutionary elements in America, such as they are, wince before it. As an appeal to the quiet anti-Semitism of American Christianity it is ill-timed. The Jews of America are enjoying a vogue. They occupy a leading place, perhaps *the* leading place in literature and the drama, and amidst the immense popularity of Jewish books and plays "Down with the Jews" grates on the ear. Negro anti-Semitism is a tragedy where it is grass roots; where whipped up as strategy it is a folly as well as a crime.

But the current popularity of Jewish books and plays, that is, books and plays written by Jews on Jewish themes, has a special character that throws a disturbing light on Jewish life and Jewish-Christian relations. Almost without exception these books and plays deal with the Jewish past, and do so in a way that waters down the distinctiveness of the Jewish branch of civilization and leaves the false impression of a better understanding between Jew and Christian. The best illustration is *Fiddler on the Roof,* a musical comedy that has become a sociological phenomenon.

Most popular Jewish books and plays deal with the Jew of yesterday in America; *Fiddler on the Roof* deals with the Jew of yesterday in Russia. Despite the lightness of its form it aspires to a serious portrayal of Jewish life under the czars, and its lightness and seriousness are equally appreciated by the public. But what it offers is as much of that life as can be understood by a Jew or Gentile who is fortified against an understanding of Jewish life. That it therefore completely traduces Sholom Aleichem, on whose material the play is based, goes without saying, but that is not important. It traduces Jewish life.

It is enough to examine the central character, Tevye the dairyman, in whom Sholom Aleichem has created the everlasting Jew in his Russian-Jewish incarnation.* Tevye is the folk Jew, simple but intellectual, not devout but religious through and through, not a scholar but not unlearned. As Sholom Aleichem portrays him he wrestles with man's eternal moral problems and confronts God with love and expostulation, with adoration and wry humor. He does so in a Jewish context, with apt quotations from the sacred writings, Bible and Mishnah and prayer book, and expresses his rebellion by following each quotation with a disastrously comical and disrespectful mistranslation into Yiddish. At every such mistranslation the average Yiddish reader, also neither a scholar nor unlearned, must put the book down and laugh heartily—and gratefully. This is just what he needed—an escape from bitterness into laughter without an escape from Jewishness and God. The true human relationship between Sholom Aleichem and his readers depends on a common background of Jewish knowledge. In *Fiddler on the Roof* an attempt is made to reproduce the relationship against a background of common ignorance. The assumption, correct enough, is that the audience has a minimum knowledge of the Bible and none at all of the other Jewish sacred books. The closest approach of the stage Tevye to his original is with, "As the Good Book says, if you spit in the air it falls back

*For a fuller discussion of Sholom Aleichem's Tevye, see below, "Man in a Forest," pp. 316 ff., and "Tevye the Dairyman," pp. 320 ff. [Ed.]

on your face"—a piece of vulgarity born of the playwright's assurance that the most hopeless ignoramus will be suspicious of the attribution. The pathos and grandeur of Tevye's faith, his profoundly wise and Jewish humanity, the tears in his laughter and the laughter in his tears, are replaced by a kind of sentimental and illiterate buffoonery.

I shall be charged with a lack of humor. A musical comedy is not a sociological study, and only a pedant will look for Jewish values in *Fiddler on the Roof.* Perhaps so, although I consider *My Fair Lady* a sound sociological study as well as excellent entertainment. But *Fiddler on the Roof* has been tremendously acclaimed precisely because, in spite of its lightness, it is supposed to be a faithful rendering of the spirit of Russian Jewry, and, in a way, of Jewry generally. Apart from which one hears on every hand that the play is good public relations—it makes non-Jews like Jews. It certainly makes Jews look like non-Jews, but what non-Jews like in *Fiddler on the Roof* is not the Jewishness of the Jews, for it is not there.

The values of contemporaneous Jewish life do not interest the Jewish writers now to the fore; this is not a fault in them, but their depiction of the Jewish life of the past betrays gross ignorance. In contemporaneous portrayals it is made to appear that Jewishness is unrelated to Jewish knowledge, and "the tradition" consists of the simple awareness of being a Jew. Again, I do not hold it against these writers that they have no feeling for Israel; I hold it against them that they ignore the place of Israel in Jewish life. Perhaps they will before long be compelled to deal with it. In *Fiddler on the Roof* Tevye is shown at the close of the last act preparing to leave for America; in Sholom Aleichem he prepares to go to the Holy Land. If the play had been written after June 1967 it might have been found better theater to stay by the original version. Sholom Aleichem, as it happens, was a Diaspora nationalist no less than a Zionist. But he was an incorruptible artist, and although Tevye never reached the Holy Land, the longing for it was bound to rise uppermost in his heart when he was left alone in the world. He is so far denaturized and de-Judaized in the play that the idea does not even occur to him. And I cannot close these observations on *Fiddler on the Roof* without mention of the rabbi, who in Sholom Aleichem is one of the most moving and most gracious Jewish figures ever created by a poet, and who in the play emerges as a rickety half-wit whose only contribution to the portrayal of the vast and manifold Jewish tradition is to bless a sewing machine.

Fiddler on the Roof is successful commercial literature; that is the only "defense" that can be put up for its inadequacies. But it does not mitigate the harmful effect of the play, which is a weakening of the prospect of a Jewish-Christian understanding. And as a defense it is rather like an attorney's plea to the jury: "Ladies and gentlemen, my client is only a pickpocket, what do you expect of him?"

The same plea cannot be made for the higher level of American Jewish writers who have captured the attention of the critics and of much of the reading public. We shall look in vain among these for data which would help us define or feel the Jewish identity. They have, moreover, so concentrated on that segment of Jewish life which is least Jewish that theirs may be defined as the "literature of the Jew who isn't." This is natural; they themselves belong to that segment, and their work is artistically honest except when they try to evoke the tradition. The Jew who finds the characters in these books almost uniformly unpleasant must not blame the author. The picture of Israelites at work becoming Canaanites, Judeans becoming Greeks, Irishmen becoming Englishmen, Polynesians becoming Westerners, anyone trying to become someone else for the sake of convenience, or under pressure, is never a pleasant one. Assimilations of peoples must always go on, old peoples must die so that new ones can be born. But the process of assimilation, the transitional time, with its half-personalities, is a sad one. Thus Latin is a great language, so is French; but Latin becoming French is barbarous.

It is pointless to object to books by Jewish writers in which we meet only unappetizing half-Jews, though it should be added that as a rule the writers go out of their way to add a gratuitous touch of nastiness to their characters. Taking this body of literature as a whole, a Jew who is warmly related to Jewish life must ask, "But where am I? And where are my friends and acquaintances, the Jews who occupy themselves with Jewish education, synagogues, philanthropies, refugees, Israel, Russian Jewry? These interests of ours don't make us less human; apart from them, and as part of them, we have problems, tragedies, crises of conscience, virtues, and, what is more important for the writers I am talking about, meannesses and absurdities aplenty. And, since this seems to be a literary *sine qua non,* we too sometimes use dirty four-letter words. Don't we rate a corner of the canvas?"

An anti-Semitic character in Joyce's *Ulysses* asks of Bloom, the all-but-assimilated Jew, "Is he a Jew or a Gentile or a holy Roman or a swaddler or what the hell is he?" One need not be an anti-Semite to ask this question of the half-Jews who fill the popular American literature of our time, and of the men who produce it; one may ask it in all friendliness. Or one may not ask it at all, being content with the impression that this is the Jew; which brings up another important question: why are these books so popular? Is it their literary merit? We know that popularity and literary merit rarely coincide; if they always did, every age would be bursting with good literature. There are always many popular books, few good ones. Fashions and fads seem to be the explanation, often inexplicable. But in the present case the explanation lies at hand: a general interest in the Jews, part of the backwash from Hitlerism. The interest is benevolent, lazy, and evasive. It does not strive for a knowledge of Judaism or of Jews in their Jewish capacity. And most Jews are content and are themselves avid readers of this literature. The vague reaction is: "It doesn't matter, as long as they're nice to us." But it matters a great deal, though only the educated and self-respecting Jewish minority perceives it. It also perceives that a genuine understanding between Christian and Jew is impossible before a much larger body of educated Jews has been created.

The Jewish education of the American-born Jew has only recently been given serious attention, and the greatest obstacle facing educators is the widely-held belief that to acknowledge oneself a Jew constitutes all of Jewishness. The bare preliminary is taken for the vast totality, and Jews who are psychologically committed in some faint degree feel that they can dispense with the spiritual and intellectual commitment. The error is compounded when the psychological commitment fulfills itself completely in contributions to Israel or to some Jewish philanthropy.

For the majority of Jews the commitment will always be more psychological than spiritual and intellectual. It is idle to dream of an American or any other Diaspora Jewry completely and deeply versed in the Jewish tradition. But a healthy Jewry has to possess enough of the tradition to become aware that its predominantly progressive and intellectual character has been largely bequeathed to it: that the line of transmission goes much further back than the recent past, further back than the Exile experience, back to a choice made by a remote ancestry in the territory now called Israel. Such a Jewry must know that its ethic and its intellectual ardor, threatened but still persistent, were infused into the people thousands of years ago and perpetuated from generation to generation. The perpetuation was conscious, systematic, disciplined. The tradition was not, and is not, in "the nature of the Jew." It had to be renewed from father to son by arduous effort; if the effort is relaxed, the character will die. Or rather, the relaxation is the portent of death.

As the choice was made in Israel thousands of years ago, so the reaffirmation of the choice throughout Diaspora Jewry is linked with the reaffirmation in Israel today. The two Jewries rise and fall together according to their common application of the tradition to the solution of their problems—general social problems, the problems of Israeli and Arab relations, of relations between Occidental and Oriental Jews, between Negroes and whites, between the Western world and the Arab world.

An American Jewry sufficiently recharged with the tradition will turn from the literature it finds so attractive today, and the change in demand will bring forth—it has already begun to bring forth—a new literature. Such a Jewry will also be dissatisfied with a Christian-Jewish pseudo-understanding. Only adolescents of all ages would rather be liked than understood; a mature and self-respecting people wants a deeper exchange with other peoples. The value of the exchange lies in the useful study of dissimilarities; the all-human similarities are the basis of the understanding.

The growing recognition of the peoplehood of the Jews is only a recognition of similarity, and this is in itself an advance. Until Israel had penetrated to the consciousness of the Western world the Jews were regarded only as members of a religious body. As such, they were not entitled to the first attribute of peoplehood, which is the possession of their homeland. There was of course also a special reason for denying the Jewish people its homeland: its permanent dispossession was implied in Christian tradition; and even where Christian faith was weak, the tradition had passed over into the secular folklore of Christendom. In its transitional stage between the two world wars Reform Judaism acquiesced in this view, but, except for a remnant in an arrested stage of development, does so no longer. It is becoming clear that the denial of Jewish peoplehood and of Israel's right to existence, with all that it implies for the Jewish people, is rooted in anti-Semitism. That the old Reform Judaism should not have recognized this need not surprise us. In other areas, too, anti-Semitism has had a subtly demoralizing effect on Jewish thought.

There is still much reluctance to accept the existence of Israel tacitly and naturally, but we must distinguish between transient political motivations and deep-rooted ideological attitudes. We must also be careful not to confuse an unfriendly attitude toward Israel with a denial of its right to exist. When de Gaulle, having settled the Algerian problem, was free to woo the Arabs, he ditched Israel. This was dictated by expediency—and *l'honneur*. Expediency and *l'honneur* change from year to year. When Mao Tse-tung discovered Nasser, and later the Syrian leaders, he also discovered the usefulness of enmity to Israel. This too was dictated by expediency—and the salvation of humanity. (De Gaulle and Mao are illustrations of the law of history that every statesman wants to stay in office long enough to undo his own work.) Russia's enmity may not be purely tactical, motivated as it is in part by anti-Semitism. In China's case, we cannot talk of a divergence of views on Israel between the leaders and the people; that the Chinese have ideas about Israel is not, to say the least, at all likely. But in Russia and the other Communist countries, ideas about Israel do exist, and they do not always conform to the ideas of the leaders. In France the distaste of the French people for the official policy toward Israel during and after the Six-Day War was so general that even de Gaulle was unable to ignore it. In England, too, the government's stand and public opinion were at odds.

Throughout the Christian world the reluctance to accept the existence of Israel tacitly and naturally as the corollary of the peoplehood of the Jews is far stronger in the Church establishments than in the laity. Here the resistance is deeply ideological, though it may sometimes be used tactically. In the Second Vatican Council's "Declaration on the Relations of the Church to non-Christian Religions," proclaimed by Pope Paul VI on October 28, 1965, the passage on the Jews contains a curious and apparently uncalled-for aside that marks it off from the passages on the other non-Christian religions. The declaration pays tribute to "the good things, spiritual and moral," to be found in the non-Christian religions, as well as to their "sociocultural values. . . . [I]n Hinduism, men contemplate the divine mystery and express it through an inexhaustible abundance of myths and through searching philosophical inquiry. . . . Buddhism, in its various forms, realizes the radical insufficiency of this changeable world. . . . The Church regards also with esteem the Moslems. They adore the one God living and subsisting in Himself, merciful and all-powerful. . . ." The last and longest passage on the non-Christian religions is devoted to the Jews.

It will be remembered that this pronouncement was a great disappointment to most Jews and to a number of Protestants and Catholics. It seemed to them that in the light of what Christians have done to Jews throughout the ages, and more particularly after what happened to the Jews under Hitler, it was at best a feeble gesture and at worst evasive on the part of the Church to declare that the Crucifixion "cannot be charged against all the Jews, without distinction, then alive, nor against the Jews of today." They were also profoundly disappointed by the passage that "reproves" where it should at least have condemned "as foreign to the mind of Christ any discrimination against men or harassment of them because of their race, color, condition of life, or religion," and again by the generalizing of the problem of anti-Semitism in the passage: "Furthermore, in her rejection of every persecution against any man, the Church, mindful of the patrimony she shares with the Jews, and moved not by political reasons but by the Gospel's spiritual love, decries hatred, persecution, displays of anti-Semitism, directed against Jews at any time and by any one." And "decries" or "deplores" are scarcely the words for what should be considered a mortal sin.

In these criticisms little attention was paid, even by Jews, to the words "moved not by political reasons" in the last passage. No such disclaimer appears in the fraternal greetings to other non-Christian religions. Its singular appearance here inevitably suggests *qui s'excuse s'accuse.* The only question is: What lies behind this politically motivated disclaimer of political motives? Which leads to the question: What political motives can the Church possibly be accused of when it "decries" or "deplores" hatred and persecution and displays of anti-Semitism? The desire to be friendly to the Jews (though not so friendly as to clear them once and for all of the hideous and superstitious charge of deicide, the key word avoided with great circumspection) is not going to be interpreted politically by Nazis and other anti-Semites. They may dislike it, while feeling relieved at its reserved tone; they are not going to say that the Catholic Church is intruding into the political field. Only one hypersensitive group is going to say it, and that is the Arab Christians who think they smell in the statement the possibility of future acquiescence in the existence of the State of Israel. And it will also be remembered with what similar circumspection the Pope, on his visit to Israel, avoided any hint of present acquiescence. We do not need accounts of what went on behind the scenes in order to know that the Arab bishops fought obstinately on the side of the conservatives for the emasculation of the stronger original statement and the inclusion of a political disclaimer.

The Church must not do anything that is likely to create a

schism or drive large numbers of its flock from the fold. It feels it has gone far enough in naming anti-Semitism among the deplorable manifestations of an un-Christian spirit. But for the Arab bishops that was going too far, and so, moved entirely by political motives, they demanded and got the disclaimer of political motivation.

I have argued that acquiescence in the existence of Israel implies acquiescence in the peoplehood of the Jews. These twin concepts run counter to classic Christian doctrine both Catholic and Protestant (they also run counter to various other notions on the nature of the Jews, but that does not occupy us here). It was therefore natural for the Christian establishments to display a shocking indifference to the facts of the Arab-Israel conflict generally and the 1967 war in particular. The voice of the churches was not heard in the gigantic protest that went up in America and elsewhere against the monstrous intent of the Arab states to wipe Israel off the face of the earth. There was no denial of the right of Israel to live; there was only a failure to rise against the planned murder.

The ideological bias of the churches, Catholic and Protestant, was strongly evident again in the discussions of the political future of the city of Jerusalem. If the advocates of its internationalization had been divided between laymen and the clergy in the relevant proportions the arguments could be discussed solely on their merits. But why should the clergy be overwhelmingly for internationalization? What this sudden concern about the guardianship of the holy places? Since the time of the Crusades the churches have resigned themselves to the Saracen and Turkish possession of Jerusalem. When, in 1948, Jordan seized Jerusalem, which was to be internationalized under the UN partition plan of 1947, the churches were easily comforted. Moslems had been the guardians for more than seven centuries, with no harm to Christianity. Access to the holy places was assured to all Christians—and why should it not be when it paid so handsomely? That access to the holy places in Jerusalem and the West Bank—Hebron, the grave of Mother Rachel—was denied to Jews not only of Israel but of every other country did not disturb the equanimity of the Christians. But *Jewish* guardianship of the places —that is quite a different matter.

The genuinely nonpolitical parts of the declaration on the Jews are offensive in their connotation that the Jews need to be absolved of the Crucifixion. The political part is offensive in its not-too-well hidden and self-exculpating affront to the State of Israel. The declaration as a whole mirrors a characteristic tendency toward reservations on the subject of Jewish relief from ancient disabilities. A feeling of impropriety is attached to the full acceptance of the Jews as the natural equals of Christians in all respects, and the Christian mind mutinies at the idea. Something must be kept as a reminder of Christian charity in admitting the Jews to equality, and this something is inevitably, and in a profound sense, a denial of equality. How craftily and with what fertile inventiveness prejudice evades discovery!

But this particular prejudice did not need to invent the support it receives from Jews whose sole interest in the Jewish people is that it should vanish as quickly as possible. Their ill-mannered intrusions into public discussion of Jewish affairs could be dismissed as a minor nuisance if it did not lead many Christians to take the view that if some Jews don't want to remain Jewish, it is wrong of other Jews to want it; and not only wrong, but actually un-Jewish. Wrong because it frustrates the Jews who don't want to be Jewish, and un-Jewish because the nice Jews, i.e., the "real" Jews, are the ones who are doing their best to stop being Jewish. Unfortunately, there are also Jews committed to the Jewish identity who are in the habit of inviting prominent "disappearers," as I call them, to air their views in publications and on platforms, while imploring them not to abandon the Jewish people in its unhappy plight. This is as futile as it is undignified. I have some valued friends among "disappearers." They would not remain my friends if they were in the habit of barging into the Jewish problem and telling Jews what to do as Jews.

The committed Jews who run after assimilating Jews, urging on them the duty and the spiritual advantages of remaining Jewish, are those whose commitment is purely psychological. If they were spiritually and culturally committed they would not feel so panicky, and they would find enough to do teaching the tradition to those who are psychologically prepared for it. The only harm assimilating Jews do us internally is to absorb energies better bestowed elsewhere, and for that we are to blame. The external harm is something; but that cannot be undone by arguing with assimilating Jews. Nor can we, on the other hand, conduct useful discussions with non-Jews who want us to assimilate, whether by religious or secular defection.

Among those assimilating Jews who won't leave us alone the Communists occupy the silliest intellectual position. But the silliness is stained with something darker, which is not removed by Communist protests against Russian or Polish or Czechoslovak anti-Semitism. Communist and Christian anti-Semitism resemble each other when they deny the Jewish people alone the rights of nationalism or peoplehood. Jewish Communists, however, have special reasons for holding their peace, or, in the Yiddish phrase, taking a mouthful of water, when the Jewish subject is mentioned. The malevolence of Communist countries toward the Jews in their midst and toward Israel belongs to the general Jewish tragedy; the role played in it by Jewish Communists belongs to the chapter called "Jewish Enemies of the Jewish People." The moral issue is painful, but it should not obscure the comicality of the intellectual aspect. One ought to be tongue-tied when one is hide-bound, but few Jews are tongue-tied, and the Communist least of all. He chants the old slogans with increasing fervor as their absurdity becomes increasingly evident. Judaism is a reactionary force! The Jewish problem, and all other problems, can be solved only by universal communism! Israel is a tool of Western imperialism! Arab nationalism is a liberating force! The cracked record seems to be made of indestructible material. And of course Israel must return unconditionally to the perilous frontiers of 1948. Marvelous to relate, the Jewish Communists of Israel, like their Arab *tovarichi*, are free to express the same opinions, if that is the right word. Some of them, having actually broken loose, and really having opinions, have ceased to be Communists. Russia has read them out of the party.

Jewish Communists in America are no longer a factor in Jewish-Christian relations, and when they were it was by exaggeration of their numbers, as of Communists generally. What stands in the way of the right creative relationship is the reluctance of the churches, rather than of the laity, to get over the first hurdle, which is to recognize the similarity of the Jewish people to all other peoples. Once this is done, an appreciation of the dissimilarities, so much more valuable in their way, becomes possible.

One more condition must be fulfilled before that possibility can be unfolded to the enrichment of American life, and that is a great lifting up of Jewish cultural standards among American Jews. It must begin in the home, with parents participating, both for themselves and for their children; it must permeate the religious centers; it calls for secular institutions, like the community centers; it calls for an extension of the Jewish day-school system and of the Jewish-oriented summer camps. We cannot speak of the revival of Hebrew as the spoken language of the Jewish home—it was never that in the Diaspora or even in the post-Babylonian Jewish commonwealth—but it has always been the additional language of the cultivated Jew, the language of his prayers and meditations and of his literary activity. But the chief mainstay of the Jewish tradition has always been and must always be its organic attachment to the land of its birth and finest flower, and a renascence of the Jewish tradition in America will be authentic only when it leads to the gradual migration of some hundreds of thousands of American Jews to Israel.

This last, climactic part of the program has many bearings. It must not be regarded as a withdrawal, much less a repudiation. Voluntary, conscious of purpose, it must strengthen Israel as the servant of both East and West. An Israel unidentifiably absorbed into the Arab world has little or no value for it. An Israel solely an extension of the West—which is what the Arabs accuse it today of being—is a disruptive intruder. An Israel remaining itself in an Arab-Israel federation—and this is bound to come—and retaining its connection with the West through millions of Western Jews, can play a unique unifying role. In his letter to Chaim Weizmann, the Emir Feisal speaks of him as "a great helper of the Arab cause." This is the natural course of Zionism, to be resumed after a long, painful, and bloody deflection.

In lifting itself to a spiritual and cultural level from which such a migration will flow, American Jewry will at last be able to establish the right relationship with Christian America. I have said that the recognition of similarity is the basis for the study of dissimilarity. One speaks of the dissimilarity between an apple and a pear because they are both fruits. One cannot speak of the dissimilarity between an apple and a triangle. Once the peoplehood of the Jews is tacitly accepted, and with it the rights Jews have in common with other peoples, the special character of the Jewish people can be examined.

It is first of all a world people and a world observer. Whatever happens anywhere—or nearly anywhere—happens to some part of the Jewish people and is communicated to the rest. If humanity is trying to create One World, Jewry is the pilot plant. At the same time, in the tenacity with which it has held on to its identity for some three and a half millennia, it proclaims the vital principle that One World does not mean One Face.

The Jewish people is an ethical people; that is to say, a Jew who identifies with his people is aware that this identification implies an ethical obligation, even if he considers himself an atheist. Whether a believer or an unbeliever, he may not, and often does not, honor the obligation; and whether he is aware of it or not, that ethic is the product of the Jewish religion. In that sense there are no Jewish atheists *pur sang;* and what we call secular Jewish nationalism is deeply involved in the Jewish religion.

This peculiarity puzzles the non-Jew, and sometimes the Jew, too. The Western world distinguishes sharply between nationality or peoplehood and religion. The reason is that religion came to the Western world from the outside, whereas the Jewish people was born as a religion. Secular Jews accept the principle of separation of church and state for Israel; but their secularism is really a variety of the Jewish religion. Reform Jews too, certainly not secularists, accept the principle, and so do many Orthodox Jews.

The Western world will be ill at ease with the Jew until it takes up an affirmative attitude toward the Jewish Diaspora as one of its permanent component elements. It must see in world Jewry a uniquely useful influence toward the harmonization of the world's nationalisms. It will do so in proportion as Western Jewry renews itself through Israel in the Jewish tradition.

From *Light on Israel* (1968)

13 BLOOD ACCUSATION: ECHOES AFTER FIFTY YEARS

I

The Blood Accusation has been an insignificant factor in the anti-Semitism of the last half-century. It has cropped up here and there in "cockroach" publications but without setting off a major agitation. One might say that it was killed by the Beiliss case,* were it not that the real killer—assuming that the death is real—was the spirit of the time. During the last fifty years the diabolism of the underprivileged has sought satisfaction not in pictures of tortured children and human vampires but in hair-raising stories of world conspiracies and universal ruin. The collapse of the Beiliss case was followed by the rise of the *Protocols of the Elders of Zion,* which did so much to soften up the world for the first phases of Hitlerian anti-Semitism, and the successful launching of the *Protocols* was the work of those Russian reactionaries who had made possible the Beiliss case.

They were undiscourageable and they were unteachable. One cannot simply say that their anti-Semitism was their undoing, for their fatal unadaptability had a far wider range; but their anti-Semit-

*In antiquity, false accusations of ritual murder were leveled against the Christians. In medieval and modern times, such accusations have been made mainly against the Jews, from the time of William of Norwich in 1144, through the Damascus affair of 1840, to the case of Mendel Beiliss in Russia, which lasted from 1911 to 1913. In 1911 in the city of Kiev, Beiliss was charged with "religious cannibalism," i.e. that he had sacrificed a Christian child in order to prepare *matzos* with the blood. Despite appeals to reason by Western countries, the czarist bureaucracy seriously pressed this charge for nearly two years, until the accused was acquitted by an all-Russian jury in November 1913. The background of the bizarre accusation are the pogroms, the disastrous war with Japan, and the revolutionary upheavals that had marked the first decade of the twentieth century in Russia. The distraction did not succeed for long and is generally regarded by historians as one more step leading to the end of the czarist regime four years later. [Ed.]

ism was an organic part of it as symbol and substance. They continued to believe that they had lost out, had been defeated and undone only because by themselves they had been unable to stand up to world Jewry; and there was only one way to retrieve their fortunes: rouse the world against the Jewish menace.

When the *Protocols* first filtered through to the West, they awakened among the large majority of intelligent people the same incredulity and derision as the first reports of the Beiliss case. That this preposterous concoction that was being spread in 1918 by the White armies fighting the Bolsheviks in Russia's civil war would be taken seriously by a large number of people seemed wildly improbable; yet almost from the first day of its appearance the forgery made its influence felt, and the initial attempts to create a Jewish homeland in Palestine ran up against it.

Chaim Weizmann, later first president of the State of Israel, was in Palestine in the spring of 1918 as head of a Zionist commission sent out by the British government to plan the implementation of the Balfour Declaration in favor of the Jewish homeland. He records in his memoirs: "In an early conversation with General Wyndham Deedes . . . I learned of at least one source of our tribulations. Suddenly, and without introduction, he handed me a few sheets of typewritten script, and asked me to read them carefully. I read the first sheet and looked up in some perplexity, asking what could be the meaning of all this rubbish. Deedes replied quietly, and rather sternly: 'You had better read all of it with care; it is going to cause you a great deal of trouble in the future.' This was my first meeting with extracts from the *Protocols of the Elders of Zion.* I asked Deedes how the thing had reached him. He answered, slowly and sadly: 'You will find it in the haversacks of a great many British officers here—and they believe it! It was brought over by the British Military Mission which has been serving in the Caucasus on the staff of the Grand Duke Nicholas.' "

II

The *Protocols* had their day. They were read by millions of people in every country. They died down, but they left a large residue of hate, suspicion, and fear throughout the Western world, or, to change the figure, a susceptibility that the Nazis exploited with mortal success in Germany and not unsuccessfully in other countries. The surviving supporters of the Beiliss case and the promulgators of the *Protocols* had the satisfaction of seeing their crusade for the liberation of the world from Jewish bondage taken up by Hitler.

Russian anti-Semitism has had a checkered career since the revolution. In the Communist creed anti-Semitism is something like the sin against the Holy Ghost, and its espousal by the Nazis enhanced, if that were possible, its depravity and hatefulness. It seemed natural, then, that anti-Semitism should be denounced as a counterrevolutionary crime that would not be tolerated in a Communist society; and it cannot be denied that during the early years—Lenin's years— of the Communist regime anti-Semitism disappeared from view in Russia. But one must say *"seemed* natural" because, on the other hand, it cannot be denied even by Communists that under Stalin anti-Semitism returned in practice while it continued to be denounced in principle.

It was not, of course, the anti-Semitism of the Nazis nor, in a certain sense, that of the czarist reactionaries. There was never a suggestion that Jews were an inferior species which had to be expelled, repressed, or exterminated for the good of the country. Nor did anyone dare to advocate the exclusion by law of Jews from any type of employment. But if Communist anti-Semitism is absolutely dissimilar from the Nazi variety while only relatively dissimilar from the czarist variety, it is because of the return of a number of familiar features.

The overall point of view of present day Russian Communist anti-Semitism may be summarized thus: there is nothing wrong with the individual Jew as such—he is as capable as anyone else of being made into a loyal citizen; but any hankering he may have for the perpetuation of the Jewish cultural tradition (hence of the group identity), whether embodied in religious or secular forms, in Hebrew (more particularly) or in Yiddish, must be studiously discouraged; by steady pressure, by the withholding of educational means, the Jewish cultural component in the all-Russian complex must be gradually eliminated.

The obvious result of such a policy will be the elimination of the Jew, for a Jew is a Jew by nurture; denied cultural nourishment Jewishness must rapidly starve to death and Jews disappear. In spiritual, though not in physical, terms it is the equivalent of the program set forth by the prerevolutionary anti-Semitic press. "The Yids must be placed under such conditions that they will gradually die out. This is one of the tasks of the government and of the best men in the country." (But it should, in fairness, be noted that Communists never use the offensive word *Zhid* [Yid, sheeny].)

Other ethnic groups in the USSR are encouraged, by subsidies and by the provision of facilities—schools, theaters, printing privileges, supplies of newsprint, etc.—to develop their special cultural possessions. Some of these groups are considerably smaller in number than the Jews, none has a richer spiritual and cultural heritage. At this writing—1966—widespread protests have moved the Russian government to a grant of derisory token facilities for Jewish cultural self-expression; but given another two or three decades of such spiritual semistarvation, these beggarly concessions will have no meaning. There will be no one to take advantage of them.

We may, with perhaps unjustifiable generosity, pass over the more primitive phase of anti-Semitism that flared up under Stalin, calling it an aberration or idiosyncrasy: the "Doctor's Plot" and the liquidation of the greater part of Russia's Jewish-cultural intellectuals. We should certainly be going too far in extending this charitable interpretation to the post-Stalin practice of emphasizing heavily the Jewish names of those who have been shot for "economic crimes." Yet even this is not the most disheartening manifestation of present-day Russian anti-Semitism.

At irregular intervals there appear in the Russian press or in special publications strange utterances on Jews and Judaism which one cannot by any stretch of the imagination fit in with the standard Communist attitude on religion as such. Nor can they be regarded as a logical extension of the Russian hostility to the idea of the State of Israel. What they are may be gathered from examination of one specimen, a book of 192 pages entitled *Judaism Without Embellishment* by Trophim Korneyevich Kichko.

It was published in the fall of 1963 and did not attract attention abroad until the spring of 1964, when vigorous protests began to be voiced, not the least among them being those of Communists outside of Russia. Contempt for religious doctrine on Marxist and "scientific" grounds is to be expected in a Communist statement on any religion, and Judaism must not ask for favored treatment; but here the accusations of obscurantism and anti-Communism degenerate into a general vilification of all Jews touched with Jewish loyalty. The almost exclusive preoccupation of this book is with what it considers the ethical indecency of Judaism as such, a religion which, it maintains, advocates theft, deception, and hatred of non-Jews.

Thus, the author claims to find in the Mishnah the following interpretation of the commandment "Thou shalt not steal": "You may not steal from or cause any other damage to your *chavers* (neighbors), i.e., Jews. As to how this applies to *goys,* to those of different religions, the Jews are free to take from them because, as Judaism teaches, 'Jehovah delivered all of the wealth of the non-Jews to the use of the Jews.' " Or again: "The Talmud morally corrupts people, instilling in them the spirit of commerce and extortion. . . . The Talmud is saturated with contempt for work. . . . The Jews like to talk a great deal about the commandment that forbids them to bear false witness. However, when the welfare of a Jew is in question, false witnessing and even false oaths are permissible. . . . While giving a false oath it is only necessary, the 'Holy Scripture' teaches, to negate the oath in the heart and soul." The charge of thievery as a religious principle is repeated with another attribution: "One of the commandments of Judaism is: 'Do not steal.' However as the *'Choshen Mishpat'* interprets, it is only from *chavers* (i.e., from your Jewish neighbors) that you must not steal. But you can steal everything from others, because, as it is written in the 'Sacred Scriptures,' Jehovah handed over to the Hebrews all the wealth of non-Jews." To which is added an interesting variant on the theme of universal Jewish power: "If the Jews did not take everything into their own hands, it was because they did not want to lose the labor power of non-Jewish workers." (This view is of course attributed to religious Jews, who are shown as presumably believing that they could "take everything into their own hands" if they felt like it.)

More generally: "The ethics of Judaism do not condemn such disgraceful actions as hypocrisy and bribery. The well-known commentator on the Talmud, Rashi, teaches: 'Based on biblical teachings, the Jew at the very outset must work with bribery in order to tempt his enemy, and in other cases he must resort to a variety of artifices.' " And: "Speculation in *matzos,* pigs, thievery, deception, debauchery— these are the characteristics of many synagogue leaders." Then follows a curious passage which needs some disentangling: "Under modern conditions the Passover holiday harms us in a great number of ways, through engendering disrespect for work and fostering elements of nationalism among the Jewish workers. In celebrating the Passover the Jews do not go to work for several days, thus they hinder production plans and violate work discipline. The celebration of the Passover is especially harmful because the entire Passover legend, all the prayers, orient the believing Jews toward returning to Israel . . . where they—free workers of our country—will become cannon fodder for Ben-Gurion's clique and for his imperialistic masters."

One would think that if holidays engender disrespect for work, the Sunday, even if observed nonreligiously, is not less injurious to the state than the Passover. But the real intent of all the slander and vilification slips out; what the writer cannot tolerate is the thought of a Jewish nationalist identity, which may awaken in some Jews the longing to live in a land of their own. Were he to make a straightforward statement to this effect, it would be objectionable enough on various grounds; but he conceals this intolerance behind a larger viciousness—a reversion to genuine anti-Semitic strategy.

For what we have here is so close a revival of Hippolyte Lyutostansky and parts of Father Pranaitis* (there is, however, no mention of ritual murder) that at least a familiarity with their work is suggested. There is the same display of recondite terms like *Mishnah, Talmud, Rashi, Choshen Mishpat, Chaver, Avot de-Rabbi Natan,* etc., suggesting scholarly depth where to the moderately informed reader there is only the wearisome, familiar old parade of misquotations, quotations out of context, and pure fabrications drawn from the segregated literature of classic anti-Semitism. The scholarly qualifications of the author in the field of Jewish religion and history are not given. There are only commendations of his work. A brief, unsigned foreword states: "The author of the book reveals to the reader the actual essence of the Jewish religion (Judaism)—one of the ancient religions of the world, which has collected within itself and condensed everything that is most reactionary and antihumane in the writings of contemporaneous religions." A second and longer foreword, signed by "Doctor of Historical Sciences Professor A. Vvedensky" and "Writer Grigori Plotkin," assures us that this is "a profound and substantial work which contains a tremendous amount of factual material conscientiously and scientifically analyzed." We are not given, either, the qualifications in the Jewish field of Professor Vvedensky or Writer Plotkin, though it is evident that the second name is Jewish.

The last sentence of the first foreword reads: "This book is intended for a wide circle of readers," i.e., its purpose is not merely to open the eyes of Jews to the viciousness of their ancestral faith but

---

*Hippolyte Lyutostansky, an unfrocked Catholic priest, was frequently quoted by the prosecution at the Beiliss trial as "a leading authority on Judaism." Father Justin Pranaitis, an obscure Catholic priest and a self-proclaimed authority on Jews and Judaism, was engaged by the prosecution to serve as the "expert" on the Jewish religion at the Beiliss trial. [Ed.]

also to inform others of it. The first printing was twelve thousand copies.

The numerous caricatures that accompany the text of this "scientific" analysis of Judaism vie with the most offensive that ever appeared in Streicher's *Stürmer:* the same repulsive faces, with blubbery, sensual lips and predatory noses, the same obscene bodies and gestures, the same suggestion of cupidity and craftiness. It was the caricatures more than the text that moved Communist organs in England, France, America, Holland, and other countries to protest; for the text, like the disquisitions of Father Pranaitis, simply does not lend itself to intelligible discussion.

Some six months after publication the Russian government began to show a little uneasiness. Tass (the Soviet news agency) and *Pravda,* one of the two leading Soviet dailies, expressed reservations about the accuracy of some of the statements in *Judaism Without Embellishment.* As Tass put it: "A number of mistaken propositions and illustrations could insult the feelings of believers and might be interpreted in the spirit of anti-Semitism." Apparently the insulted feelings of unbelievers, strongly expressed among Communists and non-Communists (among the latter were some distinguished non-Jews), did not enter into the account.

Izvestia, the other leading Soviet daily, expressed astonishment at the furor created by the book. The book was well-meant. "The intention of the booklet, by itself, can evoke no doubts," although it had to be admitted that it "contains errors" and "many of the drawings . . . can only offend the sensibilities of the devout." The Communist protests in the countries mentioned did not seem to concern *Izvestia.* It is "the bourgeois press" that "has become alarmed by a small book that has lately been issued by one of the Ukrainian publishing houses."

"One of the Ukrainian publishing houses" is technically accurate but disingenuous. The institution referred to happens to be the Academy of Sciences of the Ukrainian Socialist Soviet Republic, situated in Kiev. A twinge of memory? Of the four scientists who lent themselves to the frame-up of Beiliss, three belonged to the University of Kiev. The coincidence is painful; more so is the fact that no one responsible for *Judaism Without Embellishment,* neither author nor artist nor sponsors, has been put on trial. The book was withdrawn from circulation—though we do not know how many copies had already been sold. Thus the matter stands as of now, spring 1966.

The Russian censorship today is far more repressive and, of

course, more vigilant and more efficient than that of the czarist regime. That *Judaism Without Embellishment* should have been on sale for six months or so, that its withdrawal was ordered only under the pressure of Communist (and bourgeois) protest abroad leaves no doubt about the complacency of the government. But this is a naive understatement of the reality. The wishes of the Russian government are well understood in Russia, better, again, than in czarist days. It would have been next to impossible for Golubev and Chaplinsky to launch the Beiliss conspiracy without the cooperation of Shcheglovitov*; and it is quite impossible that a body like the Ukrainian Academy of Sciences should have ventured a publication of this kind without the sanction of Moscow. As it happened, the experiment failed. The better part of wisdom was then to hush it up.

Judaism Without Embellishment is only one of a number of anti-Semitic publications recurring irregularly in Russia, and these publications are themselves only part of the manifestation of a persistent strain of anti-Semitism in official Russian circles. Here the parallel with the evil old days thrusts itself most unpleasantly on the attention. There is no evidence that the Russian masses are disturbed by the Jewish hankering for cultural minority rights or by Jewish observance of the Passover. There is no evidence that equal treatment of the Jews in the granting of schools, the encouragement of Yiddish in literature and the arts would awaken popular resentment. As of old it is from above that the pressure and provocation (*Judaism Without Embellishment,* as addressed to non-Jews, cannot escape the accusation of provocation) are exerted. And that such should be the situation in Russia is peculiarly disturbing.

From *Blood Accusation* (1966)

*Vladimir Golubev, was a student at Kiev University and leader of local monarchist, rightist, and anti-Semitic groups. With the knowledge and consent of Chaplinsky, prosecutor of the Kiev Appellate Court, he was the inventor of the Beiliss case. I. G. Shcheglovitov, a rabid anti-Semite, was the Minister of Justice under Czar Nicholas II. [Ed.]

part four

Maurice Samuel enjoyed an association with many of the most notable Jewish personalities of the day. Some were colleagues; some he
regarded as mentors; some were close personal friends. Each has
staked out an important claim upon Jewish intellectual and social
terrain, and all are intimately bound up with various phases of Samuel's interests and achievements. His affectionate portrayals of his
associates—a sampling follows—constitute a gallery of eminent lives.
They also afford an attractive self-portrait.

TEACHERS
AND FRIENDS

14 CHAIM WEIZMANN

I

The Manchester of my boyhood was the world-renowned center of
the cotton-goods trade. "Cottonopolis" it called itself, and was; its
overseas rivals, in New England and Japan, were only flexing their
muscles in those days. In the factory areas of Manchester and of the
towns ringing it you could hear, mornings and evenings, the rush of
the cataracts of wooden clogs—the weavers going to and from work.
It was said that on a clear Sunday morning ten thousand factory
chimneys could be counted from the top of the Town Hall tower in
Albert Square; the griminess of the tower, as of every other building,
was strong supporting testimony.

But Manchester had cultural eminence, too. It was the home of
the famous Horniman Repertoire Theatre, the joint product of Horniman's Tea and Miss Horniman's passion for the stage; it was the
home of the Hallé Concerts, of the *Manchester Guardian,* second in
reputation, if second at all, to the *Times* of London, and of Manchester
University, the roster of whose faculty carried names which still echo
in the world of science and the humanities.

Ernest Rutherford taught physics there, and Niels Bohr was his
assistant. Henry Moseley, the young genius who was killed in the
First World War, had also worked there under Rutherford. Flinders
Petrie lectured on Egyptology, and James Frazer of *The Golden Bough*
came over occasionally from the sister university of Liverpool to
lecture on anthropology. Samuel Alexander taught philosophy; he
was already a name, though he had not yet published his *Time, Space
and Deity.* Arthur Schuster and Chaim Weizmann and the younger
Perkins taught chemistry, and Horace Lamb mathematics.

I can always cause a little flutter in scientific company by mentioning casually that I studied physics under Ernest Rutherford ("And did you once see Shelley plain?"). True, Rutherford taught the old, classical physics; the revolutionary experiments he was then conducting on the structure of the atom were too new to be offered to his students; Einstein's Special Theory of Relativity had already been published, but not his General Theory; the Bohr model of the atom (itself now called classical) had not yet been given to the world; the quantum was known, but quantum mechanics was still a long way off. And yet—physics under Rutherford! Something must have rubbed off on me. I am not believed when I deny it. But Rutherford was one of my many lost opportunities. All I have of him is a personal recollection: a burly, genial man, easily moved to laughter, and a superb teacher, holding, with a single exception, the attention of his large class by force of personality and ingenuity of exposition. I have tried to explain the source of my resistance to him, perhaps too kindly; but there it was. To top it all, I was chosen by the class to express its pride and gratification when he returned from receiving his knighthood (he became Lord Rutherford later); a more incongruous choice could hardly have been imagined.

Perkins and Schuster I did not meet; if I heard Frazer lecture, as is likely, I have forgotten him, and of Flinders Petrie I have only the dimmest recollection. I attended one class under Horace Lamb with no benefit whatsoever, and I remember a mild and gentle spirit detached from this world and from his students, who complained that he confided his expositions to the blackboard, not to them. My English teacher, Herford, is also a remote figure, but Samuel Alexander, whom I met once or twice, stands, or rather walks and rides, clearly before me. It was more a shamble than a walk, and the sight of him on a bicycle, familiar though it was, moved the beholders to mirth and solicitude. He was a big, stooping man with a huge beard, and looked like a cross between an old clo'man and a Hebrew prophet. He rode his bicycle meditatively, on the sidewalk as often as not, miraculous in balance and in escape from collisions. We pointed to him affectionately as our specimen, the finest extant, and the finest in university history since Hegel, of the absentminded professor. It was told of him that a policeman once asked him gently to ride off the sidewalk onto the traffic level, and was waved off with the dreamy reply: "Not now, I have just found God." It was also told that he was the owner of a metaphysical dog by the name of Griff, short for the German *Begriff* (concept).

I could have known him better, for he was accessible to all students, but I was too raw and too conceited to use the opportunity, which never came again. Another opportunity which I neglected at the time, and which came my way again, to my life's enrichment, was Chaim Weizmann.

II

I made my first contact with him when I enrolled in one of his chemistry courses, and at the interview I was too nervous to retain a clear picture of him. He examined me briefly and suggested that I sit in on one or two of his lectures. I remember, however, my astonishment that a man with such a heavy Russian-Jewish accent should be a chemistry professor. I was not thinking of discrimination; I just could not reconcile Yiddish with chemistry or anything else modern and scientific. I must have supposed that an adult mind tinctured with Yiddish had been permanently affected. I could not follow his lectures and I put it down to his accent, which, curiously enough, was no obstacle to the other students. At his suggestion I changed to physics under Rutherford, whose accent was colonial but otherwise impeccable; as we have seen, this linguistic improvement was not reflected in my physics studies.

I met Weizmann again two years later in the house of Isaiah Wassilevsky, the Hebrew teacher who introduced me to Bialik's Yiddish poetry. The memory of this encounter is uncomfortable and uneven; vivid patches alternate with areas faded almost into invisibility. I see the room, the armchair under the window in which Weizmann is seated; I see the bookshelves and the table; I hear his voice, low-pitched, guttural, slyly good-natured. But I cannot remember why I was there, accidentally or by arrangement, and sometimes it is not Wassilevsky who hovers in the background, but Massel, the Hebrew poet, who also lived in that area; and I cannot remember being reintroduced to Weizmann, or even his noticing me, let alone addressing a remark to me. Most vivid is my recollection that I wanted to be rude to him, and, as I already knew him to be a prominent Zionist, tell him that I considered the Zionist movement a paltry, shabby affair, morally indefensible and intellectually beneath contempt. This need not mean that I was then in one of my violent anti-Jewish phases. Perhaps I do not remember being noticed or addressed because I thought at the time that he did not recognize me; and perhaps I thought he did recognize me and was sparing me the embarrassment of a tacit reference to my disappearance from his chemistry class. Whatever it was, I made up my mind to dislike him.

The next time I met him was in 1922, when I was in the employ of the Zionist Organization of America, and by then he was the world leader of the movement. The moment he set eyes on me he said, with a smile that went through and through me: "Why, yes, you're the fellow I chucked out of my chemistry class." It hadn't been quite so, though next door to it; but his manner of saying it made me feel, still makes me feel in retrospect, that he was administering a friendly and facetious rebuke for my sullenness at our encounter in Wassilevsky's house ten years or so earlier. Lest this should sound like vanity, I add that his memory for faces, names, and personalities was of unbeliev- able tenacity; it extended to thousands of individuals in a dozen countries. A one-minute encounter sufficed to make a permanent impression on him, filed away and subject to instantaneous recall twenty or thirty years later. If I was immensely flattered at the mo- ment, I learned to see the incident in perspective after working with him for a few weeks.

The Zionist Organization assigned me to act as his secretary during his stay in New York. The assignment was repeated several times, and I looked forward with increasing happiness to every repeti- tion. My service with the Zionist Organization ran from my twenty- seventh to my thirty-third year; I was not and am not a hero-worship- per; the happiness I found in working with Weizmann was not simply the pride of being on close terms with greatness; it was perhaps partly that, but if so, it was his peculiar greatness, which had immense meaning for me in cultural-spiritual terms; and with this was mingled a deep personal affection.

It was an affection that remained steadfast to the end; my admi- ration changed, became more thoughtful, more critical, and far more appreciative, as the record of his achievements accumulated. When I left the Zionist Organization to become a free-lance writer and lecturer, I maintained contact with him for longer or shorter periods at longer or shorter intervals. We would meet in New York, in Lon- don, and in Israel. The last and longest contact—it would have been the happiest had we been less concerned for his health—was in 1947, when I worked with him for some months on his autobiography, *Trial and Error*. He was then seventy-three and at the beginning of the sickness he lingered in for the next five years.

III

For me, Chaim Weizmann personifies, more than any other man I have known, the best that was in the *shtetl* Jew combined with the qualities of wordly greatness, and the more I ponder the mixture the more intriguing I find it. He was at home among statesmen, but his spiritual home continued to be the townlet of Motol-near-Pinsk, in the Pripet marshes, where, he tells us, "Jews lived, as they had lived for many generations, scattered islands in a gentile ocean; and among them my own people, on my father's and mother's side, made up a not inconsiderable proportion." He spoke many languages well, he was most himself in Yiddish. He had a commanding and arresting presence; when he entered a room it became his; relaxed, among intimates, he was still the center of attention, but by virtue of a Sholom Aleichem warmth and wit. He was a scientist of international repute; but to him, as to my people in Manchester, the Bible was the supreme source of life, and its figures were his contemporaries. He had been brought up with them. Science was his instrument for the rebuilding of the Jewish homeland; the Bible was his inspiration. "Inspiration" is somewhat misleading; it suggests perhaps an exalted remoteness where there was a homey familiarity as well as reverence. He was familiar with Abraham, Moses, and Isaiah in a spirit of neighborliness. So were my people; so was Sholom Aleichem's Tevye the dairyman.

He loved and hated the *shtetl* just as Mendele Mocher Sforim had done. He loved it for the vision it had guarded for him, he hated it for the formlessness of its life, its surrender to meanness and self-pity and *shlemielishness.* He was, supremely, the man of form. Whether in submitting a memorandum to the British Foreign Office, or in planning his Rehovoth home, he had a perfect instinct for the right stance. He prepared carefully, but could improvise brilliantly. I am tempted to say that he knew all the tricks of being enormously impressive, and yet there was no trickery; his impressiveness flowed from uncalculated total commitment and immense intellectual capacity. At the same time he was amused, even tickled, by the decorative superfluities that often went along with "being impressive." The skeptical *shtetl* Jew peered, grinning, over the shoulder of the impressive statesman, and both were genuine.

I pick at random, from memory, from notes, from earlier accounts, illustrative incidents and scenes of which I was the witness.

I have described in more detail elsewhere his appearance in Jerusalem before the UNSCOP (United Nations Special Committee on Palestine) in the summer of 1947, when I was working with him on his memoirs.* The session was held in the YMCA building, and the trip to Jerusalem was a strain on him. He was no longer the magnificent figure I had known in the early days; he was to outward appearance only a sick, shuffling old man whose sight was failing him. He had to be escorted carefully on to the platform, and we who watched from the auditorium were filled with apprehension, for his voice was so low that it barely carried to the committee members before him. We could not hear what he was saying, and we knew that some of the members—particularly the Indian—were hostile; thus we were horrified when we saw him put aside the prepared statement (it had been printed for him in half-inch type). In a few moments we were at ease, for it was obvious even at a distance that he had established his old ascendancy. The faces of the most hostile smoothed out, their questions were respectful, almost deferential; they knew themselves to be in the presence of greatness.

That evening (July 8, 1947) a small group of us accompanied the Weizmanns to a performance of the Israel (then the Palestine) Philharmonic Orchestra in Rehovoth, and late that night I made the following notes:

It's like accompanying royalty to a command performance. The cars sweep up to the door after everyone has entered and been seated. The concert is held up. We come in from the side, and before our coming we sense a stirring in the audience, which rises as we enter. We advance slowly to our places in the front row; the orchestra also rises and plays the *Hatikvah* (the national anthem). All that, and the military guard at the gate of the Weizmann house (with its grounds and gardens and winding drive), and the military guard at the concert, and Weizmann's personal bodyguard, heighten the effect. I feel a bit silly in this *galère*. Applause as we enter, the heartier because of W.'s performance before UNSCOP.

Weizmann feels and believes himself to be democratic. So he is—in the way a benevolent "good" king is: laboring for his people, making no distinction between high and low, thinking of the poor, sharing their problems, planning for the amelioration of their condition, opposing the rapacity of the rich, the exploitation of the masses by demagogues or men of wealth, supporting the labor movement, feeling a deep and organic kinship with the *kibbutzim*, keeping an eye on all elements of growth in the people, concerned for spiritual values, fighting the deterioration of the Jewish spirit, loathing terrorism more for its effect on the Jewish character than for the deaths it brings, feeling himself part of every creative effort (university, music, drama —and of course science and the Weizmann Institute now in the making). In

*See below, p. 233.

short, the touch of the "ideal" king comes from this universality in relation to all that is part of Jewish life. But there is the "kingly" about him, suggestive of a court. Such a man must be wealthy, and live accordingly, with taste. W.'s house is distinguished; we call it "The White House" (also because of its color): flowers, paintings, books, cultivated talk, all sorts of people—labor leaders, British government officials, dignitaries of all countries, discreet and devoted servants, *haut ton* (much is the work of Mrs. W.).

At the same time, *heimishness* when the pressure is off; we are all on the simplest terms with him.

Much that is childish (?) in W. Eats up praise and must have it continuously. Makes him feel good and enables him to work better. All the same, isn't bamboozled by it. Knows when what he's done is good, and when it isn't; not the fool of flatterers. Doesn't relish praise—even merited—from people who don't like him. When he has done well at a public appearance, will sit and purr, and wants to be purred at. It can grow tiresome; but we go along, we realize he's just recharging.

Impressive consistency and persistency in his life's activity. Quite unable to be dishonest toward the fundamental, but can be wary, evasive, crafty, though in reality not a first-rate politician. Enjoys comfort, order, good cooking (not so much now!), tapestry, garden and trees, which he delights in showing off.

Considers himself so much *the* Jew of this generation that his ejection from the Zionist presidency in 1931 and again now, 1947, made him aghast. Who *dares* pretend to his place? And indeed all the others *are* small beside him (which is perhaps the best reason—and the one they necessarily can't have the sense and courage to give—for changing. We can't have political life thus dominated by one individual).

IV

If Weizmann's outstanding quality was his sense of form, his outstanding spiritual characteristic was his identification with the folk; he confirmed in me the link between me and my people; I do not mean here the Jewish people in the abstract, but the group which gave me life. Because of him I became clear as to its meaning beyond the framework of a particular time and place; for he was representative of the Jewish people as a historic whole, continuous in many displacements through some thousands of years.

He loved the masses in Abraham Lincoln's way; he loved the shoemaker, the carpenter, the shopkeeper, the peddler, while hating from the depths of his soul the formlessness of their lives. Pomp and circumstance as *narishkeit*, foolishness, was one thing; form as the craftsmanship of life, in science, politics, social relations, physical surroundings, morals, aesthetics, manners—that was something else. It was what the Jewish people had to acquire, and Weizmann was its teacher in personal and public life. Theodor Herzl, the founder of modern Zionism, had understood that, too, but there was a profound difference between Herzl and Weizmann which is illustrated by a Hasidic saying: "To help a man you must get down to where he is." Herzl was the avatar type, but the task called for a *shtetl* man, flesh of its flesh, bone of its bone, a *shtetl* man who had made the transformation in himself—it needed such a man to initiate the transformation, still so incomplete, in the people. He had to draw from the *shtetl* the power to overcome, against the inertia of centuries, the *shtetl's* ingrained disdain of order and system, which it had come to regard as an essential ingredient of Jewishness. To the *shtetl* man form was a *goyish* thing; it had to do with uniforms, governments, *olam ha-zeh* (this-worldliness). But *olam ha-zeh* was the very point. Our exclusion from the national essence of *olam ha-zeh,* namely, a homeland of our own, had warped the Jewish outlook, and the straightening out of this warp in the Jewish people as a whole was for Weizmann an integral part of the reconstruction of the homeland.

Weizmann was a great teacher as well as a great leader. He was particularly concerned with the unhealthiness of the Jewish attitude toward the non-Jewish world. He was himself completely at ease among non-Jews, he felt no discomfort and occasioned none. He did not—as consciously assimilating Jews often do—put his hosts under a strain practicing and tacitly requesting evasion of Jewish subjects. One of his favorite phrases was: *"C'est à prendre ou à laisser—*take it or leave it." He attributed the lack of natural self-confidence, which expressed itself in overconfidence and submissiveness, to the Jewish sense of abnormality rising from the lack of a homeland.

When I served as his secretary I used to accompany him to his mass meetings and take notes of his speeches (he always spoke extemporaneously). Here are some typical excerpts:

"You will always be treated as a guest if you too can play the host. The only man who is invited to dinner is the one who can have his dinner at home if he likes. . . ."

"Among the anti-Semites none is more interesting than the tender-hearted variety. Their anti-Semitism is always based on a compliment. They tell us: 'You are the salt of the earth,' and there are Jews who feel themselves extraordinarily flattered . . . Yet I do not consider it a compliment to be called 'the salt of the earth.' The salt is used for someone else's food, it dissolves in that food. And salt is good only in small quantities. If there is too much salt in the food, you throw out the food and the salt with it. . . ."

"We are reproached by the whole world. We are told that we are dealers in old clothes, junk. We are perhaps the sons of dealers in old clothes, but we are the grandsons of prophets. Think of the grand-sons, and not of the sons."

It was good to see—literally see—an audience catch at these points; there would be an appreciative turning and nodding of heads. The listeners knew that he had overcome these psychological hand-icaps of the Jews; they delighted in the obvious fact that when he ridiculed the assimilated Jewish notables, he could not be suspected of envying their status among non-Jews; his was indisputably higher. He could laugh at the Jewish merchants, writers, and financiers who kept repeating: "We have risen above the ghetto thing called Jewish-ness. We are moderns."

I too benefited greatly from his talks and from his general atti-tude. A fast-moving world has forgotten how the idea of a Jewish state was, not too long ago as history is reckoned, regarded as a poky, hole-in-wall oddity, classed with Rosicrucianism and the lost ten tribes. I am, in fact, not completely accustomed to the new situation; I still expect to hear: "You believe in the possibility of a Jewish state? How very interesting, you must tell me about it," meaning: "Oh Lord, how did I get into this?" How easily "What on earth is he talking about?" has become "But naturally." So forgetting, the world cannot appreciate what a long and stony road Weizmann had to tread from his dreams in Motol to the State of Israel. He called it his forty years in the wilderness, but it was longer.

V

The stoniness of that road is known only to those who accompanied Weizmann along part of it. There were large segments of the Jewish people in ideological opposition to the Zionist program; assimilated or assimilating Jews of the bourgeoisie and of the left; non-assimilat-ing Jews who wanted to see Jewishness rooted in the Diaspora with-out a homeland in Palestine, and these might be extremists in religion (Orthodox *and* Reform) or secularist nationalists; other non-assimilating Jews wanted a Jewish homeland but at all costs any-where but in Palestine. There were segments which dreaded any kind of publicity about the Jewish people, and there were segments which were indifferent. The large segment which listened sympathetically to Weizmann comprised the lower economic strata—transplanted *shtetl* Jews and their offspring. They had, on the whole, neither the will nor the means to be effective; a generation had to pass before that was changed.

Among these, Weizmann did one part of his labors, a part the more difficult because while he taught he had to raise funds; he had to be master-teacher and master-mendicant simultaneously, a double role at once spiritually rewarding and humanly humiliating. Sometimes there were well-to-do prospects among the sympathetic, and they had to be nursed and catered to. There were receptions in private homes, to which I went along with Weizmann, and some of those evenings still make me shudder. Amid vulgar and ostentatious surroundings, this man of exquisite taste and subtle intellect endured stupidly obstructive questions and coarse admonitions in the style of the *shtetl nogid* (wealthy man), in the hope, frequently deceived, of obtaining a few thousand dollars for the pioneers in Palestine. He would come away with a sick look, saying: "You have to bow to every idol on the road to Palestine."

His patience was inhuman. He had to inspire, cajole, scold, and teach. The Zionist position was paradoxical. To prove to the world that they were capable of building a homeland (for few believed they were) the Jews first had to have an opportunity to build; but to be given such an opportunity they first had to prove that they were capable of building. It was the classical problem of the beginner and "job-open—only-the-experienced-wanted." A vicious circle of this kind can never be broken; it has to be eroded; and it calls for undiscourageable self-confidence on the part of the applicant. But in the Zionist case there was little self-confidence among Jews at large; the masses didn't really believe in the capacity of the Jewish people to build a homeland.

All this Weizmann understood, and he accepted the consequences. But there were Zionist leaders who thought otherwise. They denounced his gradualism as timidity and lack of vision. As far back as forty years ago their cry was: "A Jewish state *now!*"—which in effect meant a Jewish state with practically no Jews in it. Weizmann's reply, obstinately repeated a thousand times, was: "A Jewish state cannot be created by decree, but by the forces of a people in the course of generations. Even if all the governments in the world gave us a country, it would only be a gift of words; but if the Jewish people will go and build Palestine, the Jewish state will become a reality."

Among his opponents in the Zionist movement were men of distinction. Max Nordau, the author of *Degeneration* and *The Conventional Lies of Civilization* (all but forgotten now, they made a great stir in their day), demanded, soon after the end of the First World War, that half a million Jews be transported immediately into Palestine—

sink or swim; there would be enough survivors to ensure success. Vladimir Jabotinsky, breaking with Weizmann, created the Revisionist movement—so named because he conceived it to be a return to the principles of Theodor Herzl. Herzl, too, had dreamed of a dramatically sudden *creatio ex nihilo*—an international charter to the Jews, and rapid immigration under international law. There was opposition of quite another kind, headed in America by Justice Louis D. Brandeis, who believed that the time for Zionist teaching and propaganda was past, and the work was straightforward, a business-like affair. Thus, the movement split twice—in America, with Brandeis leading *his* dissident group (he did this through deputies after he was appointed to the Supreme Court), and in the world Zionist movement with Jabotinsky leading *his* group.

Through all this, Weizmann had to negotiate with statesmen and politicians as *the* leader of the Zionist movement. He did it by the force of his personality more than by the solidity of his immediate backing. We read today of Israel's representatives being received by this or that president or foreign minister, and accept it as natural, which of course it is. But there was no of course about it in Weizmann's case; without a state's bargaining power, or at least its acknowledged right to be heard, he had to rely, for his introduction, on his official status, which was constantly challenged. His personality had to do the rest. Nor was it simply his charm, adroitness, and sincerity that won him a respectful hearing; it was the weight he carried as the concentration of Jewish history. That was his effective backing.

VI

Working with him on his memoirs in the summer of 1947 was like reliving his life with him. He was in poor physical condition, but his mind was as vigorous and supple as ever, and it was amazing to hear him pour forth his recollections and reflections for an hour or an hour and a half at a time, in ordered paragraphs, with witty and pungent interpolations. I would take it all down verbatim on the typewriter, then we would go over it, pruning and mending, before I carried the material away for final polishing and retyping. When we came to some particularly murderous sideswipe at someone, I would ask: "You don't really want that to stay, Dr. Weizmann, or do you?" His face would light up. "No, Maur-r-rice, I think we can do a little p-r-runing." Then he might add, in Yiddish: "He was, to be sure, a *mamzer,* but that wasn't his fault." *Mamzer* (bastard) is figurative in Yiddish too, but it has a wider range than in English; it may imply grudging admiration of a clever rascal or semi-rascal, as well as detestation of a low, mean character. Weizmann would use it in either sense, or in an intermediary one, and the key to his feeling was the context and his voice. He would of course have softened or deleted these passages without my suggestion, but he liked to hear me pick them out. He had a great sense of public dignity and of the responsibility of his position; in private he allowed himself outbursts of petulance, and some of his remarks were cruel, and occasionally unjust.

He had suffered much from the enforced propinquity of men he disliked or despised but who were useful to the movement. He took it out on them in the first draft, but like a man writing an abusive letter which he knows he is not going to mail. Where he writes positively and affectionately of people, as he often does, he is genuine. There were many companionships and friendships which were a deep source of joy to him.

He indulged in another kind of private savagery in the first draft, directed at political opponents with unchallengeably honest motives. He would pour out his old resentments; the heat of long-since fought-out battles would return to his blood, and he would remember his frustrations. Then, the emotion having subsided, he would wink, adding: "He was—or is—a decent fellow, you know." His most derogatory noun for a man was monosyllabic, Yiddish, and obscene. His English, which he had learned in his thirties, was excellent, calling for few stylistic corrections. Most of the work lay in the rearrangement of the material. None of the merits of *Trial and Error* can be credited to me, and I feel free to say it is a remarkable work; but what a pity that no copy of the first draft exists.

When I think back to the circumstances under which he produced the greater part of the book, I marvel again at his will power, his reserves of energy, his flexibility, and his capacity to switch his concentrated attention from one task to another. He was, at the time, preparing the Jewish case for presentation to the UNSCOP—not merely his own address, but the general policy. He was also absorbed in the development of the Weizmann Institute of Science, which had begun three years earlier. There was a constant coming and going of men and delegations at the house. And if this were not enough for an ailing man, there was the terror which was being conducted against the British by a small, desperate group of men who held themselves accountable to no one but themselves, and a campaign of insane vilification against his person and leadership. Scurrilous leaflets accusing him of having sold out to the British, for money or honors, were circulated throughout the country; walls were daubed with denunciations of "Weizmann-Pétain"; and hardest for him to bear, there was the terror itself, blind, ferocious, and demoralizing.

Weizmann writes how he saw "here and there a relaxation of the old, traditional Zionist purity of ethics, a touch of militarism, and a weakness for its trappings; here and there something worse—the tragic, un-Jewish resort to terrorism, a perversion of the purely defensive function of Haganah [the national army, clandestine till 1948]; and worst of all, in certain circles, a readiness to compound with the evil, to condemn and not to condemn it, to treat it not as the thing it was, namely, an unmitigated curse to the National Home, but a phenomenon which might have its advantages."

The terrorists were a mixed lot: idealists whose minds had become unhinged by the multimillion extermination of Jews in Europe and the calculating, callous attitude of the British rulers of Palestine; adventurers with killer instincts in search of justifiable employment; morally disoriented youngsters. Their backers, in Palestine and America, were an equally mixed assortment; the most curious element among them consisted of Jews who had never before manifested the slightest interest in Jewish affairs and who, when the homeland had been established, reverted to their former indifference. Here too there was a wide range of characters, from the genuinely intellectual type like Arthur Koestler to the squalidly picaresque Hollywood type like Ben Hecht. They were fired suddenly by the idea of "the fighting Jew"; the thinking Jew, the building Jew, the Jew who had endured and come through with unscarred psyche was and is meaningless to them. They hated Weizmann, and their campaign against him has not come to an end with his death. The supporters of the terror, to whom history assigns no role in the creation of the Jewish state, still raise their voices from time to time, not to further the work that remains to be done, but—"noteless blots on a remembered name"—to vent their frustration in continued vilification of the greatest Jew of modern times.

VII

I return from this digression to the summer months of 1947. The two or three hours I spent daily with Weizmann were of course the smallest as well as the most enjoyable part of my labors. The collating, the excision of repetitions, the verifying of dates, and so on, took much longer. Some of this was mechanical, none of it was wholly dull, for throughout I was gripped by the unfolding of a fascinating record as dictated by the man who had lived it. What moved me most deeply I have referred to in one of my notes made at the time: "impressive consistency and persistence in his life's activity." The irrevocable commitment began in his childhood, and curious recurrences of theme confirm like echoes the unity of purpose, the straight line of destiny.

As a *cheder* boy in Pinsk, little Chaim Weizmann wrote a Hebrew letter to his *rebbe,* affirming his faith in the rebuilding of Zion and prophesying that England would play the major role in it. The letter might have been written by any imaginative youngster who had grown up in a Zionist home and who had heard his grandfather tell and retell how Sir Moses Montefiore (a legendary name among Jews), held in honor by the Queen of England, had come to Russia to try to alleviate the condition of Russian Jewry, and how the Jews of Vilna had unharnessed the horses and dragged the carriage in tumultuous procession through the streets of "the Jerusalem of Lithuania." By itself a moderately interesting childhood incident, the letter is, in conjunction with the man's development many years later, an extraordinary one. For Weizmann tells how, in 1913, having been denied at Manchester University an academic promotion he thought himself entitled to, he almost left England to become a professional Zionist in Berlin. He recounts:

Whether, left to my own counsel, I would actually have taken this step, I do not know. But it was my wife who put her foot down. She disliked Germany; so for that matter did I. I cannot help thinking she was guided by something more than personal considerations, either for herself or me. In any case, I shudder to think of the possible results if I had yielded to the importunity of my friends [in Berlin] and my own momentary impulse.

He tells also how, as a boy in Pinsk, he used to take part during the Purim holiday in the money-box collections for Palestine:

Purim always came in the midst of the March thaw, and hour after hour I would go tramping through the mud of Pinsk, from end to end of the town. I remember that my mother was accustomed, for reason of economy, to make my overcoats much too long for me, to allow for growth, so that as I went I repeatedly stumbled over the skirts and sometimes fell headlong into the icy slush of the streets. I worked late into the night, but usually had the satisfaction of bringing in more money than anyone else. Such was my apprenticeship for the activities which, on a rather larger scale, have occupied so many years of my later life.

"Rather larger scale" was British understatement, which Weizmann liked and employed effectively. The organized campaigns and "drives" of the later Zionist movement have dwarfed into insignificance the collections of thirty or forty years ago, when two or three million a year from American Jewry was the limit, but Weizmann in his day was the greatest individual mendicant in Jewish history and perhaps, considering the economic strata among which he did his main work, the greatest in all history. I asked him once what difference he had found between soliciting on the ten-kopeck and the ten-thousand-dollar levels. He answered that you heard the plea of poverty more frequently on the ten-thousand-dollar level. "It's usually after an elaborate dinner for twenty; you look around at the furnishings, the tapestries and the pictures, and you feel like returning the dinner—on the spot. When a poor man is mean he makes no bones about it; he slams the door in your face, a swift and painless operation. I can remember certain houses in Pinsk where I was regularly refused with: 'I've already given.' It was a lie, as we both knew, but it was a time- and energy-saver. I liked best the man who answered coolly: 'I don't give, I'm a swine that way.' I had no quarrel with him. The rich aren't straightforward, they keep you dangling, they make a pleasurable game of it, they like to see you with your tongue hanging out. And when they do give they make you sweat for it." But he had encountered much generosity among the rich, too, and remembered it gratefully.

His apprenticeship in this field of mendicancy served him well in another field, the political. In a sense he begged his way to the Jewish state at the doors of chancelleries. There too he knew what it meant to be kept dangling, with tongue hanging out, but there too he remembered with gratitude acts of generosity and understanding. He was contemptuous of Zionists who accused him of lack of firmness when there was nothing to be firm with. "They want me to go to Downing Street and bang on the table. I could get in, and I could bang on the table once, and that would be the end of it." He used to call Downing Street his *Via Dolorosa*.

To understand the consistency of his life, one must realize that he was not a Zionist by conviction any more than one is a human being by conviction. There was nothing else for him to be. Thus, whatever vicissitudes and changes he went through as a person, the Zionist idea worked in and through them. As a child in Motol, as a youth in Pinsk, as a student in Berlin and Geneva, as a chemistry teacher in Manchester, as director of a British admiralty laboratory in the First World War, he was Weizmann the Zionist. When he came to full leadership in the Zionist movement, he had passed through all the intermediary stages; the boy, the youth, the man had lived his essential life in preparation, at meetings, conferences, congresses, traveling, speaking to handfuls in tiny halls, speaking to large audiences, arguing with individuals.

He had greatness of personality as seen from within, as well as consistency of purpose. A narrow personality united with obsessional persistence and unflagging energy can achieve much. I have known such men; by their persistence and energy they become multiple until they are like a large island of coral-reef insects; they perform wonders by the sheer multiplicity of their small, relentless selves. Nor do I mean by "greatness of personality as seen from within" the power to fascinate, the imposing or stage-filling personality, which was developed to such a high degree in Weizmann, so that people were afraid to meet him lest they be swept off their feet. Lord Balfour, a friend and admirer of Weizmann's, hearing of an anti-Zionist who refused to meet Weizmann for that reason, called the man a coward. I would not wholly agree. The power to fascinate is sometimes nothing more than itself, like the technical ability to hypnotize which I have sometimes seen displayed by trivial and unworthy men, night-club performers for instance. Weizmann had obsessional persistence as well as the power to charm, almost to hypnotize, and these qualities helped to place him on the stage of world affairs. But I can think of him as essentially the same man without these qualities and without his external achievements.

From *Little Did I Know* (1963)

15 SHMARYA LEVIN AND CHAIM NACHMAN BIALIK

Among the men who stood close to Weizmann there were two whose influence on me was second only to his. They were, like him, products of the *shtetl,* but as different from him as they were from each other. One was Shmarya Levin, whose memory as a dazzling orator is cherished by a dwindling old-time Yiddish-speaking generation; the other was Chaim Nachman Bialik, whose poetry will be read as long as Hebrew lives.

Shmarya Levin was in America when I arrived in 1914, and whenever he made a public appearance I was in the front row. I followed his addresses with difficulty at first, then with increasing joy as I acquired intimacy with the language by dint of reading, of frequent visits to the Yiddish theater—those were the great days of Maurice Moskowitz and Jacob Adler—and of conversations with Uncle Berel. My first translations were of Levin's articles in the now long-defunct Yiddish daily, *Die Varheit.* In the Yiddish phrase, I served my barber's apprenticeship on his beard. Years later I translated his three-volume autobiography. From Levin I first learned that Zionism was something more than a nationalist-political movement or a philanthropic refugee undertaking; he introduced me to the philosophy of Ahad Ha-Am, whose disciple he was, together with Weizmann, and to the biblical, folkloristic, and spiritual roots of the movement. I have many reasons for remembering him with gratitude.

Levin was a man of great gifts and little discipline; he wasted much of his life at chess, and was the unfortunate kind of addict who plays poorly and hates to lose. Even I used to win a game from him now and again, and I might have won oftener if he had not had the habit of taking back moves—which he always did in a high state of indignation and resentment, as if some invisible and stupid *kibbitzer* had forced his hand. On my visits to Palestine in later years, I would always find him at the Café Vienna, in Jerusalem, absorbed in a game of chess. At Zionist congresses he sometimes had to be dragged away from the board almost forcibly to attend to serious business in the *plenum.* He played in what we call the *yeshiva* manner, accompanying his moves with audible singsong meditations on talmudic aphorisms. He confesses in his memoirs that two arts, as he called them, chess and smoking, played an altogether too important part in his life, adding that in both of them he reached his peak early and registered no advance with the passing years. I sympathized with Levin; I too am by nature indolent, but unlike him have become reconciled to the fact that you can't beat work for getting things done.

In appearance Levin suggested a stage Mephistopheles: he was tall and lean, with a long, dark, furrowed face, brilliant eyes, the right one with a strong outward cast, a small pointed beard, and something like horns—a peculiar growth of hair standing up at the corners of his temples. On the platform he dominated an audience by his appearance, his intensity of manner, and his brilliant oratory. His Yiddish was at once formal and racy, colorful with folk allusions and quotations from Bible, Talmud, and Midrash; when I translated him I had to go round many of the passages; their point depended so much on intramural intimacies, on exegesis, and tradition familiar only to *cheder* and *yeshiva* Jews. He made the Bible alive by finding in it parallels or contrasts with current affairs; for him, as for my people, the Bible covered all possible human situations.

It was a common practice to refer to the Russian Czar as Pharaoh, oppressor of the Jews, the only difference being that the Czar was willing to let them go. Like Pharaoh, said Levin, Nicholas II kept making promises and breaking them; he called a Duma and dissolved it, called another and dissolved it. "He promised and retracted, promised and retracted," said Levin, "till the Red Sea swallowed him up."

One of his most famous parallels went back to pre-World War I Zionist history. A number of wealthy Jews in Germany were ready to contribute toward the development of a technical school in Palestine (it has become the famous Haifa Technion, Israel's M.I.T.) as a purely philanthropic enterprise on condition that the language of instruction be German, not Hebrew. In this they were acting as patriotic Germans supporting Germany's imperialist *Drang nach Osten.*

Their spokesman was a Dr. Paul Nathan, head of the Union of German Citizens of the Jewish faith, an organization analogous to the American Council for Judaism today. Levin, denouncing him, made a great play on the David-Bathsheba story and the denunciation of David by the Prophet Nathan. He cited the parable of the rich man with many flocks and herds and the poor man with only one little ewe-lamb "which he had brought and nourished up, and it grew up together with him and his children; it did eat of his own meat, and drank of his own cup, and lay in his bosom, and was unto him as a daughter." "We have one little ewe-lamb of a school in Palestine," cried Levin, "and Germany has a thousand schools. Like the rich man who forebore to take of his own flock to entertain a visitor, Germany with her thousand schools wants to take away our one little school. But who is the villain of the story today? Not David, but the false prophet. Nathan, *thou art the man!"*

Levin had a biting wit, not always under control, and some of his sallies must have been costly to the Zionist movement—but how refreshing they were! He made his first visit to America in 1907, and in spite of his identification with Zionism was invited, as a Jewish celebrity, to the home of Jacob Schiff, the anti-Zionist philanthropist. The host, anxious to make his position clear, stated it in the following terms: "I want you all to know that I consist of three parts: I am an American, I am a German, and I am a Jew." Levin, asked to address the assembled guests, wanted to know how Mr. Schiff effected the division; was it perpendicularly or horizontally? And, if horizontally, which section did he allocate to the Jewish people? There were hopes that Schiff would some day become, if not a Zionist, at least a contributor to Palestinian charities, and Levin's question was not helpful.

Levin was on friendly terms with Julius Rosenwald, another famous philanthropist who, somewhat less violently anti-Zionist than Schiff, helped Levin in a publishing venture in Palestine, as a gesture toward Jewish culture, of course, and not, God forbid, to promote Zionism. Rosenwald twitted Levin: "The most I'll do for you in a personal way is to build myself a villa in Chicago and call it Tel Aviv." "You've got it upside down," said Levin. "We want you to build a villa in Tel Aviv and not call it Chicago."

There were many Jews who contributed to Palestine philanthropic funds while disclaiming any intention to promote the building of a Jewish homeland. It was not their fault, they argued, that Palestine happened to have Jews who needed help or offered a refuge for Jews who could not find a haven elsewhere. If in effect the Zionist cause was thereby promoted, let the Zionists bear the blame. Levin, whose humor often ran to ribaldry, likened these good-natured people to a man who sleeps with a woman out of sheer kindness and washes his hands of any unintended consequences; and, in less Rabelaisian vein, to an atheist who is outraged because the only place available to the victims of a flood happens to be a synagogue.

Of a very distinguished American rabbi whose activities were multifarious, Levin said: "He's a big man, as big as the Woolworth building, and if you look closely you'll see that he too is made up of nickels and dimes." His favorite Yiddish word for a fool was the same as Weizmann's, but Levin improved on it and coined the "yam-fool." Yam is Hebrew and Yiddish for "sea," and Levin explained that this variety of fool was not to be found on land; his habitat was the ocean deep, among the other primal monsters. Thenceforth, in Zionist circles, so-and-so was a yam, without the indelicate addition. Yam could also designate a low type of person. There was, many years ago, a Yiddish journalist writing under two names for a New York daily. That he was an anti-Zionist was the least of his defects; he was equally cynical, scurrilous, and boastful under both names. When Levin discovered that the two men were one, he was overjoyed. "Thank God! One yam fewer in the world."

Levin was an unhappy man, knowing that his impatience and his indolence, in both of which he differed so greatly from Weizmann, were harmful to himself and to the cause. He lacked also Weizmann's spontaneous liking for simple people. But in spite of these limitations he was a great popular force. He lifted Zionist exposition to a new plane, and he was loved by the masses because he never spoke down to them. I learned from him a principle of the utmost importance to a professional lecturer: you may assume that an audience is uninformed in your field, but never assume that it is stupid.

The lifelong friendship between Levin and Weizmann began in Berlin in the late eighteen-nineties. They were both members, though not at the same time, of the *Jüdisch-Russisch Wissenschaftliches Verein*, a Berlin group of students who long before the coming of Herzl were advocating the creation of a Jewish state. It was in effect a group of Zionist founding fathers, extraordinary men who dreamed the maddest of dreams; for if Zionism looked freakish and harebrained in the early nineteen-hundreds, what must it have looked like twenty years earlier? By 1914, when I became a Zionist, famous men like Max Nordau and Israel Zangwill had declared for the movement. Herzl had left his indelible stamp on it. The *Encyclopaedia Britannica* of 1911 devotes two whole pages to it—and, incidentally, not much more to Communism. There were dozens of Jewish colonies in Palestine. But in the eighteen-nineties there were only the faintest beginnings of colonization, and in the Western world the movement, which was not yet a movement but an obscure and formless, though powerful, folk agitation, must have looked correspondingly madder. Yet there they were, these Russian Jewish students, nearly all of them penniless, sublimely self-confident, sublimely sure of their historic mission, talking big, but big, about the Jewish state-to-be, about international diplomacy, the alignment of the powers, the buying off of Turkey. "Mad" must be taken literally here. When Theodor Herzl showed the manuscript of his *Judenstaat* ("The Jewish State"), the classic document of modern Zionism, to a friend, he was implored to seek medical treatment. No doubt, similar counsel was given to members of the *Jüdisch-Russisch Wissenschaftliches Verein.*

The brilliance of these men and their apparent normality outside their one obsession must have strengthened the suspicion of mental derangement. All of them were gifted in various fields. Herzl was political reporter for the *Wiener Neue Freie Presse,* the *Manchester Guardian* of Europe, attached to the French Chamber of Deputies. He was an engaging feuilletonist and playwright, a man of address and wide reading, the kind of man one calls *civilized,* until suddenly, one day . . . And so it was with Weizmann, Levin, and others. If you kept Levin on Russian politics, for instance, or German literature, you could listen for hours with profit; but if you should happen accidentally to touch on the Jewish problem—"Good heavens," you thought, "what a pity!" And in a sense these men were in fact *déraillés.* That many of them forfeited distinguished worldly careers was to be expected and is not to their discredit: but in their Zionist fervor they also neglected to follow a systematic training which would have enhanced their usefulness to the movement. The impracticality of the *shtetl* clung to many of them throughout their lives. Weizmann writes:

At first I was greatly overawed by my fellow-students, among whom I was the youngest. Fresh from little Pinsk, with its petty collections and small-town discussions, I was staggered by the sweep of vision which Motzkin and Syrkin and the others displayed. There was also a personal detail which oppressed me at the beginning. I was only a student of chemistry; they were students of philosophy, history, economy, law and other "higher" things. I was immensely attracted to them as persons and as Zionists; but gradually I began to feel that in their personal preparations for life they were as vague as in their Zionist plans. I had brought with me out of Russia a dread of the "eternal student" type, the impractical idealist without roots in the worldly struggle, a figure only too familiar in the Jewish world of forty and fifty years ago. I refused to neglect the lecture hall and the laboratory, to which I gave at least six or seven hours a day. I acquired a taste for research work. In later years I understood that even deeper motives impelled me in those days to attend strictly to the question of my personal equipment for the life-struggle.

The deeper motives which underlay Weizmann's systematic approach to his life problem were connected in part with those characteristics which turned him into an able scientist; in part they were connected with his belief in himself, only tacit at the beginning, as a "man of destiny." The Weizmann archives in Rehovoth reveal how early Weizmann began to keep copious records and copies of correspondence. He probably did not foresee that they would some day be historical documents; he did not foresee, of course, that he would be the first president of the Jewish state; he was only obeying an impulse, but the "deeper motives" were already there.

There was no such subconscious *arrière pensée* in Levin's makeup. Not that he was without ambition or suffered from modesty; and he was as organically committed to Zionism as Weizmann, and was equally convinced of the inevitability of a Jewish state. I doubt whether the sharpest insight would have picked out the superior figure between these two Berlin Russian-Jewish students; but Weizmann became a world figure, while Levin's reputation is confined to the Jewish people, and even among them he is being forgotten. There was a time when he was better known than Weizmann, and not just because he was a few years older. He was a member of the Russian Duma when Weizmann was a struggling chemistry teacher in Manchester; he attracted large audiences in Europe and America. But his achievements came by fits and starts, not only because of his laziness but because his high opinion of himself was not geared to greatness. Every movement knows such men, gifted, useful, devoted, but lacking in a kind of inexorability. They don't "take hold" of history, they are not predestined leaders, their impact on people fails somewhere. Levin was admired or disliked; Weizmann had his fanatical followers and his fanatical enemies.

The third of my teachers in Zionism and Jewishness, the poet Chaim Nachman Bialik, began to mold my thinking some years before I met him in person. When I had mastered Yiddish in America, I turned again to the poem Wassilevsky had read to me in Manchester —Bialik's own translation of his Hebrew *City of Slaughter*, a bitter cry of outrage and despair wrung from him by the Kishinev pogrom of

1903. Later, when my Hebrew was good enough, I translated some of his poems from the original, and the Zionist Organization issued a small volume of my translations in 1926, on the occasion of Bialik's first visit to America. It was then that I got to know him in person. Still later I saw much of him in Palestine, especially when I lived two doors from his house on the street named after him.

I have not met or read of a poet who looked and talked less like one than Bialik. He had the round face of a clever moujik, and the build of a medium-sized but hefty butcher. He must have had in him the blood of Khazars, the medieval Tartar converts to Judaism. From his appearance you expected sound, pithy, earthy conversation, and you were not disappointed. You also expected him to be a good businessman, and he was. He had run a large and successful printing plant, first in Odessa, then, after the Bolshevik revolution, in Berlin, and finally in Tel Aviv. He was completely without literary affectation; but when you got him on to the subject of books he blazed into unquenchable enthusiasm. His Jewish erudition was enormous, and he was widely read in other literatures. Once launched, he was not to be stopped, and one listened fascinated by the range of his knowledge and the luminousness of his observations; and still, never a hint that he was a poet of the first magnitude, with few equals in the modern world and none at all in Hebrew since the time of Judah Halevi nearly a thousand years ago.

Shmarya Levin was his partner in the publishing house of Moriah, which issued a standard set of the Hebrew classics, edited by Bialik. To be in their company when the conversation veered from business to literature was a fearsome and unforgettable experience; one got a living illustration of the riddle of the immovable body and the irresistible force, for both of them were enthusiasts and tremendous talkers. One of them would be off on a streak, the other interjecting desperately every minute or two: "But let me say . . ." only to meet the ferocious response: "Don't interrupt!" The torrent continued till the speaker, pausing to catch his breath, would suddenly find himself on the outside, vainly interjecting in his turn: "But let me say . . ." The bystander, of course, didn't have a chance and didn't want one. Levin revered Bialik as one reveres a prophet, but the compulsive talker is not his own master.

In company there was a perpetual good humor about Bialik which was utterly incomprehensible when one remembered certain of his poems which could only have issued from a deeply tormented soul. In his 1926 visit to America I traveled with him to several cities where he addressed audiences in Yiddish, I in English. I was prepared, when we set out, to have a moody genius on my hands, and I braced myself for an exercise in tactfulness and understanding. It was, instead, a jolly experience. He was fascinated by the American scene, general and Jewish, and his observations, usually directed at the contrast between America and Jewish Palestine, were ingenious. I showed him, as a typically American product, a copy of *The Saturday Evening Post,* which sold for a nickel in those days. It consisted of two hundred pages, more than half of them advertising. He said: "In opulent America the problem of a magazine is: how low can we price it without losing our advertising value? In poor Palestine it is: how high can we price it without losing our readers?" "I've noticed," he once remarked, "that here in America you say: 'It's so many hours from this place to that.' The land is so big that distance loses its meaning. In little Palestine we speak of kilometers; every one of them counts." He was vastly amused when he listened to my English addresses; he understood not a word of them, but every now and again his name would bob up, and it sounded to him like: "Mumble-jumble-bumble—BIALIK—mumble-jumble-bumble —CHAIM NACHMAN BIALIK—mumble-jumble-bumble . . ." As the distinguished visitor, he always spoke after me, and he would comment in various ways on his impressions. "I have just heard my friend Samuel conducting me through long and lightless corridors. . . . I felt like a cat in a sack being beaten from time to time. . . . I felt like a swimmer on a stormy sea; now and again I came up for air, most of the time I was drowning." He had a quick eye for comical situations. I once came across him, during an all-night session of a Zionist congress, contemplating with fascination a fat delegate who had jammed himself into an armchair in the lobby and had fallen asleep. Bialik pointed at him and murmured in my ear: "A chairful of Jew."

There was no clue in his personal bearing to the misery and destitution of his childhood and boyhood. Weizmann and Levin had been born into what by *shtetl* standards were well-to-do homes. They had never known real privation of any kind, and they had been immersed in warm and happy families. Bialik was born into grinding poverty, and at the age of seven he had been sent away to live with a stern, pious, and scholarly grandfather so that his mother would have one mouth less to feed. His earliest memories were of a wretched inn kept by his sensitive father for peasants whose rude and boisterous ways he could not endure. The inn failed and the family moved to the outskirts of Zhitomir, where his father tried his hand at various occupations, never with success, so that one by one

the household possessions were sold, down to the family candlesticks
—that last symbol of Jewish respectability and piety—and the
mother had to make the Sabbath eve benediction over candles stuck
into clay. Then the father died, and the mother peddled fruit and
vegetables from door to door to feed herself and her seven children.
In the nights she mended their garments and one night a week she
baked bread for them; and as she kneaded the dough and implored
God to help her feed her little ones, she wept into the dough, so that
as Bialik tells, her children literally swallowed her tears.

A cycle of Bialik's poems is dedicated to these oppressive memories. In one he asks:

> Would you know
> From whom I have my heritage of song?
> A singer settled in my father's house,
> A humble, lonely soul who hid in corners,
> And comforted his frailty in the shadows.
> He had one song, and only one, to sing,
> The same words always, set to the same tune.
> And when my heart was frozen into silence,
> My tongue hard-cleaving to my throbbing palate,
> My stomach empty, and my cry choked back
> By my unyielding throat, his song would wake me.
> He was the cricket, minstrel of poverty.

If you knew nothing of the man's history, you would declare
from this and the other poems in the cycle that childhood misery
had set its stamp on him—were it not for another cycle in which he
celebrates the life of the Jewish village with such charm and gaiety
that you are ready to declare: "No, *this* is the experience, the other
is painful imagination and empathy." In the end, unable to reconcile the authenticity of the two extremes, you give up the quest for
"internal evidence." Equally irresoluble is the contradiction in his
attitude toward the disciplines and sacrifices of the classical talmudic education: in one place a lyrical glorification of the Jewish
will to learning and its meaning for the preservation of the people,
in another a cry of lamentation for the cruelty and waste of it. He
sounds these opposite notes in his poem, *Ha-Matmid,* in which he
describes the life of the dedicated young Talmud student, who is
fastened to his books as the Cossack is fastened to his horse in
wartime.

But the battle is one of self-conquest, and it is not fought out
under the open sky, but in a dim, candle-lit corner of a musty *yeshiva.*
Of the day's four quarters, three are given to combat, one to the

body's needs—brief sleep and meager rations. Outside, the fields are magic with summer green or winter white; the boy's eyes are fixed on the ancient text. A seductive wind steals in through the window; he does not even feel it lifting his earlocks.

> An eremite whose corner is his cave!
> With pallid face tight-drawn and puckered brows
> He keeps his incommunicable watch.
> And in the Talmud under him his soul
> Is lost and locked, forever and forever . . .
> Granite is yielding clay compared with him,
> A Jewish boy unto the Torah vowed.

There are other students in the Academy, each devoted in his degree, but he is the *matmid,* the fanatic of learning. Hunger and thirst and aching eyes have no power over him. If his mind wanders a moment from the text, it is to glance at the glory of great scholars shining across the centuries of the Jewish past, to remember how

> in the chastity of poverty
> The people and its sons have kept the faith . . .
> He tastes the prize
> He pays for with the gold of youthful days.

Is the victory worth the sacrifice? Bialik, himself once a *matmid* in the *yeshiva* of Zhitomir, stares back into the past and his mind becomes clouded.

> I in my boyhood was a listener
> Among those voices, and my youth was passed
> With those wan sufferers whose wrinkled brows
> And staring eyes implore the world's compassion.
> And every wrinkle spoke to me in silence
> Of passions stifled and of fires extinguished . . .
> My fate denied I should be lost with you,
> Unhappy ones! and to the hearth you knew
> Long, long ago I said my last farewell . . .
> The times are changed; far from your boundaries
> In alien places have I raised my altar . . .
> All, all of you do I remember still—
> The hungry childhood and the bitter manhood,
> And my heart weeps for my unhappy people . . .
> How burned, how blasted must our portion be
> If seed like this must wither in its soil.

Once again, the ambivalence of the Jew, here expressing itself in acceptance and denial of his traditional values. It is as though the poet were involved in a love which he recognizes as the source of his strength but knows to be destructive. Sometimes the love is on the intellectual level, as in this poem, sometimes on the homely level, as in his bewitching *Songs of the People.*

In all these qualities, and by virtue of his mastery of language, Bialik surpasses every contemporary in verse or prose, but they do not exhaust his greatness and complexity. One aspect of him introduces a second duality. This product of the *shtetl* detaches himself completely from his time and place in a great Miltonic poem, *The Dead of the Wilderness.* The subject is drawn from a midrashic legend which tells that the Jews who left Egypt with Moses and were condemned to perish in the desert rose in rebellion and tried to storm their way into the Promised Land against the divine decree. They were thrown back and cast into a deep slumber from which they awaken periodically and renew the attempt, again to be cast into slumber. Between the spasms of fury their gigantic bodies lie in disorder on the burning sands, the black rocks surrounding them, the hot sun beating down on their matted and monstrous faces, on the weapons paralyzed in their clenched fists, on their silent tents. It is a universal poem of man's refusal to accept the decree of fate, and the splendor of the imagery matches the grandeur of the theme.

The scenic descriptions are overwhelmingly powerful. Those who have read *The Dead of the Wilderness* and have looked on the desolation of the Sinai peninsula are filled with wonder at the evocative imagination of a ghetto Jew who had hardly strayed outside the limits of his world; he has caught the primal terror of the desert as if he had been its prisoner for many years, as if his soul had been recast by it. I once asked Bialik how these images had come to him. He said: "Outside my father's inn there was a little hill. I used to lie on it face down, thinking myself into the desert."

Bialik spurred me to the learning of Hebrew as Levin did to the learning of Yiddish; nevertheless, Bialik was a greater master of Yiddish than Levin. He could do in poetry what Sholom Aleichem did in prose—portray the lovableness of the ordinary human being; but he also had powers beyond the reach of Sholom Aleichem—a nobility of style which at one time I thought alien to the spirit of this folk language. There is much talk today of the decline and approaching death of Yiddish; it is, I think, exaggerated; but whenever I hear it I think with a pang of the lovelinesses that must be locked away forever in forgotten languages.

From *Little Did I Know* (1963)

16 MEIR OF KIKKLE

For me to write of Meyer Weisgal is to anticipate a considerable slice of my autobiography. Of the years which an irresponsible Providence has thus far allotted me, more than two-thirds echo with Meyer's presence, sometimes in close proximity, sometimes in geographic separation, but never completely suspended. His was the first friendship I formed when I arrived in America in 1914; it will under any circumstances remain the longest, for even if we were to decide to terminate it tomorrow I should no longer have the time to set up another record.

"Meir of Kikkle." The formal and *goyish* spelling is Kikol, which to me is without taste or association. I stand by the Yiddishized and therefore proper pronunciation; and the credit line should read: "By Moishe of Macin." Kikkle, a village in Poland, Macin a village in Rumania; Meyer and I, born within a few months of each other in our respective places, are two brands plucked from the burning.

I got to know him in the office of the American Zionist Federation, as it was then called, and, before long, I was a frequent visitor in his home.

The Weisgal family and the Zionist Organization were two fascinating national phenomena. The latter was undoubtedly the larger; but the Weisgal family was magnified in the visitor's imagination by the ferocious energy of its members, noisy, affectionate, quarrelsome, loyal—a tribal hullabaloo in which no personality was repressed; and there was no lack of personalities. Meyer's father was a cantor, red-bearded, scholarly, hot-tempered, quick-witted, a passionate lover of music, given to interweaving the traditional synagogue melodies with operatic arias. He had carried on an unrelenting struggle to provide for his enormous brood, of which I never got the correct count. His wife, Meyer's stepmother and first cousin, was much younger than her husband, and belonged in certain respects to another world. She was free-thinking, radical, and revolutionary, but also Zionist through and through. By the time I came on the scene the struggle for a livelihood had eased a little, for Meyer and his older brothers were already contributing to the family budget. Of some of his brothers Meyer says that he was their inferior in mental equipment; however, he was the only one of his generation to overcome the economic handicap and, by fierce persistence, to find for his gifts the scope to which they were entitled.

I make a special point of the atmosphere of that home. It was the queer mixture of group formlessness and high-level individualism characteristic of ghetto life. There was in it the vivacity of Catfish Row shot through with the cultural demands of the Jewish tradition. I, too, grew up in such an environment, but with the difference that the standards of our Jewish knowledge were much lower. What moves me to everlasting wonder is the revelation of unsuspected forces and potentialities which Meyer among others represents.

It is easy to think of a ghetto Jew, subject since childhood to intellectual compulsions, entering a university and distinguishing himself in mathematics, medicine, biology, or physics. It is not at all easy to understand the one-generation leap from ghetto other-worldliness to the mastery of modern worldly form and action.

The riddle is of course general. How did Jews set up in one generation a state which can be a helpful guide to other little states new-hatched after the Second World War? Where did we pick up the practice—not merely the theory—of parliamentary government? How did we create an army whose Sinai campaign is studied with interest and profit by graduates of West Point, Sandhurst, and St. Cyr? "Jews learn quickly!" But that is no answer, for the real question is: Why are they quick learners? Or, more correctly: Why do they make the impression not so much of learning as of recalling?

I return to Meyer. As long as I have known him he has had an unusual sense of form. I mean, among other things, that he took in at once the shape of a situation or enterprise and acted out of the awareness of its totality. In the early days it might be a parochial affair like the Ha-Shachar Zionist Society of the Bronx, in which we were fellow-members. Meyer was entrepreneur and orchestrator; he concocted schemes and put them into effect; he knew what roles to

assign to whom, and forefelt the general effect. I recited poems and
played the mandolin. The basic distinction between our contributions to Zionism has remained to this day.

Or it might be in his earliest ventures in publications. A magazine, whether it was *The Maccabean* or *The New Palestine,* was not to him
simply a collection of timely articles and news items. From the beginning, even as an office boy, he reacted with instinctive editorial and
national-political flair; these and these were the needed features,
such and such ought to be the arrangement, this and no other had
to be the size, the type, the format. And all of it integrated with his
conception of the larger needs of the movement. As the years passed
his conceptions acquired a boldness which often intimidated his
superiors. His imagination, playing about his prevision of the completed enterprise and its effects, outran committee resolutions and
budgetary apprehensions. A subordinate, he led in action. I continued to write articles; I gave lectures; I graduated into books; there
it has stopped.

As long as I was myself an employee of the Zionist Organization
I was able to watch at firsthand how often Meyer outmaneuvered the
majority of his official superiors to give the right sweep and content
to an undertaking on the final success of which *they* were later to
preen themselves. He was always in hot water—his native element,
by the way—with regard to *The New Palestine.* Except for Louis Lipsky
and one or two others, the members of the executive committee, or
whatever it was then called, hadn't the foggiest notion what a publication ought to do for a movement beyond appearing regularly and
more or less unobtrusively. I remember one excellent Zionist, a clothing manufacturer, who came one day into Meyer's office with a pair
of scissors, a tapemeasure, and pins, and gave him a practical illustration on the cutting down of publication costs. Meyer made a valiant,
voluble, and vain attempt to explain that though he was unconscious
of expense he was particularly conscious of being in the service of a
dynamic, historic movement.

And this again is a facet of his sense of form as the chief directive
in his drive to action. When the Hebrew University was dedicated in
1925, the average good editor of a Zionist publication would have
been content with some special articles and a dignified editorial.
Meyer, alert to the fact that the way news is presented itself makes
news and inspires action, aware also that the majority of the Jewish
people, and even of the readers of *The New Palestine,* would not, without the right prompting, respond to anything like the real significance

of the occasion, expanded an issue of *The New Palestine* to *twenty times its regular size*—i.e., to some five hundred pages! He called on every writer and leader in Zionism and Judaism, in every part of the world, on non-Jewish statesmen, educators, men of letters, on prominent journalists and public figures generally. To me he assigned the task of making the first English translation of Bialik's *Ha-Matmid.* That Hebrew University issue of *The New Palestine* was an event! It echoed through the country, and the reverberations still continue in the minds of oldtimers. It has a place in the history of American Zionist education. So has his three-hundred-page Herzl memorial issue of *The New Palestine,* marking the twenty-fifth anniversary of the leader's death. It lies before me, and I cull a few of the names of the contributors: Chaim Weizmann, Georges Clemenceau, Israel Zangwill, Martin Buber, Paul Painlevé, Ferdinand I of Bulgaria. . . . Meyer ransacked the world for tributes, appreciations and memoirs. To me he assigned the task of making the first English digest of Herzl's diaries.

I dwell on these events of long ago—they are separated from us by a difference in the tone of Jewish life more difficult to bridge than the mere gap of years—because they illustrate the continuity of Meyer's public craftsmanship; also because, known as they are only to the older generation, they should be remembered (together with so much more out of the past) for the sake of proportion and perspective. Our contemporaneous successes are rooted in the labor of generations. Also, the pioneers of Zionism who remained in the Diaspora were in some ways as courageous as those who took the more arduous path to the land itself. This is rarely appreciated in a generation which so tacitly accepts the Jewish state that to be pro-Israel is the most comfortable of public postures. But it is also difficult to appreciate the extent to which, even among Zionists, the readiness to belong to an almost ostracized minority, the loyalty to a ridiculed ideal, was, in those days, unaccompanied by imaginative action. I did not at the time, I do not now, regard as anything but madness Nordau's plan, born soon after 1917, to throw half a million Jews into Palestine at once and let things take their course. I have seldom sympathized with the extreme proposals of the Revisionists. It was within the Weizmannian concept of paced creativity that we fell short; and it was here that Meyer and a handful of others were goads and inspirations.

I glance along the foreshortened perspective of the years, I pick out a few of the functions Meyer filled, a few of the enterprises with which his name is connected. Of the latter I can say with complete assurance that some of them would never have been carried out without him. There would certainly have been a *New Palestine* without Meyer, and Lipsky's pen would have ensured it a high distinction; but without Meyer's furious energy we would certainly never have had the magnificent special issues; nor would the continuity of high quality have been safe. Meyer was to *The New Palestine* what Harold Ross was to *The New Yorker*. We would not have had a Palestine Pavilion at the 1939 World's Fair in New York without Meyer; and certainly it would not have been half the moral and educational success that it was. Without him we would not have had *The Romance of a People* pageant at the Chicago World's Fair of 1933, or, in 1936, *The Eternal Road,* that memorable spectacle play which Meyer conjured up outside the Zionist agencies as a superb piece of Zionist propaganda. Finally, there would have been no Weizmann Institute and no Yad Weizmann without Meyer; to this last I revert below—it is a chapter in itself.

To all of these enterprises Meyer brought a compulsive craftsmanship which cannot tolerate the second best. If we were to be represented at all at the Chicago World's Fair it had to be memorably; it had to be a majestic spectacle which twice filled to overflowing the 100,000 capacity of Soldier's Field and then was clamored for throughout the country. Nor must it for a moment be supposed that the appeal was based on mob values, on a vulgar lowering of standards. And if Meyer was to produce a Zionist spectacle play, *The Eternal Road,* Max Reinhardt had to be the director, Kurt Weill the composer, Norman Bel Geddes the designer, Franz Werfel the playwright.

Whatever a man creates, enemies are always a by-product. Even an Albert Schweitzer, whose saintliness should make an exception of him, is hated by some because "he lowers the revolutionary potential of black Africa by diminishing its hatred of the whites." Meyer confesses, perhaps not penitently enough, to a minimal endowment of saintliness. He has often had to carry through his plans in the face of inertia and timidity; he has had to bully, outshout and outswear as well as cajole and convince; if he had daring, he also had to have *chutzpah,* and there are some who concentrate their attention on his *chutzpah* because they are insensitive to his daring. And of course there is always the inevitable accompaniment of envy, which usually expresses itself in the baffled explanation: "Who? Meyer Weisgal? Why, I remember him when he was a nobody." Certainly Meyer has made enemies; but the volume and quality of his work are evidence enough that he has enlisted the cooperation, affection and admiration of a far greater number of friends.

That very phrase, "I remember him when he was a nobody," in a way expresses my view of him. He was never a nobody; he was, however, a ghetto child in Kikkle, and a ghetto youngster in Chicago and New York. He was a ghetto youth when we used to read Shakespeare together in his tumultuous home on semi-slum Brooks Avenue in the lower Bronx. Where, then, I ask again, did he acquire, I don't say the energy, the rage to do, which can erupt anywhere, but the organizational skill, which is another aspect of the sense of form?

I hear the reader say: "Why this special bewilderment? Whether it be on Meyer Weisgal's level, or above, or below, Jews have always caught on fast, or, if you prefer, have revived dormant aptitudes overnight. You cite Israel's parliamentary adaptability; have you forgotten Disraeli?" There is a crucial difference which is at the heart of the puzzle; the ability shown by assimilated Jews in the grasping and applying of the forms of the non-Jewish world is one thing; the ability of non-assimilating Jews to give modern form and effectiveness to the Jewish enterprise *within* the Jewish world is quite another. *There* the machinery of action, social and psychological, waits for the newcomer; *here* the existing machinery is of a different order, developed over the centuries, not for the creation and promotion of a state, but for the survival of a folk in adversity.

Meyer, like his revered teacher Chaim Weizmann, has been an assimilationist in reverse. He has reached out to non-Jewish form, drawn it in, and made it serve the Jewish organism. This is, if you like, one of the facets of the Zionist revolution; and that Meyer should have capped his life's work with the creation of the Weizmann Institute of Science and the Yad Weizmann is in itself an illustration of my thesis.

I shall perhaps be criticized for this last statement. I wish therefore to make myself clear. It would be absurd as well as ungracious to say that the sole credit for the Weizmann Institute belongs to Meyer, for it would certainly never have come into being without the continuous devotion of a host of collaborators. But it cannot be said of any single one of them that he was indispensable. Meyer was. Weizmann tells us in his memoirs how, on his seventieth birthday a group of his American friends "conceived a more ambitious project" than the Sieff Institute, which until that time—1944—had been Weizmann's special scientific enterprise in the Yishuv. He mentions, among others, Dewey Stone, Harry Levine, Albert K. Epstein, Benjamin Harris, Lewis Ruskin, Edmund I. Kaufmann, Sam Zachs; they had in mind "a scientific center which would embrace not only organic chemistry, but physical chemistry and other branches." Weizmann then adds: "Under the energetic guidance of my friend Meyer W. Weisgal this large project moved forward very rapidly."

Well, then, I undertake to record, for Zionist and Israeli history, the substance of my personal observation to the following effect: The "energetic guidance" Weizmann refers to was in fact the power source of the enterprise—a combination of persistence, inspiration, and demonic energy; and the Institute would never have attained its present proportions but for Meyer's visionary gift and his relentless drive.

When the idea was first broached Weizmann was already in physical decline, but his subtle and wide-ranging intellect was as unaffected as that famous charm which was the delight of his followers and the despair of his opponents. And when I worked with him three years later, through the summer of 1947, on the drafting of Book Two of his memoirs and the revision of the entire manuscript, his capacity for the organization of a large mass of material had the naturalness of a man in his prime. He was able, at our appointed hours, to eject from his attention the manifold urgent problems weighing on him at the time, and to resume dictation and discussion as if nothing of importance had intervened since our last session.

It is proper, also, to recall the circumstances. The United Nations Special Commission on Palestine (UNSCOP) was then at work in the country, and its work was of life and death importance for us. Every major witness consulted Weizmann on the material he would submit and the stand he would take; and the climax of the hearings would be the appearance of Weizmann himself. He devoted infinite care to the preparation of his long opening statement; and, as his eyesight was failing, a vexing problem arose as to how he would read it. Meyer solved the problem by staying up the whole night preceding the hearing and getting the statement printed in letters half an inch high. Weizmann's alternative solution was more radical; when he was escorted to the platform he threw away the sheets and spoke extemporaneously with unforgettable effect.

It was in the midst of these preoccupations and excitements that Meyer drove forward with the development of the Institute. Parenthetically, it was in the midst of them that Weizmann continued the setting down of his memoirs, and it is not out of place to quote from the brief acknowledgment which precedes them: "To my friend Meyer Weisgal but for whose insistent prodding and continuous help this task might still be awaiting completion." The fact is, as I can testify, that Weizmann did not enjoy writing about himself. He had too much of a sense of history to be unaware of his place in Zionism, and too much of a sense of humor to make his own public statement of it. Meyer's "prodding" and "continuous help" embraced more than a decade of filial nagging—Meyer can be a terrible taskmaster to his superiors—and of organizing the opportunities and the occasions. What Weizmann set down in 1947 could, with equal accuracy, be dated 1960; without Meyer, "this task might still be awaiting completion." And as regards the Institute, "the ambitious project" conceived by Weizmann's American friends, came too late in Weizmann's life for him to provide, among his many other responsibilities, the sheer physical attention it called for; too late, also, for him to witness its completion. He was, almost to the end, its tutelary genius, watching, cautioning, directing, infusing into every addition his high scientific spirit. The demi-urge, if I may so put it, was Meyer.

As we have seen, the original concept was fairly modest. Weizmann envisaged some important additions to the valuable Sieff Institute. He could not, at his age, carrying the burdens of office and of moral responsibility, contract as it were for a great foundation of international stature. If he had visions of that kind he kept them to himself. He was a disciple of the tanna who counseled, "Do much and say little," and to Meyer he once wrote, "Make molehills out of mountains." During my sustained contact with him in 1947, as well as before and after, I do not remember that he ever expressed the hope of having (I do not speak of seeing in his lifetime) the Weizmann Institute take on the dimensions at which it has since arrived.

I do remember, however, to what extent he relied on Meyer as his right-hand man. In 1944 Meyer was in his fiftieth year. He had done an enormous amount of work, and, whether within or outside the national agencies, it had always been in furtherance of the movement. But in spite of his many individual achievements there was nothing permanently visible and tangible to show, refer to, look at. He had scattered himself too widely and was apparently headed for the fate of many another valuable servant of Zionism—an inevitable as well as honorable fate—which is, to become part of the anonymous process, identified only as long as his contemporaries are about, consigned thereafter to footnotes in antiquarian articles. His work for the time being was still important—we used to call him the Colonel House or Harry Hopkins of Dr. Weizmann—but it seemed unlikely that his usefulness would long outlive his chief. We could not guess that it was only now, as he was entering his sixth decade, that he had found the role which was to give him an enduring niche in the history of Israel.

Meyer may not have guessed it, either; nevertheless, his inner response to the idea of the Weizmann Institute was something like: "This is it!" This was what he had been waiting and preparing for. But if he did not quite guess what he meant, neither, as I have said, did his friends. That he would become the tireless advocate of the Institute, its principal money-raiser, its outside key man, was of course expected; but that he would become the chief architect of the vast enterprise, carrying on with undiminished usefulness after the death of the master, was not.

Of formal schooling in science Meyer had had a little less than nothing; one could only say that there had always been about him a suggestion of the possibilities of atomic energy. But his intuitions were on the alert, and it is certain that his worship of Weizmann—just about this side of idolatry—made him especially susceptible to Weizmann's expressed or tacit dreams. Myself not a scientist, I am not competent to speak on the subject of the layman as director of a scientific institute. I can only speak of this specific instance, which has been under my observation from the beginning, and I am moved and confounded by Meyer's triumphant fulfillment of a commitment with which no one would *a priori* have entrusted him. I must confess, too, that even now I would hesitate to voice this personal estimate, however firmly I might hold to it, if it were not for the reputation he has won for himself with the scientific as well as the general public.

If I had been asked by Dr. Weizmann—fortunately he never sought my advice, neither did Meyer nor anyone else—about Meyer's qualifications, I would have listed the following: imagination; an abnormal capacity for sheer exertion, accompanied by an abnormal incapacity for being discouraged; an unshakable loyalty; a nose, which, to be sure, could mislead him occasionally, for the right men; and, above all, a feeling for form. I would have gone on to say that he was the best choice in sight for what we call, in the cant of Madison Avenue, "the public relations" side of the project; he would never vulgarize its significance; he would smell out the most unlikely prospects for its support and convert them into reliable assets; he would present the Institute at large to the general public exactly as the fastidious and demanding Weizmann would have done. He would also maintain, as he has done, a lively and participating interest in many other phases of Israel's development, and this would all be to the good. Having thus delivered myself I would have gone on with all the emphasis at my command: "Yes, the best man—on one condition: *keep him away from the scientists.* One must allow, I suppose, for an irreducible minimum of social contact; but in the planning of the buildings, the layout of the grounds, the calling of conferences, the invitations to scientists, either as permanent acquisitions or as participants in the conferences, for God's sake see that Meyer is completely eliminated. He'll rub those men the wrong way; he'll irritate and frustrate them; his artistic temperament, his ebullience, his high spirits, all those assets which have served his sense of form in the world of the Jewish humanities will become fatal handicaps in the scientific world."

Thus I would have pontificated; and I would have been as wrong in the conclusion as I was right in the preamble. It is with the scientists that Meyer has got along best—and not simply by keeping away. I have known several centers of learning and been friendly with numbers of university teachers. Everywhere I have found a certain amount of quarrelling, criticism, resentment, frustration, centering on the executive head. In Rehovoth it is at a minimum; and among the very distinguished visitors who have come for brief stretches, Meyer stands, thirteen years after Weizmann's death, as high as any administrative layman as I have ever heard academicians speak of. He has demonstrated a marvelous instinct for directing without interfering; and I attribute the happy relationship between him and the scientists to several related factors: an immense respect for the men and women he deals with; a resulting willingness to accommodate himself to their plans and hopes; a warm sympathy for the human side of scientists, their problems of personal adjustment and of academic ambition; an innate sensitivity to the relative capacities of men and a consequent ability to weigh conflicting programs; and, finally, imbibed from Weizmann, an appreciation of the fundamental dignity and inviolability of the scientific purpose.

It has been a curious experience to watch, over half a century, the evolution of Meir of Kikkle into the somewhat formidable person of the last paragraph. When I draw away from the personal relationship, I see him as a folk phenomenon, the representative of the hundreds of Kikkles which have been leveled with the dust and the thousands of Meyers who have gone up literally in smoke. Then, calling to mind the incalculable energies and abilities of which we have been brutally, senselessly robbed, I am filled with ever greater astonishment at what we have managed to achieve with the remnant. If we only had our six millions today! But that would have made it too easy.

From *Meyer Weisgal at Seventy: An Anthology*
(London, 1966)

part five

The *maggid* of Eastern Europe was an itinerant preacher, a member of a company of "fabulists and moralists"—the phrase is Maurice Samuel's—who traveled throughout the Jewish communities of the land exhorting, excoriating, but above all educating. Samuel himself can be regarded as a latter-day *maggid,* not only because he too was a traveling lecturer—indeed, in his time he was the most popular platform personality of American Jewry—but also because he was so quintessentially a teacher, in his writings as well as his lectures. His subject was the Jewish heritage in all its ramifications, and he was an incomparable instructor, as the following selections from his vast *"maggidic"* output demonstrate.

TRANSMITTING JEWISH VALUES

17 THE MAGGID

The first time a chairman, thanking me at the end of a lecture, made use of the kindly formula: "May he be spared many years to carry on the good work," I nearly laughed out aloud. I took it he was confusing me with another lecturer, as chairmen sometimes do. I glanced over the audience—not a smile anywhere. The absurdity of it! Why, only yesterday they had been using the other formula: "This brilliant young man . . ." Then it occurred to me that I had been addressing audiences for over half a century.

I see myself as one of the *maggidim,* the wandering preachers of East European Jewry, and my line of descent is through Shmarya Levin, himself a modernized version of the tradition. My lecture subjects are drawn mostly from books I have written on Jewish themes and books I intend to write, and, as I have indicated, I do not pretend to be merely a purveyor of information. I have an axe to grind. My general objective in lecturing, as in writing, is to help Jews acquire an interest in Jewish knowledge with the hope that they will transmit it to their children, though, with the recent improvement in Jewish youth education, the children sometimes know more than the parents, and then it is a question of encouraging the parents at least to keep up with their children. Where the interest already exists, I cater to it. My theory of Zionist propaganda is that the more a Jew knows of his people's cultural and spiritual heritage the more likely he is to be a Zionist.

It took me many years to create a market for my lectures. I had to educate audiences to like the kind of education I offered. I was told that I was too highbrow, but the curious thing was that I never heard from the people I was too highbrow for. It was always: "As far as I'm concerned, you understand, it was wonderful. I enjoy an intellectual talk; but everybody isn't like you and me." Actually, as the attentive reader—if I still have one at this point—will have perceived, there is nothing of the highbrow about me as a writer; as a lecturer I am equally unambitious. I only asked my audiences to think along with me; it called for a very modest effort, and they were more than equal to it; but they had been conditioned into a prejudice that a lecture was not the proper place for that sort of thing. What with that and my interludes of unsociability, I got few invitations even at derisory fees. After about two and a half decades, I had as many engagements as I cared to accept, at better, though still moderate, fees—a confirmation of Sholom Aleichem's aphorism that every Jew would die a millionaire if he only lived long enough.

I find this crucial difference between writing and lecturing: in the first the feeling of accomplishment or failure is deferred; in the second it is immediate. It takes me a long time to decide—if ever I do —whether something I have written has done the job; lecturing, I know from minute to minute whether I am doing well or badly; and "doing well" does not simply mean holding the attention of the audience; it means holding the attention of the audience *while presenting and conveying the ideas I want to present and convey.*

But how do I know whether a substantial part of the audience is getting the ideas? It is not by the degree of attentiveness. It is something else, a special sense, a mutual interpenetration of the audience's mind and mine, a radar effect connected, perhaps, with otherwise not perceptible changes of expression and posture, and perhaps connected with as yet scientifically undefined modes of communication between persons face to face. When I feel that I am not getting the idea across, I change the line quickly, choose another approach, start with a new supporting anecdote, quotation, recent event, historical parallel, biblical allusion. I must add that getting an idea across does not mean getting it accepted. The satisfaction lies in being understood, not in being agreed with.

There are lecturers who read from a manuscript and lecturers who have memorized their text. They belong to another species; their relationship to the personality of their audience is a mystery to me. Readers and reciters are not lecturers in my book, nor are political and religious orators; nor does the word apply to writers who take to the platform for a killing in the wake of a successful book, or to explorers just returned from a mountain peak or an ocean crevasse.

Next to the illusion of an inspired writing spell, I know of no higher pleasure than to stand before an audience and get into a streak when speech comes easily, the phrases are right, the quotations hit home, the thesis unfolds clearly and logically, and the audience follows; the highest point is reached when I suddenly perceive a novel way of presenting the material and exploit it successfully. Correspondingly, a botched lecture fills me with the acutest misery. There are times when I fail to take hold of an audience; for all the echo reaching me, I might as well be talking into a barrel of sawdust. Or, taking hold of the audience, I fail to develop the thesis, I produce only an approximation and leave an impression tangential to my intentions. The audience may be attentive, it may be working with me, it may applaud heartily at the end, but I am filled with disgust at my ineptitude.

Sometimes I get off to a bad start, and the fault may not be wholly mine. The chairman has been prolix and foolish, the audience has lost its cohesion, and my stored-up initial momentum is dissipated. This handicap can be best overcome by rebuking the chairman; the audience is pulled together by the authoritative gesture and I have worked off my resentment. But this corrective can backfire in unexpected ways. I lectured once in Bloemfontein, South Africa, on Arab-Jewish relations. My chairman was a Rabbi Rohm, who introduced me for thirty-two minutes in a lecture of his own on the same subject. When I got the floor, I asked to be forgiven for saying that I had been burning while Rohm was fiddling. The audience didn't get over it, and every few minutes throughout the lecture a chuckle would break out and spread from row to row. Sometimes the audience cannot settle down; private conversations spring up; I let them go on for a minute or two, then point my finger at the culprits and ask them either to behave or leave the hall. A latecomer will enter at the back and start walking ostentatiously to the front; it is usually a lady wearing high heels, and the impudent tap-tap echoes from wall to wall, making heads turn automatically. I break off to say: "If you can't hear well, or are shortsighted, come early." Shmarya Levin's rule was: a lecturer must treat his audience with respect, and vice versa. I was at a meeting with him when a young woman in the front row began to chew gum audibly while she stared up at him. Levin leaned over and said icily: "Madam, swallow the damn thing or spit it out." I cannot remember which she did, if either, but she stopped chewing.

Getting and holding the attention of an audience is only the first step; the second, without which the first is pointless, is to make creative use of its attention. A lecturer must have, for each occasion, and at his fingertips, ten times as much material as he needs for his purpose. He must be able to pick and choose according to the response he is getting. Even so, addressing seventy or eighty audiences a year, he is in danger of growing stale to himself and therefore listless toward his audience. Repetition is inevitable, but the varieties of combinations and their improvisation help to keep him fresh. And there is always the windfall, the unexpected new vista of exposition which opens up right in the middle of the lecture. It has its dangers, of course; you adjust quickly to make room for it, perhaps to discover that it has led you astray. You remember an important point you were about to make when the visitation interrupted, but you must not go back; you must wait for an opportunity in the question and answer period. Shmarya Levin used to say: "Going back on a deal is poor business practice, going back to a lost point is poor lecture practice."

It may seem unnecessary to add that one must be absolutely honest with an audience, but many lecturers think they are honest enough if they do not quote unreliable statistics or repeat as fact what they have heard as rumor. Honesty demands that you never offer a plausible argument hoping that no one in the audience knows the effective counterargument. It is dishonest to shrink from the prospect of a hostile reaction, or to veil your convictions in deprecatory language, or to ingratiate yourself by turning folksy. These are the devices of the politician and the orator, not of the lecturer.

Like Gaul and Mr. Schiff, my average audience is composed of three parts; an informed and sophisticated core, an intelligent receptive mass, and a small nondescript periphery—harmless people with minds as difficult to locate as the whereabouts of an electron. For these last, attendance at a Jewish affair is an act of piety, a gesture toward the higher life. I can always identify them by their eagerness to thank me at the close of the evening. They are given to protracted handshakes with a pumphandling or rotatory motion or a complicated grip like a lodge signal. Their congratulations are warm and undiscriminating: "Mr. Samuels"—it is never Samuel—"you were absolutely marvelous. Last month we had a man who did card tricks. He was very good too." They expect to be remembered on the slenderest grounds. "Mr. Samuels, don't you recognize me? I was at your lecture in Knoxville twenty-five years ago." When I shake my head regretfully, they add: "It was a very rainy evening."

For most lecturers the question and answer period is a sort of afterbirth, to be disposed of quickly and hygienically; for me it is the climax of the evening, and I make it as long as possible. It is during this period that I check on my intuitions, and it is during this period, too, that I learn something of what is going on in the mind of American Jewry, or at least a certain sector of it. A thousand questions directed at me every year by audiences drawn from the most varied communities constitute a Gallup poll in reverse; and the changes in the type of question over a period of nearly fifty years build up a skeleton history of Jewish public opinion.

I prefer the spoken to the written question; I like to see the questioner, it helps me to understand him, and I will take the risk that he will want to outline his autobiography. Sometimes the questioner flounders about; I have to guess at what is troubling him and find the words for it; it is pleasant to see his face light up when I succeed. I do not mind delivering five or six capsule lectures on top of the main lecture if the questions touch on important issues, the less so as they help me to bring up the good point I lost while chasing the new insight.

Some of the questions are merely silly, some simple and factual, and a few unfathomable. After a lecture on the character of Leopold Bloom in James Joyce's *Ulysses* I was asked: "Mr. Samuel, are you in favor of human nature?" and after a lecture on Sholom Aleichem, whether I was in favor of vivisection. Late in the night after the Sholom Aleichem lecture I recalled having used some phrase like "dissection of human beings," but I never established a connection for the first question. There need not have been any; my questioner no doubt belonged to the small army of amiable cranks who haunt meetings in order to put in a word on vegetarianism, free love, Esperanto, faith healing, Bahaiism, moral rearmament, Yoga, spiritualism and kindness to animals; they form part of the periphery. The pest questioner is in a tiny class by himself; he attends every lecture and always has a question. He betrays himself the moment he opens his mouth by the pitch of his voice, which for some reason is half an octave or so higher than the average; the practiced lecturer can also identify him in advance by the dismay of the audience, which vents itself in a groan of resignation at the sight of him.

The loquaciously hostile questioner who wants to debate the issue with you from beginning to end must be disposed of decisively the moment he stops to catch his breath. An anti-Zionist rabbi named Foster rose after one of my addresses in Newark and began to deliver himself on the inadvisability, impossibility, and un-Americanism of creating a Jewish state in Palestine. At the first opportunity I slipped in the remark: "Sir, do not worry; the Jewish homeland will be built by the children of Israel, not the foster-children." After that the audience was deaf to him. In 1928, speaking on the Arab-Jewish problem, I found the same gentleman in my audience. I have referred, in telling of my last meeting with my old *rebbe,* to the anti-Jewish riots which swept over Palestine in the fall of that year.* The Haganah, or defense army, then clandestine, was in its primitive stage, and over a hundred and fifty men, women, and children were killed and thousands wounded before the British restored order. Even the anti-Zionist Jewish Communists of America, caught off guard, joined in the worldwide protests until they were ordered by Moscow to reverse their position, which they did with that bland and unembarrassed celerity which is, or used to be, such an engaging feature of dedicated Communism. Rabbi Foster put his question briefly this time: "Mr. Samuel, what would *you* do if you were an Arab?" I counterquestioned: "Rabbi Foster, what would you do if *you* were a Jew?"

Oddities remain imbedded in my memory, freak incidents, incongruities that are a joy forever, incredibilities that startle me afresh whenever I think of them—somewhat as if I had heard the train announcer at Grand Central say distinctly: "The Goddam five-twenty-five for Bridgeport is now ready on track nineteen." The first prize belongs to a 1933 meeting. At that time world Jewry was divided on the issue of Jewish colonization in Russia. Most Zionists correctly saw in it nothing more than a device to divert Jewish funds to Russia; but some of them were taken in and one of them challenged me earnestly: "Mr. Samuel, don't you think it's better to give relief to Jews wherever they need it until we can build the homeland and all go and relieve ourselves there?" The atmosphere was so serious, the turn of phrase so unexpected, that the audience was paralyzed. In a similar stoniness an audience once heard me commit a ghastly spoonerism in a metaphor which intended to refer to a piston pushing. In spite of the sudden chill at my heart, I had the presence of mind to hurry on without correcting myself, thus creating a doubt in the minds of my listeners. I do not know whether it was incredulity or courtesy which prevented the audience from bursting into a shout of laughter when I was introduced at a meeting in the

*See "The Twig Is Bent," p. 19. [ED.]

Bronx, where I was then living, in the following terms: "We have with us tonight Mr. Maurice Samuel, who is well known throughout America and in the Bronx as well. As the chairman of this evening, I will not bore you for long, since we have brought Mr. Samuel here for that purpose." This story has become something of a legend, and has been attached to various speakers, but unless my chairman of that evening reinvented the gem—he was too kindly and unsophisticated a man to have been quoting—I claim it as part of my saga.

An introduction is not, or should not be, an idle and hasty formality; its function, difficult and responsible, is to pull the audience together and dispose it to listen. It should be neither too long nor too short, neither fulsome nor dry, neither facetious nor pompous. It must contain mention of the subject and some polite remarks on the lecturer's qualifications for dealing with it. A nervous chairman infects the audience, and precious minutes are lost before it regains its composure. If the chairman has been chosen as a reward for various services but happens to know nothing about the subject or the lecture, he should confine himself to reading the introduction furnished by the lecture bureau. Had this rule always been followed, one flustered lady would not have introduced me as Mr. Furtlewanger because the late Lion Feuchtwanger had addressed the organization the previous month, and another as Sholom Aleichem because I had written a book about him.

The most difficult part of an evening comes when, being at leisure and glad to engage in conversation even after a two-hour stretch on the platform, I am buttonholed by the wrong people. Some have private grievances against the organization or the community leadership and want me to adjudicate in their favor; others want to tell me of a long and complicated personal experience which bears out or disproves part of my thesis; and there are those who ask: "Mr. Samuel, do you *really* believe" something or other I said in the course of the lecture, as if they expected me to confess that I had only been fooling. But some are troubled by serious questions which they were too shy to ask in public, and these are among my best teachers.

The change in the character of my audiences, and in the matters which interest them, is, as I have hinted, a commentary on Jewish development in this country over the last half century. It is also an indicator of general changes. It goes without saying that the immigrant element has largely disappeared; those that come to hear me are eighty to ninety percent American-born, more than half of them of American-born parents. One curious result has been the almost total disappearance of a perplexity that used to haunt my audiences thirty and forty and fifty years ago. It went under the name of "dual allegiance." Was it possible to be a "good American" with half one's heart attached to the idea of a Jewish homeland in Palestine? The question is still put here and there, but it emanates from a small, identifiable, extremist assimilationist minority.The more American the Jews have become, the more natural does it seem to them to be, if not ideological Zionists, vigorous supporters of the State of Israel. It is not only that the timidity of the newcomers has dissolved in the tacit Americanism of their descendants; it is also that America herself has lost a good deal of her provincialism. The growing consciousness of the fateful world role which has devolved on her makes her sympathetic to the value of additional attachments. (I avoid the word "allegiance" because it is part of a loaded formula.) "Americanism" loses all contemporaneous meaning unless it is hyphenated with "One-Worldism," and One-Worldism finds encouragement in emotional and cultural bonds with other peoples; there cannot, in my opinion, be too many of them, for America's good and the world's. Certainly these double or multiple affections (I myself feel strong ties to England and France) will create problems occasionally, but how can the great transition which is now mankind's imperative be made without problems?

The transition is to something far more significant than a state of guaranteed peace. Beyond the danger of human self-annihilation lies the danger, less spectacularly horrifying but hardly less horrible to contemplate, of the annihilation of the human self, the gradual disappearance of those human group differentiations in which a self is rooted. In the introduction to Teilhard de Chardin's *The Phenomenon of Man,* Julian Huxley speaks of the tendency, emerging from technological progress, "which might destroy the effects of cultural diversification and lead to a drab uniformity instead of to a rich and potent pattern of variety in unity." Before us looms the specter of a planet inhabited by six or ten or fifteen billion nobodies-in-particular (and why we should consider it an achievement to infect distant planets with such biological specimens is beyond me).

The recoil in American Jewry from an earlier melting-pot theory of assimilation is in part a response to the threat of depersonalization. It is mixed with other factors; the extermination of six million Jews and the birth of the State of Israel have left deep psychological effects; and the general American movement toward religious affiliation, often—and more or less correctly—characterized as a purely social phenomenon, has set up a kind of machinery for Jewish self-recovery. But it is quite wrong to stop at these factors. The young Jewish physicists, chemists, mathematicians, engineers (I have met hundreds of them) who find they have to provide some Jewish instruction for their children, and join a temple or a synagogue for that reason, are often puzzled at themselves. "Look" they expostulate, as if anxious to disassociate themselves at once from their superstitious grandfathers, "look, I'm beyond that sort of thing, but I want my son at least to know who he is." I mention the scientists because it is presumably the scientific outlook which is most intelligently (or should I just say articulately) at odds with the notion of Jewish affiliation; also because among them one might expect a certain amount of clear thinking on the subject. I probe and find confusion. I ask: "Can't your son be a Presbyterian and know who he is?" They answer: "I don't believe in any religion, but if my son has to get a certain amount of religion to know who he is, at least let it be Jewish." I continue: "But why on earth do you want him to know that he is a Jew?" Sometimes they answer: "Better for him to find it out from me than from an anti-Semite"; sometimes: "A man shouldn't be ashamed of his origins"; and sometimes: "Well, if he isn't a Jew, what is he?"

Now, this concern with the child's need for self-identification is genuine, and the answers have meaning for the speaker, on one level or another; what the parents often do not perceive is that they, finding themselves the begetters of a new generation, are urgently in search of their own self-identification. The unformulated anxiety runs: "We've got children! What shall we tell them about ourselves? And, for that matter, *who are we?"*

The spiritual confusion of the physicist, mathematician, etc., is not different from that of the doctor or lawyer in the same predicament, or, given a certain level of intelligence, of the plumber or pantsmaker. It begins with a misconception in the religious field. A member of an audience once said to me: "As a physicist I do not believe in the existence of God. I know that things take place in accordance with unchangeable laws. In years of experimentation I have never come across an instance of interference with those laws by an outside power." I commented: "You seem to be under the impression that only a physicist, or a scientist generally, is aware of the inexorability and inviolability of the natural laws of cause and effect. But a pantsmaker, too, has the right to say: 'As a pantsmaker I do not believe in the existence of God. I know that in the making of a pair of pants there are inexorable and inviolable laws of cause and effect, and in all the years of my pantsmaking I have not come across a single instance of interference with these laws by an outside power. Never, never, in the making of thousands of pairs of pants have I seen a single pair come out right if the cutting was wrong.' His scientific experience hasn't the range and subtlety of yours, but it is as decisive."

Belief in God does not by itself make a Jew, just as calling oneself an atheist does not make one an atheist (the intellectual discipline of atheism is extremely exacting). The Jew who thinks himself an atheist and, looking for self-identification, can find it only in the Jewish people, relies on the fact that Jewishness, unlike Christianity, regards *peoplehood* as an expression of religion. And peoplehood does not mean nationality or nationalism; it means a group-cultural personality within which the individual comes to birth, and this in turn means being rooted in the culture.

But by a certain age—say the late twenties or early thirties—much exertion is needed to send down new roots or to reactivate old ones that have withered. Usually something is still there, and not only because of reminders from the outside, a personal experience, an overheard jibe, exclusion from certain areas of employment; something beyond the fact that Jews habitually consort with Jews; something that nags quietly, or starts suddenly to life without apparent provocation, a regret, a sense of self-alienation and self-devaluation, an obscure perception of some kind of impiety. The something that is still there is also felt, often enough, as a confounded nuisance: "I didn't ask for it! I refuse to let myself be pestered by it. To hell with the past." Hence an ambivalence of attitude, a simultaneous hankering and resentment, respect and derision. "The Jews, Jewishness—you can't just wave it away; the Jews, Jewishness, just a lot of antiquated rubbish."

Thus, a popular Jewish woman novelist opens her autobiography with: "All my life I have been inordinately proud of being a Jew," and some fifty pages farther on explains: "It has always been my contention that the Jew, left in peace for two hundred years throughout the world, would lose his aggressiveness, his tenacity, his neurotic ambition, would be completely absorbed and vanish, as a type, from the face of the earth." Now, surely the lady cannot be "proud" of these Jewish characteristics, and surely she must look forward to the day when a world purified of hatreds will permit this somewhat repellent type to disappear. But no, what she is proud of in her Jewishness is the noble sentiment she quotes from the Bible as the motto of her book: "Now, therefore, if ye will obey My voice, and keep My covenant, then ye shall be a peculiar treasure unto Me, above all peoples; for all the earth is Mine and ye shall be unto Me a kingdom of priests and a holy nation." On the other hand, it appears from her account that if the Jews have in some slight degree approximated to this lofty ideal, they owe less to God and the prophets than to certain questionable historical characters: "For centuries we have been kept from complete absorption or utter oblivion by such fanatics and megalomaniacs as a Pharaoh, or Ivan of Russia, or Philip of France, or Edward the First of England. . . . Adolf Hitler has done more to solidify and spiritualize the Jews of the world than any man since Moses."

Novels which depict Judaism or Jewishness as nothing more than a persistent historical trauma, and the Jewish people as the locale of a baffling non-filterable virus called anti-Semitism which has the curious faculty of keeping the host organism alive for centuries, are very popular with Jews engaged in the struggle for self-recovery; they find there relief for one side of their ambivalence. Whatever my subject at a lecture, I am sure to be asked for my opinion of such books while their brief and lucrative season is on; and since I consider it my duty to have an answer, I must, like the reader for the Catholic Index, regularly imperil my soul, or my sanity, for the benefit of my audiences.

I also imperil my soul occasionally by the intemperateness of my comments; but what other kind of comment can one make on the following piece of advice, which another Jewish novelist puts into the mouth of one of his sympathetic Jewish characters: "What you're afraid of, George [a fellow-Jew], is the world of the Gentiles. Somewhere, God alone knows the location, you've picked up and believe the same notions about Gentiles that *so many* Gentiles have about Jews. That they're creatures of another planet, with cloven hoofs and spiked tails and *a passion for drinking human blood* [my italics]." The author does not know where on earth some Jews have picked up these monstrous beliefs about Gentiles! It is for him no miracle that when the concentration camps opened they did not let out on the world a horde of lunatic survivors. It surprises him that even among those who have only learned something about the camps there should occur occasional delusions(!) of persecution. One must assume that this is his attitude, for a proper comment on the hideously coarse statement I have quoted occurs nowhere in the novel. There isn't a Jew or Gentile in it with intelligence enough to make it. And how ingeniously he turns the tables—"that so many Gentiles have about the Jews. . . ." Jewry and Christendom are even stephen. Gentiles misunderstand Jews, Jews misunderstand Gentiles; there is an unfortunate mutuality of self-perpetuating misunderstanding without a basic cause on either side. The crowning touch is "the passion for drinking human blood." The author might have spared us this oblique reference to the ritual blood libel, so often thrown by Christians at Jews but never by Jews at Christians. He might, in order to fill out the picture with the honesty expected of a novelist, have had someone say: "Yes, I know, George, certain terrible things have happened over the centuries, and recently, too; all the same. . . ." No, instead he has another perceptive Jew admonish George: "Don't hide. Don't dig a hole for yourself. . . . Do what your heart tells you, not your religion. It's more important to be a man than a Jew." It appears that, for the author, "Jew" and "man" are in some way incompatible.

The recurrent impulse to get rid, somehow, of this burden of Jewish identity, and the endless, banal discussion of it, are often characteristic of Jews who are fundamentally attached to Jewishness. Perhaps it is only a particular form of the longing that all human beings occasionally experience to be someone else for a change. So I am frequently asked: "Can't we assimilate?" and I answer: "Some of us certainly can, and do, but you must not make a programmatic thing of it; that would be like screaming at people: 'Relax!' "

Some years ago an "ex-Jew" wrote an article in *The Atlantic Monthly,* describing how, by the exercise of the proper tact, ingenuity, and determination, he had managed to "pass" completely. He wrote under a pseudonym, of course—otherwise he would have ruined his life's work—and offered himself as proof conclusive that "it can be done"; and Jews who complain that the gentile world won't let them assimilate are deceiving themselves; it is their own clannishness or self-assertiveness that stands in the way. No one, he reported, but no one except himself now knew him as an ex-Jew; and he advised Jews at large to follow his example.

I was surprised by the number of Jews who read the article and wanted to know what I thought of it; there must have been quite a run on that issue. I pointed out to my questioners that in addition to the particular qualifications which enabled the "ex-Jew" to carry out his farsighted plan, he had to thank that vast majority of Jews who lacked both his qualifications and his ambition. It is obvious that if all the Jews of America were to make a concerted attempt to "disappear," the country would be set by the ears, and the more widespread the attempt, the fewer, in the final account, would be the instances of success. Let us imagine the courts of New York, Philadelphia, Boston, Cleveland, Chicago, and Los Angeles suddenly flooded with petitions for change of name—in most instances the first prerequisite; let us then imagine a miraculously rapid and uniform favorable disposal of all the cases; then let us imagine the disappearance of the serried columns of Cohens, Caplans, Levys, Horowitzes, Hurwitzes, Samuels, and Slomowitzes from the telephone books. What a hue and cry there would be, here and abroad! *"Where are the Jews of America!"* The political commentators would be in their element, propounding theories: at one extreme that the Jews had gone underground in accordance with the sinister plans outlined in the *Protocols of the Elders of Zion;* at the other that they had been massacred in a tremendous and marvelously organized St. Bartholomew's night which had not left behind so much as a single *corpus delicti.* (I ignore the various problems of relocation, transportation, and economic reintegration: one need only think of the chaos in the social security offices.)

What I really held against the "ex-Jew" was not his imbecility but his ingratitude. He was like the millionaire who earnestly counsels the poor to emulate him and repeat his success, forgetting that a few people can be millionaires precisely because other people, much more numerous, cannot. Those who have the necessary combination of ability, craftiness, single-mindedness, imaginativeness, avariciousness, and love of power (not to mention luck) will become millionaires without his encouragement; others are merely disturbed from time to time by the reflection: "He's right! I could have made it, too," when in fact they haven't a dog's chance, not only because of social handicaps, but because they just aren't built that way.

"Ex-Jew" was built in a certain way, and because of it he was able to realize his ambition, though not quite as completely as he imagined. There was one person, very important to him, to wit, himself, who was in on the secret, and how he took it is not clear from his statement. He may have chuckled at the situation, thinking how he was diddling his neighbors, the Jewish people, and history. He may have winced slightly when a good friend of his made an anti-Semitic remark—say, something on the order of: "A Jew can try to disguise himself as much as he likes, but I can tell one a mile away" by some unpleasant characteristic or other—and then laughed up his sleeve: "Poor devil! He doesn't suspect he's been having one in his home for years." It is possible that he entered a mild demurrer, just

to test his feeling of security: "Oh, I don't know. . . ." I have sometimes wondered whether some of his best friends were Jews; and I
have wondered what became of him. There is the horrid possibility
that he was exposed by a chance encounter, and perhaps even by
himself—a slip of the tongue at a Christmas Eve party where he had
taken a drop too much and was irresistibly impelled to hint at the
relationship between him and Jesus, or, God knows, in a moment of
unaccountable revulsion. But if he carried on successfully to the end,
his children would be quite secure, assuming, as we must, that when
they asked him about his parents or other relatives he made up some
cock and bull story. Or he may have decided not to risk marriage and
fatherhood. The fact is that there is no such thing as an assimilated
Jew any more than there is a digested potato. There are only assimilating Jews, and they are never absolutely safe. One may be
second-generation baptized, and a United States senator to boot, and
a granddaughter will take it into her head to join a *kibbutz* in Israel.

Assimilationism as an organized movement, with national headquarters, organs, slogans, chapters, and chairmen, is an absurdity
from the practical as well as from the moral point of view. Boris
Pasternak, himself a convert to Christianity, urges something like it
in *Dr. Zhivago.* Referring to the sufferings of the Jewish people, he
cries: "Of what use is it to anyone, this voluntary martyrdom? Whom
does it profit? For what purpose are those innocent old men and
women and children, all these subtle, kind, humane people, mocked
and beaten up through the centuries? Why didn't the intellectual
leaders of the Jewish people ever go beyond *Weltschmerz* and ironical
wisdom? Why have they not disbanded this army which keeps on
fighting and being massacred nobody knows for what? Why don't
they say to them: 'Come to your senses, stop. Don't hold on to your
identity. Be with all the rest. You are the first and best Christians in
the world. You are the very thing against which you have been
turned by the worst and weakest among you.' "

These generous words about the Jewish people—I should like to
think they are deserved: "the best Christians in the world!"; isn't it
a bit overdone?—make nonsense of the proposal. Why should David
Gordon, the Christianized Jew in the novel (he is one of the self-
images of Pasternak), want the dissolution of so exalted an example?
If Jewishness produces "the best Christians," oughtn't the world to
turn Jewish? Which is perhaps what Jesus, the home-grown Jew,
intended, and Paul, the Hellenized Jew, could not understand.

Assimilation takes place quietly, more or less simply, and is a natural thing. Sometimes I will be invited by a questioner to express disapproval of Jews who drift away, intermarry, and initiate the slow process by which Jewish identity dissolves. I am unable to comply. A Jew has the same right to intermarry as an American or an Englishman has to emigrate. All peoples regularly lose contingents of their sons and daughters; to hold them by force when they have the opportunity and the desire to leave is an abominable act of tyranny, an infringement of the basic right of the human being to seek his happiness where he thinks he can find it. Or else I am invited to express alarm at the volume of Jewish assimilation. Again I cannot oblige; for such distress as I feel is occasioned, not by the diminution of our numbers, but by the insufficiency of Jewish content and Jewish values in that mass which will persist with a Jewish designation into all the foreseeable future.

Jewish values! Again and again I am asked: "But what *are* those Jewish values you keep talking about?" and I must answer again and again that one doesn't explain them, one acquires them by a conscious effort; they are associated with a body of Jewish knowledge; and that body of Jewish knowledge is in turn associated with the Jewish view that without knowledge there is no Jewishness. This is the specific Jewish tradition of intellectuality, the dissipation of which is a loss to every country with a Jewish community. I think sometimes of the role that Jews ought to be playing in America as her intellectual pacesetters. We are still, I believe, in front, but only by the momentum of the past. Most of our young intellectuals are not with us; their children will be strangers to the tradition which carried their fathers. That is a pity, but the loss is not irreparable. The matrix is still here.

If the anti-Jewishness bias of some writers does not trouble me too much, the pro-Jewishness of others does. I am referring to the sentimental books, novels or memoirs, which are filled with exhibitionistic and smiling affection for our recent ancestry. "Nothing," says Professor Herbert Muller, "is more undignified than a past become quaint." Such books achieve the same popularity as their opposites and do more harm because they purport to tell us something about Jewishness. I had a boyhood friend in Manchester, Louis Golding, who grew up to be that sort of writer. When we were youngsters we were very fond of each other, and his father, a Hebrew teacher and a sternly Orthodox Jew, used to thrash him for frequenting the company of a notorious apostate like me. In later years Louis and I developed a strong aversion toward each other's books, and we used to meet at intervals, in London and New York, to express it; if the intervals were too long, we wrote each other abusive letters about each other's latest productions. He died recently and I miss him, because I never really lost my fondness for him. Besides, my personal acquaintance with other writers of his type, where it exists at all (I don't move in literary circles), is too slender to provide me with this outlet. But the type will fade away as immigrant memories recede.

Though I am sure that my lectures do no harm, I cannot be sure that they do any good. The measure would lie in the number of people who have been prompted by them to take up Jewish studies. That number is steadily increasing, but who knows if I have had anything to do with it? Lectures about the value of Jewish culture can indeed be samples of Jewish culture, and that is what I try to make them; but if the listener is content to nod approval and leave it at that, he is like the man who goes to church or synagogue as an expression of his faith in the value of faith, which is a fair description of much of our contemporaneous religious revival—and nothing new, at that. Gissing said of the Victorian Englishman: "His religion, strictly defined, is *an ineradicable belief in his own religiousness*" (his italics). I place in the same category the Jew who "believes" in Jewishness, his own Jewishness, and makes no effort to give it substance. From time to time I am asked wistfully why the Bible can't be made as attractive as Bible movies, and why an immortal work like the Talmud can't be reduced to twenty-five simple lessons. I have to drive home the point that these inane longings, or rather velleities, are hostile to the very material, as it were, of Jewishness, its specifically moral-intellectual discipline and substance.

In that substance the spirit expresses itself, having no other means of expression for us. The One God of whom I get glimpses speaks to me, as a Jew, *in that substance,* making it the starting point and medium of my perception of the world, my mode of entrance into it and my identification with it. Exactly when that substance, in its earliest form, became the heritage of the group which evolved into the Jewish people, is to me a mystery. I cannot accept as literal the account of Genesis. I suggest that instead of God having spoken to Abraham (or Abram), He put into the heart and mind of the primitive group, no doubt through a prophetlike figure, the myth of His having spoken to Abraham. What He is thus purported to have said to Abraham concerning the destiny of the group, namely, that in it the families of the earth should be blessed (what a mad notion!), the group accepted as the *raison d'être* for its existence. When did this happen? That, I have said, is a mystery to me, and I cannot think it will ever be resolved. But the notion stuck. It was and is periodically repudiated and reasserted, disregarded and renewed in ascending perception. The records are superficially confused, the thematic consistency and continued clarification perfectly clear. The renewal of Jewishness can take place only in these terms, and if the re-creation of the State of Israel is conceived in other terms, that is (as certain ultra-Orthodox Jews assert, without, alas, being themselves an acceptable example) one of the periodic repudiations. Either Israel ultimately helps the Jewish people to be a world-serving community or it is, however successful in other respects, Jewishly speaking a failure.

These are the very high ideas I try to infuse into some of my lectures. They are seemingly so out of kilter with the ordinary tenor of our lives that one is tempted to laugh, to dismiss them as so much hot air. But either there is God and purpose, and then this ordinary tenor, with all its failures, absurdities, and shenanigans, indicates a meaningful direction, or else there is neither God nor purpose, and then, as I asked in my youthful years, what difference does it make if we inflate ourselves with empty delusions?

From *Little Did I Know* (1963)

18 THE NATURE OF JEWISH MONOTHEISM

I

The Jewish Bible does not, contrary to the popular impression, shared by many Jews, state or imply that the first acknowledgment of the One God was Abraham's peculiar achievement or that He was unknown to others than Abraham's descendants. God spoke to Adam and Eve before the Fall, and received the offering of Abel after it; He also carried on a colloquy with Cain; and His identity was known to all four. For that matter, He addresses Himself, directly or in dreams, or through messengers, to unbelievers like Lot and Laban and the Abimelechs and Pharaoh. Noah and his sons too, long before Abraham, were addressed by God and knew Him. We are also told in the fourth chapter of Genesis that as far back as the second generation after Adam "men began to call upon the name of the Lord." Before the Flood, "Enoch walked with God, and he was not, for God took him." In the time of the Flood, Noah stood in an intimate relationship to God. In the time of Moses there was Balaam, a prophet of God belonging to another people than the Israelites. The Jewish Tradition exalts Enoch (Jewish boys, too, are still named after him), and places Balaam in the highest human rank imaginable to it, making him the equal of Moses, and adding that he was given to the non-Jewish peoples in order that they might not complain of discrimination.

Outside of the Bible there are instances of the recognition of God in ancient times, the most famous, perhaps, being that of Ikhnaton. Certain of the Stoics—Cleanthes, Epictetus, Marcus Aurelius, and others—might be included. But the argument as to who first conceived the notion of the One Universal God is as pointless as the arguments that once went on as to who first discovered and located the planet Neptune, the Englishman Adams or the Frenchman Leverrier, or who first worked out the differential calculus, Newton or Leibnitz. Not in the "discovery" of God lies the meaning of the Jews, but in what they did with that discovery. For whereas many individuals in moments of brilliant insight made the discovery before and after them, the Jews alone as a people sweated out (the Yiddish word *oisgekrenkt* is better than "sweated out") their monotheism over the millennia; they alone made it their obsession as a people and somehow or other hung on to it with unbelievable doggedness from its first emergence four thousand years ago until this day; and the record of the first half of this multimillennial torment is that collection of books known as the Jewish Bible. One may properly say that Judaism is meaningless without the Jewish Bible, not because it tells of the discovery of God, but because it mirrors the struggle of recalcitrant man with the consequences of his discovery.

Thus we are dealing not with a discovery, but with a process. The Biblical record is a continuing drama. It is fragmentary, a sacred anthology of excerpts in which there is frequent reference to other records, now lost. And yet, with all its incompleteness, it is magnificently consistent and instructive. The theme is struggle: inspiration, defection, return, near-obliteration, re-emergence against all probability, the picture of a people possessed by a divine destiny reluctantly assumed, everlastingly repudiated, everlastingly reclaimed.

Professor Arnold J. Toynbee does not understand, does not seem to be willing to understand, that this is the peculiar drama of the peculiar people. He repeatedly gives ancient Judaism the aspect of a feature common to the "Syriac Civilization." Thus he writes of "the Syriac legend of the creation of the Physical Universe when 'God saw everything that He had made' "! This attribution of the Genesis account of the Creation to the Syriac civilization utterly confounds the significance of the Jewish Bible at its outset. The late Solomon Goldman opens his vast, uncompleted study of the Jewish Bible with these striking words: "The Book of Genesis is the great clearing which the fashioners of the Jewish saga made in the jungle of primitive folklore." This is correctly and powerfully put. But the Book of Genesis is more than that. It is the repudiation by the Jews, the deliberate, willed, daring, single-handed repudiation of the Syriac and all the other ancient civilizations in the matter of their wild God-ideas. It is the *shofar* blast before which the towers and temples and groves, with their images of demons and dragons and phallic and theophagous gods, collapse. The ruins of the buildings and their inhabiting monstrosities are scattered throughout the Jewish Bible, to the confusion of the literal-minded and the gratification of the cynical.

It is the proper task of the archeologist of ideas to try to identify the fragments: Was the *t'hom* ("the deep") originally *Tiamat,* the Babylonian dragon? It is worth thinking about, though not worth losing sleep on. Whence the story of the sons of God mating with the daughters of man to produce a race of giants? To what particular or general source may we trace the serpent? And so on, through not merely Genesis, but many of the biblical books. Here is, indeed, a fruitful field for the study of cultural interrelationships. But these very fragments bring into bolder relief the unique nature of the effort which, beginning with the trumpet peal of the first sentence, gives the Book of Books its perdurable position among human utterances. In the ancient world that effort, so far as we know, is unique; as Professor Toynbee himself says, neither the "Syriac," nor the Egyptic, nor the Babylonic, nor the Minoan civilizations participated in it; and that effort, bound up with the everlasting struggle against inertia, relapse, and apostasy, expressed itself in the record that constitutes the Bible.

So much has been written, and by the most gifted writers, of the magnificence of the exordium to the Bible, that it would be absurd of me to seek to emulate them. I am concerned only with the definition of the Jewish drama as a peculiar and, thus far, humanly inexplicable experience. I am concerned with it here because an understanding of it destroys the theory of the one-time or nonrecurrent inspiration as the basis of Judaism.

The drama of the Jewish people seems to proceed in a series of life-and-death crises, like one of the continuous movies of forty years ago. There is hardly a century in which the outside observer would give Judaism a dog's chance of surviving. At the very outset, during that theophany at Sinai which is remembered forever after as the binding agreement, the Israelites make themselves a molten calf; and the infuriated Deity bids Moses stand aside, "and My wrath shall wax hot against them, and I will make an end of them, and I will make of thee a great nation" (Exodus 32:10). What an inauspicious start! Who, thereafter, would have counted on a future for this people? But this was not the only occasion on which immediate and total destruction threatened it from the very Source of Life even before it had set foot in the Promised Land. When the Israelites let themselves be frightened out of their wits by the reports the spies brought back from the still unconquered land, God said to Moses: "How long will this people despise Me? And how long will they not believe in Me, in spite of all the signs which I have wrought among them? I will strike them with the pestilence and disinherit them, and I will make of you a nation greater and mightier than they" (Numbers 14:11 f.).

On both these occasions God inspired Moses to dissuade Him from His fierce purpose, but the Israelites did not escape severe punishment. On the first occasion they were decimated, on the second they were sentenced to perish in the wilderness—only their children, a generation hence, should inherit the Promised Land. The Israelites, reacting blasphemously against the punishment for blasphemy, made their own forbidden attempt at immediate conquest and were disastrously repulsed. They proved their unworthiness again at Baal-peor, where they yielded to the attractions of the temple prostitutes of the local idol and thousands of them died in the disciplinary action that followed (Numbers 25). But is it necessary to dwell on the defections of the desert generation? Has it not become a byword among the nations?

One would have expected that the generation born in the desert, and the generations that followed, those which were in fact privileged to enter and conquer, would show a steadfastness lacking in the slave forebears whom Moses had led out of Egypt. They were no better. For we read, immediately after Joshua's death:

And the children of Israel did evil again in the sight of the Lord, and served the Baalim; and they forsook the Lord, the God of their fathers. . . . They went after other gods, of the gods of the people round about them, and worshipped them. . . . And the people of Israel did that which was evil in the sight of the Lord, and served the Baalim and the Asheroth. Therefore the anger of the Lord was kindled against Israel, and He gave them over into the hands of Cushan-Rishathayim, King of Aram-Naharayim. . . . But when the children of Israel cried out unto the Lord, the Lord raised up a deliverer for the people of Israel . . . Othniel the son of Kenaz . . . and the people of Israel again did that which was evil in the sight of the Lord; and the Lord strengthened Eglon the King of Moab against Israel. . . . But when the people of Israel cried out unto the Lord, the Lord raised up a deliverer for them, Ehud the son of Gera. . . . And the people of Israel again did that which was evil in the sight of the Lord . . . and the Lord sold them into the hands of Jabin King of Canaan. . . .

Then it was Deborah the Prophetess who was sent to their rescue; and after forty years of tranquillity the monotonous chant is resumed:

The people of Israel did that which was evil in the sight of the Lord, and the Lord gave them into the hand of Midian seven years. . . . When the people of Israel cried unto the Lord on account of the Midianites, the Lord sent a prophet unto the people of Israel. . . .

and the prophet chose Gideon to deliver the Israelites.

But the people of Israel again did that which was evil, and served the Baalim and the Asheroth, the gods of Syria, the gods of Sidon, the gods of Moab, the gods of the Ammonites, and the gods of the Philistines, and they forsook the Lord and did not serve Him . . . [Judges, *passim*].

One is tempted to say that the Israelites and God could neither get along together nor let go of each other. The period of Judges ends when the Israelites in one of their ever-recurrent assimilationist moods demand a king of Samuel.

All the elders of Israel gathered themselves together and came unto Samuel at Ramah. And they said unto him: "Behold, thou art old, and thy sons walk not in thy ways; now make us a king to judge us, like all the nations." But the thing displeased Samuel, and Samuel prayed unto the Lord. And the Lord said unto Samuel: "Hearken unto the voice of the people in all that they say unto thee; for they have not rejected thee, but they have rejected Me, that I should not be king over them. According to all the works which they have done since the day when I brought them up out of Egypt even unto this day, in that they have forsaken Me, and served other gods, so do they also unto thee" [1 Samuel 8:4–8].

If the reader objects, saying: "All this is legend. It was set down many centuries after the purported time," I answer that the consistency of the story with the later behavior of the Jewish people bespeaks more than legend. I also ask: "What purpose was there in the creation of such a discouraging legend by those who were obviously trying to influence the people to greater faithfulness? Far more intelligible would have been the usual romanticizing of the past into an example of purity and fidelity." To this, indeed, the prophets did resort now and again, as when Jeremiah exclaims: "I remember thee, the kindness of thy youth, the love of thine espousals, when thou wentest after Me in the wilderness, in a land that was not sown" (Jeremiah 2:2). And: "When Israel was a child, then I loved him, and out of Egypt I called My son" (Hosea 11:1). But these praises of the dead past are few, while innumerable and crushing are the condemnations of Israel's ever-recurrent defections.

The pattern is maintained until the destruction of the Jewish kingdoms. A brief and not wholly satisfying interlude is afforded by the reigns of David and Solomon: already Solomon, for all his wisdom, and for all God's favor, failed in his later years:

> For it came to pass when Solomon was old, that his wives turned away his heart after other gods. . . . For Solomon went after Ashtoreth the goddess of the Zidonians. . . . And Solomon did that which was evil in the sight of the Lord . . . [1 Kings 11:4–6].

And after Solomon the Kingdom is split into Israel and Judah.

If there are two periods of particular discouragement in the story, they center on Elijah in Israel and Jeremiah in Judah. We abandon all hope for Israel in the days of Elijah, when Jezebel, with the people collaborating, had liquidated all the prophets of Jehovah; and Elijah, a broken-hearted refugee in the wilderness, pours out his plaint to God, and asks for death:

> It is enough; now, O Lord, take away my life. . . . I have been very jealous for the Lord, the God of hosts; for the children of Israel have forsaken Thy covenant, and slain Thy prophets with the sword; and I, even I only, am left; and they seek my life, to take it away [1 Kings 19:4, 14].

The last spiritual convulsions of the doomed Northern Kingdom are portrayed with terrifying vividness in Ezekiel:

> [Samaria] played the harlot when she was Mine: and she doted on her lovers, on the Assyrians, warriors, clothed in blue, governors and rulers, handsome young men all of them, horsemen riding upon horses: and she bestowed her harlotries upon them, the choicest men of Assyria, all of them; and on whomsoever she doted, with all their idols she defiled herself . . . [Ezekiel 23:5–7].

And so the Northern Kingdom of Israel was destroyed, and the ten tribes were scattered, never to be reassembled. The Southern Kingdom of Judah saved itself, or was saved—how and why we do not know if we take the narrative literally; for her behavior was apparently no better than that of the Northern Kingdom; if anything it was, according to the prophet last quoted, worse. Jerusalem's lust for the worldly, the flashy, the vulgar, the successful, the militarily triumphant, the self-destructive, surpassed that of Samaria:

She was more corrupt in her doting, and in her harlotries more than her sister in her harlotries. She doted upon the Assyrians, governors and rulers, warriors clothed most gorgeously, horsemen riding upon horses, all of them handsome young men. And I saw that she was defiled; they both took one way. And she increased her harlotries, for she saw men portrayed upon the wall, the images of the Chaldeans, portrayed with vermilion, girdled with girdles upon their loins, with pendant turbans upon their heads, all of them captains to look upon, the likeness of the sons of Babylon . . . [Ezekiel 23:11–15].

But survive the Kingdom of Judah did—for a time; and the drama of the people and its God is now focused on that remnant of territory. Now surely the end must come, not only of the kingdom, but of the people that inhabits it. For now that God has shown that He can destroy five-sixths of His people, what hope for the remaining unrepentant sixth? Who can read the closing chapters of the Second Book of Kings, and the life of Jeremiah as it unfolds in his Book, without being tempted to exclaim: "Surely the remnant of this people disappeared from the face of the earth long ago, and these are its last utterances, miraculously preserved for a far-off future and—fortunately—deciphered by the labors of ingenious scholars. Or perhaps this people never existed, the record is such an improbable one. Perhaps it is all a fable, not quite intelligible to our modern mind. Perhaps it is a fabrication—perhaps—perhaps . . ."

To such reflections we would be tempted if the improbable record were not topped by the even more improbable survival of the people into our own day, and its vigorous protests against premature burial.

I will not rehearse here the stages of the fall of Judah; but I must point to the *completeness* of the demoralization as portrayed by Jeremiah at the time of the First Destruction. Even the remnant that might guarantee a future is defiled. When the Babylonian conqueror, unwilling to "create a desert and call it peace," leaves a portion of the people in Judah to carry on a minimum of economic activity and appoints a Jewish governor, Gedaliah, who pleads for submission and peace, the war party assassinates him; and to this day Orthodox Jews observe an annual fast for Gedaliah. The handful flees the country into Egypt, dragging with it the protesting Jeremiah. There he still exhorts them, an old man, shattered in body, unshattered in spirit, pleading with his people till the end. His admonitions are greeted with mockery:

Then all the men who knew that their wives offered unto other gods and all the women that stood by, a great assembly, even all the [Jewish] people that dwelt in the land of Egypt, in Pathros, answered Jeremiah, saying: As for the word that thou hast spoken unto us in the name of the Lord, we will not hearken unto thee. But we will certainly perform every word that has gone forth out of our mouths, to offer unto the Queen of Heaven, and to pour out drink-offering unto her, as we have done, we and our fathers, in the cities of Judah, and in the streets of Jerusalem . . . [Jeremiah 44:15–17].

The Tradition adds that Jeremiah was finally stoned to death by the Jews in Egypt.

And now let us note again that this is commonly regarded as the period of Israel's or Jewry's unchallengeable spiritual greatness. Where is that greatness? In the single soul of Jeremiah? Or shall we add his contemporary Ezekiel? Is this the greatness of a people? We shall have to return to this strange question: it is fundamental to our discussion.

Meanwhile, we move with the centuries. After an interval of two generations, a number of Jews returned from Babylonia to Judah, encouraged and assisted by the Emperor Cyrus. You will read of their condition and of the "promise" they held out, in the books of Nehemiah and Ezra and the last prophets, Haggai and Zechariah and Malachi. It is the old story! For they failed again. It was to rescue them from the spiritual abyss into which they had fallen that Ezra and Nehemiah came to them from the Persian Empire with a new group of zealots (and how did *these* happen to arise?). We read the words of Nehemiah the son of Hachalia:

Now it came to pass in the month of Chislev, in the twentieth year, as I was in Shushan the castle, that Hanani, one of my brethren, came out of Judah, he and certain men; and I asked them concerning the Jews that had escaped, that were left of the captivity, and concerning Jerusalem. And they said unto me: "The remnant that are left of the captivity there in the province are in great affliction and reproach. . . ." And it came to pass when I heard these words, that I sat down and wept . . . [Nehemiah 1:1–4].

And now three hundred years pass, between the days of Ezra-Nehemiah and the days of the Maccabees, and for these three hundred years nothing is known of the history of the Jews in Judah. A few names have come down to us; an institution, the Great Synagogue, is mentioned; it is assumed that the Jews lived submissively under the alternating overlordships of the Egyptian Ptolemies and the Syrian Seleucids, the heirs of Alexander. And when the record resumes we find, to our stupefaction, that a people has been reconstituted, a people so powerful that it can take up with undiminished vigor the everlasting drama! Powerful enough, that is, to go on struggling internally, to split, to be faithful, and to continue a relationship with God.

Of all the miracles of Jewish history I find none more baffling than this one. How did the handful of demoralized Jews—they cannot have numbered more than one hundred thousand—who in Ezra-Nehemiah's time were without Sabbaths and without festivals, who were dissolving out by intermarriage with idolatrous wives, how did this shapeless mass of Judeans, who, it would seem, were hardly better than the slaves who came out of Egypt, become the people that yielded a renegade half to the Asiatic Greeks and with the other half rescued itself for the far-off future? Ezra has been given the name of "the second Moses." If he was indeed responsible, by the laws and customs he instituted, for the re-establishment of the people, he merits the title. But we do not glimpse in him the magnificence of the first lawgiver; and we cannot understand, in the terms of this personality, how the mounting process continued for those three hundred years. We only know that in those blacked-out centuries the Books, with all their denunciations and tales of horror, but with all their incomparable visions of the One God, were edited, and perhaps some of them written; the Oral Tradition became a mighty thing; the Jewish Bible took on about the form in which we have it today; the foundations of the Mishnah were laid; the Pharisees emerged to leadership; the focus of vitality passed from the Temple to the synagogue, from sacrifice to study, from the building to the Book.

The stories of the Jewish people's survival of the Seleucid and Roman attempts to destroy it are not less improbable than the earlier stories. To the north and south of Maccabean Judah were the Seleucids and the Ptolemies. Edom, Moab, Ammon, Philistia were vanishing—Judah should have vanished too. It did vanish under the Roman assault, but not before it had succeeded, while fighting off the Seleucid assault, in consolidating the new fortress, that of the spirit ("the ethos of Johanan ben Zakkai"), which was to withstand the battering of eighteen centuries. It perfected, beyond the power of time to destroy, that instrumentality of beliefs, rituals, traditions, and attachments which was to ensure the resumption, in the same place, of the same Jewish effort to come to terms with God.

II

When the sins of the Jews are cited against them on the authority of the prophets, it is easily forgotten that the prophets themselves are products of the Jewish people. The record of their ministrations from Moses to Malachi shows that a continuous force was at work in the people, and its survival as a Jewish people is connected with the persistence of that force. One cannot tell where the force resided, or in what proportion of the people. Clearly the denunciations of the prophets are hyperbolic: a people as rotten as they represent the Jews to have been could not have survived for a single century.*We see an instance of this exaggeration in Elijah's case. He complains to God: "The children of Israel have forsaken Thy covenant, and slain Thy prophets with the sword; and I, even I only, am left." And God answers: "Yet will I leave seven thousand in Israel, all the knees which have not bowed to Baal, and every mouth which hath not kissed him." And in fact by the time Elijah was carried to heaven in the fiery chariot, a considerable school of prophets had already been established by Elisha (2 Kings 2).

"Whatever lives," says Goethe, "deserves to die." This is as true of the Jewish people as of every other. But the Jewish people does not die. Its refusal to do so is bound up with an obstinate principle of search which keeps on triumphing over successive failures. Somewhere in the folk, even when the largest part of it has fallen away, the principle reasserts itself and maintains the line. It is as though the folk-soul were saying to itself: "I am not going to die until I have found out what this is all about." The principle which runs through the Bible and gives a special meaning to its monotheism, making it infinitely more than a single flash of intellectual insight, runs also through the later history of Jewry; the story continues with a consistency that reflects a convincing verisimilitude back on the Bible narrative, and we shall see that while the Bible has given that principle classical expression, it has not exhausted its operation.

From *The Professor and the Fossil* (1956)

*Cf. Samuel Dill's observations on Juvenal's extravagant denunciations of Roman society, which "suggest a doubt whether the cancer of luxury had struck so deep as satirists thought into the vitals of a society which remained for so many centuries erect and strong" (*Roman Society from Nero to Marcus Aurelius*, 1920, p. 67). [M.S.]

19 THE ETHOS AND TECHNIQUES OF SURVIVAL

Judaism is not only an ethos. Judaism is an outlook on life which is associated and interwoven ideologically with the history of a people. Let me put it in a simple way. If somewhere in China today an individual were to work out for himself all the ethical and theological principles of Judaism, and live up to them, would that make him a Jew? My answer is no. He would be as good a person as any Jew, and better than most Jews; but he would not be a Jew until he had associated himself with the fellowship, and had accepted the responsibilities and instrumentalities of that fellowship.

By the instrumentalities I mean not only a ritual; and, as to the ritual, we must remember that the Jewish ritual is the expression of the history of a people that, when faithful to Judaism, sees history as a manifestation of God's will. Judaism cannot be separated from the Jewish Bible, the Mishnah, the Talmud, the commentators, the Kabbalah, Hasidism, the Exile, the Restoration, the total fact of the Jewish experience: it cannot be separated from these and restated in the form of a series of ethical and theological theorems. From time to time in the popular press there appear articles on the beliefs of Jews, most of them written by Jews. These efforts to transpose the key of Judaism into the key of a religion of a different order are usually a testimony to the amiability of the editors who encourage them and to the goodwill-mindedness of the writers who make them. Certainly there are things that the Jews believe; but before these can be understood, one must establish the character of the Jewish people in its peoplehood. When that has been done one may proceed to inquire: "What do Jews *know* and believe?" For in the case of the Jew, to accept certain tenets of faith as abstractions, without a knowledge of the Jewish people and an informed self-identification with it, does not constitute true and reliable membership in it.

What, then, is the Jewish people? It is a continuing association of individuals, now some thirty-five hundred or four thousand years old, working out an experiment in the relationship to God. It is partly a hereditary association, though not on principle or by deliberate choice. Proselytes of any race are accepted. On the other hand, it would seem that only a limited number of proselytes can be accepted; beyond that number the relationship between the faith and peoplehood would break down. This looks like exclusion on principle. For suppose the hypothetical Chinese were joined by hundreds of thousands or millions of others, all ready to join the association. What connection could *they* have with the faith and ritual centered on peoplehood and the Restoration? The question is unanswerable; and it is unanswerable precisely because it approaches the messianic area of ideas. Judaism in Jewry is an experiment in time; when the Messiah will have come, when all peoples will have accepted the faith, the experiment will have been successfully concluded. We shall be beyond history, and we cannot picture to ourselves in secular terms the post-historic condition of mankind.

Until that conclusion approaches, the experiment cannot be detached from the people and its modes of expressing the faith. Neither is it the kind of experiment in which one can at successive stages put the details of the previous stages in the files with the notation: "Facts A, B, and C have been definitely established." The early stages are continuously present as contemporaneous experiences. One must always be reliving the Bible and the later records of the people. A knowledge of them is therefore indispensable to the continuing of the experiment. How the people reacted to the consciousness of the One God three thousand years ago, and two thousand years ago, and one hundred years ago is, as knowledge, part of the faith and part of the present reaction. Imperfection in that knowledge is imperfection in one's Jewish identity.

Of course that knowledge can never be perfect, for man cannot be perfect. There are, moreover, two general types of knowledge, that of the scholars and that of the folk. In neither of them is purely cerebral knowledge enough, for I am not speaking of an academic acquaintance with certain remote events (facts filed away), which an outsider and unbeliever may also acquire. The knowledge must be of the affective kind which amounts to a renewed participation in the events—what Thomas Mann called "the recurrent festival of pre-sentness." Thus folk-knowledge, when tinged with this self-identification, is truer than scholar-knowledge, from which it is absent. There can, of course, be a combination of the scholarly and affective, and that is best.

The affective element in Jewish knowledge is kept alive by a ritual in which the events are plastically embedded and their meaning and circumstances brought near to us and into us. The Passover ceremony of the Seder contains the injunction that every man, woman, and child participating must feel that he or she in person was liberated from Egypt, and the ceremonial is designed in the spirit of that injunction. The celebrants relive the Exodus. The legend form of this injunction puts it thus: all the unborn generations were present at the giving of the Law from Sinai, and every unborn Jew uttered the words: "*Naase v'nishma*—we will do and we will obey." The millennial insistence on the retention of Hebrew at least for prayer and sacred study is another aspect of the technique of intimate self-identification with the total Jewish experience. The retention of the harvest festivals geared chronologically to the Palestinian seasons, and ignoring the seasonal realities of the lands in which the Jews actually live, is still another. The regular Jewish prayer for "the former and the latter rains" in climates where such things are unknown is one more. Certainly to one who watches these rituals from the outside, or who performs them perfunctorily, the impression is of petrification, or of fossilization. How incorrect that impression would be with regard to believing Jews we may see from the fact that all these practices kept the people alerted, as it were, for the Restoration and for a resumption of life in Palestine. The Seder foretold the Return; the harvest festivals and the prayers for "former and latter rains" made easier the adaptation to the Palestinian landscape and seasons; the retention of Hebrew, if only in prayer, made possible—though with an effort—its revival as the language of daily intercourse. It is true that not all observant Jews were to go to the new Jewish state, but all of them maintained a kind of training for it. Thus a whole army is kept in training and only a part of it goes into battle.

But, if one may so put it, the most important part of the ritual is *study:* and the difference between Jewish and other study is clarified once and for all when we remember that for others a knowledge of the history of their people is a civic duty, while for Jews it is a sacred duty. It is considered God's will not only that we shall be good, but that we shall know what He did to us and what we did about Him.

The view is that we cannot, in fact, know what He wants us to do without that knowledge of what happened between Him and us, between Him and the world, and among all three of us. There is a sense in which Jews consider *all* knowledge sacred, and all study—unless it leads toward apostasy—a religious exercise.

These techniques and methods—or whatever other names one might choose—are as inseparable from the ethos as the form is from a work of art. It therefore follows that to state the ethos in other terms is very difficult, if not impossible; Judaism is livable rather than describable. And yet the ethos is distinct enough. It is based on the One God who made everything, the universe and man, light and darkness, good and evil. His relationship to man, His special and crowning creation, is direct and forbids diminution or confusion by the interposition of intermediaries. It will not tolerate, either, the shading away of the Singularity by the suggestion of any special Emanation carrying with it the actual nature of the Divinity. Where such deviations occur in Jewish thought they are considered dangerous and are not in the mainstream of Judaism.

Just as the relationship will not suffer diminution by intermediaries, so it cannot be consistent with the delegation of moral authority to men or to things. The moral laws are not derived from political or social expediency. Man shall be good not for the health of the state but because it is God's will, transmitted by the prophets. The moral laws shall not be deduced from sociological or anthropological study; they do not have to be, and in fact they cannot be; for they are not relative things. If the crimes of Clapham are indeed crimes, and are nevertheless considered chaste at Martaban, Clapham has not been cleansed thereby, whatever the grounds on which Martaban is considered chaste. We must desire peace not because wars between nations never settle anything—a doubtful proposition anyway; nor because, as Professor Toynbee says, they are usually civil wars between members of the same society—the existence of societies in his sense is a debatable proposition too. We must desire peace because it is God's will. Morality is not an "enlightened egotism," and the industrial enterprise which declared in an advertisement that it was trying to cut down accidents because they made for "bad public relations" was not on the right track. Nor is morality a philosophic system. Every effort to seek elsewhere than in God the ultimate authority for goodness and peace is a form of idolatry, not the less so when it is a "scientific" search.

This does not mean that idolators and atheists cannot be good people, any more than that professors of God cannot be bad people. Nor does it mean that belief, any more than unbelief, is always total. ("We called the chessboard white, we call it black," says Bishop Blougram to Mr. Gigadibs.) Within the range of Judaism, as of Christianity, are to be found formal unbelievers who derive their ethos from sources that they challenge, and sometimes the sincerity of the challenge is a tribute to the power of the ethos.

Now I must repeat that the Jewish people associates the striving toward its ethos with its history, and does so the more strongly because no people among which it lives considers its own history a sacred drama. There have of course been Christian philosophers who have seen history at large as the unfolding of God's will; but their peoples study God's will on Sundays, their own, and world history, the rest of the week. Thus when a Jew considers his Americanism or his Englishhood a substitute for Judaism and a replacement for his feeling of participation in the Jewish peoplehood—which is what vast numbers of Jews actually do—he secularizes himself out of his Jewish identity.

The refusal to give up its peoplehood-in-God is another way of saying "the cultivation of the ethos of Judaism." To the Jews the world did not seem "serious" because its victories and defeats, its glories and tragedies, were not being enacted in the consciousness of a sacred purpose. Its wars were extensions of the frivolities of the racecourses and the jousting lists. In this Jewish outlook we find the clue to that continuity of identity through the centuries which we are seeking.

That the gentile world was, even with all the brilliance and attractiveness of its most creative periods—not excluding the most modern—a frivolous world, a "vanity," remained a deep-rooted feeling in those Jewish masses which clung to their peoplehood. They did not feel that the Jewish people in ancient Palestine had done well, had "behaved" better than any other people. On the contrary, they repeatedly admitted that it was because of their sins that they had been exiled from their homeland. But the two episodes of the first and second states had been serious; they had contained the kind of effort at working out the relationship with God that was not to be found in the histories of other states.

Thence the longing to make the third attempt remained in the people, deeply worked into its religious identity, and constituting the most powerful of those "techniques" which, without looking on them as explanations, we may observe in the Jewish survival. That the Jewish people could not perish because it had to "make good" in Palestine became for its faithful elements an integral part of the ethos. For, *per contra,* the idea that the Jewish people should perish in exile or remain there till the end of time carried the inescapable implication that its history, thus truncated or permanently suspended without the proper rounding off or dénouement, could not have been sacred.

In this complex of views and beliefs it endured century after century, to the growing astonishment and finally the awe (not unmixed with exasperation) of the surrounding world; and the longer it endured the more obvious was, of course, the conclusion that it was not enduring for no reason. Nor could that reason be a trivial one, like the reason for the survival of certain biologic species, the turtle or the oyster, for example, which have found safety in arrested evolution behind a mechanical carapace. For the endurance of the Jewish people is a continuous exertion of the will in the face of adversity, of creative ingenuity in the midst of change.

We need not speak of the courage it needed to die for one's faith at the stake, or to become for its sake a wanderer in a hostile world. More impressive in its way was the ability to stand up to the choreography and décor of humiliation which the Middle Ages added to their economic and physical maltreatment of the Jew: the ghetto, the yellow badge, the spitting ceremonials, the insults, the naked footraces, the blood libels, the accusations of poisoning the wells. Hundreds of thousands of little people accepted the verdict of an ever-renewed malevolence without a thought of purchasing security and comfort by defection. And escape was so easy, so simple! The "racial" rejection of the Jew was unknown in the Middle Ages. It was all a matter of belief. The churchmen were eager to win souls; the conversion of the Jews was an ideal; and there were prelates of a genuine Christian disposition who, protecting the Jews in times of popular bloodthirstiness, made the offer of Christianity in a spirit that was particularly tempting. The answer of the faithful was No. The Jewish people had a task to complete and would not quit in the middle.

From *The Professor and the Fossil* (1956)

20 THE PROPHETS AND THE NATION

There is a curious connection between prophetism and the Jewish people. Unless we realize this, we shall not reach an understanding of the Jewish character throughout the ages, the Jewish position in the world today, the relationship between Christendom and Jewry, the origins and purpose of the State of Israel. For my personal thesis, this connection explains how my parents and my *rebbe* came to be what they were, and how I came to be what I am.

After a number of readings of the prophets, and of the historical biblical books from Judges to Kings, prophetism begins to take on an undeniable pattern. We perceive, to our astonishment, that the prophets are not random eruptions of the spirit. What lies before us is an organic historical episode with a clear trajectory of development.

The prophets begin dimly. We read first of magicians, medicine-men, dervishes, augurs, manipulators of divining-bones and sacred figurines. They seem to be part of the general picture of the East where—as elsewhere but more markedly—magic exertion (the strategy of animism, as Theodore Reinach calls it) is accompanied in the individual by violent psychic disturbances. Then follow schools of prophets, wandering bands of enthusiasts, such as Saul joined. They have their techniques, one of which is music, for casting themselves into their clairvoyant trances. They are of the shaman type, with its mixture of priestly and prophetic functions. They are in part professionals. They can be hired for special jobs, or even set up in business by an entrepreneur. The concept of the prophet is very primitive at first; gradually it lifts itself into higher meaning.

To illustrate the beginning of the process:

We read in Judges that a rich man in Ephraim, named Micah, bought himself a set of sacred implements—gods, ephods, and teraphim, or figurines—and engaged an itinerant Levite to be his priest, permanently attached to his household, in exchange for board and lodging and annual payment of ten shekels and a suit of clothes. A band of Danites, on the prowl for new territory for the tribe, consulted the young Levite, and liked him so well that they carried him off, together with the sacred paraphernalia. When he protested, they said: "Hold thy peace, lay thine hand upon thy mouth, and go with us, and be to us a father and a priest." In this early and curious instance of forced labor the chronicler, aware of certain irregularities, mentions that in those days there was no king in Israel. But he does not imply that this prophet-priest was unreliable, or that his craftsmanship was affected by the irregularities.

The characteristics of these dawn-figures of prophetism lingered on into later generations, when the pre-prophetic was evolving into the prophetic, when the Jewish type was lifting itself clear from the general matrix of the surrounding world. Samuel, in the period following the Judges, was half priest and half prophet. But he also did little divining jobs. He was consulted, for a small fee, on the matter of some strayed and stolen asses. In a later period Elisha, when asked to prophesy in regard to a war against Moab, called for music so that he might achieve the right condition of ecstasy. The association of prophecy with magic foresight and the performance of miracles never died out completely. At the highest stage Isaiah was intermediary for a miracle, in which the motion of the sun dial was reversed for King Hezekiah. But by that time the miracle was an altogether unimportant element in prophetism.

We do not know what the dawn-prophets taught, if they taught anything beyond the techniques of their craft. The first great ethical prophetic utterance is that of Nathan, directed at King David. But it is Elijah, that wild, tremendous folk-figure, who is the clearest compound of the primitive and classical types; *and historically he stands halfway between them.* Elijah was priest, magician, and morality prophet. He sacrificed in successful competition with the court prophet-priests. He was prodigal with miracles: he brought a dead child to life, he renewed the meal and oil of the poor widow, he burned captains and soldiers with a word, he foretold drought and rain. He becomes the morality prophet in the story of Ahab, Jezebel, and Naboth. There, like Nathan before him, he sounds the authentic note. But, again like Nathan, he falls short of the highest achievement.

Both Nathan and Elijah, by the power of their utterances, unveiled the moral insight that is beyond the retributive principle; that is, beyond prudence, calculation, and reason. But they dealt with the individual. It was not until a century after Elijah that Amos initiated that phase of Jewish prophetism which is its complete fulfillment: the identification of nationhood with moral purpose. From now on the national destiny is placed under the sign of moral perception.

As in all historical developments, so in the development of prophetism the old persisted side by side with the new, in a diminishing ratio. Primitive manifestations of prophetism never died away completely—they merely lost importance. Nathan began the moral tradition of prophetism; but another prophet at the court of King David, Gad, Nathan's contemporary, is the embodiment of the taboo tradition. Gad brought punishment to David not for a moral misdemeanor, but for having transgressed the taboo against the taking of a census. The contrast between Nathan and Gad is startling: juxtaposed, they make one think of an illustration in a popular book on anthropology: homo sapiens and ape-man.

Instructive, too, is the contrast between the destinies of the two stories associated with Nathan and Gad. The story of the slaying of Uriah the Hittite, and of the annihilating rebuke it drew down on King David, is never forgotten; centuries afterwards it is quoted in the biblical text, a blot on the memory of David. The story of Gad sinks into obscurity, and David's contravention of the taboo makes no impression on later generations.

When Amos and Isaiah and Micah and Jeremiah were fulfilling the supreme functions of prophecy, some contemporaries of theirs, mentioned in the history books of Kings, still lagged behind in earlier stages. A superficial reader of the Bible, failing to distinguish between these strata, also fails to grasp the evolutionary process that is here presented. He is also apt to be confused by the fact that many of the climactic passages in the highest prophets are—as we shall see —later additions. But that is of no importance in the establishment of the pattern. *What matters is that these additions were conceived in the original spirit of the prophets.* The mold had been created.

The prophets have been called the archetypes of the democratic tribune, the defenders of the common people against the kings, of the poor against the rich. This view, which has much truth in it, is liable to abuse. We must note that the prophets were not demagogues: they did not take up the attitude that the poor are sinless, that the oppressed are, as such, always and naturally and axiomatically in the right. They did not assume that the masses are not in want of moral admonition, being the helpless victims of "the system." Victims the masses are, to be sure, but to deprive them of moral choice is to complete the victimization. The main burden of the prophetic accusation is, of course, turned against those who are in power, for they have a larger range of choice. The princes, the men of substance, the counselors, the judges—these are in the first line of attack: "What mean ye that ye beat my people to pieces, and grind the faces of the poor? saith the Lord God of Hosts." And there is also extenuation for the sins of the weak: "O my people, they which lead thee cause thee to err, and destroy the way of thy paths." But we have just seen that when Jeremiah assembled the refugees in Egypt—and they must have been very poor to recall with such longing the "victuals" of the happy time in Judea—he threatened them with even greater calamities for their perverse and obstinate loyalty to the uncleanliness of the Astarte cult.

To defend the poor without toadying to them, without pauperizing them spiritually, was of the essence of the prophetic purpose. In oppression and poverty the masses must not be encouraged in the destructive belief that they are devoid of responsibility. That leads to mechanism, and mechanism is either all or nothing. For if one cannot talk of responsibility to the poor, one cannot talk of it to anybody; the rich, too, are "victims of the system."

The prophetic vision was not of a prosperous, well-managed nation, but of a nation permeated with the moral spirit; that is what issues from amidst the stratified confusions and occasional obscurities of the prophetic utterances. The prophets (the classical prophets, that is) were nationalists exclusively in this spirit; and though it is correct to call them the guardians of Jewish nationalism, we must always remember what purpose they ascribed to it. For them a nation that was not a moral instrument had no reason for existing, and had no "right" to exist. This is the substance of the prophetic national policy. The formula is not: "Let the nation live though all moral value perish," but: "Let the nation perish if it has no moral purpose." This is the symbolic meaning of the threats of total national destruction.

Sometimes the prophets sentimentalized about the past. Hosea, in the time of Jeroboam the Second (eighth century b.c.e.) thinks back to the idyll of the national birth, and prophesies a renewal of the spirit of old: "And she [the Jewish nation] shall sing there [in Jerusalem], as in the days of her youth, and as in the day when she came out of Egypt." Jeremiah, nearly two centuries later, speaks thus to the sinful people in the name of God: "I remember thee, the kindness of thy youth, the love of thine espousals, when thou wentest after me in the wilderness, in a land that was not sown."

Yet, not long before Jeremiah uttered these poignant words, another prophet, unnamed, delivered this blasting message from God to the apostate King Manasseh: "I will forsake the remnant of mine inheritance, and deliver them into the hand of their enemies . . . *because they have done evil in my sight, and have provoked me to anger since the day their fathers came forth out of Egypt, even unto this day.''* The record, which must have been known to Hosea and Jeremiah, bears out this anonymous prophet, at least in regard to the misbehavior of the Jews who left Egypt. It would be pedantic to take Hosea and Jeremiah to task for historical inaccuracy; the contradictions of great spirits add up—it is only those of small spirits that cancel out. The final effect adds up to this: the vision of the nation as a moral organism, the vision of the moral spirit as a self-subsistent reality, and the vision of the world fulfilling itself in that spirit.

The curve of the prophetic growth is associated with the curve of the history of the Jewish people from the time of the judges to the Babylonian exile. In six or seven centuries the people passed through a tremendous series of experiences. They saw the monarchy established, and within a century after the anointing of the first king they saw the nation split into two parts. Two centuries later the larger part, Israel, the Northern Kingdom, where the first of the universal prophets had ministered, was wiped out by the Assyrians. The remaining part, the Southern Kingdom of Judea, forefelt its doom; a century and a half later it was wiped out as completely—to all appearances—as the first. Within those centuries the prophets evolved from the medicine-man of Micah and the wandering schools of the days of Saul—those who left no message—to the uniquely individualized types of Amos, Isaiah, and Jeremiah, whose written messages were carried into the Babylonian exile.

The trajectory of prophetism is not associated with the trajectory of national power, but with the trajectory of national experience. The prophets were a projection of the people in growth. They were the people in utterance or, to borrow from psychoanalysis, the national superego struggling with the id. Their denunciation of the nation as such was a national self-denunciation; though they were often persecuted by the rulers, there never occurred a popular uprising against them. In all the long record, there is not one instance of a prophet being slain by the people (an interesting reflection on the story of the Crucifixion). The masses as a whole, they who were less guilty than the rulers, felt—without always obeying—that the prophets were the national mouthpiece, even though they often foretold universal and indiscriminate destruction.

This thesis of the national-structural character of prophetism is of such importance in the understanding of the Jewish people and its potentialities that it is impossible to ignore the criticisms which the more informed reader will bring against it, and which the less informed reader knows to exist.

There are scholars who believe that Jewish ethical monotheism developed very late in Jewish history, fighting upward against Canaanitish and surrounding polytheisms. There are others who believe that Jewish monotheism, ethical or taboo, is older than the existing records, and that the oldest codes of law which we possess derive from a common source of still greater antiquity. There is, in biblical criticism, a great to-do about plagiarism and priority of ideas as between the Hebrews and other ancient peoples. We are told on the one hand that ethical monotheism was known to Egyptian and Babylonian priests before it was known to the Hebrews; we are warned on the other hand against seeking the origins of prophetism or of ethical monotheism in the practices and institutions of other peoples. Two features usually dominate the discussions: one is emotional interest in giving credit to the Jews or withholding it from them; the other is a journalistic addiction to phrases like "the more modern theory is . . ." and "more recent research shows . . ." (For a brilliant résumé of this material the reader is referred to Solomon Goldman's *The Book of Human Destiny.*) As for the prophets, a great distinction is made between those whose names are attached to their own books—the "literary prophets"—like Amos and Isaiah, and those who appear only in the historical accounts, like Nathan and Elijah. (The historical accounts are, for this purpose, the books of Samuel, Kings, and Chronicles.) It is noted that the "literary prophets" are not mentioned—with a few unimportant exceptions—in any of the historical records covering their periods. Various deductions are made from this circumstance, the most important being that we must not confuse the two types of prophets and their relative influence, if any, on the Jewish people.

We are told, further, that practically all of the prophetic books and nearly all of the historical books were produced very late—say in the Babylonian exile, or even in the following centuries—long after the periods with which they purport to deal. They are (some say) products of the third, fourth, and fifth centuries B.C.E., and are utterly unreliable as pictures of what took place in the sixth to the tenth centuries B.C.E.

None of these analyses and conjectures have any bearing on the crucial phenomenon—historically speaking—of Jewish prophetism: namely, its patterned deployment within the framework of Jewish history, the internal, unshakable proof of its *national* character. If this phenomenon is an illusion, we should have to accept one of two wildly improbable theories:

(1) Out of a hodgepodge of plagiarisms, of tangled and intermingled texts separated by centuries, there accidentally emerges the consistent and cohesive historical picture I have presented.

(2) The writers of the biblical texts, living more than two thousand years ago, anticipated our modern and sophisticated sense of the historical. Groups of Judean Jews, writing and editing in the third, fourth, and fifth centuries B.C.E. collaborated—consciously or unconsciously—to throw backward into the sixth, seventh, eighth, ninth and tenth centuries B.C.E. a pattern of development satisfactory to the historical sense of our twentieth century.

Since I am not a believer in miracles, I am compelled to reject both of these astounding theories. But this is not by any means equivalent to ignoring the higher criticism. We can accept a great deal of it; we can break up Isaiah, and sundry other prophets, into first, second, third, and fourth; we can fragmentate and reshuffle the historical books; and we are still left with the historical pattern of prophetism. It is so insistent that on grounds of common sense, and of every human probability, it withstands all but the most chaotic misuse of conjecture. It imposes a limitation, because it dominates logically. Even so, as we shall see, there is ample room for disagreement on the dates of specific passages. And I shall be compelled to discuss these disagreements because it is imperative to establish, for the understanding of contemporary meanings in Jewish-Christian relations, the limits of the intrinsic values of the Bible.

I have said that what was added to the prophetic books, whether in the Babylonian time or later, does not change the national-structural character of the prophetic episode. When we read the second —or second and third and fourth—Isaiah, we can see clearly, from the historical allusions, that the passages were written centuries after the first Isaiah; at any rate, centuries after the first Isaiah is purported to have lived. And there are sections here—as there are interpolated sections in the first Isaiah—which are not inferior to the highest productions of the classical prophetic age. But they are fragments— even if inspired fragments—of insight. The pattern had been established long before; the phenomenon was there, the Jewish view of nationhood and morality had been established. Prophetism as a national production—a unique thing in the world—had crystallized. The last of the self-recording prophets, following the return from Babylon, no longer had the original stature; they are epigones.

Finally, the reader may wonder at the omission of Moses from a survey of the prophets—he who is regarded by the Jewish people as the greatest of them, and of whom it is said: "There arose not a prophet since in Israel like unto Moses." But Moses stands apart in many ways. He is unquestionably a reconstruction. He is outside the trajectory of prophetism, and he is not subject to classification. There are patriarchs, kings, prophets, priests, who fall into patterns. There is only one Moses. And though he is regarded as the greatest of the prophets, he is, because of his atypicality, never called the prophet, like Elijah or Isaiah. He is called "our teacher." He presides over the birth of the Jewish national history but does not fit into it. This gigantic figure is the nearest approach in the Jewish record to a superhuman personality, a God-man. It was perhaps because they were conscious of dangerous possibilities in the Moses story that the editors of the Passover Haggadah omitted mention of him; with the astonishing consequence that when the Jews assemble annually to commemorate, with elaborate ritual, with ancient prayers and sagas, the incident of the Exodus, the central human figure in its execution is "repressed."

From *The Gentleman and the Jew* (1950)

21 THE MANAGER: REBEKAH

"Managerial," is the best overall word for Rebekah, the wife of Isaac; and after it "intuitive," "unerring," "competent," all with a touch of greatness. I am dazzled by her masterly grasp of things, and by her executive dash. If I had a problem in human relations it is Rebekah I would want to consult. What, not Naomi, the subtlest and most loving schemer of them all? No, not Naomi, who, I suspect, would solve my problem by making me into the kind of person who doesn't have that kind of problem.

We remember Rebekah chiefly as the principal in the *cause célèbre* of the embezzled blessing. She is the woman who hoodwinked her blind old husband into deeding to their son Jacob the family legacy that should have gone to Jacob's older twin brother, Esau. Thousands of monographs, and stories, and plays, and poems, have been written round the rights and wrongs of the affair. My stand in the immemorial controversy will become apparent in due course, but by way of preface I have this to say: whatever the formal rights and wrongs, the character of the legacy was such that to have loaded it onto Esau would have been fantastically cruel—assuming that the fantastically impossible could have happened—namely, that Esau could have received it.

Certainly Rebekah's handling of that involved and explosive situation, in which murder was latent, is the climax of her career, and it is proper to think of it first when her name is mentioned. But please note: the climax of her career; not an isolated incident, not one of those sudden, breathtaking displays of will and skill which make us gape at the performer and exclaim: "The devil! Who would have thought he had it in him!" On the contrary, anyone who has studied Rebekah and her life with Isaac would expect and even demand it of her. She was born for it, she prepared for it, and she alone could have carried it off.

It amuses me to compare the image I formed of Rebekah in my childhood with my present evocation of her. I was influenced then —as I still am, though how differently!—by her entry into the story, by her meeting with Eliezer, the wife-seeking emissary, for which she is remembered almost as often as for her deception of Isaac. As a pictorial subject "Rebekah at the Well" is one of those compulsive insipidities which are standard equipment for Bible illustrators. All of us have seen hundreds of Rebekahs with a sweet and earnest simper proffering water to the weary, wayworn wanderer and his camels. The pious *rebbe* whose life I helped to shorten aided and abetted the artists by his discourses on Rebekah's moral perfections. And I am amused because my present image is so dissimilar in the midst of so much similarity.

Let us go to the Text.

Eliezer, the old and trusted servant of Abraham, has come from Canaan, all the way across the desert that Balaam traversed, to seek a wife for Isaac, his master's son. He stands by the well outside the city of Nahor, perplexed. His instructions, clear in some respects, are in others obscure. Here is what his master said to him before he started out: "Put, I pray thee, thy hand under my thigh. And I will make thee swear by the Lord, the God of heaven and the God of the earth, that thou shalt not take a wife for my son of the daughters of the Canaanites, among whom I dwell. But thou shalt go unto my country, and to my kindred, and take a wife for my son, even for Isaac."

These are already strange terms of reference. The choosing of a wife for Isaac is henceforth Eliezer's exclusive responsibility, and Isaac's acquiescence in the choice is taken for granted, while Eliezer assumes the responsibility as a matter of course. We read only that he foresaw a possible obstacle: "Peradventure the woman will not be willing to follow me unto this land; must I needs bring thy son back unto the land from which thou camest?" And he received this categoric reply: "Beware that thou bring not my son back thither." Then Abraham continued: "The Lord, the God of heaven, who took me from my father's house, and from the land of my nativity, and who swore unto me, saying: 'Unto thy seed will I give this land'; He will send His angel before thee, and thou shalt take a wife for my son from thence. And if the woman be not willing to follow thee, then thou shalt be clear from this my oath."

What troubled Eliezer now was the phrase in the first part of the instructions: "Unto my country and to my kindred." Was "kindred" an absolute condition? If so, why "unto my country," seeing that Abraham had no kindred outside Mesopotamia? In the second part Abraham had said: "Thou shalt take a wife for my son from thence," as if the country were the absolute condition, and "kindred" only a preference. As far as Eliezer knew, Abraham's family, the people among whom he had done his first missionary work, had shown no susceptibility to his vision. There had been one exception, Lot, and he had come to a bad end. Why the family at all, in fact?

Eliezer prays: "And he said: 'Lord, the God of my master Abraham, send me, I pray Thee, good speed this day. Behold, I stand by the fountain of water; and the daughters of the men of the city come out to draw water. So let it come to pass, that the damsel to whom I shall say: "Let down thy pitcher, I pray thee, that I may drink"; and she shall say: "Drink, and I will give thy camels drink also"; let the same be she that Thou hast appointed for Thy servant, even for Isaac; and thereby shall I know that Thou hast shown kindness unto my master.' And it came to pass, before he had done speaking, that, behold, Rebekah came out, who was born to Bethuel the son of Milcah, the wife of Nahor, Abraham's brother, with her pitcher upon her shoulder. And the damsel was very fair to look upon, a virgin, neither had any man known her; and she went down to the fountain, and filled her pitcher, and came up. And the servant ran to meet her, and said: 'Give me to drink, I pray thee, a little water of thy pitcher.' And she said: 'Drink, my lord'; and she hastened and let down her pitcher upon her hand, and gave him drink. And when she had done giving him drink, she said: 'I will draw for thy camels also, until they have done drinking.' And she hastened, and emptied her pitcher into the trough, and ran again unto the well to draw, and drew for all his camels. And the man looked steadfastly on her."

I should think he would. Seldom has a prayer been answered so promptly and with such point-to-point fulfillment. Yet it was not so much what the girl did as the way she did it. She hastened, she ran, and withal she was so deliberate. She let him finish drinking before she offered to water the camels. And she had to do a lot of running back and forth with her pitcher, as anyone knows who has seen camels drink after a long journey. But no hesitations, no questions, no ill-timed courtesies, which would perhaps have been lost on a thirsty man and certainly on thirsty camels; just quick action, thorough, and completed before the conversation was resumed.

I like that girl. So did Eliezer. It does one good to watch her. I can imagine more than one man, especially among such as have found the world a bit too much for them, watching with us and saying, or rather thinking: "That's the kind of girl I should have married."

II

It was the kind of girl Isaac should have married, and did. Whereupon the reader may comment dryly: "Let us rather say the girl he was married off to, no less than she was married off to him." I understand. The reader does not like marriages for the good of without the consent of. Neither do I. Even when they turn out well, yes, even if it could be shown that on the whole the system works better than ours, we should still object. We live in order to grow and develop, and where there is no freedom of choice there is no development. For me, too, this view is self-understood, and because its implications are so important, let us pause while Rebekah is running up and down the steps emptying and filling her pitcher—it will take her quite a time —and let us see what bearing our view has on Isaac and Rebekah, and for that matter on the People of the Book generally.

In the instance before us it is undeniable that one of the parties —the man—was disposed of without consultation; and not by the woman, a thing that is liable to happen in the most emancipated societies, but by his father; and even by his father's chief servant. However, it will be seen that Isaac's was a special case; and what really troubles us is the status of biblical woman. She can be shown by honest quotation to have been a chattel, a serf, a commodity, a sexual plaything, a degraded, disfranchised, second-class human being. One need go no farther than the crushing fiat issued against Eve after the fall: "I will greatly multiply thy pain and thy travail; in pain shalt thou bring forth children; and thy desire shall be to thy husband, and he shall rule over thee." And if today, even in our society, the woman's desire is still toward her husband—in other words, if even today women are more anxious to get married than men—some of the blame attaches to the influence of the Bible. But thank God, or rather, no thanks to God, we have made some progress.

A superficial perusal of the Isaac-Rebekah story strengthens the shocking effect of those words from the third chapter of Genesis.

Eliezer comes to Nahor to find a wife for Isaac. The woman he picks will accept the husband sight-unseen. Yes, it is conceded that she might not be willing to follow Eliezer. Let us not make too much of that; the unwillingness might be her family's. And what is Eliezer's criterion? That the woman shall know her place—namely, as the ministrant to a man's needs—and those of his camels. Having found a satisfactory candidate, he puts bracelets on her hands and—how significant!—fastens a ring on her nose. He proceeds to her home, negotiates with the family, settles everything without a word from the young woman, and leads her off—we might say by the nose. What more does one want as proof of women's degradation in the Bible?

Speaking for myself, I want a careful scrutiny of the Text. And now that Rebekah has at last watered all the camels without any assistance from Eliezer or his men, let us resume the reading, and let us go slowly:

"And the man looked steadfastly on her, holding his peace, to know whether the Lord had made his journey prosperous or not. And it came to pass, as the camels had done drinking, that the man took a golden ring of half a shekel weight, and two bracelets for her hands of ten shekels weight of gold. . . ." Later that day, when Eliezer is telling the family about it, he is more detailed. He says: "I put the ring upon her nose and the bracelets upon her hands." Then: "He said: 'Whose daughter art thou? Tell me, I pray thee. Is there room in thy father's house for us to lodge in?' And she said unto him: 'I am the daughter of Bethuel, the son of Milcah, whom she bore unto Nahor.' She said moreover unto him: 'We have both straw and provender enough, and room to lodge in.' "

I insist: mark that pretty chit well. She does not lose her head when the stranger produces the valuable presents. She is still deliberate and systematic. Having given him her parentage, she pauses, then assures him with the right emphasis that his unexpected arrival will not embarrass the household. And when he says: "Blessed be the Lord, the God of my master Abraham, who hath not forsaken His mercy and His truth toward my master; as for me, the Lord hath led me in the way to the house of my master's brethren," when he utters these astounding words, she still does not lose her self-possession, still does not pester him with questions. We read immediately: "And the damsel ran, and told her mother's house according to these words."

I hope I have established the image of Rebekah as it rises for me from the Text: lively, intelligent, quick in action even as a girl; a person with—as I have said—"a grasp of things." This is not the submissive and servile Oriental female of popular tradition. And yet —she sits by silently while Eliezer speaks at length with the rest of the family, describing the condition of his master Abraham, the man of wealth, declaring the purpose of his visit, recounting all that has happened at the well, his prayer and the answer. He ends with these words: "And now if ye will deal truly and kindly with my master, tell me; if not, tell me; that I may turn to the right hand or to the left." The men of the household, Laban and Bethuel, the brother and father, make answer: "The thing proceedeth from the Lord." As in the case of Balak we cannot tell what "Lord" they mean when they echo Eliezer's word, but they continue piously: "We cannot speak unto thee bad or good. Behold, Rebekah is before thee, take her, and go, and let her be thy master's son's wife, as the Lord hath spoken."

This is really too much. There she is. Take her. Go. And not a word from Rebekah. But why should she speak if she likes what is happening? Just to show us that she has a will of her own?

We read on: "And it came to pass that, when Abraham's servant heard their words, he bowed himself down to the earth unto the Lord. And the servant brought forth jewels of silver, and jewels of gold, and raiment, and gave them to Rebekah; he also gave to her brother and to her mother precious things. And they did eat and drink, he and the men that were with him, and tarried all night; and they rose up in the morning, and he said: 'Send me away unto my master.' And her brother and mother said: 'Let the damsel abide with us a few days, at least ten; after that she shall go.' And he said unto them: 'Delay me not, seeing the Lord hath prospered my way; send me away that I may go to my master.' And they said: 'We will call the damsel, and inquire at her mouth.' And they called Rebekah, and said unto her: 'Wilt thou go with this man?' And she said: 'I will go.' And they sent away Rebekah their sister, and her nurse, and Abraham's servant, and his men."

I turn the phrases this way and that, and I linger over the question to Rebekah, and her answer. The matter has been settled, has it not? "Wilt thou go with this man?" refers not to the sale but only to the time of delivery. If it referred to the sale it would be an empty formality and a mockery. As it is, the question can only mean: "Will you go at once or linger a few days?" And the girl's unfeeling answer means: "At once. This very morning." What are we to make of it?

Was Rebekah so unhappy at home that she could not wait

another day if only for her mother's sake, not to mention father and brother? And if that was how she felt, where was filial respect, or the show of it? Or was she so resentful of the high-handed transaction that she said in effect: "I am no longer your property. Deliver me without delay to my purchaser"? These are not idle questions. We are looking for the spirit of the situation.

But we are on the wrong scent. Let us bethink ourselves that Rebekah and her mother—and no doubt the nurse, too—sat up half the night, talking about this fairyland turn in their lives. It is not recorded that they even asked Eliezer what his master's son looked like, or how old he was. They saw the miracle as a whole *à laisser ou à prendre,* and since it was *à prendre,* Rebekah understood that one did not linger over such things, one did not draw them out with increasingly tedious banquetings and farewells. It was all thrashed out in the night. Even the preparations were begun. How else could she have left on such short notice? When Rebekah's mother joined Laban in saying: "Let the damsel abide with us a few days," she did so out of deference to her son, perhaps also her husband, who is very much in the background. And when she joined in the question, it was with foreknowledge of the answer.

Something more, and that of crucial significance. Instinct—by which I mean the totality of her character—told Rebekah that it would be good for her husband to know, and to remember for the rest of his life, that when she was called to him she turned to her family and said: "I will go—at once."

III

Thus everything falls into place, and it is a willing bride, a ready, capable, clever, and attractive young woman, who goes out to meet her destiny. "And Rebekah arose, and her damsels, and they rode upon the camels, and followed the man. And the servant took Rebekah and went his way. And Isaac came from the way of Beer-lahai-roi; for he dwelt in the land of the South. And Isaac went out to meditate in the field at the eventide; and he lifted up his eyes and saw, and, behold, there were camels coming. And Rebekah lifted up her eyes, and when she saw Isaac, she alighted from the camel. And she said unto the servant: 'What man is this that walketh in the field to meet us?' And the servant said: 'It is my master.' And she took her veil and covered herself."

How this passage expands and unfolds for me, enriched by its enclosing past and future, and enriching them! How fitting it is that when Rebekah first sees Isaac he should be walking in the darkening field, sunk in meditation! She knows him. She makes her camel stop and kneel; she dismounts; and only then does she ask Eliezer: "What man is this that walketh in the field to meet us?" There are other first meetings of a man and a woman in the Bible conceived in key, perfect overtures. Isaac's son, Jacob, when he meets Rachel, for whom he will serve fourteen years, begins with an act of service; exhausted as he is by his long journey across the desert—the same journey as Eliezer has just made, but alone, not with a caravan, and not with presents —exhausted as he is, he insists on rolling away the stone from the well with his own arms, and on watering Rachel's flock. Moses the Liberator meets Zipporah at a well, too; and his first act is to defend her and her sisters against the ruffianly shepherds who are driving them away. But of all such preludes none reaches so deep as this one for Rebekah and Isaac, the woman of action and the man of meditation.

We learn from the Text that Isaac was forty years old when Rebekah came to him—a man set in his ways. He did not just happen to go out in the field that evening for the purpose of meditation; it was a habit with him—that is to say, a need. We could guess from the preceding account of his life thus far, without drawing on later confirmation, that he is a man who reacts rather than acts. His struggles are internal. Things are done for him and to him; his function is to get at the good in them; and if anyone confuses this with passivity, let him try it for a while.

When Isaac was a child he lost his only companion, a half-brother, Ishmael, not by death, but by unnatural separation. Ishmael, older than Isaac by a few years, was driven out into the desert together with his mother, Hagar; and the one who drove them out was Sarah, Isaac's mother. The cause, it appears, was arrogance on Hagar's side, vindictive jealousy on Sarah's.

If we want to get some idea of what Isaac had to meditate on, we can begin here. And without inventing anything, leaning solely on the Text, we shall discover that though arrogance and vindictiveness were motives and proximate causes in the Ishmael episode, they were irrelevant as far as Isaac was concerned. Seen from within the purpose of his life, the forces were quite different.

We go back to the days when Sarah was still called Sarai, and Abraham Abram; that is, before they were given the new names which declared their destinies, before Ishmael and Isaac were born. We read:

"Now Sarai Abram's wife bore him no children; and she had a

handmaid, an Egyptian, whose name was Hagar. And Sarai said unto Abram: 'Behold now, the Lord hath restrained me from bearing; go in, I pray thee, unto my handmaid; it may be that I shall be builded up through her.' "

Such was the custom of the time, and Abraham's grandson, Jacob, was likewise to make use of it, and much more frequently than his grandfather. It is one of the many features of woman's life in the biblical record which justify the indignation of moderns. On the other hand, it does not seem to have been regarded in this light by Hagar—or by the servants of Jacob's wives. For we read that when Hagar "saw that she had conceived, her mistress was despised in her eyes." Already then Sarah drove Hagar into the wilderness; but there an angel appeared to Hagar and bade her go back. He also told her that God had great things in store for her offspring: "I will greatly multiply thy seed, that it shall not be numbered for multitude . . . thou shalt bear a son, and thou shalt call his name Ishmael, because the Lord hath heard thy affliction. And he shall be a wild ass of a man, and every man's hand against him. . . ."

Where did this take place? Here, at Beer-lahai-roi, where Isaac is now walking, sunk in meditation.

Hagar returned to her mistress, and some years later, when Sarai had borne Isaac, and her name was Sarah, as Abram's had become Abraham, the second and final expulsion took place. We read: "And Sarah saw the son of Hagar the Egyptian, whom she had borne unto Abraham, making sport. Wherefore she said unto Abraham: 'Cast out this bondwoman and her son; for the son of the bondwoman shall not be heir with my son, even with Isaac.' "

Those words "making sport" have a special meaning, as we might suspect from the "wherefore" which follows them. Let the reader turn a few pages of the Text to the chapter that tells of Isaac as a married man trying to pass off Rebekah as his sister, when they were among the Philistines. There we read: "Abimelech king of the Philistines looked out at the window, and, behold, Isaac was sporting with Rebekah his wife. And Abimelech called Isaac and said: 'Behold, of a surety she is thy wife.' " I may add, once more, that the point is driven home somewhat more sharply in the original, for in the two places the same verb is used in the same tense, gender, number, and mood. But it is clear enough from the English that the wild and precocious son of Hagar was a danger to the child Isaac.

Some thirty-five years have passed since then, and Isaac is walking in these same fields of Beer-lahai-roi. His half-brother is a desert rover, and every man's hand is against him. Between things remem-

bered and things told him Isaac pieces it all together, and understands, as heir to the blessing, the purpose of the loss. For the con-
templative man past and future are reversible in meaning; they mold
each other; purpose and cause are interchangeable terms; and for two
men the same event can have two separate purposes and therefore
two separate causes. To each of them the cause that serves the other's
purpose is only a pretext. To Ishmael, Sarah's thought for Isaac's
well-being was a pretext, her hatred of Hagar the cause. In Isaac's
book Sarah's hatred of Hagar was a pretext, her thought for his
well-being the cause. He understands, he accepts, he submits.

He also sees why Abraham consented to the expulsion, though
only after God had promised him—for the second time—that the boy
would live, to become the founder of a great people. But Abraham
had suffered, he had found it "very grievous"; and thus, as a cause,
had identified himself with the purpose. Abraham had risen before
dawn, and had himself sent them away, his concubine and his son,
into the desert, with a loaf of bread and a bottle of water, all he could
lay his hands on in the darkness, rather than leave the expulsion to
Sarah. Whenever Isaac thinks of that parting he stops walking, he is
paralyzed for a moment. Yes, he understands, he accepts, he submits;
and still the struggle is not over; it never will be, and the pain will
never become a mere memory.

When Isaac was twelve years old, or perhaps thirteen—the Text
refers to him there as a lad—a terrible thing was done to him. He was
offered up as a sacrifice, a burnt offering, on Mount Moriah, by his
old and loving father. But this was done to him with his wholehearted consent; and let us not call it a near-sacrifice just because at
the last moment he was unexpectedly bidden to go on living. He did
not anticipate the reprieve, neither did his father; for if they had
done, the incident, which left such a mark on him—as it has on the
world—would have been childish mummery. He gave up his life; he
passed through the valley of the shadow of death; and he came back,
and took up his life again. Surely in this alone there was material for
a lifetime of meditation.

For me the most interesting role here was played by the mother,
who played no role at all. She was not consulted—that is definite. She
was never told about it—that is implied. She was excluded from the
most significant single event in the life of her son, the event that was
her vindication. Isaac must often have pondered this extraordinary
fact: she who had guarded him for God was not permitted to know
how God claimed him and found him perfect.

The Text informs us that when Isaac was awaiting Rebekah,

only two years had passed since Sarah's death, and his heart was still heavy for her. Her tent stood vacant, waiting for her who was to be the wife of the heir to the blessing. And he was not the chooser of his wife any more than he had been the chooser of his mother. Why need he be? The unchosen mother had acted for his good; why should the unchosen wife do less?

Let her come, and let her come quickly; that will be a sign. He reckons the days. Seventeen each way across the desert, and an indeterminate number for the search. Or perhaps, since an angel might have gone before, no search. Thirty-four days, then, for the coming and going, and a week or ten days for preparations and farewells; and only thirty-four days have passed since Eliezer set forth.

But for an unknown reason he has this evening taken the direction from which the caravan will arrive. He has walked a long way, sunk in thought, and suddenly, again for an unknown reason, he raises his eyes from the ground, and against the fading light in the west he sees a line of camels approaching soft-footed over the ridge. Still for an unknown reason he continues his walk instead of turning aside or back, and his heart beats faster. It cannot be. She cannot have come thus, without a moment's delay. And still he continues, and he sees the foremost camel halt, and kneel, and a woman descends. There is an upwelling in his heart, and unspoken words tremble on his lips: "I might have known."

Then we read: "And the servant told Isaac all the things he had done. And Isaac brought Rebekah into his mother Sarah's tent, and she became his wife; and he loved her; and Isaac was comforted for his mother."

From *Certain People of the Book* (1955)

22 THE COMIC AS FOOL: AHASUERUS

I must begin by dispelling the popular notion that there is no humor in the Bible. I am not speaking of ironical passages here and there, or of figures held up for the complacent derision of the godly. I am speaking of sustained comic writing and of deliberately comic figures, of which there are many varieties: comics as fools, as dolts, as knaves, as grotesques, and even as beneficent gnomes. I shall present them in turn between the serious personalities; and I open with Ahasuerus the Emperor.

The humor of the Bible is deadpan. The narrative never abandons the stately rhythms that come through to us even in the translations, and an implacable solemnity seems to brood over individuals and incidents: let me say a suspiciously implacable solemnity, because it is inconceivable that the whole biblical world should have lived its life in such a sustained severity of mood. Long ago I suspected that in many places the majestic façade only half concealed an invitation to mirth: a progressive mirth, developing from a startled and timid grin into a joyous chuckle, to explode at last into a convulsion of the diaphragm. And here I attempt the all but impossible task of infecting the reader with laughter at second hand, choosing the Book of Esther as material for the first experiment.

It opens with Ahasuerus, who is introduced in royal panoply: "This is Ahasuerus who reigned, from India even unto Ethiopia, over a hundred and twenty-seven provinces. . . . And in the third year of his reign he made a feast unto all his princes and servants; the army of Persia and Media, the nobles of the provinces, being before him. He showed the riches of his glorious kingdom and the honor of his excellent majesty many days, even a hundred and fourscore." And after the great feast a smaller feast, for the residents of Shushan the capital, in the palace gardens. "There were hangings of white, fine cotton, and blue, bordered with cords of fine linen and purple, upon silver rods and pillars of marble; the couches were of gold and silver, upon a pavement of green, and white, and shell, and onyx marble. And they gave them drink in vessels of gold, the vessels being diverse one from another. . . ."

We have been lulled into dignity by the gravity of the style, awed into respect by the splendor of the setting. And we read:

"On the seventh day, when the heart of the king was merry with wine, he commanded Mehuman, Bizzetha, Harbonah, Bigtha, and Abagtha, Zethar, and Carcas, the seven chamberlains that ministered in the presence of Ahasuerus the king, to bring Vashti the queen before the king with the royal crown, to show the princes and peoples her beauty, for she was fair to look on."

It is time to put the Text down and to close our eyes. The narrator might have said simply that Ahasuerus commanded the queen to appear before him; or that he sent messengers; or that he himself went for her. No. Massively epic, the periods inform us that Ahasuerus appointed an imperial commission, and that it consisted of the seven chamberlains whose names are entered on the eternal scroll. Let us repeat them reverently: Mehuman, Bizzetha, Harbonah, Bigtha, and Abagtha, Zethar, and Carcas.

A wit has made a seasonal classification of fools: the Winter Fool and the Summer Fool. The winter fool enters concealed in parka, overcoat, earmuffs, galoshes, muffler, and gloves, a formidable figure of a man. He removes the wraps ceremoniously one by one, and what do we behold? A fool, an authentic and unmistakable fool, in unencumbered command of his inimitable talents, and already performing. The summer fool, on the other hand, rushes in bareheaded and in shorts, without defenses or pretenses, a fool at first sight. Ahasuerus is a winter fool.

Behold the seven commissioners, befuddled, disconcerted, and conscious of high responsibility, in official procession from the king's banqueting hall to the queen's. There is no established protocol for their unprecedented assignment. Never before, to their knowledge, has a Persian consort been commanded to exhibit her imperial shapeliness at a state banquet. The commissioners must improvise. Shall they enter in a body or select an envoy? What is the proper wording? His Imperial Majesty had said: "Go fetch the queen. I want the boys to see her. And tell her to be sure to put the crown on." The language was irregular; where was the preamble, where were the distinguished guests, goodwill, innovation, Her Majesty's gracious cooperation? Mehuman, Bizzetha, Harbonah, Bigtha, and Abagtha, Zethar, and Carcas consult in the vestibule of the queen's banqueting hall. Time is short; action is imperative; minds are confused. "You go in, Bigtha." "No, Abagtha is the man." "Not I. What's the matter with Harbonah?" In a burst of confidence Mehuman squares off and exits.

We read: "But the queen Vashti refused to come at the king's commandment by the chamberlains."

Reenter Mehuman, glassy-eyed and all but speechless. "Well?" "She won't come." "What do you mean, she won't come?" "She won't come. She threw me out. She practically insulted me." Incredulity followed by consternation among the seven chamberlains, Mehuman, Bizzetha, Harbonah, etc. Bigtha looks at Abagtha, Abagtha looks back at Bigtha, all seven look at each other. This is the Ahriman of a situation. "Let's try again. You go, Carcas." "The Ahriman I will! Go yourself!" "Who'll tell Ahasuerus?" "Not I." "Let's go home, maybe he'll forget, he's pretty high."

Meanwhile Ahasuerus, flushed and convivial, throws anticipatory glances at the door and knowing winks at the guests, and waits all unaware of the incredible turn of events. And the guests wait; and a whispering rises at the back. The seven commissioners straggle in, distraction written on their faces, and there is an agonized interchange, *sotto voce,* on the dais. We are familiar with the scene; we have all been at banquets where something has gone wrong, and the chairmen have gone into a panic of sibilation. But this is no ordinary banquet, and never was the miscarriage of a program fraught with more far-reaching consequences. The commissioners stutter: "O King, live forever—Her Imperial Majesty—that is, Queen Vashti—" "Speak up!" hisses the ruler of one hundred and twenty-seven provinces from India to Ethiopia. "What is it?" "Let not His Imperial Majesty be angry with his servants—the queen—unexpected—indisposed—" "Don't talk like an idiot. She was perfectly well this morning. You found her at the banquet, didn't you? Are you drunk, by any chance?" "No, Your Imperial Majesty, we are all sober, especially I—but the queen—I mean—indisposed to come—certain reasons—protocol—" The whispering at the back swells into a buzzing. Tittering is heard. The hearts of the guests are as merry with wine as the king's.

We read: "And the king was very wroth, and his anger burned in him. Then said the king to the wise men . . ." In brief, the wraps are off, and the performance is in full swing.

II

Always in the grand manner, without the flicker of an eyelash, the narrator now gives us the names of the seven imperial councilors whom Ahasuerus called into session in this hour of crisis: Carshena, Sethar, Admatha, Tarshish, Meres, Marsena, and Memucan. The single item on the agenda, we read, was formulated by the king himself: "What shall we do unto the queen Vashti according to law, forasmuch as she hath not done the bidding of the king Ahasuerus by the chamberlains?" The narrator clearly hints at a rewording: "What shall we do that it be known unto all the empire and unto all the generations that the king Ahasuerus did become exceeding drunk at the imperial banquet?" For it was to this problem, whatever their other intentions, that the best brains of the empire, the seven councilors, princes of Media and Persia, Carshena, Sethar, Admatha, Tarshish, Meres, Marsena, and Memucan, really addressed themselves, and with a success to which we are even now testifying.

Of the proceedings taken down by the imperial speedwriters nothing has survived except the brilliant summation by councilor Prince Memucan, which, standing alone, is an invaluable addition to our knowledge of classical Oriental statesmanship. Said councilor Memucan: "Vashti the queen hath not done wrong to the king only, but also to all the princes, and to all the peoples that are in the provinces of the king Ahasuerus. For this deed of the queen will come abroad unto all women, to make their husbands contemptible in their eyes, when it will be said: 'The king Ahasuerus commanded Vashti the queen to be brought before him, but she came not.' And this day will the princesses of Persia and Media who have heard of the deed of the queen say the like unto all of the king's princes. So there will arise enough contempt and wrath. If it please the king, let there go forth a royal commandment from him, and let it be written among the laws of the Persians and the Medes, that it be not altered, that Vashti come not before king Ahasuerus, and that the king give her royal estate unto another that is better than she. And when the king's decree which he shall make shall be published throughout all his kingdom, great though it be, all the wives will give to their husbands honor, both to great and small."

Memucan showed high skill in giving the question such wide moral and political perspectives. Admirable, too—at least on the surface—is his concern that not a single princess of Media or Persia shall remain ignorant of Ahasuerus's behavior at the banquet, and of what flowed from it. Ahasuerus liked the proposed measures; it is one of the advantages of being a fool of means that one need not languish in obscurity. His council liked it, too. We read: "And the word pleased the king and the princes; and the king did according to the word of Memucan; for he sent letters into all the king's provinces, into every province according to the writing thereof, and to every people according to their language, that every man should bear rule in his own house, and speak according to the language of the people."

III

This Ahasuerus: he was not a man to be trifled with. He was stern —nay, inexorable—but just: majestic in anger, deliberate in chastisement. That was how he saw himself in the affair of the contumacious queen. But only for a time. We read: "After these things, when the wrath of the king Ahasuerus was assuaged, he remembered Vashti, and what she had done, and what was decreed against her. Then said the king's servants that ministered unto him . . ."

What were they to say? He was remembering Vashti, but with wrath assuaged. He was remembering what she had done to him, but also what he had done to her. He had to remember, further, that he was inexorable, he was the personification of "the laws of the Medes and Persians," which do not change. It was depressing. Vashti had sinned, and she had been punished. But perhaps she had had a change of heart; and "she was fair to look on." Clemency becomes a king. One is inexorable, certainly, but does one have to go to extremes? Can one not be inexorable within reason? If there were only some way—unfortunately all those letters had gone out, to all the provinces, each in its own language.

Ahasuerus brooded. Like all fools he had a new picture of himself for every need. He was always saying of himself, gaily or gloomily, impetuously or thoughtfully: "That's the kind of person I am, take it or leave it." Those of us who are not completely fools lapse into this practice only after a few drinks, and it is then that we utter the *cri de coeur:* "I've got to be myself, I've got to be honest with myself; I know it's not clever of me, but I can't help it." Ahasuerus, alas, added to his natural talents a weakness for the bottle. At the famous banquet, just before Vashti's ill-advised defiance, he had been old King Ahasuerus-Cole, democratic, hail-fellow-well-met. Immediately after it he had been an outraged and inexorable majesty. The picture he now had of himself was of the tragic man-god-ruler, sacrificer and sacrifice, fated to inexorability and yearning in the midst of his awful grandeur for the common human touch.

It was a tricky business, this of keeping pace with Ahasuerus's internal pictorial changes, and brief was the life of a councilor without an eye for art. Here, finally, is what his servants said to him:

"Let there be sought out for the king virgins fair to look on; and let the king appoint officers in all the provinces of his kingdom, that they may gather together all the fair young virgins unto Shushan the castle, to the house of the women; and let their ointments be given them; and let the maiden that pleaseth the king be queen instead of Vashti."

In effect, this was only a cleverly phrased reminder. Vashti had been deposed in accordance with the decree; but the decree also provided that "the king give her royal estate to another that is better than she." The delay was making it appear that the king despaired of finding a better queen than Vashti, and this, besides causing the king to eat his heart out, played into the hands of the subversives. We read that when his servants had spoken, "the thing pleased the king, and he did so." The servants were lucky that day; it pleased him only in the sense that he was lonely, and resigned to his duty. He showed no enthusiasm, and did nothing to hasten the leisurely proceedings. The officers had to be appointed; the candidates had to be chosen in one hundred and twenty-seven provinces and brought to Shushan. What with the local tryouts, the distances, and the travel conditions of those days, this cannot have taken less than several months. After they had been assembled, a whole year was consumed by the preparations for the finals. "So were the days of their anointing accomplished, to wit, six months with oil of myrrh, and six months with sweet odors, and with other ointments of the women."

No committee presided at the awarding of the first prize. Ahasuerus was the sole judge, without appeal, and he must have anticipated the exercise of this untransferable royal prerogative with some uneasiness. For we read: "When the turn of every maiden was come, to go in to king Ahasuerus . . . in the evening she went, and on the morrow she returned to the house of the women. . . . She came in unto the king no more, except the king delighted in her, and she were called by name." There is no roster of unsuccessful candidates

—a tactful piece of reticence. We can only guess at their number. It cannot have been less than two hundred and fifty-six—one winner for each of the one hundred and twenty-seven provinces and the capital, and for each one runner-up. The law was strict; Ahasuerus was not permitted to reject a candidate on sight, no matter how unfavorable his immediate impression. Like every other candidate she was entitled to her night in court. It therefore stands to reason that he could not arbitrarily suspend the competition at a point of his own choosing and declare himself satisfied. We read, in fact: "And the king loved Esther above all the women, and she obtained grace and favor in his sight more than all the virgins; so that he set the crown royal upon her head, and made her queen instead of Vashti." There were no omissions, and Ahasuerus probably got more of the common human touch than he had yearned for. It came to an end at last, and, whatever his criteria, we must assume that Ahasuerus found Esther not only better than all the other candidates, but, as prescribed by the decree, better than Vashti, too. In any case, the policymakers had no grounds for complaint; Esther made a submissive and obedient queen; that was how she twisted Ahasuerus round her little finger.

Was he very much in love with her? We have only a comparative statement: "above all the women." She had great influence over him, and he thought highly of her—but love? We know that he would let weeks pass without sending for her, and since she was already queen the competition could no longer be blamed. If she came to him uninvited it was at the peril of her life. When her people was threatened with extermination by Haman, and her cousin Mordecai besought her to intervene personally with Ahasuerus, she had to return this message: "All the king's servants, and the people of the king's provinces, do know that whosoever, man or woman, shall come unto the king in the inner court, there is one law for him, that he be put to death, except such to whom the king shall hold out the golden scepter, that he may live; but I have not been called in unto the king these thirty days."

It was a general law, but that Esther was afraid to test it on herself reflects unfavorably on Ahasuerus as a lover. We cannot accuse her of undue mistrust, either, after he had ignored her for thirty days. And she was thoroughly afraid. Mordecai had to put strong pressure on her. He sent back word: "Think not with thyself that thou shalt escape in the king's house, more than all the Jews. For if thou altogether holdest thy peace at this time, then will relief and deliverance arise to the Jews from another place, but thou and thy father's house will perish; and who knoweth whether thou art not come to royal estate for such a time as this?" Esther made the decision in trembling, and sent this message to Mordecai: "Go, gather together all the Jews that are present in Shushan, and fast ye for me, and neither eat nor drink three days, night or day; I also and my maidens will fast in like manner; and so will I go in unto the king, which is not according to the law; and if I perish, I perish."

It appears that when the queen disobeyed the king he could do no more, according to the law, than depose her, whereas if she approached him unasked for and unwanted, the penalty might be death. Disobedience in a queen was a civic offense, nagging could be treated as a capital crime. The royal prerogatives in Persia were not uniformly onerous.

IV

We are told next how Haman asks Ahasuerus for permission to liquidate a sizable part of the population of the empire.

Haman, Ahasuerus's current favorite, had been affronted publicly by Mordecai the Jew. The circumstances are not given, and Mordecai's disregard of the Jewish position, unexplained except by rumors in the Tradition, is hard to understand. We read: "When Haman saw that Mordecai bowed not down, nor prostrated himself before him, he was full of wrath. But it seemed contemptible in his eyes to lay hands on Mordecai alone. . . . Wherefore Haman sought to destroy all the Jews that were throughout the whole kingdom of Ahasuerus."

He went about it with the propaganda which, unchanged in any detail, has remained standard to this day. Like Memucan, he made his speech where it would do most good: in the ears of a fool; but unlike Memucan, privately, for the exclusive benefit of Ahasuerus: "There is a certain people scattered abroad among the peoples in all the provinces of thy kingdom; and their laws are diverse from those of every people; neither keep they the king's laws; therefore it profiteth not the king to suffer them. If it please the king, let it be written that they be destroyed; and I will pay ten thousand talents of silver into the hands of those that have charge of the king's business, to bring it into the king's treasuries."

Did King Ahasuerus ask for the name and identity of the people? He did not. Did he ask for the sources of Haman's information? He did not. When Vashti had disobeyed him he had called into session the Supreme Council of Seven to deliberate on the consequences to the welfare and morale of the empire. Did he consult anyone as to the possible effects that the extermination of this unnamed people might produce on the economy of the empire? Or want to know how long this had been going on, and why? He did not. Having listened to the speech, "the king took his ring from his hand, and gave it unto Haman, the son of Hammedatha the Agagite, the Jew's enemy. And the king said unto Haman: 'The silver is given to thee, the people also, to do with them as seemeth good to thee.' "

And forthwith the secretaries were called in, and the couriers flew along the imperial roads, "unto the king's satraps, and to the governors that were over every province; and to the province of every people; to every province according to the writing thereof, and to every people after their language. . . . The posts went forth by the king's commandment, and the decree was given out in Shushan the castle; and the king and Haman sat down to drink; but the city of Shushan was perplexed."

The last time the posts went out "to every province according to the writing thereof, and to every people after their language," it was to have them round up virgins for the king; this time it was to have them slaughter the Jews. It is an ingenious contrast, which teaches us something about the diverse uses of power in the hands of a fool.

In what terms did Ahasuerus dramatize himself to himself as he sat drinking with Haman after issuing the order for the extermination of the Jews? I may be wrong, and my career as adviser to Ahasuerus might have been a brief one, but I feel that they amounted to the damn-decent-sort-even-if-I-am-an-inexorable-man-god-king pic-ture, the sort who does a man a favor off-hand, without prying and hedging and stalling and acting the stuffed shirt with: "Don't you think one ought to consult the council?" and: "Let me look into it and I'll let you know tomorrow." Perhaps there was also a hint of the and - they - say - I'm - incapable - of - a - simple - kindness - they'll - never - know theme. At any rate, he told Haman to keep his money: "The silver is given to thee, the people also, to do with them as seemeth good to thee." That was the kind of person he was.

Somewhat surprisingly he was still that kind of person—or was it again?—a few days later when, after her long fast, "Esther put on her royal apparel, and stood in the inner court of the king's house, over against the king's house; and the king sat upon his royal throne in the royal house."

He had not seen her for thirty days, and there she stood, uninvited, unexpected, and unannounced, that most acutely embarrassing of intruders, the neglected wife come to remind her husband of his conjugal obligations. It might have ended badly for her. Ahasuerus was, as we have seen, a busy man whose life was weighed down with cares of state. Women don't understand, they take such a personal and self-centered view of things, and many a husband would have sympathized with Ahasuerus if he had flown into a temper and put his scepter behind his back. Fortunately he was not that kind of person. We read: "And it was so, when the king saw Esther the queen standing in the court, that she obtained favor in his sight; and the king held out to Esther the golden scepter that was in his hand. So Esther drew near, and touched the top of the scepter. Then the king said unto her: 'What wilt thou, queen Esther? For whatever thy request, even to the half of the kingdom, it shall be given thee.' "

It was a generous offer. Kings have been known to give up the whole of a kingdom for love, but not to a wife. And in those days kings had more to give up. How proud Ahasuerus must have been when Esther made her reply: "If it seem good to the king, let the king and Haman come this day unto the banquet that I have prepared for him"! He had reason to be proud. How wisely and with what masterly insight he had picked her out from among the hundreds of contestants with nothing more than a single night's acquaintanceship to go on! How different she was from Vashti! Not a hint of reproach for his prolonged abstinence. It was of him alone that she was thinking. How adoring the woman was, how humble, how good-looking! And if he had only known, how hungry!

"Then the king said: 'Cause Haman to make haste, that it may be done as Esther hath said.' " In his excitement he forgot to give the queen her title. No matter; he was not the kind of man to stand on ceremony. The order to Haman was, we may be sure, superfluous. Haman had no idea that Esther was a Jewess. Neither had Ahasuerus. She had kept it secret on the advice of Mordecai, her cousin, and adoptive father, and general counselor. But it would have made no difference. In every generation, from Berenice to Magda, there have been Jews and Jewesses to whom Jew-haters could say in all sincerity: "If only the others were like you!" Not that Ahasuerus was a Jew-hater; he was merely the kind of person who votes a Haman into office and then says: "Buchenwald? I never heard of the place." Also, in the more familiar phrase: "Why, one of my dearest friends is a Jew"—or "a Jewess."

Haman was there on time; so was Ahasuerus, who, whatever else he was, was never late at a banquet, especially when it was prepared by his Esther, on whom he could rely for the right menu. We too may rely on her to be more attentive to her husband's thirst than to her own hunger. So we read: "And the king said unto Esther at the banquet of wine: 'Whatever thy petition, it shall be granted thee; and whatever thy request, even to the half of my kingdom, it shall be performed.' Then answered Esther and said: 'My petition and my request is—if I have found favor in the eyes of the king, and if it please the king to grant my petition, and to perform my request— let the king and Haman come to the banquet that I shall prepare for them, and I will do tomorrow as the king hath said.' "

Have I done Ahasuerus an injustice? It does seem from the above that he was not entirely taken in by Esther's loving solicitude, and that he suspected her of having something up her brocaded sleeve. If this is so, if he was not merely talking court language, I am glad to apologize. But let me add that after years of intimacy with the man and his record I have found just this one flaw in Ahasuerus's fatuity. Nevertheless my apology is wholehearted. I shall not be evasive; I shall not resort to the subterfuge so beloved of Bible scholars, and say: "This passage is an obvious interpolation." When I am wrong I am always ready to admit it. For better or for worse, I happen to be that kind of person.

But by no stretch of the imagination can we discover in Haman even a glimmering of suspicion. We are now treated to a marvelous portrayal of blissful self-complacency poisoned by a single frustration: "Then went Haman forth that day joyful and glad of heart; but when Haman saw Mordecai in the king's gate, that he stood not up nor moved for him, Haman was filled with wrath against Mordecai. Nevertheless Haman refrained himself, and went home; and he sent and fetched his friends and Zeresh his wife. And Haman recounted to them the glory of his riches, and the multitude of his children, and everything as to how the king had promoted him, and how he had advanced him above the princes and servants of the king. Haman said moreover: 'Yea, Esther the queen did let no man come in with the king unto the banquet that she had prepared but myself; and tomorrow also am I invited by her together with the king. Yet all this availeth me nothing so long as I see Mordecai the Jew sitting at the king's gate.' "

We could profitably spend more time on Haman as a subtype; for if Ahasuerus is the Pure or Blithering Fool, Haman is the Masterful or Self-Destroying Fool. He had everything to make him happy except Mordecai's homage, and that was his undoing. "All this availeth me nothing, as long as I see Mordecai the Jew sitting at the king's gate." But our subject is Ahasuerus, and the other characters, as well as the rest of the story—the plot to destroy the Jews, the foiling of it by Mordecai and Esther, the downfall of Haman—must be subordinated to it. It must suffice here to mention that Zeresh and the friends of the family offered Haman the following gratifying advice: "Let a gallows be made of fifty cubits high, and in the morning speak thou to the king that Mordecai may be hanged thereon; then go thou in merrily with the king unto the banquet." The "thing" pleased Haman; and he caused the gallows to be made. Not a moment was lost, for we read that they were ready by the next morning.

Nor shall we linger over Haman's humiliation before his execution, except in so far as it sheds additional light on our main subject. A rare thing happened to Ahasuerus between the two banquets: he passed a sleepless night. "And he commanded to bring the book of records of the chronicles. And it was found written, that Mordecai had told of Bigthana and Teresh, two of the king's chamberlains, of those that kept the door, who had sought to lay hands on the king Ahasuerus. And the king said: 'What honor and dignity hath been done to Mordecai for this?' Then said the king's servants that ministered unto him: 'There is nothing done for him.'"

I cannot account for the directness of the reply and the forbearance of the king. It would have been no more than right if he had hanged a few officials for such criminal negligence. Here a man had saved the king's life by uncovering a palace conspiracy, and some months later the king's servants blandly reveal that no reward had been made, no distinction conferred, nothing, but nothing, done about it. Did they expect him to think of everything? And suppose he had not happened to pass a sleepless night, or had not asked for the chronicles, or they had picked on another passage—was he to assume that the incident would have been buried forever, and he would be made to appear, before his contemporaries and posterity, a monster of ingratitude?

But Ahasuerus did not make a scene. He was perhaps too tired, and too disgusted. Besides, what was the use? He was now the man with a thousand servants who, when he wants a thing done, has to do it himself. Tired as he was, he acted promptly. "And the king said: 'Who is in the court?' Now Haman was come into the outer court of the king's house, to speak unto the king to hang Mordecai on the gallows he had prepared for him." Well, there at least was a servant who would not let him down. And he called Haman in, and put the question to him: "What shall be done to the man whom the king delighteth to honor?"

As we know, or ought to know, and would expect by now if we did not know, Haman took the question as applying to himself. In his state of mind it was perfectly natural. Whom else would the king want to honor first thing in the morning? They must have told Haman, too, that Ahasuerus had hardly slept that night—such tidings spread swiftly through a palace—and it was a profoundly moving thought that what had kept the emperor awake was his anxiety to heap fresh honors on his favorite and his inability to hit on something appropriate. Indeed, Haman was so moved that he forgot to ask for permission to hang Mordecai. That is a pity. I have often wondered what Ahasuerus would have said under the special circumstances, and what personality he would have assumed for the occasion.

He was spared the effort. In a transport of joy Haman cried: "For the man whom the king delighteth to honor, let royal apparel be brought which the king useth to wear, and the horse that the king rideth upon, and on whose head a royal crown is set; and let the apparel and the horse be delivered into the hand of one of the king's most noble princes, that they may array the man therewith whom the king delighteth to honor, and cause him to ride on horseback through the streets of the city, and proclaim before him. 'Thus shall it be done unto the man whom the king delighteth to honor.'"

Good man! It was a solid, detailed answer such as Ahasuerus expected from a competent adviser. He said: "Make haste, and take the apparel and the horse, as thou hast said, and do even so to Mordecai the Jew, that sitteth at the king's gate; let nothing fail of all that thou hast spoken."

At this moment we can be quite sure of Ahasuerus's projection of himself. He had shown once more that he knew how to pick his advisers; he had discharged a debt of honor; he had made good an outrageous administrative oversight. Let the world now look on the king who never forgot a service. He was, if possible, more than usually satisfied with himself as he watched Haman depart on his mission, and it is altogether unlikely that he noticed the peculiar green tinge that had crept over Haman's face.

I permit myself another brief digression. Haman's feelings on this occasion are indicated in the record. After he had performed the ghastly ceremony, he "hastened to his house, mourning and having his head covered." Nothing is said about the way Mordecai took the extraordinary episode. But he cannot have been any happier than Haman. Here he was, dressed in the king's robes, riding the king's caparisoned and crowned horse, being led through the city by his inveterate and despised enemy, who croaked at irregular intervals: "Thus shall it be done unto the man whom the king delighteth to honor." And all the time he was sick with worry over the impending massacre of the Jews. It was mad.

V

We are at the high point of suspense in our story, and we must stop for a moment to take stock. I have just said that to Mordecai the whole thing was mad. But none of the principals, except Ahasuerus, can have felt sure that day of the sanity of things. For that matter, the uncertainty must have extended to the entire population of Shushan the capital as it stood on the sidewalks and stared, more perplexed than ever, at the astounding spectacle. Orders were out for a St. Bartholomew's Night, a Sicilian Vespers, a November Burning of the Synagogues—there are unfortunately synonyms enough for what was awaiting the Jews of Persia—and here the leading member of the Jewish community was being accorded the highest honors by the man responsible for the orders. To add to the confusion, everyone knew that it was Mordecai's noble dignity, or reckless insolence—the description depended on one's point of view—that had set off Haman's hatred.

One could not make sense of it. What had happened? Had Haman suddenly been cured of his anti-Semitic complex? Had a reconcilation taken place? Then why did Haman look as if he had been dead for several days? And if he was doing it against his will, and the orders for the massacre had been canceled, why had not the city been told, and why did Mordecai look even worse than Haman? We can better imagine than reproduce the debates which rent the air that day in the homes and saloons of Shushan, and on the street corners. At the center of it all Ahasuerus, and he alone, moved serenely about his business, if we may so put it, never doubting the essential sanity of a world that his intelligence directed.

On the day of the dénouement Ahasuerus's business, after his exacting labors on behalf of Mordecai, was to prepare for the evening. "So the king and Haman came to the banquet of Esther the queen. And the king said again unto Esther on the second day at the banquet of wine: 'Whatever thy petition, queen Esther, it shall be granted thee; and whatever thy request, even to the half of the kingdom, it shall be performed.' "

Honor where honor is due. In this matter Ahasuerus was a gentleman. Drunk or sober he remembered his promise to his wife, and he did not, as some husbands will, take advantage of the delay to whittle it down. He had said: "half the kingdom." He did not now say: "three eighths of the kingdom," or "a third, things haven't been going too well this week." Always assuming, of course, that it was not merely an Oriental court formula. And now Esther made her request, and we are about to view one of the world's greatest paintings: "Fool Getting a Jolt."

"Then Esther the queen answered and said: 'If I have found favor in thy sight, O king, and if it please the king, let my life be given me at my petition, and my people at my request; for we are sold, I and my people, to be destroyed, to be slain, and to perish. But if we had been sold for bondmen and bondwomen, I had held my peace, for the adversary is not worthy that the king be endamaged.' "

I have more than once met the suggestion that the famous Esther was just a pretty puppet manipulated by the brilliant Mordecai; it was her body and his brains, her voice and his inspiration—the original Trilby-Svengali combination. The view owes more to masculine vanity than to common sense. We need not underrate Mordecai's part in the affair, or deny that he had much to do with formulating the general policy. He may even have suggested the foregoing speech. But to deliver it at the right moment with an air of spontaneity, to balance it so neatly, to know exactly when to stop and on what note, was beyond the capacity of a puppet. If ever the reader finds himself under the necessity of pleading for his life with an Ahasuerus, let him study Esther's diplomatic technique. In the absence of her physical advantages I cannot guarantee success, but it is impossible to improve on the psychological approach.

The real purpose of the speech, gathered into its climax, is to protect the king's good health. Nothing but the threat of death—her own and that of her people—could have induced Esther to endanger it. Everlasting bondage was preferable to such a crime. As for Haman, he did not count at all. Nobody counted but Ahasuerus. There was even a certain presumption in trying to save one's life, and prevent a general massacre, at the cost of the king's peace of mind. But the flesh is weak—he would understand and forgive.

"Then spoke the king and said unto Esther: 'Who is he, and

where is he, that durst presume in his heart to do so?' And Esther said: 'An adversary and an enemy, even this wicked Haman.' Then Haman was terrified before the king and queen. And the king arose in his wrath from the banquet of wine and went into the palace garden.''

We have come full circle and are back at the beginning! Ahasuerus is at a banquet; he has been drinking; he has been affronted; he is angry. There it was Vashti; here it is Haman. The difference is immaterial. Let happen what will in the outside world, Ahasuerus's interior life follows its own cycle. This time he is angrier, perhaps drunker; words fail him, and he must go into the garden to cool off and think things over. We know him well enough by now to be sure that, with him, thinking things over will not lead back to any such question as: "Who was it gave Haman permission to exterminate an entire people without so much as asking for its name, and then sat down to have a drink on it?" The nearest he will come to it, and even this is unlikely, will be: "Why didn't the scoundrel, the snake-in-the-grass, the traitor, tell me it was the queen's people?" What his mind is busy with is the choice of the personality he ought to put on. In what capacity shall he face the situation? Who is he? The betrayed monarch? The brilliant uncoverer of another conspiracy? The knight errant of justice? The merciful father of his people? The disappointed friend? There is such a wide range of selves, and he looks among them frantically, unable to decide, and this makes him angrier and angrier. What ingratitude, to put him in such a quandary without a moment's warning! And he must act without delay, to show his queen—tears of pride mingle with tears of rage as he thinks of her —who he is. No time to call the imperial council into session. She is waiting for him, his Esther, his chosen one, to show her and that villain who he is. Yes, but who is he?

He is still undecided when he rushes into the banqueting hall, and there, Ormuzd be thanked, he finds that the solution has been prepared for him.

Haman had remained "to make request of his life to Esther the queen; for he saw that there was evil determined against him by the king. Then the king returned out of the palace garden into the place of the banquet of wine; and Haman was fallen upon the couch where Esther was.''

It comes to Ahasuerus like a flash of lightning. We read: "Then the king said: 'Will he even force the queen before me in the house?' '' But of course! How obvious! How natural! The problem is solved, the crisis is over. He is the outraged husband.

"As the word went out of the king's mouth, they covered Haman's face. Then said Harbonah, one of the chamberlains that was before the king: 'Behold also, the gallows fifty cubits high, which Haman hath made for Mordecai, who spoke good for the king, standeth in the house of Haman.' And the king said: 'Hang him thereon.' " That was magnificent. He was the man of lightning-like decisions. "So they hanged Haman on the gallows he had prepared for Mordecai, and the king's wrath was assuaged."

As for the rest of the story, how the king handed over the house of Haman to Esther, and how he exalted Mordecai in Haman's place, and how he sent out orders to the Jews in the provinces to defend themselves against their enemies, and how the Jews slaughtered those who attacked them, and how they did the same in Shushan the capital, and how Haman's ten sons were hanged—behold, is it not written in the chronicles of the Book of Esther?

What is not written there is what happened to the marriage in later years, and whether the king ever regretted his choice, and how long he reigned. But we can be certain that there were many banquets, and Ahasuerus was never sober for long, and his wrath was often roused and assuaged, and, whatever happened, he was that kind of person and he proclaimed it to the world. For it is written the dead will rise, and be alive, and black will become white, and the crooked shall be made straight, but the fool will remain a fool.

From *Certain People of the Book* (1955)

23 THE PROPHET ELIJAH

Of all the People of the Book, the prophet Elijah alone lives in my mind as a double take; the image brought along out of my childhood refuses to stand apart; it overlaps the image rising from the closely scrutinized Text, often getting the ascendancy over it.

I bring out of childhood the unfading picture of a gentle, playful, compassionate, ubiquitous, and protean friend of the poor and forlorn, a venerable merry-andrew of righteousness, a chuckling incarnation of all the world's benevolent pixies, a prestidigitator of parcels for the poor, a dispenser of free tuition to penniless students, a sneaker-in of keys to the unjustly imprisoned, a milk-warmer and cradle-rocker for neglected babies, a mischievous spoiler of mischief, a finger-on-nose admonisher of the uncharitable rich, a malicious but not murderous marplot among oppressors, usually invisible to them, a knight-errant righter of wrongs armored in prayer shawl and phylacteries, a graybeard boy-scout performer of odd jobs for the bedridden and arthritic, a kidnapper of cares, a pickpocket of unrighteous mortgages, capable of a thousand forms, human and animal, and even vegetable and mineral, an all-year-round (may he forgive me!) Daddy Christmas—in short, the never-failing eleventh-hour intervention of Providence without its portentousness.

He is all this because of a multitude of folk stories current among the grown-ups who surrounded my childhood; stories that lived in the spoken word, and stories read by kerosene and candlelight out of ill-printed, tattered brochures supplied by a one-eyed bookdealer, and passing from hand to hand; stories that I remember only in the aggregate, but which make me marvelously and lovingly envious of old Elijah, who has nothing to do but gad about all over the world,

faster than the jet plane, and even with simultaneous multiple appearances in different places, relieving distress, wiping away tears,
bringing consolation, vindicating the pious. What a life! And he will
live this life until he announces—and this will be his most glorious
good deed, universal in scope, the greatest wholesale benefaction
with which an ordinary mortal can be entrusted, the climax of his
career, to be followed by an eternity of blissful contemplation—until
he announces the Messiah himself. And as the announcer of the
Messiah he is surrounded not only by stories, but by folk melodies
which are filled with the sweet, sad yearning for the messianic, that
ultimate assurance of the palatability of goodness.

Such is the Elijah of my childhood. But when I contemplate the
Elijah of the Text, what do I see? A tempest of suffering, a whirlwind
of rebuke, a wild figure that emerges in drought and vanishes in a
chariot of fire. An avenging destroyer, a wielder of lightning, a killer,
he is either in furious motion or in passionate meditation; and laughter withers in his presence. Only with one person was he gentle—
with the widow of Zarephath; and for her he behaved in the manner
conforming to my childhood vision of him. For the rest he was a
flame and a fury, a portent and a fugitive, like a human comet. And
like a comet, his flesh wasting in the incandescence of his motion, he
would appear, to the terror of evil-doers, and disappear for long
intervals in outer space.

How can this be? Whence these two opposed and apparently
irreconcilable versions? I asked this question over and over again
until it dawned on me that in his earthly life Elijah had only one
opportunity to reveal and exercise his essentially kindly nature—and
that was with the widow of Zarephath and her son. His life was one
long, cruel frustration; and Ahab and Jezebel, and yes, the Israelites
of that time, made of him what he did not want to be, and what, in
being, he endured with infinite suffering. He was martyred by the
people he had to deal with—principally Ahab, and indirectly Jezebel.
That's the kind they were. And as for the people, the folk: it is doing
penance until this day. It is compensating him for his earthly exertions and experiences in its behalf by letting him revel in the bestowal of an infinite variety of ingenious and unexpected benefac-
tions. "There," it says, "dear, good old Elijah, have a happy time until
the end of the world's badness; and you yourself shall be the termi-
nator of your employment, on the day when your activities will no
longer be needed."

From *Certain People of the Book* (1955)

part six

One of Maurice Samuel's special talents, the one for which he was perhaps best known, was that of Jewish cultural mediator. Most particularly, his efforts have served to make the language, culture, and literature of Eastern European Jewry accessible to generations of non-Yiddish readers. *The World of Sholom Aleichem, Prince of the Ghetto* (which deals with that other Yiddish giant of literature, Y. L. Peretz), and *In Praise of Yiddish* constitute a kind of "trilogy" which has no precise parallel in the English language. They are solid and seminal works which have never been displaced by any of the numerous successors they inspired and helped to produce.

INTERPRETER
OF YIDDISH

24 THE WORLD OF SHOLOM ALEICHEM

Of Certain Grandfathers

This book is a sort of pilgrimage among the cities and inhabitants of a world which only yesterday—as history goes—harbored the grandfathers and grandmothers of some millions of American citizens. As a pilgrimage it is an act of piety; on the other hand it is an exercise in necromancy, or calling up of the dead, which was the sin of Saul. For that world is no more. The fiery harrows of two world wars have passed closely across its soil within the lifetime of a generation; and in between it was a participant in one of the world's great revolutions. Fragments of it remain *in situ;* other fragments, still recognizable but slowly losing their shape in the wastage of time, are lodged in America. From these fragments alone, were there no records in memory or writing, we should be as hard put to it to reconstruct the warm, breathing original creation as to recapture the proto-Indo-European language from the syllables embedded in a score of modern languages.

The world of Sholom Aleichem is mostly—not wholly—the internal world of Russian Jewry forty, fifty, sixty, and seventy years ago. It is—again mostly—the world of the Jewish Pale of Settlement, with special emphasis on a section south and west and east of Kiev. Hereabouts Jews had lived their separate life from very ancient times. There were synagogues in the Crimea long before there were churches, and Jewish pedlars long before there were pogroms. Hereabouts, too, there was once—eleven and twelve centuries ago—a Jewish kingdom of converted Tatars. Kiev boasted its first pogrom in the twelfth century; we have the names of rabbis of that period; and we know that Jews of that period went west for their education. But the world of Sholom Aleichem had no connection except by collateral descent with the original communities of southeastern Russia. Khazar kings and Hebrew merchants were absorbed by masses of Jewish immigrants who came eastward under the pressure of the Crusades, bringing with them the language which developed into Yiddish and a way of life which retained its identity for a score of generations.

In the innocent childhood of our century the Russian-Jewish Pale of Settlement was the disgrace of Western humanity, the last word in reaction and brutality. We have traveled far since then. Just as our world wars may look back on the piddling squabbles of our first decade—our Boer wars, our Russo-Japanese and Balkan wars—and ask contemptuously: "Do you call *that* a war?" so Hitlerian anti-Semitism can look back on the discomfort of Jews under the Romanovs and ask: "Do you call that persecution and oppression?" Perhaps the Jews of a generation or two ago owe history an apology for having set up such a clamor about the occasional slaughters—they never amounted to more than a few hundred men, women, and children at a time—the wholesale robberies, the expulsions, discriminations, and humiliations. It was a principle of Russian law that everything was forbidden to Jews unless specifically permitted. But by an oversight which Germany has since corrected, the right to remain alive was not challenged. Within the vast semi-ghetto which was the Pale and outside of which the Jews could not settle, Jewish life grew and unfolded. Russia acquired her Jews reluctantly, through the partitions of Poland; having acquired them, she fastened them down where they were, deprived them of land, instituted for them, in the high schools and universities, the *numerus clausus* or system of educational rationing, and did her best generally to discourage in them the appetite for life. But Russia lacked—as we shall see in the course of the pilgrimage—the high ideal of wickedness. Perhaps, then, the clamor of the Jews was justified only as a warning to the world. They managed to survive and even to flourish; but the world which failed to understand the possibilities behind the persecutions was to pay a heavy price for its callousness or sloth.

They managed to survive and even to flourish. But their prosperity was spiritual rather than material. They maintained a remarkable civilization, with values which the world cannot spare. Simply as a demonstration of character in adversity, that civilization should not be forgotten. If it was inevitable that the good perish with the bad, we must perhaps shrug our shoulders and repeat the Occidental equivalent of the Arab's "Kismet"—"That's history." But it is not inevitable or desirable that the memory of that world should wholly perish.

One man became the mirror of Russian Jewry. His name was Sholom Rabinovitch, and he adopted the pen-name "Sholom Aleichem," the common daily greeting of Jews, which originally meant "Peace be unto you," but which usage has whittled down to something like "How do you do?" He was a part of Russian Jewry; he was Russian Jewry itself. It is hard to think of him as a "writer." He was the common people in utterance. He was in a way the "anonymous" of Jewish self-expression, achieving the stature of a legendary figure even in his own lifetime.

Many other writers have left us records of Russian-Jewish life, and some of them compare well with the best-known in the Western world. None of them had this natural gift for complete self-identification with a people which makes Sholom Aleichem unique. He wrote no great panoramic novels in the manner of a Balzac or a Tolstoy. He did not set out with the conscious and self-conscious purpose of "putting it down for posterity." He wrote because of a simple communicative impulse, as men chat in a tavern or in a waiting crowd with their like. He never tried his hand at solemn passages and mighty themes, any more than people do in a casual, friendly conversation. But his language had an incomparable authenticity, and his humor—he is the greatest of Jewish humorists, and in the world's front rank—was that of a folk, not of an individual.

Thus it comes about that the phrase "the world of Sholom Aleichem" has two meanings in one. It is the world in which Sholom Aleichem lived, with which he suffered and laughed, himself its focus or miniature. It is also the world which appears in his books. We pass without a break from his descriptions, his men, women, children, cities, and townlets, to historic Russian Jewry, as we might reconstruct it (though not so well) from other sources. We pass back again, fusing external and internal material in a natural whole. We could write a *Middletown* of the Russian-Jewish Pale basing ourselves solely on the novels and stories and sketches of Sholom Aleichem, and it would be as reliable a scientific document as any "factual" study; more so, indeed, for we should get, in addition to the material of a straightforward social inquiry, the intangible spirit which informs the material and gives it its living significance.

Sholom Aleichem is almost unknown to millions of Americans whose grandfathers made up his world. This is not simply a literary loss; it is a break—a very recent and disastrous one—in the continuity of a group history. Jews who get a certain spiritual tonic from the reflection that they are somehow related to the creators of the Bible and of its ethical values forget that the relationship was passed on to them by the men who begot their fathers. Who were these men? Under what circumstances did they nurture the relationship for transmission? What tone and color had their lives? What purpose did they conceive themselves to be serving in their obstinate fidelity to the relationship? What hopes had they for themselves—and for their grandchildren?

Are these questions irrelevant, or perhaps even improper, in a world which is in the throes of a tremendous transformation and must keep its eyes on the future? Not if they are put in the right spirit —one of human curiosity, of affection, and, if you like, of decency. We might even add, of modesty. It is not a wholesome thing to believe that we and our posterity will find all the answers; for some of them were discovered in the very imperfect past. The study of history will never become obsolete, and a knowledge of one's grandfathers is an excellent introduction to history. Especially these grandfathers; they were a remarkable lot.

Man in a Forest

A clumsy wagon drawn by a dispirited nag crawls along the narrow path which leads through the forest from the city of Boiberik to the village of Anatevka. The man on the driver's seat, a little, bearded Jew in a ragged capote, keeps his eyes half closed, for he has no inclination to look on the beauties of nature. His stomach is empty, his heart is in his tattered boots. All day long, from summer dawn to summer dusk, he has been loading and unloading logs of wood, carting them from the edge of the forest to the railroad station of Boiberik. He started out without breakfast, did without lunch, and has yet to have his supper. It will not be much of a supper. The ruble a day he earns—when he earns it—will not buy a day's food for ten stomachs, one of them a horse's, even though nothing is deducted to clothe nine bodies—his own, his wife's, and those of his seven daughters. Seven of them, and not a single son; seven hungry daughters and a hungry wife, waiting for him and his ruble at the other end of the path. Little wonder if, for all his hunger, he shows no haste as he sits up there driving homeward.

Driving? That is hardly the word. He has not the strength to drive, and it is all the horse can do to keep the ramshackle wagon crawling along, while the shadows of the trees grow longer and longer until they seem to become, as the man mutters to himself, "as long as the Jewish exile."

The forest is silent; no leaf rustles, no bird sings. Nothing is heard except the creaking of the cart, the dull klop-klop of the horse's hoofs and, occasionally, the mutter of the man's voice when his disconsolate meditations become audible. Now and again he does indeed make a driver's gestures; he lifts up the whip and brings it down again, but it is done listlessly and without conviction. What sense is there in lashing the animal? He expostulates with it instead, or, rather, explains the situation, for he is the kind of man who, however bitter his heart and however empty his stomach, does not lose sight of the larger aspect of things.

"Pull, miserable monster!" he mutters. "Drag, wretched beast in the likeness of a horse! You're no better than I am! If it's your destiny to be Tevye's horse, then suffer like Tevye, and learn like Tevye and his family to die of hunger seven times in the day and then go to bed supperless. Is it not written in the Holy Book that the same fate shall befall man and beast?"

Then the man Tevye bethinks himself and takes back his argument. "No!" he says. "It is not true. Here I am at least talking, while you are dumb and cannot ease your pain with words. My case is better than yours. For I am human, and a Jew, and I know what you do not know. I know that we have a great and good God in heaven, who governs the world in wisdom and mercy and loving-kindness, feeding the hungry and raising the fallen and showing grace to all living things. I can talk my heart out to Him, while your jaws are locked, poor thing. True, a wise word is no substitute for a piece of herring or a bag of oats; and if words could fill stomachs my old woman, God bless her, would be supporting all of us, and half the world besides. 'Children he wants me to bear,' she says, 'seven of them, no less. What shall I do with them? Throw them into the river? Breadwinner! Tevye of the golden hands! Answer me!' She said it yesterday, and the day before, and the day before that, and she'll say it tonight. Sweet homecoming! What shall I answer? Nothing. For she is a woman, and the Holy Books are closed to her, the sayings of the sages are beyond her. Her wisdom, alas, is of another kind: an expert without equal at handing out a dinner of curses and a supper of slaps. What else should she have learned, being the wife of Tevye?"

The shadows of the trees are beginning to merge into one vast dimness. The sadness deepens in Tevye's heart, and all kinds of unbidden thoughts rise up in him—not the rational thoughts of a thinking man, but primitive ideas and imaginings. He sees the faces of friends and relatives long dead peering out at him from the rising wall of darkness. He remembers doleful stories of untimely deaths, of murder and robbery, of demons which haunt the forest in unimaginable likenesses, dragons, serpents with tongues a mile long, many-headed monsters.

"As the Holy Book says," he mutters, "man is dust, and his foundations are of the dust; which, rightly interpreted, means that man is as weak as a fly and stronger than steel. Thou hast made us a little lower than the angels. It depends what you call a little, doesn't it? Lord, what is life, and what are we, and to what may a man be likened? A man may be likened unto a carpenter; for a carpenter lives, and lives, and lives, and finally dies. And so does a man."

So, against the rising tide of despair, Tevye tries to spin the thread of rational discourse. But he feels the waters engulfing him, and he knows it will not do. Despair is a sin and a blasphemy, despair is unbecoming to a man and a Jew. He will not give way. He will address himself to the Throne of Grace, he will have it out with the Almighty, with the One who lives for ever. And suddenly Tevye realizes that the hour for *Minchah*—afternoon prayer—is almost gone. Ah, that explains it! He pulls up, steps down from the cart, and, holding the reins, begins to pray. And he prays in a manner all his own. He repeats by heart the prescribed prayers, word for word, from beginning to end, exactly as they are set down in the book; but while his tongue follows the ritual, his mind accompanies it with interpolations and interpretations and commentaries which have never been heard before.

"Blessed are they that dwell in Thy house (Right! I take it, O Lord, that Thy house is somewhat more spacious than my hovel!). . . . I will extol Thee, my God, O King (what good would it do me if I didn't?). . . . Everyday I will bless Thee (on an empty stomach, too). . . . The Lord is good to all (and suppose He forgets somebody now and again, good Lord, hasn't He enough on His mind?). . . . The Lord upholdeth all that fall, and raiseth up all that are bowed down (Father in heaven, loving Father, surely it's my turn now, I can't fall any lower). . . . Thou openest Thy hand and satisfiest every living thing (so You do, Father in heaven, You give with an open hand; one gets a box on the ear, and another a roast chicken, and neither my wife nor I nor my daughters have even smelt a roast chicken since the days of creation). . . . He will fulfill the desire of them that fear Him; He will also hear their cry and will save them."

Having thus reached the end of the *Ashre,* the first part of the afternoon prayer, Tevye turns his face away from the setting sun and looks eastward into the darkness, in the direction of the Holy Land, taking up his station for the Prayer of the Eighteen Benedictions, which must be repeated in complete immobility. But scarcely has he begun with "God of Abraham, God of Isaac, God of Jacob" when a demon takes hold of his horse; for without warning, without visible or comprehensible cause, the exhausted creature breaks into a wild and idiotic gallop, and Tevye, clinging to the reins, pants after it, sobbing breathlessly:

"Thou feedest all things in mercy, and keepest faith with the sleepers in the dust. (Stop! Indecent creature! Let a Jew say his prayers, will you? If ever there was a sleeper in the dust, O Father, it's me, Tevye, the father of seven. Did I say dust? In the mud, O Lord, in the filth of life! A thousand million curses in your bones, wretched animal! Couldn't you find a more fitting moment for displaying your talents? Lord of the world! Those others, the rich Jews of Boiberik, who do not have to lug wood to the railroad station for a ruble a day, but live on the fat of the land in their country cottages, *they* know Your grace and kindness. Father in heaven, why not I? Am I not a Jew, too? Where is justice, I ask, where is fairness?) . . . Look Thou upon our poverty (no one else cares to look upon it—stop!). . . . Send us a healing, O Lord, for our sickness (we managed to get the sickness without Your help, thank You). . . . Have mercy upon us and be compassionate unto us (that means me and my wife and my hungry children—and may this horse be carried off by a black year!). . . . And may it be Thy will that we be restored (yes, that we, all Thy children, the children of Israel, return once more to the Holy Land, and rebuild Thy temple, and offer Thee sacrifice, to the singing of the priests and the Levites as in the days of yore). . . ."

At this point, as suddenly and as imbecilically as it had set off on its wild gallop, the horse comes to a dead stop, and Tevye finishes his prayer standing still and facing east, the sweat pouring down his face and beard.

Tevye the Dairyman

This is Tevye the dairyman you have just met—Tevye, the best-known and best-loved figure in the world of Sholom Aleichem. A little Jew wandering in a big, dark forest, symbol of a little people wandering in the big, dark jungle of history. For the moment he is only Tevye the drayman, the wage-slave; the God in whom he believes with all his heart, whom he loves and prays to at least three times daily, whom he addresses intimately with affection, irony, sympathy, reverence, impudence, and indestructible hope, the Omnipotent One who sits on high while we grovel here below, has not yet wrought with his child Tevye the great miracle concerning which you shall learn in the proper place. We meet Tevye for the first time while he is still the Jewish Man with the Hoe, bowed (who deeper?) with the weight of centuries; the burden of the world is on his back, but—here is the supreme difference—the emptiness of ages is not in his face.

It must be repeated, because it is the key to our understanding of Tevye: the emptiness of ages is not in his face. We must approach him with caution, curiosity, and liking, but not with the impulse to classify. He is not to be disposed of so simply. If he were just Markham's brother to the ox, you could write heroically about him and make him the springboard for a grand, revolutionary utterance. But Tevye will not let you strike an attitude in his behalf; he is not docile material for your fits of cosmic righteousness. Should you begin to orate at him he will listen, despite an empty stomach, with the closest attention, and just when you think you are at your irresistible best he will interrupt you with a disastrous misquotation from the Holy Books; he will disconcert you with the suggestion that he cannot be patronized on that high level. You want to remake the world? By all means! Let's sit down and talk it over. You would remove oppression, injustice, want, and persecution from among mankind? The idea is not at all bad. But first of all I should like to know who you are, and I should also like you to know who I am.

In short, Tevye is the indestructible individualist, and this is not to be misinterpreted as anarchist. He is, in a baffling way, a blend of

individualist and traditionalist. Yet he is also something of the revo-
lutionist; and, indeed, it is more revolutionary to believe in God and
take Him to task sensibly than not to believe in Him and denounce
Him in unmeasured language. Here too, however, Tevye is in the
tradition. The Orthodox Jewry of which he is a part is not unac-
quainted with protests directed at the Lord of the Universe for His
mismanagement of human affairs. There was, for instance, the Saint
of Shpolle, "the grandfather," who once summoned God to a regular
trial. Yes, he of Shpolle appointed nine other judges and, himself
acting as the tenth, cited the Eternal to appear before them. Or,
rather, since God is everywhere, the judges simply entered into session and took the presence of the Defendant for granted. Three days,
behind closed doors, the Court of Ten prayed and fasted and consulted the records, the Torah, the books of the sages, and the re-
sponsa. And then, not hastily, not in the heat of argument, they
issued their verdict, which was against the Defendant. They pronounced Him guilty on two counts: first, that He had created the
spirit of evil and had let it loose among the Jews; second, that He had
failed in His manifest duty to provide adequate sustenance for Jewish
women and children.

Not that it seems to have done much good, Tevye is ready to
admit. Still, you can't dismiss it as a trifle. Such great and learned
rabbis cannot have been wasting their time. And, in any case, you
simply cannot leave God out of the reckoning. You cannot ignore His
Torah and the long line of the generations which have died to keep
it alive. So, whatever you propose to do for Tevye and the world,
kindly remember that he is an Orthodox Jew, and no rearrangement
of the universe is acceptable or even thinkable which will not leave
room for his religious practices.

For instance every morning, at sunrise or shortly before, Tevye
has to say his long morning prayers, the *Shachris,* and he has to say
them, on weekdays, with the prayer shawl over his head, and the
phylacteries on brow and arm. It's no good arguing with Tevye on
this point. It is worse than useless to talk to him of superstition,
mummery, and the opiate of the masses. He will have only one
answer, delivered in a talmudic singsong: "If all the persecutions of
the ages, and all the bitternesses of exploitation, could not prevent
me from repeating the prayers of my fathers, shall I be made to fall
away from them in a world of freedom?" But the *Shachris* is only a
beginning. During the day Tevye must take time out—and he does
it, as we have seen, under the most discouraging circumstances—for

certain other prayers. Do what you like with Tevye, chain him to a galley, yoke him to a chariot, starve him, break him, he is going to say his three prayers daily. And when the Sabbath comes, he will not work. You must make up your mind that Tevye the coolie, or Tevye the dairyman, simply will not work on the Sabbath, from sundown on Friday to sundown on Saturday. No labor leader in the world has ever been so insistent on the forty-eight or forty-hour week as Tevye on his six-day week. The Sabbath is the Lord's day; that is, it is Tevye's day for rest in the Lord. He will not work on that day, he will not carry money about, he will not touch fire or tear paper or do anything that savors of the slavery of the body. He will not work, either, on the two days of the New Year, or on the Day of Atonement, or any other of the festivals. You will neither bribe, bully, nor persuade him into such transgression. For the Sabbath and the festivals are all that are left to him; they are the last citadel of his freedom. On those days he will pray, meditate, and refresh his spirit with a little learning. He may be hungry; he will contrive to rise above it. He may not know where the next day's food will come from, either; he will contrive to forget that, too.

There never was such obstinacy! It must not be thought, either, that Tevye, crushed under the double burden of the Jewish exile and the worker's slavery, clings to these practices merely as a grim protest. Not by any means. He enjoys them, thoroughly. He loves the Sabbath and the festivals. He loves prayer. And when the Passover comes around, he rejoices in the liberation from Egypt exactly as if he himself had just marched out of bondage. On Purim he is gleeful over the downfall of Haman, and on the Day of the Rejoicing of the Law he is ecstatic over the gift from Sinai.

Where does Tevye belong, and why is he so beloved of the Jewish masses—that is, of the Yiddish-speaking proletariat? At this point we can say that Tevye was not proletariate, not even in the days when he sweated hungrily from morning till night lugging the felled tree trunks from the forest to the railroad station. Nor was he middle-class, not even after the miracle, when God had raised him from the dunghill and transformed him into Tevye the dairyman. He is always just a Jew making a living, and he is proletarian in the sense that he believes in only one way of making a living—namely, by the labor of one's hands. As Tevye the dairyman he worked, and the family worked with him. Wife and daughters milked the cows and goats, churned the butter and pressed the cheese; Tevye was the delivery-man, traveling back and forth through the forest between his cottage near Anatevka and the rich summer homes of Boiberik.

Just the same, Tevye is something of a businessman too; and at once we must set against this the fact that the ways of the business world are not in him. The idea of making money by the handling of money, or by the mere manipulation of words and documents, is alien to him. In this he is at the opposite extreme from his distant relative Menachem Mendel, who is perhaps the second most famous figure in Sholom Aleichem's world. Menachem Mendel is the *luft-mensh* (the manipulator), the *shlemiel* of the exchange, the wild man from whose dreams of sudden riches and pyramided finances God guard all of us. And to clear Tevye completely, we must add at once that Menachem Mendel is not even his relative. He is related to Goldie, Tevye's wife, being a second or third cousin three or four times removed.

Only once did Tevye let himself be tempted into Menachem Mendel's insane world, when he took out all his savings, every bit of one hundred rubles, and gave them to Menachem Mendel to turn into a fortune. He lost them, of course, for Menachem Mendels do not make money, either for themselves or for others. "Serves me right!" was what Tevye said, and spat out three times. "Is it money you want, Tevye? Then sweat for it, break your back, tear your guts out, plow the sands with your nose—but don't expect anything for nothing."

In talking of Tevye we must avoid at all cost the highfalutin; still it must be said that he represents, fundamentally, the inextinguishable spirit in man. Created for laughter by the greatest of Jewish humorists, he turns out to be, on more careful scrutiny, a type of aristocrat. He is a descendant of martyrs and scholars; and whatever happens to him, the marks of his lineage are ineradicable. He cannot abide ignorance and grossness in human beings. He will not even admit that poverty and oppression are adequate excuses for utter want of spiritual interest; and certainly he will not accept the blanket exoneration: "What can you expect of a man under such a system?" System or no system, a human being must retain some residue of uncorrupted spirit, or forfeit Tevye's respect.

This much is implied for Tevye in being a Jew, for he thinks of himself as an ordinary, everyday Jew. He would laugh heartily if someone called him an intellectual or a scholar. He cannot interpret the intricacies of the Talmud or the mysticisms of the Kabbalah. But he is at home in the Bible, and in Rashi's great commentary on it. On Friday evenings and Saturday afternoons he will not fail to read through the week's portion of the Pentateuch, translating it into the vernacular. In leisure moments he will dip into the Mishnah, or into the Ethics of the Fathers, where it is written: "Say not: 'I will study when I have the time,' for then you will never have the time." Such things Tevye considers the minimum requirements of the simple Jew; these, and decency, and faith in God, and a drop of brandy on occasion.

The chronicle of Tevye's life is, except for the miracle near the beginning, one of uniform calamity. Yet it is read for laughter by tender-hearted people. Not what happens to Tevye is funny, but how he takes it. We might call him Tevye the unextinguishable. We might add, rather helplessly, that sometimes he puts us in mind of a Job with a sense of humor and without the happy ending, and sometimes of Charlie Chaplin.

The Judgments of Reb Yozifel

"Lilies that fester smell far worse than weeds," sang a poet unknown to old Kasrielevky—a poet old Kasrielevky might have loved because as many commentaries have been written on him as on the Talmud, and as many interpretations grown up round his text as round that of the Torah. The Kasrielevkites were so organically interpenetrated with religion that they had nothing to be good with except religion, and nothing to be bad with except religion. (Somewhere among the old prayers there is one which runs approximately thus: "O Lord, let me worship Thee not only with my good inclination, but also with my evil inclination.")

Shalachmones, the sending round of sweetmeats on the festival of Purim, was not a religious rite, properly speaking. But it had a semireligious character, and in any case it was a charming tradition; certainly it added, or was supposed to add, to the jollity of the celebration and the sweetness of life.

The Kasrielevkites sent one another plates of *hamantashen*, of *teiglach*, tiny squares of dough boiled in honey, chopped nuts and spices, of cakes, tarts, biscuits, cookies, scones with raisins and scones with currants; they sent one another everything that the ingenuity of the housewife could devise with flour, eggs, milk, sugar, fruits, and an oven. All day long boys and girls, messengers and maidservants, scurried through the streets of Kasrielevky, carrying gift and return gift from neighbor to neighbor, acquaintance to acquaintance, relative to relative, and receiving a little cash reward—Purim money. A lovely and gracious tradition it was, which gave a special tone and color to Purim, the most secular of the festivals.

Lovely and gracious, that is to say, in the spirit, and for that matter in the execution too, most of the time. But how can one ensure a lovely and gracious tradition against petrifaction into the formal and snobbish? How can we prevent the gifts of Father's Day and Mother's Day and Wedding Day and Birthday and Christmas from degenerating into—well, into missiles instead of missives? Consider a housewife of Kasrielevky, with her Purim list of relatives, in-laws, friends and acquaintances, each one of whom had to be considered individually. There were gradations and standards and precedents, featherweight distinctions in the sending and return of *shalachmones;* particularly in the return, if you happened to be the first recipient. For instance, two *hamantashen,* five cookies, a currant scone, and a slice of honey cake called exactly for one *hamantash,* two tarts, eight biscuits, and a raisin scone, or its equivalent, three slices of honey cake, a slab of *teiglach,* two currant scones, and three cookies. Of course the size of the slices and the density of the baking also entered into the reckoning.

You had to know your way about these usages; it was a question of feeling rather than of weights and measures. You had to be the possessor of a massive memory, as well as of a delicate sense of social values. For a disparity in gifts was permissible, or, rather, expected, as between the poor and the well-to-do; the former were not abashed to receive a plateful of good things out of all proportion to their own sending; the latter did not expect in return more than a token greeting. But God help you if you sent more than you received to one whose inferior status was not established and acknowledged; or less than you received if your own inferiority was not similarly established and acknowledged. The *nogid,* or rich man, ranked everybody except the other *negidim;* the trustees of the synagogue were in the upper brackets; the rabbi, the cantor, and the ritual slaughterer were in the middle class for substance, but high up for honors. There were class and personal distinctions, individual and group subtleties—all in all an etiquette as complicated as the hierarchies of the Byzantine court and the rigid ceremonial compulsions of the hidalgos. And people knew their rights and stood on them.

A particular sense of delicacy was needed by the first sender of *shalachmones,* especially as the gifts might be crossing and still had to correspond to the weights and measures of the code. Here was where memory came in, the *shalachmoneses* of previous years, the relative standing of the parties, and the interpretation thereof in *shalachmones* rating.

How deep the code went, and what calamities might follow from the contravention of it, we learn from the incident of the two Nechamahs, or rather of their employers. Nechamah the black and Nechamah the red were two servant girls. Nechamah the black worked for Zlota, the wife of Reb Isaac the storekeeper, and her pay was four and a half rubles the season—six months—with clothes and shoes. Nechamah the red worked for Zelda, the wife of Reb Yossie the storekeeper, and her pay was six rubles the season, no clothes and shoes. On a certain muddy Purim—that is to say, on a certain Purim, for the festival occurs in the early spring, when the unpaved streets and alleys of Kasrielevky were covered by six inches of ooze—Nechamah the red and Nechamah the black came face to face as they were carrying their covered trays of *shalachmones,* Nechamah the red on her way to the employer of Nechamah the black, and vice versa. A happy meeting! The girls were tired with delivering gifts in all quarters of the town. So they sat down on a doorstep to swap experiences, compare tips, and revile their employers.

Thence they proceeded to show each other the contents of their respective trays. Nechamah the black was the bearer of an appetizing square of strudel, two big honey cakes, a fish-shaped cake stuffed with ground nuts and sugar, and a slab of poppyseed cake rich with honey. Nechamah the red carried a fat *hamantash,* black with poppyseed, two "cushion cakes," so called from their shape and softness, a golden cookie starred with black raisins, a slab of tart, and two cherub cakes. As any Kasrielevkite expert could have told you, the gifts were balanced to a nicety, both in respect of each other and of the relative social status of the senders.

Who would have thought that from this casual encounter of two servant girls would ensue a *cause célèbre* never to be forgotten in the annals of Kasrielevky? And who but a Kasrielevkite could understand, and even sympathize with, the circumstances? Beginning with loose, idle talk, the two Nechamahs, tired and hungry, as well as rebellious and envious, passed from the scrutiny of each other's trays to the consideration of conspiracy. What would be the harm, they asked, if an equal quantity of sweetmeats were removed from each tray, leaving the balance where it had been? Thus, if the strudel disappeared from the tray of Nechamah the black, and the golden cookie from the tray of Nechamah the red, the gifts of Zlota the wife of Reb Isaac and of Zelda the wife of Reb Yossie would still be perfectly matched. One could go further: if a honey cake faded from the tray of Nechamah the black, accompanied by a cushion cake from the tray of Nechamah the red, the equilibrium would still remain undisturbed. And was it not more fitting that the said strudel and honey cake and cookie and cushion cake should go to the feeding of the stomachs of the Nechamahs rather than the vanity of their employers?

Said and done; which showed they were only two foolish servant girls; for they left two fatal considerations out of the count. Zelda the wife of Reb Yossie and Zlota the wife of Reb Isaac would remember what they had sent, but see only what they received. There was, moreover, the unalterable status established and maintained throughout the years.

Thus it was: Nechamah the black brought her depleted shipment to Zelda, the wife of Reb Yossie, who uncovered the tray, took one glance, and uttered a shriek which woke from his afternoon nap her husband Yossie, Yossie the Washrag as the Kasrielevkites had named him because he was the most henpecked husband in Kasrielevky.

"Tell your mistress," hissed Zelda to Nechamah the black, "that I hope she lives till next Purim and doesn't get a nicer *shalachmones* than this from anyone in town."

Nechamah the red brought her diminished offering to Zlota, the wife of Reb Isaac, who uncovered the tray and almost fainted. She could not call to her husband, Reb Isaac, because he was not at home. One-a-year Isaac was *his* nickname, because every year, without fail, his wife brought forth a baby. That was the way of the Kasrielevkites; they gave a man a nickname and it stuck. Reb Isaac might live to the age of ninety, and cease to procreate at the age of seventy, but it would be One-a-year Isaac till the day of his death.

"Look at this *shalachmones*," gasped Zlota. "May all the nightmares of my life, and the nightmares of the lives of all my ancestors, be visited upon the heads of my enemies! Is this a *shalachmones* or a joke? Take this back to your miserable mistress, do you hear?" Wherewith the wife of One-a-year Isaac thrust out of doors Nechamah the red and sent her back to Zelda, the wife of Yossie the Washrag.

It would have been bad enough if One-a-year Isaac and Yossie the Washrag had been mere acquaintances. They were friends, which was odd enough since their two dry-goods stores stood side by side on the marketplace and they were forever snatching away each other's customers. But friends they were. They lent each other a couple of rubles now and again, they came to each other's homes on Friday evenings for the Sabbath benediction, and in the winter they went into each other's stores to warm up at the stove or play a game of checkers. Their wives, too, were on friendly terms, exchanging pots and scandal, pouring out their hearts to each other, and taking counsel on their domestic problems. Friends have, of course, larger foundations on which to erect a quarrel than have mere acquaintances. On the morning following this Purim, Reb Yossie the Washrag and One-a-year Isaac, well primed by their respective wives, opened their adjacent stores as usual and stationed themselves at their respective doors, each one waiting for the other to say "Good morning" in order that he might not answer. Customers being scarce that raw spring day, Reb Yossie and Reb Isaac stood there grimly, hour after hour, till their wives arrived.

"Isaac," said Zlota, acidulously, "why don't you thank your friend for the wonderful *shalachmones* he sent us yesterday?"

"Yossie," said Zelda, poisonously, "have you returned adequate thanks for the noble present you received?"

"I don't speak to a Washrag," announced Reb Isaac loudly.

"I wouldn't answer a One-a-year," responded Reb Yossie.

There you had it! The battle was joined. In less time than it takes to put on a prayer shawl, the husbands were in each other's beards, the wives in each other's hair. The marketplace came to life; half the town assembled to separate the combatants or to join in the mêlée. The air was filled with questions and answers: "*Shalachmones,*" "insult," "*Shalachmones,*" "fit for a beggar," "*Shalachmones,*" "*Shalachmones,*" "*Shalachmones.*" Before the day was over, One-a-year Isaac and Yossie the Washrag invaded the office of the prefect, Pan Milinievsky, to lodge charges of libel, assault and battery, and malicious slander. With them came their wives, relatives, acquaintances, and enemies.

It is as shocking to report as it would be dishonest to deny that recourse to Pan Milinievsky the Gentile on matters connected exclusively with internal Jewish differences was only too frequent. Particularly was this true in the autumn, round the time of the Festival of Booths and Simchas Torah, the Rejoicing for the Law. But no season of the year was exempt from such scandals. There could always be an explosion over precedence in the synagogue, over privileges denied or honors misplaced. Feivel, the son of Chantze Mirke, got the most coveted section of the Torah to read out on a Sabbath morning when obviously it should have gone to Chaim, the son of Leah Dvosse; Kiveh One-eye was called twice in one month to roll up the sacred Scroll, and Deaf Itzig not even once in two months. Pan Milinievsky, a Russian with a high forehead and a vast beard, had been prefect of Kasrielevky so long that he spoke Yiddish like a native and even understood something about the delicate problems of precedence and social status in the synagogue. A decent enough man, considering that he was a gentile and an official; reasonable enough in the taking of bribes and, though an anti-Semite, devoid of viciousness. A trifle impatient, though, as he showed again on this occasion. For having tried for over an hour to get a word in edgewise between the accusations and counteraccusations of Zlota, Zelda, Isaac, Yossie, and their partisans, he rose to his feet and roared: "Get out! Get out! The whole kit and kaboodle! Go to your rabbi!"

So the litigants and their partisans streamed toward the house of Reb Yozifel, the old and honored rabbi.

Patient, wise, long-suffering Reb Yozifel! He cannot be introduced casually. I must digress and present Reb Yozifel according to his merit. He was an old man even in old Kasrielevky, and he lived on into the wonders and terrors of new Kasrielevky. The word "rabbi" has been denuded, among us moderns, of the connotations which clung to the word *"rav."* Reb Yozifel, the *Rav* of Kasrielevky, has not his like among us. To say that he was a scholar and saint is to give him his formal due. He was the conscience of Kasrielevky, its purer self and its suffering heart. Himself without sin (you would not have dared to suggest this in his presence), he did not believe in the sinfulness of others. He saw only childishness and error. No man, in his view, was wicked by choice. It was all misunderstanding. If you only listened to the "sinner," if you gave him a chance to talk himself out, you would discover nothing but good intention gone astray.

Now, just as an instance of Reb Yozifel's way with "sinners" (let Zelda and Zlota and Isaac and Yossie and the rest of them wait awhile), there was the matter of the old people's home which Reb Yozifel set his heart on, and of the rich Jew—not a Kasrielevkite—who donated the money for it. This was in later years, in the period of new Kasrielevky, when they were building the station for the railroad which the Kasrielevkites did not believe in. The rich Jew in question was a contractor; a St. Petersburger; a modernized man; one of the Poliakovs, whose name was mentioned in an awed murmur, like that of the Brodskys and Rothschilds; and he came to Kasrielevky on business.

When a Jew comes to Kasrielevky on business the town organizes itself round him. His room is beleaguered by merchants, messengers, brokers, pedlars, and commission men. Within an hour of his arrival Kasrielevky must know his name, his occupation, the nature of his mission, the size of his income, and the probable length of his stay. Privacy? Reticence? Kasrielevky knows not these things. All Jews are brothers; all Jews have a share in the world to come and in each other's present business.

But this man Poliakov—of *the* Poliakovs or not—was an unnatural phenomenon. First, he took two whole rooms for himself at the Kasrielevky inn; second, he shut himself up and refused to receive anybody; third, he stationed a man at his door (did you ever hear the like?), and if you wanted to see him, you had to be announced.

Reb Yozifel and two of the leading householders of Kasrielevky, the *crème de la crème* of its respectability, called on the said Poliakov, and for some reason or other the guardian at the door had left his post. So they entered unannounced, whereupon the fantastic St. Petersburger, coming out from the inner room, fell upon them in a rage and ordered them out as if they were, God forbid, robbers, or beggars.

The two householders fled, but Reb Yozifel, frail, tottering old Reb Yozifel, stood his ground, and began to explain, in his quavering voice, that this was a holy matter, an old people's home for which he was collecting funds, and that he was offering the stranger a share in paradise in exchange for a donation. The man Poliakov, beside himself at the impudence of the funny old Jew in the medieval gaberdine, lost himself completely, and before he knew what he was doing, he had slapped old Reb Yozifel in the face, so that Reb Yozifel's skullcap fell to the floor, and he stood there bareheaded for several seconds, perhaps for the only time in his life.

Slowly and thoughtfully Reb Yozifel bent down and picked up his skullcap; slowly and thoughtfully he faced the stranger.

"That," said Reb Yozifel, "was for me. Now what will you give for the old people's home?"

When Reb Yozifel came out and rejoined the terrified committee, his face was flushed—one cheek being unaccountably redder than the other. But he had the promise of the man Poliakov of St. Petersburg that an old people's home would be built in Kasrielevky.

That, as I said, was years later. At the moment Reb Yozifel's home has been invaded by the tumultuous crowd turned away so unceremoniously by Pan Milinievsky. And here the scene was repeated, with this difference, that Reb Yozifel made no attempt to wedge in a word. He let the hours pass while the room resounded with the clamour of accusation and counteraccusation: *"Hamantash," "Shalachmones,"* "insult," "beggarly," "Washrag," "One-a-year."

They quieted down at last and demanded judgment, which Reb Yozifel, as *Rav,* was bound to render. Never had he been known to fail in this duty, no matter how complicated or embittered the dispute. Indeed, Reb Yozifel was famous for his judgments, not less than for his sanctity.

But before judgment came the summation of the case, which Reb Yozifel began with a heartbroken sigh.

"We stand," he said, "on the threshold of the Passover, the great, the holy festival—the festival, it may be said, without an equal. Thousands and thousands of years ago our ancestors went forth from Egypt in freedom, and traversed the Red Sea dryshod. What a festival! What a sea! What a miracle! Forty years they wandered thereafter in the wilderness, having received the Torah at the foot of Sinai, that marvelous Torah in which it is written *ve-ohavto,* and thou shalt love, *re'echo,* thy neighbor, *komocho,* as thyself. Ah, what a Torah God gave us! And how shall we honor it? With quarrels, with foolish disputes, with vanities? Is it not a desecration to prepare thus for the Passover? Come, children, we have serious business before us. We must begin to consider what shall be done in this town of ours for the poor, who must celebrate the Passover like all the others. Have we yet made a list of what they need, in the way of eggs and potatoes and chicken fat—not to mention *matzos,* of course? But stay! There is a quarrel to be composed, a judgment rendered. Let us begin the summation once more. The Passover is approaching! The Passover! What a festival! Our forefathers went out of Egypt in freedom, and traversed the Red Sea dryshod. And after that they wandered forty years in the wilderness, having received the Torah at the foot of Sinai! What a Torah! A Torah without an equal! Do you know what that means? . . ."

And so Reb Yozifel went on with his summation, in his weak, sad voice, and one by one the partisans began to sneak from the room; one by one they withdrew, and after them the litigants, each one going thoughtfully and shamefacedly home, to wonder what the excitement had been about, and to prepare for the great and holy festival of the Passover.

Could King Solomon have done better?

Death in Exile

For Sholom Aleichem the pilgrimage was permanently broken off on Saturday, May 13, 1916. The way station where he died was an apartment house at 968 Kelly Street, the Bronx, and the time was the middle of the First World War.

Those were dark, bitter years to die in, for a Jew sensitive to the fate of his people. The Yiddish-speaking world of Europe was the battlefield in the vast war of movement between Russia and Germany. Nicholas I was still on the throne—what hopes could the Jews repose on a Russian victory? But Germany was the cradle of modern anti-Semitism. Simon Dubnow, the greatest Jewish historian of our time, has pointed repeatedly to this fact. His *History of the Jews of Poland and Russia,* published in 1913, made the dilemma clear even before the First World War began. What hope, then, was there for the Jews in a German victory? No wonder Sholom Aleichem himself said, in his *New Arabian Nights,* the record of the Jewish agony in the First World War: "Of course this is a Jewish war—its purpose is the annihilation of the Jewish people." The spirit of the time, and his own share in the flight from Europe, helped undermine the resistance which he had put up for nearly a decade against tuberculosis and diabetes; and the death of a son came to him as a solemn forewarning of his own impending departure.

He did not foresee that worse was to follow for the Jews; the Polish pogroms and the mass slaughters organized under the Ukrainian hetman Petlura (one cannot speak of them simply as pogroms) were yet to come. And in the not too remote future, after a breathing-spell in Poland and a liberation in Russia, there was to follow the total eclipse of Hitler's advance over the remnants of the Yiddish world. But what he lived to witness was bad enough—and he closed his eyes to it, defeated at last.

There he lay, used up and burned out, in the little apartment in the Bronx. Three bearded old Jews of Pereyeslav, the townlet of his birth, had performed the last rites for him, washed his body, wrapped it in cerements, swathed him in his praying shawl. For thirty-six hours—two nights and a day—a permanent guard of Yiddish writers stood over him, while an interminable line of mourners wound through the adjoining streets to take a last look at the tired, clever, puckish face, relaxed in death. They tiptoed in, stood for a few moments staring down at the waxen features under the candlelight, and passed on. Fifteen thousand of them managed to get a last glimpse of Sholom Aleichem in the flesh, and thousands more came too late on the morning of Monday. A hundred and fifty thousand lined the streets at the stopping places of the cortege, at the Ohav Tzedek synagogue at One Hundred and Sixteenth Street and Fifth Avenue, at the Jewish community center at Second Avenue and Twenty-first Street, at the offices of the Hebrew Immigrant Aid Society, and at the building of the Educational Alliance on East Broadway.

In a sense it might be said that his pilgrimage was not broken off—it had come to its end. Those who believe that the tempo of a man's work is dictated unconsciously by the number of years placed at his disposal may add Sholom Aleichem to the evidence. It was in 1908, the forty-ninth year of his life, that he was first struck down by sickness. But that same year was marked, all over the Jewish world, by an extraordinary celebration of Sholom Aleichem's completion of a quarter of a century of literary activity. It was a demonstration which probably has not its like in the exilic history of Jewry. In hundreds of towns in Russia, Poland, England, the Americas, South Africa—wherever Yiddish was read—in the Kasrielevkys of the Pale, Kasrielevky on the Hudson, Kasrielevky on the Pampas, Kasrielevky in the Transvaal, there were meetings at which his works were read forth, and the *Kasriels* in exile laughed with Sholom Aleichem and at themselves, wept with him and over themselves. He had by then achieved a place in the folk which was final and unchangeable. He wrote much that was great in his last eight years; when he died he was engaged in great work and had great works in mind. They would have added to the delight of his readers, not to his name.

In another sense, too, he had completed his pilgrimage. He had known all the vicissitudes of a Jew, he had tasted all the experiences which were peculiar to the history of his people. He had been a *cheder* boy in old Kasrielevky, and a Russian Gymnasium student; he had passed from the medieval to the modern; he had been a tutor, a Crown Rabbi, a businessman; he had dealt in sugar, had gambled on the Yehupetz stock exchange, had turned insurance agent; he had been very rich and very poor. He had been a Maecenas of literature, and he had known what it was to need a Maecenas and not to find one. He had published lavishly the works of lesser writers and had been unable to find publishers for his own. He had been adored and ignored. He had had his plays turned down by producers, he had been bullied by New York newspaper editors who told him they knew better than he what the public wanted. And always he had written. He wrote in health and sickness; he wrote on trains, in droshkies, on the kitchen table, at his business desk, in the midst of ledgers, balance sheets, and IOU's. He wrote even on his deathbed. He was driven by an intolerable creative strength. The excessive imagination, the gifts of observation and of memory, and the irresistible impulse to mimicry which had made him a portent in his *cheder* days stayed with him to the end. But never was he the less a man, living with his fellow men, because he was the writer; and as a man he had lived through all that his people had suffered.

It is not a formality to speak of the thousands who poured out into the streets of New York on that day as "mourners." It was not formality that caused hundreds of unions, brotherhoods, societies, Zionist clubs, benevolent orders, and Socialist organizations to call hasty meetings on the Sunday of May 14, and to send their representatives to the cemetery on the morning of the 15th. It was not formality that brought delegations to New York from every town in America within overnight distance. Nor was it Sholom Aleichem himself that they mourned. It was a part of their life which had been torn away from them. They were attending the rehearsal of their own obsequies, saying the *Kaddish* in advance over their way of life, for they knew that none would say it afterwards. Brighter days might indeed come for the Jewish people, but the savor of their world would not be tasted by their children, and they would be a mystery to their own posterity.

This "they" felt. And who were "they"? None other than the people he had written of. Tevye himself left his milkcart at the corner of Intervale Avenue and came with Goldie to say farewell to Sholom Aleichem. Menachem Mendel the *shlemiel* came with them. Not far off was Sholom Ber of Teplik, no longer the *nogid* but a rag pedlar; and behind him limped along Berel the Lame, who had gone to Heissin in his company on a memorable day. Mottel the cantor's son, and Ellie the tailor, and Leizer Wolf the butcher, and old Reb Yozifel, the pietists and the revolutionaries, the skullcaps and the bowler hats —they filed through the living room where he lay in state, they darkened the streets of the Lower East Side, they waited for him at the cemetery. They heard the singing of the requiem—"God, full of mercy"—and it was as though a people were being consigned to the grave. Why, then, should they not mourn? Who was to speak for them now that Sholom Aleichem was dead, and who was to remember them if he was forgotten?

Sholom Aleichem lies buried in Mount Nebo Cemetery in Cypress Hills, Brooklyn. He had asked that his body be transferred, after the war, to the cemetery of his beloved Yehupetz; but this could not be done, and it is better so. In other respects the provisions of his testament were carried out. His grave is simple, and only his epitaph distinguishes it from those that surround it. He had said: "Let me be buried among the poor, that their graves may shine on mine, and mine on theirs."

From *The World of Sholom Aleichem* (1943)

25 PERETZ ON HASIDIC ECSTASY

Hasidism was many things: a religious movement, a social protest, a national renaissance, and a great explosion of spiritual folk energy. But above all it was an ecstatic seizure. It was an exalted mood among the masses of the poor of Eastern Europe. It was a singing, dancing, worshipping, loving approach to God and the world. It was a mighty Yea-saying. Like all such unpredictable manifestations of the human spirit, it ultimately died down into strange forms and broke up into strange contradictions. But in the days of its first joyous blossoming, a hundred and fifty to two hundred years ago, among the Jewries of Russia and Poland, it was one of those rare illuminations which break from time to time upon the somber surface of human history.

But definitions and descriptions of Hasidism, literary or historical, will not get us very far. One must listen to the Hasidim themselves. And there's the difficulty. They had a language of their own, unintelligible to outsiders. I do not mean that they used a special dialect of Yiddish or of Hebrew. Not at all. Their language was the simplest imaginable. But they infused into their talk—which was of course the mirror of their experience—such a quality of exaltation that the outsider understood all the less precisely because every one of the words was misleadingly familiar to him.

They could not explain themselves to others; their views and feelings had to be transmitted by emotional infection. Therefore it was inevitable that their foremost spokesman to the outside world should not have been one of them. Y. L. Peretz was not a Hasid. He was as far removed from the Hasidim in his beliefs and daily preoccupations as any modern Jew could be; or, let us say, in his conscious beliefs and preoccupations. But it was his peculiar gift to have caught and made accessible to us—to whatever extent it can so be made— the spirit of the Hasidic world. It is of course open to the skeptic to suggest that we have no means of knowing whether what Peretz gives us is really Hasidism. But the alternative is to believe that Peretz created the contents of a whole religious movement—that which no single person has done in the history of the world. (Skepticism often makes big calls on our faith.)

Peretz was not a praying Jew; he could be bitterly rationalist on the subject of prayer. He rarely if ever went to a synagogue, and he certainly never put on prayer shawl and phylacteries at home—at least, after he left his father's house. But, as we shall see, he transmits the bliss of Hasidic prayer with an intensity that the Hasidim knew only from within. Peretz paid no attention to the dietary laws, and he never made the benediction before eating a piece of fruit or drinking a glass of water—or of brandy. But what the benediction before food and the grace after it meant to a Hasid, he alone makes the non-Hasid understand. Peretz did not use the physical symbols of the ritual, did not wear the woven fringes under his shirt, did not (except perhaps by accident) have a *mezuzah* on the lintel of his door, did not build a booth for the Feast of Tabernacles. And yet if we who resemble him in these matters want to understand with what intimate joy they were invested for the Hasidim, we shall do best to go to Peretz.

"Look you," says one of his Hasidic characters. "We Hasidim take a drink of brandy, and *they* take a drink of brandy." ("They" in this context are either Gentiles or non-believing Jews). "Why do *they* drink? They don't even like it. They pull a face as they pour it down their throats. It's the evil inclination, the Devil's will, that drives them to drink. You can see their souls shrinking from it, their faces wrinkling up. But when *we* take a drink we make the benediction over it and invoke the name of the Blessed One. In fact, we take the drink only for the sake of the benediction. The mention of God's name is the purpose of the drink. And therefore the soul enjoys the drink, and wants to drink.

"*They* are forever proclaiming: 'Happiness! We want happiness! We want to enjoy the good things of this world!' And I tell you that happiness and the good things of life are ours alone. For He is the source of all happiness and of all good things; from Him alone they stream forth."

Another of his Hasidic characters talks of the Rabbi of Nemirov, one of the most exalted figures in their tradition.

"It is known to the whole world that he of Nemirov served the Eternal One in purest joy. Happy is the eye that was privileged to behold the radiance which spread from him and shed its light on all about him. The Jew within range of it forgot the exile, forgot all pain and tribulation; nay, he forgot himself. All the souls were poured into one soul, and that was the soul of Him of Nemirov.

"And what shall I say about his singing, and his sacred dances? Words and movements were steeped in the Holy Spirit. And once, in an ecstatic moment, he called out: 'I hereby do proclaim and reveal to mankind that the whole world is nothing more than a singing and a dancing before the Holy One, blessed be He. . . . Every Jew is a singer before Him, and every letter in the Torah is a musical note. Every living soul is a letter of the Torah, wherefore all souls taken together make up the Torah—and souls and Torah are a song to the King of Kings of Kings, the Holy One, blessed be He.'

"Then he went on to say that just as there are many singing voices, so there are many musical instruments; and every melody is suited for some particular musical instrument, which alone can render it; and for every instrument there are particular melodies. For the instrument is the body and the melody is the soul.

"Every man, too, he told us, is a musical instrument, and his life is a melody, a gay or mournful melody. And when the melody has been played out, the soul—that is, the melody—flies out of the body and joins in the great melody before the Throne of Glory.

"And alas for the man, he said, who lives without a melody; for it is like living without a soul. It is no life at all."

The speaker reports further what the Rabbi of Nemirov had to say concerning the formalists and scholars, the Talmudists and men of learning, against whose icy dominion over Jewish life Hasidism was the revolt.

"Such scholars," said he of Nemirov, "whose learning, however great, is only on the surface, are like visitors to a royal palace who are permitted to see its outside, but are forbidden to enter. They have not even the courage to knock at the door, for fear it will not be opened. They see the walls, the windows, the doors, the chimneys, and the banners flying over the roof. Sometimes they see smoke ascending from the chimneys; and sometimes they even catch from afar off the voices of servants passing through the vestibules. . . . But those who let their souls sink into the spirit and meaning of the Torah are like visitors for whom the doors stand open, and they are welcomed into the King's glory."

And again, he of Nemirov likened those dry scholars, those unadmitted visitors about the palace, to workmen who know how to make a musical instrument, or how to mend it, but cannot play on it. "Their hands are often skillful, but their ears are stopped up; and when someone plays the instrument they have made, they cannot hear. Or else their hearts are stopped up; they hear but do not understand. And if there is among them an exceptionally gifted workman who does occasionally put the instrument to his lips, all he can do is imitate someone else's melody.

"I," added he of Nemirov, "am no scholar; that is, no workman. I cannot make an instrument nor mend one. But, God be thanked, I can play on all of them."

Now, concerning the "inwardness" of prayer among Hasidim, which is like the inwardness of the Torah, another Hasid described a great experience. He does not mention the name of the Hasidic rabbi who was at the center of it; it may have been he of Nemirov; it may have been another. Nor do I know whether Peretz invented the incident or whether he found it in the tradition.

"Joy within joy" he calls the experience—a special visitation of ecstasy. It was connected with the services of the New Year—the time of the annual accounting and judgment of mortals in heaven. "And as you know," he reminds us, "we Hasidim make a happy occasion of it. We aren't like the other Jews, the Misnagdim, who are terrified by the approaching judgment. We know that we are not being haled before a foreign potentate. It is our own Father in heaven who is going to judge us; and so, after prayers, we take a couple of glasses of brandy, and we dance."

But on this New Year of which he tells, something quite out of the ordinary happened and made it the most memorable New Year in the annals of that Hasidic group.

The Rabbi stood before the congregation, leading it in prayer. And what a prayer leader he was! All day long his voice poured out supplication and praise; for on the New Year he permitted no one to take his place. And who would have wanted to? Who would have dared? As he stood there, the messenger of Israel to the Throne, his voice was like a pathway from earth to heaven. It stretched from prayer to prayer, broad and unbroken, bearing the hopes of his people.

And then suddenly, a dreadful pause, a break. He had reached the prayer that begins: "To God who prepareth judgment." The words rang out clearly. But those which followed: "To Him that searcheth hearts, to Him that uncovereth the deeps," were uttered uncertainly. And when he came to the words: "To Him that buyeth His slaves in the day of judgment," his voice broke completely, and a frightful silence followed.

One second, two seconds, three—and every second an eternity. Terror spreads through the congregation; up in the gallery women fall down, fainting.

And then the Rabbi comes to. A shudder passes through his body, and the tense and terrified silence is broken by a joyous cry: "Who taketh mercy on His people on the day of judgment." And the Rabbi prolongs the words in happy turns and roulades, while his feet begin to move, as of themselves, in a jubilant dance. And the rest of the morning prayers continue with renewed strength.

Between the first and the second morning prayers the Rabbi explained what had happened. A very trifling matter, you would imagine; but wait.

As we know, when a man reads from the prayer book, the eyes run ahead of the lips. The lips say "uncovereth the deeps," the eyes are already at "buyeth His slaves in the day of judgment." And thus it happened with the Rabbi that morning of the New Year service. But there and then it occurred to him that the words made no sense! He simply did not understand them, had never understood them. What possible interpretation could one put upon these words, which declared that "God bought His slaves in the day of judgment"? And in the utter confusion of that moment the Rabbi suspended his prayer and became silent.

As you may well imagine, the break was noted at once in the Upper Circles. Our Rabbi's prayer suspended! A calamity! Not to be endured! Immediately the decision was made to reveal to him, in a vision, the meaning of the words, so that he might continue with the prayer.

And as the Rabbi closed his eyes in perplexity, the heavens were cleft before him. This is what he saw:

The chamber of the heavenly court. It is still empty. The prosecuting attorney, counsel for the defense, the judges, all are yet to arrive. The Rabbi looks around. The chamber has five doors: one in the right wall, with the sign: "Counsel for the Defense"; one in the left wall: "Prosecuting Attorney"; three doors at the back, in the eastern wall, and in front of them the table and the scales. The middle door at the back, which is closed, bears the legend: "Hosts of the Blessed"; the other two doors at the back are open. Through the one on the right the Rabbi sees the garden plots of paradise. There the patriarchs and the sainted ones are seated, steeped in the effulgence of the Divine Light, studying the Torah. Their crowned heads are bent over the sacred texts: for them there is no judgment day. Through the door to the left the Rabbi sees the labyrinths of hell. Hell is empty and silent; on a holy day the souls in hell are given respite, there is no torment and no punishment. The fires still burn —it is "the everlasting fire which shall not be extinguished"—but the demons are occupied with a special task.

And now the door in the right wall opens, and counsel for the defense enters, carrying under his arm the records of the good deeds of mankind for the past year. Alas, a very small sheaf. A poor year it has been for good deeds. Counsel for the defense observes that the door opposite is still closed. A bad sign, that. It is taking them too long to collect *their* records. The harvest of mankind's misdeeds fills the granaries of hell. Counsel for the defense drops into a seat and closes his eyes sadly.

The door in the left wall opens, and two demons enter, staggering under the load of the first bundle. The Rabbi hears their bones creaking under the burden. They throw down the bundle and sing out loudly: "That isn't even a tithe of the harvest. The demons are still collecting—whole treasuries are yet to come."

Counsel for the defense covers his face and groans. He apparently feels that no one hears him. The court is not yet assembled, the residents of paradise are busy with the Torah, hell is empty.

Counsel for the defense is mistaken! Among the residents of paradise there is the beloved, the unforgettable Hasidic rabbi, Reb Levi Yitzchok of Berdichev, the Compassionate One. *He* hears the groan of anguish that bursts from the lips of counsel for the defense. He alone among the children of bliss has not forgotten those who dwell in darkness and the shadow of death; he alone remembers that for *them,* on earth below, there is still a judgment day. And if someone groans in heaven, it is undoubtedly for them. Reb Levi Yitzchok interrupts his studies, looks up, and through the open door perceives the crushed figure of counsel for the defense.

Levi Yitzchok of Berdichev, tenderest of all Jews, most vigilant in defense of his sinful people, rebuker of the Almighty for His severity toward mortals, Levi Yitzchok of Berdichev steals into the chamber and understands at once what is toward: he sees the slender sheaf under counsel's arm, the vast bundle on the table. It takes Reb Levi Yitzchok just one instant to decide. He bends down and, straining himself to the utmost, picks up the bundle of adverse records; he flings it through the door at the left, down into the flames of hell.

Again two demons enter, bent double under a load of records. The moment they leave, Reb Levi Yitzchok deals with this bundle as he dealt with the first. And so with the third and the fourth and the rest.

Finally it is the Ashmedai himself, Asmodeus, the Devil and prosecuting attorney, who enters, a broad grin on his face. What is this? Help! The records! Not a sign of that opulent harvest. He looks around, sees the last bundle burning in hell; looks around again, and sees Reb Levi Yitzchok sneaking back toward paradise. He runs over, grabs him by the arm, and yells:

"Stop, thief!"

The cry resounds through all the seven heavens. Patriarchs and saints start up from their studies and rush into the chamber. The center door at the back opens and the members of the court file in. Counsel for the defense starts up.

"What is it?"

Before this heavenly assembly the Devil declares how he caught Reb Levi Yitzchok red-handed. He points to the fires of hell, where the last bundle—it was the heaviest of all—is still smoldering.

Truth is truth! Reb Levi Yitzchok confesses. Justice is justice! The Devil is asked what sentence he demands. He too decides on the instant. He quotes the Scriptures—he would!—"The thief shall be sold for his theft." Let Reb Levi Yitzchok be sold as a slave publicly, to the highest bidder. The Devil will of course join in the bidding. And no matter what it costs him, he intimates, he will find it worth his while.

This is the law, and there is no appeal from it. Let the auction begin!

So they stand facing one another, the Devil on one side, the children of bliss on the other, Reb Levi Yitzchok between them. The members of the court take their seats; the bidding opens.

Father Abraham makes his offer: his heavenly credit for the priceless gem of the Covenant, the first Jewish commandment; and he adds as bonus his credits for his famous hospitality. After him comes Isaac, whose contribution is almost as large: the credits for his readiness to be sacrificed on the altar by his father. Jacob follows: his possessions are his simplicity, his devotion to learning in the days when his brutish brother Esau went hunting in the fields. Then comes Rachel, with *her* special distinction, the love-mandrakes; and after her the other matriarchs, each contributing her own glory. And row upon row of saints follow, each putting up, for the purchase of Reb Levi Yitzchok, whatever reward he had garnered during his sojourn on earth.

But it is the Devil himself against whom they are bidding, and he has treasures beyond computation. For every addition to the right scale he throws a corresponding price into the left scale. He ransacks the earth, brings out forgotten wealth from beyond the hills of darkness, till the eyes are dazzled by the display. The saints have exhausted their stocks, the two scales stand level, and in a last flourish the Devil takes the crown off his head and flings it into the auction. He must have Reb Levi Yitzchok at any price. The scale on the left begins to sink; it falls lower, lower.

Counsel for the defense advances and throws in on the right the meager records of the year's good deeds. In vain. They are not substantial enough to arrest the downward flight of the scale on the left.

A crooked and vindictive grin spreads over the Devil's lips, and triumph flickers in his eyes. Oh, what a catch, what a haul, what a victory for hell! Reb Levi Yitzchok of Berdichev, perhaps the most glorious figure in the Hasidic world after the founder himself, the Master of the Name! Before the scale has touched bottom the Devil places a hand on Reb Levi Yitzchok's shoulder and points significantly to the door on the left, the door opening on hell. "This way, please."

Horror runs through the ranks of the blessed. What! Reb Levi Yitzchok lost? It cannot be! And yet—what is to be done?

The horror and confusion increase—until they are suddenly stilled by a Voice. It is the Voice from the Throne of Glory.

"*I* buy him!"

And again through the deathly silence: "I raise the bid! 'For Mine is the earth and the fullness thereof'—and I give the whole world for Reb Levi Yitzchok."

The Devil's face became black as thunder.

Gleefully the Hasid finishes the story:

"That's what the Rabbi told us in the pause between first and second prayers that New Year's morning. And you, you non-Hasidim, you Misnagdim, you unbelievers, can you understand what happiness was ours that New Year?

"First, there was the record of our sins destroyed—which means a happy and prosperous New Year as good as in our pockets. Second, Reb Levi Yitzchok redeemed. And third, to top it all, and best of all, the secret of a text at last revealed. 'To Him that buyeth His slaves in the day of judgment!' "

That was the "inwardness" of prayer among Hasidim, an intimacy of communion between man and God that made the word *Father* literal. It was part of the general mystic self-identification with divinity which Hasidism revived and popularized from the esoteric doctrines of the Kabbalists, extending to the simple masses what had been the privilege of the spiritual elite.

As Hasidism grew older and developed its careerist rabbis, its wonder-workers and dynasties, it also developed its sects. The followers of Shneour Zalman of Ladi, at the beginning of the nineteenth century, were thinkers, scholars, and ascetics. Shneour Zalman was by intellectual equipment much closer to the Gaon of Vilna—who turned him from his door, or rather refused to open it to him—than to the founder of Hasidism. And again, the followers of the Rabbi of Kotzk did not hold with prayer; they were more for study as the expression of man's relation to the Divinity. But the original strain of Hasidism, surviving in the bulk of the movement till the present day, was interpenetrated with the ecstatic experience; for the classic Hasid prayer was the most difficult of human exercises—the deliberate daily renewal of inspiration.

Peretz gives us a story of the Ba'al Shem—the founder of Hasidism—at a seder ceremony, and puts into his mouth (though the story and explanation are of Peretz's invention) a typical Hasidic exposition of prayer.

The Ba'al Shem wanted his listeners to understand in what manner prayers mounted from earth to the Heavenly Throne. Not all prayers proceeded straightway to their destination, he said. The rates of ascent differed. A's prayer, offered long after B's, might register long before. It depended on the purity of the prayer. Prayer, said the Ba'al Shem, consists of body and soul; the words are the body, the intent is the soul. The more soul or spirituality a prayer possesses, the straighter is its upward path. But if a prayer is deficient in these lightening elements, it meanders, it rolls about, it is pushed hither and thither by the winds, it is swallowed up by fogs, drenched by rains, perhaps even forced downward, to become tangled in the growths of jungles. In the end it reaches heaven; it must, for the letters of the Hebrew words are sacred, they are of heavenly origin, and all things must return to their origin. Sooner or later, then, the prayer comes home. Thus it comes about that although Jews pray at stated hours of the day, and for longer stretches during certain days of the year, the arrival of prayers in heaven is continuous, and not intermittent. That is the meaning of the verse: "The Guardian of Israel neither slumbereth nor sleepeth." Compassion forbids that He should not always be alert to the arrival of a prayer.

Now, it sometimes happens, the Ba'al Shem went on, that a Jew will be standing up during the solemn prayer of the Eighteen Benedictions, murmuring the words, but thinking all the time of his purchases of grain. That prayer, God help us, is then loaded down with sacks of wheat and other gross earthly things. A prayer so handicapped may well wander about in the wilds of space for a hundred years or more before it shakes itself free of its burden and makes the ascent. Meanwhile the man has died! He is called to trial. The prosecuting attorney piles his evil deeds on the left-hand scale, counsel for the defense stands there empty-handed. "But God Almighty," screams the Jew, "where are my prayers, at least? I know I prayed." Alas, his prayers have not even started their ascent. And the court, to vindicate its reputation for justice, opens a window and lets the man look down. Far away on the earth below, somewhere in a farmyard, he sees his wretched prayers still struggling to get out from under the weight of the sacks.

As to what happens to this unhappy man until his prayers arrive, we will say nothing.

From *Prince of the Ghetto* (1948)

26 *DALES* (POVERTY)

I

Dales, "poverty," has become hypostasized in the Yiddish folk mind, and is a living presence. The poet Mani-Leyb sings:

> *In dem oremland fun lite*
> *Zingt a foygl in a shmite,*
> *Un derfar oyf yedn rog*
> *Zingt der dales yedn tog;*
> *Zingt der dales un der oylem*
> *Zingt mit im oyf ale keylim.*

> In the poverty-land of Lithuania
> A bird sings once in seven years,
> But to make up for it, on every corner,
> Poverty sings every day.
> Poverty sings, and all and sundry
> Sing along with all their organs.

Of a poverty-stricken home one hears it said: *der dales fayft fun ale vinkelekh,* "Poverty whistles from every corner"; *der dales tantst in mitn shtub,* "Poverty dances in the middle of the room"; or, in the early stages, *der dales hot zikh arayngeganvet in hoyz,* "Poverty stole into the house."

But I should like to establish *dales* in English with some of its Yiddish status; I shall capitalize it henceforth, and I shall not translate it, but speak of it as one does of the Muses, Clio for history, Melpomene for tragedy, and Dales, the tenth, for poverty, a masculine Muse unknown to Parnassus, the dominant voice in the life of the Yiddish-speaking masses of Eastern Europe.

Some may argue that *parnose,* "livelihood," was not less a presence in the Jewish mind than Dales, and is entitled to equal honors. Certainly the word was as familiar and as often on the lips of city and *shtetl* Jew alike, and it is not easy for American Jews of today to think themselves into the desperation with which their grandfathers prayed on the High Holy Days, and especially on Yom Kippur, for *parnose* in the new year. *Vos tut nit a yid tsulib parnose?* "What won't a Jew do to provide for his family?" reflects the humiliations of the oppressed Jew. Sometimes *khayune* stands for *parnose;* in Poland and Hungary they also called it *pinosi,* which Jews elsewhere parodied.

God is the *mefarnes,* "He that provides," but God was occasionally forgetful, as Berel the tailor protested in Peretz's story. Since the *parnose* of so many Jews was, or came from, a tiny, wretchedly stocked shop, or a stand in the marketplace, or a basketful of produce (usually tended by a woman), a word closely related was *leyzn,* "to take in money (on a sale)"; and *git mir tsu leyzn,* "Buy something from me," was the pitiable refrain from thousands of throats.

But if I give Dales precedence over *parnose,* it is because he was so much more present as a reality; he haunted the Jewish mind. In the opinion of Professor Dov Sadan, perhaps the foremost authority on Yiddish, Dales was once actually a demon, a malevolent spirit with an independent existence which was acknowledged in countless sayings.

Vu der dales klept zikh on ken men fun im nit azoy laykht poter vern, "Where Dales has once fastened on, it's no light matter to get rid of him, shake him off"; and a similar sentiment runs to rhyme, *der dokter ken ales ober nit aroystraybn dem dales.* "The doctor can do everything except drive out Dales." For Dales is the ever-present threat; *farn (far dem) toyt un farn dales ken men zikh nit bavorenen,* "There's no insurance against death and Dales." Moreover, *der dales hot a grobn kop,* "Dales has a thick head," i.e., where Dales reigns one sees not the brains, which is confirmed by another saying, *der dales farshtelt di khokhme,* "Dales conceals (a man's) wisdom."

Farvos fayft der dales? "Why does Dales whistle?"—that is, why does he make his presence so manifest? The answer is, *vayl er hot nor a dude,* "Because a whistle is all he has." Again, in the same spirit, *farvos klapt der dales?* "Why does Dales make such a racket?"; *vayl er geyt in klumpes,* "Because he wears clogs."

Dales has grades and degrees—*a dales vi a kurfirst,* "a Dales like an Imperial Elector," or a *kuflshmoynediker dales,* "a Dales of eightfold amplitude," or a *draygorndiker dales,* "a Dales three stories high," when two-story buildings were a rarity—and Dales is hard to disguise, for *az me makht dem dales a kaftn vert der kaftn klener,* "If you clothe Dales in a cloak, the cloak shrinks."

Dales iz nit pasles, "Dales is not dishonesty," says one proverb, and is contradicted by another, *dales makht pasles,* "Dales occasions dishonesty"; however that might be, the Grundy sector of the Yiddish world was as ashamed of Dales as of a crime. There was another side that accepted poverty with resignation, even with cheerfulness and gaiety; there were some who considered it the proper condition of the Jew, according to the talmudic saying, "As a red ribbon becomes a white horse, so does poverty become the Daughter of Judea."

This was the view to be found among the workers rather than among the lower middle classes. Most Jews were poor, pious, and prolific, but the workers seldom dreamed of wealth, while the middle classes seldom dreamed of anything else. Among the privations of poverty none was harder to bear than its humiliations, and the desire to dissimulate it was as passionate as the desire to rise out of it.

Mit a barsht un mit a nodl bahalt men dem dales, "With a brush and a needle you hide Dales," says one proverb, and another, *mit a groshn leym makht men dem dales reyn,* "With a pennyworth of clay you clean up Dales." *Farshteln dem dales,* "concealing (the presence of) Dales," was a social imperative, failure to do so a moral disgrace. But how difficult was concealment! *Der dales leygt zikh tsu ersht oyfn ponem* (Heb.), "Dales settles first on your face." Of what use then were needle and brush and a pennyworth of clay?

II

Round the central personification, Dales, are grouped various figures and concepts. The chief of these, second only to Dales, is the *kaptsn,* "the poor man." Alas, to translate *kaptsn* as "a poor man" is to depersonalize the word, reduce it to the status of the simple Germanic *oreman,* which seems to say the same thing but by comparison says nothing at all. There are "poor men" among all peoples, but the *kaptsn* was to be found only among the Jews. He was an affirmation, an institution, in a sense the chief representative of the Jewish people. He was everywhere: *vu me geyt un vu me shteyt dreyt zikh der kaptsn in mitn,* "Whichever way you turn, the *kaptsn* is there in the midst of everything." And he was everywhere as of right, even when the well-to-do rebuked him contemptuously with *kaptsn vu krikhstu (krikhstdu)?,*" *"kaptsn,* look where you're going," or *"kaptsn,* know your place!"

The *kaptsn* was of course haunted by Dales, but he was not the embodiment of it, for Dales conveys indigence of spirit as well as material want, whereas the *kaptsn* could also be a *kasril,* an irrepressibly cheerful pauper, *orem ober freylekh,* "poor but merry."

He would acknowledge that *der shverster ol iz a leydike keshene,* "The heaviest yoke is an empty pocket," but he carried it with panache. He jested about it; he brought to bear upon it, in high mockery, the scraps of learning left over from *kheyder* years and collected from religious ceremonies and the visits of wandering *maggidim,* "preachers." He created an intellectual culture of poverty whose like I have not met elsewhere, and which it is all but impossible to convey in a language other than Yiddish.

Let me nevertheless make an attempt. I offer here an example of the wit of the *kaptsn,* with a bleak explanation (the best I can work out) for those without Yiddish or Hebrew. It was sung with an imitation of the *kheyder* melody of childhood.

> *Vayiten lekho* (Hebrew)
> *Keyn gelt iz nishto* (Yiddish)
> *Mital hashomayim* (Hebrew)
> *Nishto vu tsu layen* (Yiddish)
> *Mishmaney ho-orets* (Hebrew)
> *Dos gelt iz baym porets* (Yiddish)

Every Yiddish line rhymes with the Hebrew line preceding it, but instead of being a translation it is a completely irrelevant statement, which, however, makes sense in itself and in connection with the other Yiddish lines. The Hebrew lines contain, almost word for word, part of the blessing bestowed by Isaac upon Jacob (Genesis 27:28) under the impression that he was Esau.

Now to repeat the lines with complete translation:

> *Vayiten lekho* (Hebrew), "He will give unto thee"
> *Keyn gelt iz nishto* (Yiddish), "money there's none"
> *Mital hashomayim* (Hebrew), "of the dew of the heavens"
> *Nishto vu tsu layen* (Yiddish), "there's nowhere to borrow"
> *Mishmaney ho-orets* (Hebrew), "of the fat of the earth"
> *Dos gelt iz baym porets* (Yiddish), "the landowner has the money"

In this laborious elucidation nothing remains of the black gleefulness pervading the original. Here was not only a delicious piece of verbal ingenuity bringing a grin to the faces of the hungry; it was also an exercise in pious mockery, respectful irreverence, and bantering blasphemy. For the Hebrew text is from the Torah, and what could be more submissive? The translation(!) is from life, what could be more relevant? And of course the pleasure of it rose from "insideness," from that familiarity with the sacred texts in the original which was the mark, and the exclusive privilege, of the Jew still faithful to the God of the Fathers.

Still faithful, and still rebellious in faithfulness. The ambivalence extended to God's people not less than to God Himself, for no one is more bitterly critical of the Jewish people than the Jew lovingly committed to its perpetuation. Not that there is in Yiddish anything like the blood-curdling denunciations of the prophets of old. The Yiddish form of Jewish self-denigration is in low key, sibilant, sardonic, and subtle, occasionally blasphemous, *a kleyn folk, ober paskudne,* "A small people, but a loathsome one"; *a got hobn mir, aza yor oyf undz, un a folk hot er, aza yor oyf im,* "A God we have, such a year on us, and a people He has, such a year on Him." Concerning piety there is a folk saying: *tsu vos darf a yid hobn fis? az in kheyder muz men im traybn, tsu der khupe firt men im, tsu koure brengt men im, in shul arayn geyt er nit, tsu shikses krikht er, haynt tsu vos darf er hobn fis?,* "What does a Jew need legs for? To school he has to be driven, to the marriage canopy he is conducted, to burial he is brought, to synagogue he does not go, and he crawls after gentile girls; so what does he need legs for?"

III

It is Sholom Aleichem who has given to the world, for its everlasting edification, the prototype of the Yiddish-speaking Eastern European Jew whose natural habitat was Dalesland and whose natural condition was that of the loving, sardonic, conforming, and contumacious child of God and His people. It is true that by the grace of that same God, Tevye the dairyman escaped from semidestitution into semidemi-affluence, acquiring, *mayse nes,* a cow, a goat, and thirty-seven rubles of working capital, and leading thenceforth a life of labor free from actual want. But all his days he remained the original Tevye, whose inquiring mind and challenging spirit mirrored the physical neediness and spiritual indestructibility of the Yiddish masses. Come what might, Tevye would hold onto his identity as thinking man, believing Jew, and protester against God's mistreatment of the Jewish people.

He expressed this harmonious triune personality by his avenging mistreatment of sacred texts, sardonic mistranslations conceived not in the callow manner of the apostate but, more subtly, in the expostulatory spirit of the submissive devotee. He believed that God had a Jewish sense of humor, and far from being displeased by a display of mutiny, would smile understandingly as long as all was couched in the wit of the Torah. It was for Teyve a basic tenet that God hates an ignoramus, or more exactly, an *amorets,* a devotee and pillar of ignorance.

And here lies the painful tragedy of the attempt to portray Tevye in English without his fundamental instrument of self-expression, namely, his manhandling of sacred Hebrew texts in ingeniously blasphemous Yiddish. It was a form of folk humor, and we see a specimen of it in the parody of Jacob's blessing. In Sholom Aleichem it became a personal style. But when Tevye is remodeled on the English stage for audiences innocent not only of Yiddish and Hebrew, but even of the Bible—not to mention the *siddur,* the Mishnah, and the Talmud —he is denaturized into a kindly imitation of a Shakespearean clown without the wit we expect, but steeped in a low sentimentality made to order for *amkho,* Jewish and non-Jewish. Thus transformed, he has been received round the world with loving lachrymosity and complete misunderstanding. For the clearest and most refreshing characteristic of Tevye is the mocking brightness of his mind, without which as background his sentimentality is simply mawkishness; it is as though we were to judge Heinrich Heine by *Du bist wie eine Blume* without knowing that he was also the author of *Atta Troll.*

Some of the background needed to appreciate Tevye's wit, such as a knowledge of the Jewish Bible, should be but is not universal; some acquaintance with the prayer book, Talmud, and Midrash might be expected among a majority of Jews but is found only among a self-respecting minority. Even so, the curriculum is not complete; without enough Yiddish (and therefore Hebrew) to follow him in the original, even the sharpest and most perceptive mind, relying on translation, must guess at the inner Tevye. To be sure, what can thus be glimpsed is impressive enough, and since miracles do happen, a genius may yet find a way of reproducing Tevye's monologues in English without loss of their essence. God speed the day!

To clarify the nature of Tevye's gnomic mutilations, we must imagine an American college graduate addressing an audience of his intellectual peers. We must further imagine that all of them once took a course in Latin and have preserved in their memories the familiar tags with which "cultivated" essays were peppered a century or two ago. The speaker throws them in from time to time accompanying them with English paraphrases and explications which are sometimes utterly nonsensical, sometimes ingeniously tangential, sometimes both, and always with a vague suggestion of authenticity and relevance.

Here are some imperfect examples (the game can be played by any number):

Sic transit gloria mundi, "Here today and gone tomorrow."
Reductio ad absurdum, "A fool and his money are soon parted."
Caveat emptor, "A pig in a poke."
De mortuis nil nisi bonum, "Once you're dead it's for good."
Ars longa vita brevis, "That's the long and the short of it."
Semper fidelis, "The more the merrier."
Delenda est Cartago, "Neither a borrower nor a lender be."
Carpe diem, "Shoot the works."
Non compos mentis, "Look who's talking."
Aere perennius, "Airy nothings."
Alea est jacta, "Throw the bum out."

Another condition must be added: the texts thus deliberately deformed in translation must be, without exception, sacred, belonging to prayers that have been an immemorial consolation, an everlasting shelter from the storms of history. What, then, is the meaning of this indecorous frivolity, this burlesquing of ultimate values? Strange as it may sound, it is an antipodal declaration of loyalty, an assertion of independence in submissiveness.

Among the most beloved of the biblical "scrolls" is the Song of Songs, and among the (now trite) similes used by the king concerning his shepherdess is *keshoyshane beyn hakhoykhim,* "like a lily among thorns." Sholom Aleichem "translates" it as *vi a finfter rod tsum vogn,* "like a fifth wheel to a cart."

In the valedictory prayer to the Sabbath, when the visiting Queen is ushered out, there occurs the phrase: *hamavdil beyn koydesh lekhoyl,* "He that maketh division between the sacred and the profane." Sholom Aleichem accompanies this with the translation: *ver es hot di klingers dem iz voyl,* "If you've got the ringers (coin), bully for you" (the Shakespearean phrase is "happy man be his dole").

In the daily *shimenesre,* also called the *amidah* ("standing prayer"), occurs the supplication *refueynu venerape,* "Heal us and we will be healed." This emerges as *shik undz di refue, di make hobn mir shoyn aleyn,* "Send us the healing, we've managed to get the affliction without Your help."

And a final example: In the *pirke oves,* Ethics of the Fathers, a mishnaic book familiar to many of the simple folk, there is a famous admonition: *shloyshe sheokhlu al shulkhn ekhod,* etc., "Three that have eaten at one table and have not exchanged words of the Torah, it is as if they have eaten of sacrifices to idols." *Shloyshe sheokhlu* became the key phrase to the entire passage, "Three that have eaten." Sholom Aleichem, once seeing a Jew gormandizing at table exclaimed, *shloyshe sheokhlu, er hot gegesn far dray,* "He was eating like three."

IV

The Sholom Aleichem spirit played about the concept of poverty, explored all its possibilities, and created a multitude of denominations. We are not yet done with the *kaptsn,* "pauper," of whom there were many subspecies: a *kaptsn vi der shabes hagodl,* that is, having the grandeur of the Great Sabbath that preceded the Exodus from Egypt; not the *kaptsn* in person, of course, but his *kaptsones,* his *kaptsnhood,* one might say, awesome in its sweep, its venerability and its indestructible grandeur; and then a *kaptsn mit ale kheyngribelekh,* "a *kaptsn* with all his dimples," meaning, of course, again his *kaptsones,* and not his doubtless unprepossessing self. Very homey, too, is a *kaptsn in zibn poles,* "a *kaptsn* in seven garment-skirts," that is, a bedraggled and ragged *kaptsn,* swathed, figuratively, in sevenfold castoffs.

Oni and *evyen* are likewise synonyms for "poor man," but they have not the status of *kaptsn. Oni* is connected with *anives,* "humility," and *evyen* with the name given to a dissident Jewish sect of the first century, the Ebionim, "the poor (of understanding)." Conscious of their separate weakness, the two words joined forces in the phrase *oni ve-evyen,* an emphasis by addition, "A poor man, poor man," while the *evyen-shebe-evyoynim* was emphasis by intensification; he was "the poor man's poor man," as one speaks of the poet's poet. Then, in a sudden turn of modernity, the folk created *oni-ve-evyon et kompani,* which may be freely translated as "Poverty, Inc.," itself confronted by the rival firm, *kaptsnson un hungerman,* "Pauperson and Hungerman."

One way of grinning at poverty was in tender love names. A *kaptsn* became *kaptsenyuk,* an *evyen* an *evyok;* or in bittersweet diminutives set to rhyme:

In eyvele keyn fendele
In shtaygele keyn hendele
In baytele keyn rendele.

In the little stove no little pot,
In the little coop no little chicken
In the little purse no little coin.

Nor must we forget the *dalfn* (by coincidence the second son of Haman). Etymologically he stands close to Dales, for *dal* is Hebrew for poor, and *dalfn* has a special ring because of its similarity to *khalfn,* a money changer. A *khalfn* is one whose business is to change money, a *dalfn,* one whose business it is not to have any. He is sometimes called *a dalfn vi in posek shteyt,* "a *dalfn* such as is written into the biblical verse," that is, fulfilling all his functions and obligations as a *dalfn. Vi in posek shteyt* does not mean that there is a biblical verse on the subject; it is an idiom in wide use meaning "the real thing plus," or "in spades."

Kaptsn, oni, evyon, dalfn are all of Hebraic origin; the Germanic equivalents are not nearly as colorful. *Oreman* is unemotionally descriptive; *betler,* "beggar," when not actually indicating a mendicant, has some sting; so has *shleper,* "low person, vagabond, hobo." Both are offensive words, and have never been touched with the sardonic pathos of the Hebraic. *Shnorer* has accumulated some color; literally it means "beggar," but *betler* is more commonly used of one who goes from door to door, or stands cup in hand on the street. A *shnorer,* more generalized, is a sponger, a deadbeat, even a parasite; but the verb *shnorn* is also used semihumorously for fundraising in good causes.

I may seem in these observations on privation and humiliation to be indulging in the sin I have just denounced, sentimentalization. There was nothing jolly and hilarious about the destitution that lay like a curse on millions of Jews in the Yiddish-speaking world; and it would be grotesque to speak of Sholom Aleichem's and Mendele's *kaptsonim* and *evyonim* as "poor and happy." They were miserable, and knew it; but the question that haunts us historically is, why did they not disintegrate intellectually and morally? How were they able, under hideous oppression and corroding privation, under continuous starvation—the tail of a herring was a dish—to keep alive against a better day the spirit originally breathed into man? The answer lies in the self-mockery by which they rose above their condition to see afar off the hope of the future.

From *In Praise of Yiddish* (1971)

27 "TRANSLATORS ARE TRAITORS"

It is impossible to penetrate to the Yiddish world by mere translation; there must be, on the part of the reader, a willingness to devote some attention to the peculiar, revealing character of Yiddish, to whatever extent this character can be conveyed in English. We will begin by admitting and discussing the limitations; we shall then see what can be done about them.

It is useless to try to explain why the rules of good English forbid you to say: "He made himself a nonperishable name by inventing an imperishable food." You let it go with the remark that that happens to be the genius of the English language—and then add hastily that "genius" as here used does not mean extraordinary gift of native power, but pervading spirit. Every language has its genius, which is nontransferable; and on one level Yiddish differs from English or French or Italian just as these differ from one another.

It differs in the same way from the German, even though it has taken from a German dialect about eighty-five percent of its raw material. In one very important sense the primitive roots of a language are like foods absorbed by different persons: the end results are incommensurable. Ivan eats a potato and it becomes Ivan. Hans eats the same potato and it becomes Hans. From this point of view it is wholly wrong to identify Yiddish with German, and especially silly to call it, as some do, a corrupted German. (It is of course equally absurd to suggest, as others are tempted to, that German is a corrupt Yiddish.) When the Jews of the Rhine valley had, after some centuries, digested the German roots, these were no longer recognizable as far as the spirit is concerned.

True, the Yiddish words *tish* (table), *mensh* (person), *kop* (head), *ferd* (horse), are, as raw material, pretty much the same as in German, and a pidgin German-Yiddish conversation can be carried on by their means. But the moment spirit enters, the communication is broken. A couple of instances will suffice:

The simple Yiddish phrase *dem rebbens shnur* (the rabbi's daughter-in-law) is in one sense easily understood by a German, only he would say *die Schnur des Rabbiners,* although *Schnur* is now archaic and *Schwiegertochter* is the modern equivalent. Actually *dem rebbens shnur* and *die Schnur des Rabbiners* are worlds apart, for reasons which, even if we could elucidate them, would not help us at all to make the two worlds one.

Dem rebbens shnur! It is a phrase loaded with many values, each of which is brought out by its appropriate intonation. Say it one way and it is quiet and dignified, evocative of Friday-evening candles and the Sabbath loaf. Say it somewhat differently—pulling in your chin a little—and it becomes an epitome of small-town snobbery: the young woman walking down the street, *her* chin pulled in a little, and the whisper passing from door to door: *"Dem rebbens shnur!"* A third manner, and the physical image vanishes; it becomes an abstraction, a function in a lofty tradition, an institution for which there is no substitute. But *die Schnur des Rabbiners,* like *the rabbi's daughter-in-law,* is merely a young woman who married the son of a rabbi—a statistical fragment.

There is a curious and charming portmanteau word in Yiddish, *staitch!* which can best be described (if described at all) as an expletive of expostulation. If one Jew has told another a tall story that can be neither accepted nor denied, it is not impolite to answer with the exclamation: *"staitch!"* In this sense it may be tormented into English as: "Bless my soul! You don't tell me!" Or if someone has committed a misdemeanor (as distinguished from a serious crime), he may be reproved with a somewhat distressful: *"staitch!"* which amounts more or less to: "But, my dear fellow, one can't do that sort of thing!" Or if someone makes an unreasonable demand, you counter with an appeal to the sense of proportion: *"staitch!"*—which now becomes an ironical but not unfriendly: "How d'you get that way?" And still again, recalling to an ingrate the benefits he once received, *"staitch!"* approximates to: "Man alive! In the face of all I've done for you?" And in a similar spirit, though on other grounds, it may be addressed to the Almighty Himself, meaning then: "Father in heaven! After all our faithfulness!"

It all depends on the intonation, which may be:

1. courteously skeptical (the tall story)
2. fraternally admonitory (the misdemeanor)
3. amicably derisive (the excessive demand)
4. speechlessly distressful (the ingrate)
5. intimately but unresentfully accusatory (the Almighty).

And I do not speak of the possible permutations and combinations of these numbers, which, in the mouth of an unusually expressive person, may achieve incredibly edifying results.

Now the word *staitch!* has been traced back to the German phrase *"wie heisst's auf Deutsch?*—What do you call that in German?" It may originally have been an innocent question or a provocative challenge. I have heard Americans, confronted with some baffling or offensive statement, cry back: "Say, what's that in American?" Or, as Maria says to the clown in *Twelfth Night,* "Make that good." *Wie heisst's auf Deutsch* was gradually constricted from four syllables into one, and the shorter it grew in pronunciation, the wider it grew in implication. What connection is there now between the Germanic raw material and the Yiddish finished product? Who can translate the latter back into the former? As well try to unscramble an omelet and hatch a chicken from it. It is of course interesting and instructive to trace the transmutation; but the information this provides brings the outsider no nearer to the insider's *"staitch!"* And in the same way, if someone were to trace the steps by which *imperishable* and *nonperishable* acquired their specific tonalities in English, he would not thereby learn the usage of the words; that comes from practice plus instinct, rather than from logic.

Personal names are fascinating instances of spiritual molds. Why is it that the English name *Tom* has become synonymous with manliness and honesty?—in combination, naturally, with honest and manly surnames. Fielding's Tom Jones and Hughes's Tom Brown are two of the most famous exemplars of English solidity of character. To be sure, they corresponded to widely divergent ideals; Tom Brown would have shrunk from Tom Jones as a gross and sensual early Georgian, and Tom Jones would have grinned at Tom Brown as a mid-Victorian milksop. But each was to his age the embodiment of grand old English grit and mettle. I feel that it is useless to seek the why of this distinction; at best we may get part of the where and when. Still, why is it that *Caleb,* on the other hand, is naturally a villain, a tricky lawyer, a heartless collector of mortgages? One is tempted to look back at the Hebrew original: *kelev,* a dog. But Caleb was not a name of evil association among the Hebrews. On the contrary, a well-known Caleb—namely, ben Yefuneh—shares with

Joshua ben Nun the distinction of having brought back from Palestine the first favorable minority report. Of the twelve spies sent in by Moses, only these two were undaunted by the dangers of the conquest. We see, then, that names, passing from one language or people to another, may undergo transvaluations just like other words. And what can translators do about it?

The extent to which Yiddish has remolded the raw material it has taken over may be studied in proper names. *Shprintze* is an especially lovable girl's name in Yiddish. It has gaiety and goodness. One thinks of Shprintze as young and bright-eyed; one sees her running, basket on arm, to the village market, her shining, pointed nose innocent of powder, her lips parted in a happy smile. She is poor but jolly, betrothed, or recently married, to a sturdy workman, who is admittedly not much of a scholar, but respectful of learning, observant of the tradition, and prepared, of course, to give his children the finest education obtainable. That is Shprintze. The name is derived from the Spanish *Esperanza,* and was brought (it is surmised) by Spanish Jews at the time of the expulsion into the valley of the Rhine, where Yiddish was already in an advanced stage of crystallization.

Now, I do not know what suggestions the name Esperanza carries with it for most Spaniards. The word means "hope," but that may go for nothing. A girl called Hope in English unfortunately suggests one from whom there is little to be hoped, just as *Friedrich,* in German, suggests anything rather than its literal meaning, "rich in peace." For me (and since I do not know Spanish my feeling about the name has nothing to do with its Spanish overtones) Esperanza suggests alternately the cloister and the guitar; on the one hand a nun's name, but also, on the other, the name of the young woman whose eyes, "more darkly bright than love's own star," were hidden by the lattice from those of the serenader below. Well, whoever Esperanza was, she has become Shprintze, altogether unrecognizable; and never again will Shprintze be Esperanza.

In a like way the Yiddish girl's name *Yente*—it is really not a girl's name, somehow one thinks of it always as belonging to a grown woman—goes back to the Italian *Gentilia.* Yente has become for the Yiddish world synonymous with noisiness and vulgarity, with some implications of rough good-heartedness: it is the equivalent of "washer-woman." It would be absurd, in translating a Yiddish story into Italian, to make Yente Gentilia again; but neither does the Italian get a hint of the author's intention if the name is left as it is.

Possibly the extremest instance of such a transformation is found in the Yiddish name *Feivish*, which began as Phoebus Apollo. Now Feivish—especially when coupled with Yukel—is perhaps the most comical-trivial man's name in the Yiddish-speaking world. Zangwill found an equal for it in Soshe Shmendrik, which is, however, synthetic. Not only is Feivish utterly remote from any physical suggestion of Phoebus Apollo ("He was a man born with thy face and throat, lyric Apollo," sings Browning in "The Dead Grammarian"); no writer would dream of assigning to a Feivish the smallest task calling for dignity, common sense, learning, or even clear enunciation.

I have referred to the immense range of intonation that endows the word *staitch!* with countless variations of meaning. Spoken Yiddish differs, again, from spoken English, in relation to their written models, in a manner which I obviously cannot hope to convey here; but the spoken language has naturally reacted back on the written; and in Yiddish the context of a phrase or word carries a larger hint of intonation than in English.

All this is intended to illustrate that Yiddish has its separate genius, and more particularly to make clear that the etymological origins of Yiddish words are no longer a clue to their living identity. As a result it is just as hard to translate classical Yiddish into German as into English or French. I have always been skeptical of the language-scholars who try to clarify the meaning of living words by reference to their roots in a dead language: skeptical, that is, on this one point; their material has great value and interest in other regards. Actually it is harder to translate classical Yiddish into German than into French or English or Italian, precisely because of the physical affinity of German and Yiddish. There is an additional obstacle. When a ghetto Jew wanted to sound cultured in the modern sense, superior to his surroundings, and tony generally, he Germanified his Yiddish; that is, he tried to reassemble the omelet. Thus a serious translation of Yiddish into German savors of the outlandish and affected, at least to the Yiddish ear, so that the translator is thrown off balance. Besides which German, either in its involved and stately mood or in homely mood, is not so apt as Anglo-Saxon English to convey whatever can be conveyed of Yiddish to a non-Jew.

Of the languages I know, Yiddish is by far the best for reading aloud—as the reader must surmise from what I have already said about it. But the reading aloud of even a good English translation from the Yiddish is extremely dangerous. I once witnessed an English performance of Ansky's *Dybbuk;* the acting was good, and the translation—as I thought back on it—not at all bad. But the actors had an Oxford-cum-Harvard accent, and their cultured epiglottal voices, issuing from the bearded faces of gaberdined Hasidim, turned the tragedy into a grisly comedy.

Now, when Jews speak of the "impossibility" of translating Yiddish into English, they have in mind just those differences of spirit and idiom which are the ordinary barriers between all languages. They will ask, for instance: "How on earth can you say in English: *Heyr oyf tzu haken a tchainik?"* *Haken a tchainik* (literally, to chop or wallop a teakettle) is to talk nonsense long and earnestly on a given subject. *Heyr oyf* is "stop," or "give over." To make it harder they will cite: *"Er hot gehakt a tchainik oyf vos die velt shteyt"* (he walloped a teakettle on what the world stands on), meaning "incessantly," "interminably," or, in idiom, "to beat the band." But when such instances are given—and it should be noted that we have to do here with words of non-Hebrew origin—they are really beside the point as far as the particularity of Yiddish is concerned. *These* difficulties do not make of Yiddish a uniquely untranslatable language; they merely show that Yiddish is neither more nor less translatable than other languages and has nothing special to complain of. There is another level on which Yiddish is in fact unique.

I am willing to concede that perhaps Yiddish is in fact somewhat more difficult of translation than other languages even on the ordinary level. I have called Yiddish a "knowing language" because of the special intramural hints, allusions, and interjections in which it abounds; it is also that because of intonation and gesticulation. I have not yet come across a theory which explains why some languages—Chinese, for instance—give the same syllable-words entirely unrelated meanings on different pitches. I am tempted to suggest that the early crystallizers of Yiddish, speaking a dialect that was then much nearer to the originating language, and therefore intelligible to the hostile strangers around them, began to develop a technique of gesture and intonation which enabled them to converse on two levels simultaneously, one for themselves, one for the outsiders. There is a popular Yiddish story about a Jew who is being tried for the theft of a chicken: asked by the judge—via an interpreter—whether he pleads guilty or not guilty, he answers in quiet despair: *"I* stole the chicken!" The interpreter, obviously not a Jew, translates: "Guilty," whereas a Jew would have known from the intonation that *"I* stole the chicken," thus uttered, means the exact opposite, and in its extremest form.

Later, when Yiddish was spoken (in Poland, Russia, Rumania) among surrounding peoples that could not have understood it, the presence of a Gentile may have impelled the Jew to develop the gesture as an auxiliary of speech, and occasionally as a substitute for it. But gesticulation is common, though in varying degrees. The French gesticulate much more freely than the English, the Americans, or the Germans. But I do not find in French gesticulation the peculiar congruence with meaning which I find in Yiddish. The Frenchman seems to gesticulate because he is energetic, the Jew because he is subtle; the Frenchman emphasizes his meaning by a tone, the Jew changes it.

There are of course Yiddish phrases and idioms that are the crystallization of purely Jewish experience or social form. *Dem rebbens shnur* is what it is in Yiddish because of the accumulation of associations round a specifically Jewish institution. A phrase like *areinfallen vie a yoven in sukkah* (to blunder like an ignorant boor into a festival tabernacle) condenses a world of circumstance. The *sukkah* is the ritual tabernacle that Jews put up during the festival of Sukkoth. To adorn the *sukkah* beautifully, to take one's meals in it ceremoniously, to sit there whenever possible, is a commandment and a delight; there is about the *sukkah* a peculiarly intimate and tender complex of memories and emotions. The image of an insensitive stranger blundering into a *sukkah* as if it were an ordinary hut or lean-to is therefore vivid and painful. *Yoven,* a Greek (figuratively, any boorish fellow), may be an echo of Maccabean times. "Bull in a china shop" is the best I can do with the phrase in English.

There are phrases and turns of speech which are quite hopeless from the translator's point of view. A certain type of Jew is described as *a shadchan a badchan a ganev a lamdan a yid.* Literally, a *shadchan* is a marriage-broker, a *badchan* a wedding jester, a *ganev* a thief (but the word is used jestingly, too), a *lamdan* a scholar, a *yid* a Jew. But these professions or attributes are each embedded, for the Yiddish-speaking Jew, in entire subworlds of association, and a man who is all those things put together is a one-man civilization. The best I can produce here, for rhythmic effect and friendliness of tone, is: "a rascally son-of-a-gun of a scholarly matchmaking Jew." Not very helpful.

Sometimes there is an incredibly felicitous approximation. *Got di neshomeh shuldig* (literally, owing God his soul; i.e., blameless as a babe unborn) is hit off perfectly in English by "butter wouldn't melt in his mouth." The phrases cover each other perfectly, nothing missing, nothing left over. And it is amusing—as well as rather touching—to observe how two such disparate peoples as the Jews and the English, and two such disparate languages, have found the identical attitude of good-humored derision toward impudent rascality parading as injured innocence.

Alas for the good souls who dream of a universal literal language, Ito or Esperanto or Basic English, even as an auxiliary. Man is born to idiom as the sparks fly upward. The difference between literal language and idiom is the difference between barracks and a home. From the intimidating efficiency of the first we turn to the coziness and privacy—and dangers—of the second. And if we live in barracks for more than a week or two, we create little corners in it, corners for ourselves and our clique, to which outsiders are aliens: little intimacies, attachments, and idiosyncrasies spring up about the shape of the wall and the places of the cots. What a hullabaloo there will be in the Esperanto world when—as they must sooner or later —idioms spring up unbidden. Or have some appeared already? (I severed my connection with the language after a high-minded and barren affair with it many years ago.) No doubt more idioms will be needed in Esperanto to express the consternation of the Esperantists at the first deviations from literalness.

I come back to my Yiddish and its idioms, and repeat: in respect of the points I have discussed so far, Yiddish is a language like others, with certain inalienable values and an inalienable spirit; these are not my reason for stating that classic Yiddish cannot be translated. Extraordinary things have been done in the way of translation. The Bible in English at once springs to the mind, and after it Shakespeare in German. Almost as great as these, for ingenuity and insight, is Scott-Moncrieff's translation of Proust. And as an instance of what can be done by way of murdering someone in a foreign language, we have only to look at the English translations of *Faust.* There is a special delight in reading the Bible with the Hebrew and English side by side, or Shakespeare with the English and German: there are neatnesses and profundities of transmission which bring a sudden smile of joy to the lips. I say "joy"—for it is that kind of happiness which attends the breaking down of seemingly insuperable barriers between one people and another, one language and another. And yet: one becomes alive to the paradox that very often the better the translation, the more it wrongs the original. The less it reads like a translation (and is not that the conscientious translator's aim?), the more uneasy the original creator, wherever he may be, must be feeling at the transformation. "Very wonderful," he murmurs wryly, "but is that really me?"

From *Prince of the Ghetto* (1948)

Maurice Samuel was, in every sense of the term, a man of letters. There was hardly a literary form that he did not attempt. In addition to his polemical and expository writing, he was the author of five novels and a number of short stories. He was also a journalist, an essayist, a critic, and a writer of verse (his earliest publications consisted of poems he contributed to the British magazine *Voices,* where he appeared in the company of, among others, D.H. Lawrence). The following selections, taken from a variety of sources, represent this wide-ranging aspect of Maurice Samuel's work.

WRITER
AND READER

28 AL HAREI CATSKILL

My uncle (father's side), a remnant dealer,
Was wont to say: "Of all that deal in remnants
The God of Israel was the first, for He
(His name be blessed), looking on our despair
And knowing, too, the bitterness of exile
(Is it not written *Shechinta begalutha?*),
Found comfort for Himself and us in this:
'A remnant of My people shall return!' "

This was the proper style of the Creator
Since first He made a covenant with us:
He took a remnant and He made a people.
He took a remnant of the seed of Terach
And in the land of Goshen wrought a people.
He drew a remnant from Mizraim forth
And in Judea made Himself a people,
A Law, a Temple, and a Prophecy.
A handful left the plains of Babylon,
Its bursting fields, its markets, and its glory,
The envy of the nations and their prize:
A remnant turned again to make a people—
A land of armories and synagogues,
Of bearded warriors of intemperate will,
Of saints and sages gentler than the dove—
The Maccabean fury and the love
That wakened in the wise old eyes of Hillel,
Akiba's sweetness and Bar Kochba's rage.

My great-grandfather was a honey-gatherer,
And he had thirteen sons and all are dead.
His birthplace is unknown; his resting place,
A family legend tells, is Palestine.
His name, his occupation, and his grave
Is all that's left to rumor and record.
One son, my father's father, lived and died
In Glodorlui, which if ten living Jews
On this side the Atlantic know the name,
It's nine more than I'd dare to take an oath on.
My uncles, father's cousins, second cousins,
By pairs and handfuls cover the world.
Some peddle socks in the Nalewki; some
Sell diamonds on the *Faubourg Cracovie.*
The former sing their Yiddish with an *ly,*
The latter condescend to German only.
I've met a sprinkling of the stock in Paris
("Mon fils unique est mort pour la patrie"),
A minor tribe has England for its home
But mingles badly with the lost ten tribes;
Some live beside the Golden Gate, and some
Beside the *Brandenburger;* some, I hear,
Are Talmud students in the Gaon's city,
Vilna the old—and some are "Harvard men,"
While I, who live in Babylon the New,
Preach the Return to startled Jews, and spend
This summer in the Catskill Mountains here.

The honey-gatherer, who sent his seed
To inherit graves a thousand miles apart,
Had never heard of Catskill: for the rest,
Paris and London, Warsaw and New York,
Were one to him. His straight geography
Knew only of two worlds—Golus and Zion.
He did his duty to the former—thirteen sons
After some generations do their share
Toward filling earth; and with his duty done
He packed his portion in a bundle, took
The wanderer's staff (that's how I picture him)
And sought the latter out to die in peace.

My grandfather, his son (the one who lived
In Glodorlui, of old Wallachia)
Was likest to have followed in his steps.
He, while the fresh wind of a Western world
Troubled his brothers and inclined their steps
In quick succession toward the setting sun
(Some, disillusioned, sought the East again
And came by stolen frontiers into Poland)
Alone inherited the father's dream,
Which made of all his life a pilgrimage
Between his birthplace and his grave in Zion.
But something in his actions and his ways—
Perhaps the passion for antiquity,
Perhaps his oriental inclinations,
Perhaps his nose—displeased his peasant neighbors.
Moishe the Jew (I got my name from him—
'Twas given me in the hope that I would prove
A tzadik, or a martyr, for his sake)
Became impossible; and thus, one night,
A band of them, with murder in their hands,
Broke in on him while he, by candlelight,
Was deep in Babylonian mysteries.

Something, a *soupçon* of the Talmud chant
My sainted granddad loved, rings in my ears.
It comes from younger lips. Judea's daughters
(Modern edition, but as like as peas
To those intolerant Isaiah once
Cursed with such detail anatomical)
Accompanying the lilting phonograph:

> *O Katerina, O Katerina,*
> *Please—get leaner . . .*
> *Bettina, my Bettina,*
> *I can't eat my farina,*
> *Ta-ram-ta-ra-ra-ra-ra,*
> *Ta-ram-ta-ra-ra-ra-ra.*

The crowded porch is hidden from my view
While here I scribble in a nest of pines,
But I can see them: hips and shoulders jolly,

The body subtle-swaying, eyes half-closed,
And soft waves galloping from top to toe
Like waves of shadow through a field unshorn.
Is it romantic fancy that invests
Their twanging melodies with shadow tones
Strayed from the pages of my granddad's *Shas?*

My Paris uncle, mourning for his son
(*"Mon fils unique est mort pour la patrie"*)
Speaks of his fatherland with tears of pride.
"La France quand-même. Is there in all the world
The peer of her? Mother of liberty,
Gay with immortal youth! Alone she solves
The double mysteries of faith and joy.
She worships life with laughter. From of old
The nations laboring dourly at the task
Of merely living, turn to her for breath,
And catch from her a moment's merriment.
Yet she is strong. Behind her laughing eyes
Lurks steel—a rapier in a dazzling sheath.
Greatness and grace! Tradition in a jest
And wit the soul of wisdom! *C'est la France!"*
In faultless French delivered: but the flame
That flushed his temples had a somber hue,
A something deadly, something too intense.
My granddad's curse! If I had never known
The martyrdom of Glodorlui, or if
They had not told me why I bore my name
I would not look for the exotic East
In uncle's patriotic sentiments,
Or hear the echo of the arghool's drone
In voices chanting to the ukulele.
And yet—and yet—why do the heathen rage?

The singing on the porch dies quick. A stir,
A mighty shout goes up—I can't resist.
"I held four aces, with the joker out!
Four aces with the joker out and lost!"
"Suppose you held four aces? What of that?
Four of a kind was held before and lost."
"I held four aces with the joker out!

Four aces and no joker!" "Did you see?
A straight flush from the nine! He bought the Jack!
An inside straight!" "I held four iron aces!
I held four aces and the joker out!
Four aces!" *By the streams of Babylon.*

I turn back to my shelter, through a field
Of sunlit grass; with every onward step
A bursting cloud of grasshoppers goes up,
And patters down again. A squirrel sits
And flicks his armpit with a rapid leg.
He sees me, starts, outstares me for an instant,
And passes in a flash. I dream again.

My cousin by the *Brandenburger Tor*
Is scientific-international.
Last night an intellectual youth was here
Put me in mind of him. "I mix with Jews
By accident of contiguity.
That's all, my friend. Don't look for deeper cause,
Traditions, missions, and the rest of it.
This is an age of science. What's a Jew?
What cranial index has a Chosen People?
What's the description of a Race of Priests
That answers to laboratory tests?
The *Jew* is an illusion: Jewishness
A dying system of transmitted dreams.
That settles it."
That might have settled it,
But all unwary and unwitting he,
Enfranchised of transmitted dreams, broke forth
In unprovoked apocalyptic terms:
"Behold, the brotherhood of man draws nigh,
The night of error and delusion passes.
The light of reason dawns on all the earth,
And war shall die."
Isaiah, Chapter Two,
Has something to the same effect, I thought,
Though rather better phrased. But what's the sense
Of polemicizing with an obstinate Jew?
The way of faith is hard—and just as hard

The way of unfaith, both by checkered loops,
Twist within twist, each tinier than the last,
Lead back to wonderment and weariness.
"The Jew is an illusion!" Is not life,
All life, self-watching, an illusion too?
"There's no belief!" But thinking is believing,
And merely living is an act of faith.
Since living and believing are the same,
The Jew, believing most, the longest lives.
That's pretty! Let's see what the Jew believes.

My Paris uncle, he who lost his son,
Believes that France illumines all the world.
My cousin in Berlin, the Ph.D.,
Believes that science will redeem mankind.
My second cousin, in the *Vilner kleisel,*
Believes whatever's written in the *Shas.*
My Harvard relatives believe the Jew
Must suffer till he learns how to behave—
To wit: to talk discreetly, take to sport,
And temper his uncivilized *élan*
Either in argument or eating soup.
Another, by the Golden Gate, believes
We have a mission, which, in brief, is this:
To teach the world that God is only One,
That peace is good and war is bad: that men
Are all of them the children of One Father.
But all our teaching must be done politely,
Without insistence or obstreperousness—
So gently that the world will not perceive
That we are different from the rest of it.

And here in Catskill what do Jews believe?
In *kosher,* certainly; in *Shabbos,* less
(But somewhat, for they smoke in secret then),
In *Rosh Hashonoh* and in *Yom Kippur,*
In charity and in America.
But most of all in Pinochle and Poker,
In dancing and in jazz, in risqué stories,
And everything that's smart and up-to-date.

("Milton, thou shouldst be living at this hour,"
To hear the Catskills ringing with thy name.)

Is that what Jews believe? Give up the ghost then!
You've lived with shadows, not with living men.
If this were all, how simple were the story!
There's something else! "A remnant shall return . . ."
Define that something else! Pluck out the secret,
And lay it on the table for dissection.
Yes, if creation were a formula
And life a scientific incantation.
But here's a something that no man can read
Or ever will: the book before *Bereshith.*

Menorah Journal, December 1925

29 MY THREE MOTHER-TONGUES

I

How fortunate and fitting it is that I should have been born myself
and not somebody else, and therefore that I was born into the Jewish
people. How fortunate and how fitting, also, that I was born into the
English language and did not have to read Shakespeare and Gibbon
in a foreign language or, God forbid, in translation. I would have it
that English is peculiarly suited to me, it fits me so neatly and so
intimately, I could not, as I am a Jew, have done without it. ("Praise
God," said the monk, "for that he did cause rivers to flow through
great cities!")

Shakespeare and Gibbon have held before me the standards of
the English language as an art. Shakespeare is as precious to me as
a personal teacher, and I hold with Samuel Johnson that he is greater
in the comedies than in the tragedies. Greater is an odd word here,
but let it stand. Let me add that I have a special delight in the playful
(pagan?) aspect of Shakespeare and in the countless little jewels (I
cannot help citing a few instances) that sparkle out unexpectedly as
I fare through his pages. They always take me by surprise, though
I know that each in its place has been lying in wait for me. What is
more, I can see how they have been planted. When I think of the
adjacent text, I see how the supreme master, pursuing the theme in
hand, has thrown in uncalled for and superfluous little miracles, not
to advance the action, or fill in a scene, or even to enrich a character,
but just for the fun of it.

So old Montague, unburdening himself of his worry over his
distraught son, breaks unconsciously into lovely verse. He fears to
see in Romeo

> the bud bit by an envious worm
> Ere he can spread his sweet leaves to the air
> Or dedicate his beauty to the sun.

Who would have thought the old man had it in him? At this point he might suddenly feel somewhat confused: "Did I say that?" Or, in *As You Like It,* fuddy-duddy, kindly Monsieur le Beau, courtier and filler-in, when he addresses himself to Orlando:

> Sir, fare you well:
> Hereafter, in a better world than this,
> I shall desire more love and knowledge of you.

The heart stops for a moment to take in the charm of it. One wants to go back and protest; only kings would talk like that—if they could. There is the same experience with Charles, the wrestler, in the preceding scene. He is speaking of the banished Duke in the forest of Arden: "They say many young gentlemen flock to him every day, and fleet the time carelessly, as they did in the golden world." Should any mortal, let alone a vulgar and boastful wrestler, a prizefighter, you might say, be allowed to throw this singing line so off-handedly to the world?

Or, in *Twelfth Night,* it is just a little less impermissible for Viola, all teasing loveliness and grace, to declare of herself as her hypothetical sister,

> she never told her love,
> But let concealment, like a worm i' the bud
> Feed on her damask cheek.

She is entitled by virtue of her role to exercise the highest enchantment latent in language, but one feels she ought not to have carried it quite so far. The words leave behind them an ache of beauty; they cannot be spoken, they can only be thought.

II

Speaking of fun, there's much to be got out of comparing Shakespeare with Gibbon, *The Histories* with *The Decline and Fall,* the one taking in all of life for its own sake, the other, the doctrinaire, seeing in all of life a thesis: "I have described the triumph of barbarism and religion." Can't you just imagine the fat little man passing a church with averted gaze and muttering, like an old-time fanatical Jew,

"Shakets teshaktsenu vesa'av tesavenu—Let it be abominated and let it be desolated, for it is anathema," after which you turn in your thoughts to Shakespeare taking his ease between rehearsals at The Mermaid Tavern. I have had many a good inward laugh on the subject, and a rush of quotations, but I must hurry on, for an even more important subject has been waiting, suppressed, since the first paragraph of this essay.

III

Which speaks to me more intimately, the Bible in Hebrew, with which I am long familiar, or the English King James version? I read, *"Ubavel tsvi mamlakhot tiferet ge'on kazdim*—And Babylon, the glory of kingdoms, the beauty of the Chaldees' excellency, shall be as when God overthrew Sodom and Gomorrah. It shall never be inhabited, neither shall it be dwelt in from generation to generation: neither shall the Arabian pitch tent there; neither shall the shepherds make their fold there. But wild beasts of the desert shall lie there; and their houses shall be full of doleful creatures; and owls shall dwell there, and satyrs shall dance there. And the wild beasts of the islands shall cry in their desolate houses and dragons in their pleasant palaces: and her time is near to come, and her days shall not be prolonged." Then I read the English and the Hebrew alternately, as I have done countless times these many years, and I wonder, am I nearer to the prophets in the Hebrew or in the English? Does not the Hebrew—*ubavel tsvi mamlakhot*—ring for me with the grandeur of Elizabethan England and the religious passion of the Protestant England of that time? How can I fix the tonality of the original Hebrew as it was intended for or received by the ears of the first listeners? And when, where, for whom was it put into the present permanent form? If a super-committee of the foremost living scholars were to answer these questions in a chorus of unanimity, I still would not know.

The Jewish Publication Society translation of 1917 puts "pride" for "excellency," "cats" for "beasts," "ferrets" for "doleful creatures," "ostriches" for "owls," "jackals" for "wild beasts," and "wild dogs" for "dragons." There is no doubt that the scholars of the J.P.S. translation knew Hebrew better than King James's men, but King James's men (and the dead Tyndall they leaned on so heavily) knew English better, and I am certain that in religious earnestness they were not second to the scholars of the J.P.S. Some doctrinal changes in the text are absolutely necessary if we are not to be misled; and if we want to possess a sound biblical Hebrew we must be chary of the King James text at some points. But did "ferrets," "owls," "jackals" reproduce in the ears of the first listeners—not to speak of later audiences and listeners who knew Hebrew after the Babylonian exile and the Diaspora—the associative effects they have for us? Who can tell? Do we know whether Isaiah was thundering or scolding? Was he sublimely denunciatory or in a tearing rage? Proust says of Swann that "he suffered from the eczema of his race and the constipation of the prophets." As we say in Yiddish, that too is a point of view.

The learned Virginia Woolf has an essay "On Not Knowing Greek" (of which she had a sound knowledge), and the scholarly Henry Ryecroft, from whom I have taken a hint or two, writes: "Among the many reasons which make me glad to have been born in England, one of the first is that I read Shakespeare in my mother tongue. . . . I am wont to think that I can read Homer, and, assuredly, if any man enjoys him it is I, but can I for a moment dream that Homer yields me all his music, that his word is to me as to him who walked by the Hellenic shore when Hellas lived?"

What English Protestantism in its purest form got from the Hebrew Bible can also be seen in Hazlitt's description of his father, the old dissenting Unitarian minister, who thought of Jesus not as a god but as the greatest of mankind. In his penurious and high-principled life this friend of Coleridge might have been taken for a Jewish scholar because of his complete immersion in the Hebrew Bible. But he was innocent of the language and had to content himself with the King James translation. Content himself? The Old Testament gave him a steadfast happiness which he could not have purchased with the highest and most distinguished benefice at the bestowal of the Church of England. In an obscure English village, missing only "the converse that he loved," he passed his days in the study of the Bible "and the perusal of the commentators—huge folios, not easily got through, one of which would outlast a winter! . . . [T]o his lacklustre eyes there appeared within the pages of the ponderous, unwieldy, neglected tomes, the sacred name of JEHO-VAH in Hebrew capitals . . . there were glimpses, glimmering notions of the patriarchal wanderings, with palm trees hovering in the horizon, and processions of camels at the distance of three thousand years; there was Moses with the Burning Bush, the number of the Twelve Tribes, types, shadows, glosses on the law and the prophets; there were discussions (dull enough) on the age of Methuselah, a mighty speculation! there were outlines, rude guesses at the shape of

Noah's Ark and of the riches of Solomon's Temple; questions as to
the great lapses of time, the strange mutations of the globe were
unfolded with the voluminous leaf, as it turned over; and though
the soul might slumber with an hieroglyphic veil of inscrutable mysteries drawn over it, yet it was in a slumber ill-exchanged for all the
sharpened realities of sense, wit, fancy, or reason. My father's life
was comparatively a dream; but it was a dream of infinity and eternity, of death, the resurrection, and a judgment to come!"

The incomparable style of William Hazlitt the son ("We are
mighty fine fellows," said Robert Louis Stevenson, himself a stylist
of rare grace, "but we cannot write like William Hazlitt") must have
come to him at least in part through his father and his father's
ceaseless readings of the King James Bible.

Shakespeare was in his forty-seventh year when the King James
translation appeared in 1611, and he wrote only one play, *Henry the
Eighth,* after that. He must have read Tyndall's translation. We cannot
think of Shakespeare as either religious or irreligious, as an atheist
like Christopher Marlowe, that unsettling Dostoievskian spy apparition blazing fitfully through Elizabethan England, even less. Ridicul-
ing the Puritans, he was nevertheless Protestant English through and
through—and many more things besides. He is the classical world,
the Renaissance, the first awareness of America ("the vex't Ber-
mouthes"—Bermuda); he is the end of medieval man. James Joyce
calls him a genius and a time-server. Yes, he was Establishment and
toadied a little to the mighty, and he turned an honest penny, they
say, turning out *The Merry Wives of Windsor* for the Queen. But though
Renaissance, he was not amoral, and though he used Shylock for a
comedy (how odd that *The Merchant of Venice* should be, as Shakespeare intended it to be, among his comedies), he more than hinted
at the tragic element in the Jew. He was a kindly man. We see it at
once in the famous Macbeth puzzle. What is the meaning of that
third murderer who appears in the night, unannounced, unexplained,
uncontracted for, to help in the doing in of Banquo? Why, he is only
a needy actor to whom Shakespeare threw a bit part at the last
moment.

Subsuming it in a flash, I the English-born* American Jew, with
my heart equally in America and Israel, accept the Shakespeare-
English Bible-Hebrew Bible synthesis that is me gratefully and com-

*Technically Rumanian-born and brought to England at the age of five. Of
the Rumanian language the only traces in me are some words I picked up in the
Rumanian subsection of the Manchester ghetto. [M.S.]

pletely. If there are odd bits of me elsewhere, that is so much to the good. And if I seem to consider the Bible as nothing but literature, that is because to do more would take me out of my depth.

IV

If I may use an Irishism, the third element in the synthesis of me, Yiddish, is a thing apart. I grew up with it as a child, I grew away from it as a youngster and a young man—so much so that when I arrived in America at the age of nineteen I could speak only a babu Yiddish—and found it again on the East Side of New York. It was a strange encounter, at first apparently accidental, but when I got down to systematic study the language rose inside me to welcome the prompting from the outside. It has become almost as much myself as English, but less so than Hebrew. Lecturing on occasion in Yiddish, I have had to go begging for many words and locutions; in English everything comes flying toward me at the slightest inward nod. But then again I have not read Yiddish with anything like the fullness of English—though Lord knows how much of English literature is a blank to me.

What sets Yiddish apart for me is a sort of despair. It is so difficult to translate, and the difficulty receives circular reinforcement from the absence of a solid body of Yiddish literature translated into English—or for that matter, any other modern language. It is a self-perpetuating alienation from what we call "the great world." It gives me quite a turn, as we used to say in England, to think that the Yiddish poetry of Chaim Nachman Bialik (he was equally great in Hebrew and in Yiddish) and of Aaron Zeitlin and Jacob Glatstein and Chaim Grade will probably never be known beyond the faithful circle of Yiddish readers. Each of them has "struck one clear chord to reach the ears of God," but He has not seen fit to let its echo come to the ears of others than the faithful. The meager translations that exist, though sometimes better than passable, are an infinitesimal fragment of the whole corpus.

The same melancholy pervades me when I brood over the Yiddish prose writers. Sholom Aleichem is a resounding exception, and I am satisfied to be remembered as his herald in English. Two other Yiddish writers seem to have broken the spell—Sholem Asch and Isaac Bashevis Singer; on examination it will be revealed that they are not Yiddish writers—that is, insofar as they have found a large English audience—but writers in Yiddish. Though they treat of Jewish subjects there is no Yiddishness in them. This is especially true of Sholem Asch. In his successful books he kept an eye on the outside world and translatability—which is why I found him so easy to translate. I never "translated" Sholom Aleichem; I wrote round him. I did the same with Y. L. Peretz, who is almost Sholom Aleichem's equal, but he never caught on. One man haunts me with special insistence as an inheritor of unfulfilled renown: Zalman Shneour, who, like Bialik, wrote with equal freedom and grace in Hebrew and in Yiddish. I should have done with Shneour's *Shklover Yidn* ("The Jews of Shklov") what I did with *The World of Sholom Aleichem.* Now it is too late, unless a younger generation of translators is prepared to take the gamble.

The faithful will be around for quite a time; their numbers may even increase. By "the faithful" I mean those readers and speakers of Yiddish who have fastened to the language as I did, not the happy-go-lucky pickers-up of phrases here and there, or those who remember only what they overheard from parents and grandparents and remember that little badly. How did the scores or hundreds of Yiddish words and phrases—often distorted and debased or given new shadings—find their way into American English? I believe vaudeville in the big cities, with their high proportion of Jewish spectators, explains much of it. These last were always good for a laugh when a familiar Yiddish word was thrown in: the sudden, scattered laughter was infectious ("What did he say?"), an explanation from the performer usually followed, and the fashion spread. In the borsht circuit, where nearly the entire audience nurtures a vestigial Yiddish, the appeal to gregariousness, security, separateness, insideness, being in the know is irresistible. Between them, the two overlapping types of audience launched the words on a public always susceptible to novelty, the latest thing, and the exotic. What happened to Yiddish in the sequel is beyond the Divine compassion.

The horror of it may be mitigated by an awareness that this gallimaufry of *disjecta membra* of the Yiddish language is not the Yiddish language, as most Jews with a smidgin of Yiddish believe. Their belief has a touching quality of obstinacy and pride—"Sure I know Yiddish: *chutzpah, beigel, gefilte fish, boychik, nudnik, mazel tov, kosher, feh, shtik, shema yisroel!"*—reflecting a newfound affection. Some of the words have permanent value, and will rise out of the vulgar and vernacular into general acceptance; others will sink into outmoded slang and disappear. It is an interesting collection but a thing of anguish to the faithful.

V

Like the Bible, the Yiddish language loses its meaning if not seen under its meta-literary aspect. Both were the product not of art for art's sake but of art for God's sake. Yes, Yiddish too. You cannot read Yiddish intelligently as a whole without feeling God, the Sabbath, the High Holidays, the Exile, the Return at the center, all created by the Bible. If you are a *veltlecher*—a secularist, an unbeliever—you get at least an echo of them.

It is the Exile, or Diaspora, so vividly evoked on the Mountain of Curses, that predominates in Yiddish life and literature, even when, perhaps particularly when, over against it there rises the gaiety and playfulness of Yiddish life. The seal of a horror which the Mountain of Curses could not overtop has been set upon Yiddish. We shall find ease and welcome in America, and we shall answer with love; but freedom, even in Israel, cannot, should not erase the memory of the Holocaust. Jeremiah lamenting, "Behold, and see if there be any sorrow like unto my sorrow" may be accused of arrogance, for there had and *have* been exiles, exiles unnumbered, though no such repetition of exiles as Jewish Diaspora history. But beyond description and understanding is the Holocaust, for none but we can grasp the conception of it: *that the Jewish people wherever it can be found all over the world shall be sought out and exterminated.* This is not merely Hitler's Nazism. In 1901 Eugen Dühring, a German philosopher of high standing, wrote, "On the threshold of the new century it is no longer relevant to speak of the usual half-methods or merely palliative means to be used against the Hebrew evil *among the peoples.* As far as I am concerned the only adequate answer to the Jewish question lies in the wiping out of the *whole questionable species.* "

Even thus we must not fall into an arrogance of sorrow. Since no one will *want* to understand, we must carry this memory with us unspoken, only hinted at. We must also remember that Yiddish is a mirror of the Diaspora in its totality, with *all* its possibilities. Thus it must be remembered in Israel too. There and in the Diaspora a cultivated—I will not even say scholarly—Jew cannot do without at least a fair grounding in Yiddish, just as the pious Talmud Jew took and takes it for granted that he should be able to read and understand the Aramaic of the Zohar, the *Kaddish,* the *Kol Nidre,* the *Ho Lachmo Anyo* of the Passover Haggadah, and a *ketubah* (wedding contract). Thus, to sum it up, the educated American Jewish Jew must be grounded in the English of Shakespeare and the King James Version, the Hebrew Bible, and Yiddish. At a pinch he can substitute for Shakespeare quite a number of geniuses all the way from Chaucer to W.H. Auden, but the King James translation and the Hebrew Bible (and yes, the *siddur*) are indispensable.

Midstream, March 1972

30 THE CONCEALMENTS OF MARCEL: PROUST'S JEWISHNESS

Among modern literary creations there are on my list three which I believe cannot impart anything approaching their full values without long and sustained intimacy. They are James Joyce's *Ulysses,* Thomas Mann's *Joseph and His Brothers,* and Marcel Proust's *Remembrance of Things Past.* In each case, one may in a single reading experience the kind of joy and wonder which once every few years are awakened in us by a new book; but if we let it go at that we have merely circumnavigated an island continent whose interior would repay years of exploration. Of the three works mentioned, *Remembrance* (for short) is the most rewarding. Gide, on reading part of it, exclaimed: "Dazzled!" So one is. A second, a third, a fiftieth reading, ten and twenty and thirty years of browsing in it gradually overlay the feeling of astonishment with one of mingled awe and gratitude.

Fellow Proustians will of course endorse this panegyric; but when I add that the great work is full of contradictions, confusions, and impossibilities they will undoubtedly raise their eyebrows as if to say: "And isn't Shakespeare, too?" I go on, however, and remark, perhaps to their surprise, that quite otherwise than in Shakespeare the contradictions, confusions, and impossibilities in *Remembrance* are necessary qualities of its greatness. The structure and purpose demand them, the exacting and labyrinthine style fits them. This is not because we are in a half-hallucinatory world like Kafka's; we are among real, very real people, incidents, and circumstances; we are in the historical Paris, France, and the world of about 1879 to 1922. What we are confronted with, however, is a unique concept of the novelist's mission.

II

The most immediate area of confusion and inner contradiction, lead-ing into the others, is that of the book's purported authorship and personal base. *Remembrance* is presented as a fictional autobiography —fictional in a double sense or in the second degree. The inside author calls himself Marcel—and he is not Proust. At that, whoever he is, he is using his own name to designate an imaginary person, which he, the fictional Marcel, has himself thought up.*

Very well; we accept the device as soon as we perceive it and proceed contentedly till we are pulled up by certain passages which make us blink and ask: "For heaven's sake, where are we supposed to be? Is it in the real world, is it in Marcel's world, or is it in that of his hero?" Thus, we read about a certain rich, retired café owner and his wife who come to the rescue of a widowed niece-in-law and work for her without pay to replace the husband who has fallen in the war. Marcel, in a transport of admiration, exclaims:

In this book of mine, in which there is not one fact which is not imaginary, nor any real person concealed under a false name, where everything has been invented to meet the needs of the story, I ought to say that these millionaire relatives of Francoise . . . are people who are really alive . . . and it gives me a childlike pleasure and deep emotion to record here their real name, Lariv-ière. . . . [II, 276]†

The first effect is as though the principal actor in a play within a play were to step out from the interior play and address the stage audience of fellow actors: "Ladies and gentlemen, I beg your permis-sion to stop this performance while I tell you about certain wonderful real-life people, the Larivières, to the following effect. . . . I thank you. The performance will now be resumed." Whatever this may be supposed to mean to the play-acting audience, the announcement is, at first, still part of the play to the real-life audience; that is, to the readers of Proust. On quick second thought, however, it becomes clear that Marcel is speaking as Proust. The Larivières *are* real people; whether or not they have been found and identified by Proustian researchers is immaterial. But Marcel cannot be Proust at some points and an unidentified Marcel elsewhere. Within the body of *Remem-*

*I shall speak of Proust when I mean the known author, and of Marcel when I mean—sometimes interchangeably—the fictional author and the nonexisting man he is writing about. [M.S.]

†All references are to the Random House edition of *Remembrance of Things Past,* translated by Scott-Montcrieff, in two volumes. [M.S.]

brance the sudden exteriorization dislocates the entire structure. The elaborate pretense of a fictional "I," Marcel, telling someone else's story, collapses. Once Marcel is Proust he is Proust for good.

There are other instances of this involuted self-contradiction. Marcel is an old man when he begins to write seriously, more exactly, when he contemplates the decision to do so. In the marvelous *envoi* —one hundred and thirty large, closely printed pages—he deals with his return from a sanatarium to attend a high society reception, where he realizes what time has done to him and his contemporaries.

I was discovering this destructive action of Time at the very moment when I was about to make clear and to intellectualize in a literary work some realities that had no relation whatever to Time. [II, 1038]

Instead of writing, I had lived in idleness, in the dissipation of a life of pleasure, amid sickness, care of my health, and strange humors, and I was taking up my work on the eve of my death, with no knowledge of my craft. [II, 1118–1119]

This is a throwback; the enterprise is completed; it lies before us. Marcel is referring to the time when he thought himself ready for death and doubted that he would live long enough to complete his immense design. We have to assume that *Remembrance* was produced after the belated decision and in an eremitic isolation (as in fact it was). Marcel has nothing to tell us about the actual production. The years of self-immurement and labor are a blank. All he permits himself about them is a few lines immediately preceding those last quoted above:

I had decided to devote to it [the work] all my strength, which was leaving me slowly. . . . Soon I was able to show a few sketches. No one understood a word. Even those who were favorable to my conception of the truths which I intended to carve later in the temple congratulated me on having done them with a microscope, whereas I had, on the contrary, used a telescope. . . . They called me one who grubs for petty details. Moreover, what was the use of undertaking it? I had had a certain facility as a young man. Bergotte* had declared my schoolboy writings "perfect."

Nevertheless, six hundred pages earlier we find this:

And yet, my dear Charles—whom I used to know when I was still so young and you were nearing your grave, it is because he whom you must have regarded as a little fool has made you the hero of one of his volumes that

*When the chips are down, Bergotte is Anatole France, and Proust is referring to his first published book, *Les Plaisirs et les Jours*. [M.S.]

people are beginning to speak of you again and that your name will perhaps live. If in Tissot's picture representing the balcony of the Rue Royale Club . . . people are always drawing attention to yourself, it is because they know that there are traces in you of the character of Swann. [II, 519]

What do we have here? First, once more a specific denial on Marcel's part that he has invented *his* Marcel; second, the information that at the close he already knew himself to be famous and was even entertaining hopes of immortality for his work.

But in the enormous throwback postscript, filled with retrospection, self-analysis, and analysis of his destiny as a writer, Marcel ignores the crucial admission of his "reality" within the novel, and the equally crucial fact, so bound up with his development as a writer, of his success. He has come back to the impossible stance: "I'm using my name, which doesn't represent a living personality, to cover a person of my invention, an aspiring writer whom I portray as vanishing from the world unfulfilled." The reader cannot disentangle the skein; he is not supposed to try; he must remain, for Marcel's (and, we shall see, for Proust's) purpose, in a state of receptive bafflement.

III

Related to the necessary confusion of identities and truth-fiction is the equally necessary confusion of Time (and of time).

Time (with a capital) is one of the principal characters in *Remembrance,* or one of its dimensions, fused with the other three in an Einsteinian continuum. The French title *A la recherche du temps perdu* means literally "In Search of [the] Lost Time"; more accurate titles would have been *The Overcoming of Time,* or *The Liberation from Time.* In the famous passage on the piece of cake dipped in tea, Marcel relates an experience which recurs toward the end of the book in connection with the tinkling of a spoon and the feel of a sunken flagstone under his foot. It is a crucial key experience. Unplanned, unpredictable in its effects, the tasting of the piece of tea-soaked cake sends a shudder through his body.

An exquisite pleasure had invaded my senses, but individual, detached, with no suggestion of its origin. And at once the vicissitudes of life had become indifferent to me, its disasters innocuous, its brevity illusory—this new sensation having had on me the effect which love has of filling me with a precious essence. . . . I had ceased now to feel mediocre, accidental, mortal. Whence could it have come to me, this all-powerful joy? [I, 34]

By a tremendous effort he calls up the connection out of the depths of his memory. It was "the taste of the little crumb of madeleine which on Sunday mornings at Combray . . . when I used to say goodbye to her in her bedroom, my aunt Léonie used to give me dipping it first in her own cup of real or of lime-flower tea."

Then follows the loving evocation of all the far-off world of his childhood. But the bliss, the precious essence, which flowed at first from the actual tasting is absent from the effort to establish the connection and also from the resurrected picture. *That* sensation had come, unbidden, unamenable to recall, from the fleeting transcendence of Time, brought about by a seeming triviality; and the transcendence of Time is the transcendence of the mediocre, the accidental, and the mortal in man.

What is portrayed here as the highest form of human self-realization parallels closely Schopenhauer's description of the happiness which follows the transcendence of the will. One need only substitute "time" for "will" almost everywhere in the following:

When some external cause or inward disposition lifts us suddenly out of the stream of willing, delivers knowledge from the slavery of the will, the attention is no longer directed to the motives of willing, but comprehends things free from their relation to the will, and thus observes them without personal interest, without subjectivity, purely objectively. . . . Then all at once the peace which we were always seeking, but which always fled from us . . . comes to us of its own accord, and it is well with us. It is the painless state which Epicurus prized as the highest good and as the state of the gods . . . we keep the Sabbath of the penal servitude of willing; the wheel of Ixion stands still.

It is this blessedness of will-less perception which casts an enchanting glamour over the past and distant. . . . We can deliver ourselves from all suffering just as well through present objects as through distant ones whenever we raise ourselves to a purely objective contemplation of them, and so we are able to bring about the illusion that only the objects are present and not we ourselves. [*The World as Idea,* Bk. III]

The function of art, the mission of the artist-novelist, as seen in *Remembrance,* is to conquer or overcome time, not in the obvious sense of creating an immortal work, but in the personal experiencing and imparting of mastery over time, the elimination of our wretched awareness of subjection to time.

Liberation from time plays hob with "time" in the story. As we have seen, Marcel complains (as Proust did, openly) that his friendly critics congratulated him on having used the microscope, whereas he had used the telescope. He uses both—simultaneously. The result is aesthetically thrilling, editorially impossible.

Thus we learn that Marcel and his first love, Gilberte, the daughter of Charles Swann and the former Odette de Crécy, are of about the same age, and that Gilberte was about fourteen or fifteen when Marcel used to play with her on the Champs Elysées (I, 365). We also learn that Swann and Odette met at about the time of the Murcia floods (I, 173), which took place in 1879. A long and for Swann unhappy love relationship existed between him and Odette before they married. Swann had ceased to love her. He cries out at one point: "To think I have wasted years of my life, that I have longed for death, that the greatest love I have ever known has been for a woman who did not please me, who was not in my style" (I, 292).

And then Swann and Odette disappear from the story to reappear later as a married couple (though frequent mention of Swann and his "unfortunate marriage" occurs much earlier, before the Swann story is broached). Swann and Odette cannot have married before 1884. Therefore 1885 is approximately the date of Marcel's birth. Nevertheless he represents himself as a young man about town when the Dreyfus affair, which has a prominent place in the story, broke upon France. That happened in 1894 when Marcel, according to "chronology," cannot yet have been ten years old.

He represents himself as a doddering, elderly man soon after the close of World War I. At the high society reception mentioned (1919? 1920?) he overhears himself referred to as "Papa"—and since he is not married, a moderately advanced age, at the least, is indicated. But he was, again by the "factual" record of the story, just past his middle thirties, if that. The grotesque havoc which the years have wrought on him and on some of his contemporaries is inexplicable, but necessary. He needed a long contemporaneous perspective, that of a sexagenarian, at least; and so he juggles with time, he telescopes it, and he also brings the material close for microscopic examination. This wonderful performance enables the reader, while noting the unacceptability of the account in a corner of his consciousness, to participate in the overwhelming reality of Marcel's conquest of Time.

IV

We have here and there, especially toward the end, inconsistencies of the ordinary kind, as if the author's memory were failing him. These are of no significance. Significant and remarkable is the purposeful system of inconsistencies and contradictions into which are built the (here related) subjects of homosexuality and Jewish identity.

Both occupy dominant places from beginning to end, and they are often intermingled in a curious, one might say a dizzying, fashion. By his own account, meaning only by his own flat statement, Marcel is neither a homosexual nor of Jewish descent. His love affairs are exclusively with women; and if he himself is not a believing Christian, he has grown up in an irreproachably French, impeccably Catholic home, and retains a sentimental affection for its religious observances. However, his obsessive preoccupation with homosexuals and Jews, with homosexuality and Judaism, and, still more, his frequent linking of the two, coming on top of his special evasiveness, as set forth below, drive us to certain strange conclusions.

To begin with the homosexuality. Apart from his absorption in the subject, Marcel exhibits a knowledge of its obscurest symptoms and effects which, we imagine, can be found in a heterosexual only if he is a psychiatrist specializing in this field. The heterosexual layman must assume that the knowledge is real, but in any case the manner in which Marcel acquires it soon awakens the suspicion, then crystallizes the certainty, that he is "hiding" from us something that he is disclosing without a formal confession. This too is a not uncommon device in the novel, but here the implications carry us beyond the fictional.

Marcel has his first glimpse of homosexual relations when he is a youngster. By accident he sees and hears Mlle. Vinteuil and her girlfriend making love in the former's house at Montjouvain (I, 122 ff.). As a youth, and again by accident, he sees the Baron de Charlus wooing the ex-tailor Jupien in the courtyard of the Guermantes mansion, part of which has been rented to Marcel's family; and on this occasion Marcel manages by an intricate maneuver, itself full of the accidental, to get next to the room which the men are using, and to overhear them through the transom (II, 1 ff.). It is quite by accident —I am omitting a number of other instances—that toward the end of the book, walking through the darkened streets of wartime Paris, Marcel stumbles into a little hotel in which, again by an intricate maneuver, he is able, this time, to watch Charlus, now a convulsive masochist as well as a homosexual, being ministered to by young men hired for the purpose by Jupien.

One has to think of Marcel as a voyeur with a special bent and unbelievable good luck. Winking at the reader's suspicions, he writes mockingly: "The affairs of this sort of which I have been a spectator have always been presented in a setting of the most imprudent and improbable character, as if such revelations were to be the reward of an action full of risk, though in part clandestine" (II, 8).

Besides being reduced to these impossible shifts to account for his expertise, which anyhow declares his sexual proclivities (and outside this framework, those of Proust), Marcel, going helplessly, necessarily, and by the law of artistic truth a step further, complicates (and by the same token clarifies) the situation by dwelling endlessly on the compulsion of every homosexual to dwell endlessly on himself and his peculiarity. In short, Marcel positively insists on revealing his invert fixation by means of serio-comic inadvertencies to which you could not hold him in a court of law; and when he reproduces the interminable chatter of Charlus, the homosexual *par excellence*, he is deliberately drawing attention to himself and his own compulsion to talk.

Thus Charlus is asked whether a certain person is a homosexual, and we read:

Charlus drew himself up with a forbidding air. "Ah, my dear Sir, I, as you know, live in a world of abstraction, all that sort of thing interests me only from a transcendental point of view," he replied, with the touchy suscepti-bility peculiar to men of his kind, and the affection of grandiloquence that characterized his conversation. "To me, you understand, it is only general principles that are of interest, I speak to you of this as I might of the law of gravitation." But these moments of irritable reaction in which the Baron sought to conceal his true life lasted but a short time compared with the hours of continual progression in which he allowed it to be guessed, dis-played it with an irritating complacency, the need to confide being stronger in him than the fear of divulging his secret. [II, 590]

V

The two features in Marcel's treatment of Jews and Jewishness which point to his burden of Jewish identity are: first, his close interweaving of homosexuality—once it is clear that he is a homosexual—and Jewishness (the word "Jewishness" has no cultural-religious conno-tation here, it indicates only awareness of Jewish descent, partial or entire); second, his strikingly ambivalent attitude on Jewishness— respect and contempt, attraction and loathing, each expressed in such extreme emotional terms that it is impossible to see him as anything but a Jew. With the first of these features I deal immediately; the second (which already appears as a motif in the first) I leave to the confrontation with Proust as the author of *Remembrance.*

It is once more the figure of Charlus that moves Marcel to his self-revealing utterances. Charlus, the French *grand seigneur,* is most decidedly not Jewish, and Marcel's interweaving of homosexuality and Judaism does not imply that he believes homosexuality to be especially prevalent among Jews. What one suspects is that only a Jewish homosexual with a deep, hidden malaise about his Jewishness and his homosexuality (and perhaps not so hidden, for we have heard him refer to his own "strange humors") could have turned out the following passages, in which homosexuality and Jewishness are seen as parallel and equivalent destinies:

He [Charlus] belonged to that race of beings, less paradoxical than they appear, whose ideal is manly simply because their temperament is feminine and who in their life resemble only in appearance the rest of mankind. . . . Race upon which a curse weighs and which must live amid falsehood and perjury, because it knows the world to regard as punishable and scandalous, as an inadmissible thing, that which constitutes for every human creature the greatest happiness in life . . . friends without friendships, despite all those which their charm, frequently recognized, inspires and their hearts, often generous, would gladly feel; but can we describe as friendship those relations which flourish only by virtue of a lie and from which the first outburst of sincerity . . . would make them to be expelled with disgust, unless they are dealing with an impartial, that is to say a sympathetic mind . . . just as certain judges assume and are more inclined to pardon murder in inverts and treason in Jews for reasons derived from original sin and racial predestination. [II, 13]

Their honor precarious, their liberty provisional, lasting only until the discovery of their crime . . . excluded even, save on the days of general disaster when the majority rally round the victim as the Jews rallied round Dreyfus, from the sympathy, at times the society of their fellows, in whom they inspire only disgust at seeing themselves as they are . . . like the Jews, again (save some who will associate only with others of their race and have always on their lips ritual words and consecrated pleasantries), shunning one another, seeking out those who are most directly their opposite, who do not desire their company, pardoning their rebuffs, moved to ecstasy by their condescension; but also brought into the company of their own kind by the ostracism that strikes them, the opprobrium under which they have fallen, having finally been invested, by a persecution similar to that of Israel, with the physical and moral characteristics of a race, sometimes beautiful, often hideous . . . and, going in search . . . of cases of inversion in history, taking pleasure in recalling that Socrates was one of themselves, as the Israelites claim that Jesus was one of them. . . . [II, 13–14]

In this last quotation Marcel is speaking mostly about the assimilating Jew. Elsewhere he extends the view to the Jewish people as a whole, or to one or another of its nonassimilating elements:

. . . when they [certain homosexual types] seek to communicate their taste to others, they approach not so much those who seem to them to be predisposed towards it . . . as those who seem to them to be worthy of it, just as others preach Zionism, conscientious objection to military service, Saint-Simonism, vegetarianism, or anarchy. [II, 17]

I do not know of a more moving lament over the historic condition of the Jewish people than the sentences which begin with "Race upon which a curse weighs" and "Their honor precarious, their liberty provisional"; or anything as grotesquely comical, intentionally or not, in the very midst of deep pathos, as the last words of the section entitled *Cities of the Plain* (in the French *Sodome et Gomorrhe*):

These descendants of the Sodomites, so numerous that we may apply to them that other verse of Genesis: "If a man can number the dust of the earth, then shall thy seed also be numbered," have established themselves throughout the entire world; they have had access to every profession and pass so easily into the most exclusive clubs that, whenever a Sodomite fails to secure election, the blackballs are, for the most part, cast by other Sodomites, who are anxious to penalize sodomy, having inherited the falsehood that enabled their ancestors to escape from the accursed city. It is possible that they may return there one day. Certainly they form in every land an oriental colony, cultured, musical, malicious, which has certain charming qualities and intolerable defects. . . . I have thought it well to utter here a provisional warning against the lamentable error of proposing (just as people have encouraged a Zionist movement) to create a Sodomist movement and rebuild Sodom. For, no sooner had they arrived there than the Sodomites would leave the town so as not to have the appearance of belonging to it. . . . They would repair to Sodom only on days of supreme necessity, when their own town was empty, at those seasons when hunger drives the wolf from the woods; in other words, everything would go on very much as it does today in London, Berlin, Rome, Petrograd,* or Paris. [II, 25–26]

These are Marcel's considered judgments. Brief pronouncements in the same sense occur elsewhere as *obiter dicta.* A summing up leaves us uncertain whether he looked on homosexuality as, on the whole, a privilege or an affliction. He plays with this question as he has Charlus (and himself) play with the question of his sexual fixation:

He [Charlus] refused to see that for the last nineteen hundred years all conventional homosexuality—that of Plato's young friends as well as that of Virgil's shepherds—had disappeared, that what survives and increases is only the involuntary, the neurotic kind, which we conceal from other people and disguise to ourselves. And M. de Charlus would have been wrong in not denying frankly the pagan genealogy. *In exchange for a little plastic beauty* [my italics, M.S.] how vast the moral superiority. . . . It is the homosexuality that survives in spite of obstacles, the thing of scorn and loathing, that is the only

*"Petrograd" tells us that Marcel could not have written this before 1914 or after 1924 (but Proust died in 1922); he therefore wrote it between the ages of twenty-nine and thirty-seven, a wild anachronism if he began the novel as an aging man. [M.S.]

true form, the only form that can be found conjoined in a person with an enhancement of his moral qualities. [II, 524]

"Involuntary . . . neurotic . . . disguise to ourselves . . . enhancement of his moral qualities. . . ." The statement flies apart under our gaze. How can the enhancement of moral qualities, springing from a compulsion neurosis, go hand in hand with a reluctance to acknowledge the beneficent source of the improvement? If a man knows himself to be more moral because of a certain psychic disturbance he may hide the source of his merits from the persecution of the world; but he will not be ashamed of it within himself.

Yet the concealment from others and from himself is only intermittent. The teasing of his listeners by Charlus (and of his readers by Marcel) does not let up. Thus, concerning the affair between Charlus and the violinist Morel:

. . . speaking generally, let us say that M. de Charlus, notwithstanding the aggravation of his *malady* [my italics, M. S.] which perpetually urged him to reveal, to insinuate, sometimes boldly to invent compromising details, and did intend, during this period in his life, to make it known that Morel was not a man of the same sort as himself and that they were friends and nothing more. This did not prevent him . . . from contradicting himself at times . . . whether he forgot himself at such moments and told the truth, or invented a lie, boastingly, or from a sentimental affectation, or because he thought it amusing to baffle his questioner. [II, 528]

The equivalence of homosexuality and Jewishness is in some passages mingled with the analysis of the homosexual's alternations between reticence and exhibitionism:

. . . a vice (so M. de Charlus used at one time to style it) to which he gave now the genial aspect of a mere failing, extremely common, attractive on the whole and almost amusing, like laziness, absentmindedness or greed. Conscious of the curiosity which his own striking personality aroused, M. de Charlus derived a certain pleasure from satisfying, whetting, sustaining it. Just as a Jewish journalist will come forward day after day as the champion of Catholicism, not, probably, with any hope of being taken seriously, but simply in order not to disappoint the good-natured amusement of his readers. . . . [II, 527]

VI

Perhaps it will be suggested that Marcel was no more a homosexual, with all his absorption in the subject, than he was a snob, with all his absorption (in both senses) in high society. We shall be reminded

394 THE WORLDS OF MAURICE SAMUEL

that he often decries and lampoons snobbery; so he does, as the
self-made millionaire often philosophizes on the vanity of riches and
goes on accumulating them, and a king on the happier lot of the
plowboy without having the slightest desire to change places with
him. We are begging the question; the fact remains that Marcel is and
wants us to know that he is a homosexual. He is, and apparently does
not want us to know that he is, Jewish.

"Apparently," but not in the ordinary sense; it is more like: "I
can't help revealing that I'm a homosexual and a Jew, but I disclose
the first playfully; the second reluctantly, *à contrecoeur.*" Why the
distinction, the difference in method? Perhaps it is that Marcel, despite Swann's brilliant social success, looks on homosexuality as less
of a bar than Jewishness in the fahionable world which he must enter
and describe, so that the technical admission would complicate his
task; perhaps he (thence Proust) thinks himself the kind of Jew
whose Jewishness has been forgotten, is never commented on,
though he himself must advert to it. He is nevertheless well aware
of society's long memory. A Mme. Gallardon says of Swann: "I know
he's a converted Jew, and all that, and his parents and grandparents
before him. But they do say that the converted ones are worse about
their religion than the practicing ones, and that it's all a pretense"
(I, 257).

There is more to be said for the idea that at times Marcel lost
track of his identity. The "Overture" to *Remembrance* opens with Marcel, an aging man, trying to fall asleep. In the various stages between
waking and sleeping he imagines himself now a child in his old
bedroom, long ago demolished, now in the house where he actually
is, now in other places where he once lived, and, reconstructing his
surroundings according to the relevant illusion, he sets them whirling
in the darkness. Walls, furniture, windows slide about him as he
passes from scene to scene. As for himself: "When I awoke at midnight, not knowing where I was, I could not be sure at first who I
was" (I, 5). Something like this has happened to all of us; that Marcel
chose the experience for the opening to the "Overture" is certainly
not accidental.

VII

The question whether study of an author's life enables us to see
deeper into his novel or play, and get more out of it, has recently been
revived in connection with Proust's work. For myself, I cannot re-

member having been helped in this way with Proust or anyone else. It is always possible to say, of course, that the help is indirect and works through a heightening of interest, but this is not what is meant; or that the help is contained in subliminal suggestions, and if this is what is meant it does not make for intelligible discussion. On the other hand I owe much to studies which treat an author's work wholly or chiefly as a self-contained world. Milton Hindus's *The Proustian Vision,* though not the only study of its kind to raise the subject, sent me to a rereading of Schopenhauer. My conclusions are not quite the same as Mr. Hindus's, and the passages I quote support a different point of view. Nevertheless, Schopenhauer, too, has added to my appreciation of Proust. Thus it may be argued that a biography which tells us that Proust was deeply influenced by Schopenhauer would be useful. But that is already "interior" information. Also, the affinity with Schopenhauer may be a coincidence, would have existed if Proust had never looked into Schopenhauer. Moreover, familiarity with an author's life may warp our judgment. Knowing what I do about George Gissing, I invest *The Private Papers of Henry Ryecroft* with a degree of poignancy which the text probably does not justify.

I am wholly in agreement with Mr. Hindus when he says: "It seems best not to fall into the genetic fallacy, and to treat Proust's ideas in themselves. We ought not to assume too easily that we know their source or that we may dismiss them because of their origin."

Against Mr. Hindus appears George D. Painter in his scholarly *Proust, the Early Years.* Mr. Painter is emphatic to the point of "pleasant truculence" (as Angus Wilson says) in his espousal of the contrary view:

It has become one of the dogmas of Proustian criticism that his novel can and must be treated as a closed system. . . . Monsieur X. is praised for having "emptied his mind"—did he have to empty it of so very much?—"of all Proustian matter extraneous to the novel. . . ." "I do not propose," says Professor Y., "in this study, which is an attempt to interpret Proust's great novel, to discuss the external facts of his life. . . ." But they like to have it both ways. . . . I have not tried to deny Proust's homosexuality—on the contrary, I have given the first full account of it based on evidence. . . . It is surely relevant to know of Proust's novel what the novel meant to the author. . . . What do they know of *A la recherche* who only *A la recherche* know?

In the first part of this essay I have tried to prove that an attentive and uninhibited reader of *Remembrance* must conclude that Marcel, and therefore Proust, was a homosexual and a Jew. Whether he was exclusively homosexual is unimportant. The "evidence" produced by Mr. Painter is in my opinion trivial by comparison with the massive confession in the book itself. It puzzles me that Mr. Hindus should have had to lean on Gide's diaries for the final "pinning down" of the facts. Certainly, as the following quotation shows, Gide opens the eyes of the blindest and puts an end to all speculation (from the entry May 14, 1921, published, according to Justin O'Brien, translator of the journals, in 1939):

Spent an hour yesterday evening with Proust. . . . Although having begun, as soon as I arrived, to talk of homosexuality, he interrupted himself to ask me if I could enlighten him as to the teaching of the Gospels. . . . When I say a word or two about my *Memoirs:* "You can tell anything," he exclaims, "but on condition that you don't say *I*." But that won't suit me. Far from denying his homosexuality he exhibits it, and I could say almost boasts of it. He claims never to have loved women except spiritually and never to have known love except with men.*

"You can tell anything, but on condition that you don't say *I*"! What can Mr. Painter mean (unless he wants to call Gide a wholesale fabricator) with his "the first full account of it [Proust's homosexuality] *based on evidence?*"

Later we find in Gide the following, and other passages like it: "I have read Proust's latest pages . . . with, at first, a shock of indignation. Knowing what he thinks, what he is, it is hard for me to see in them anything but a pretense, a desire to protect himself, a camouflage of the cleverest sort . . ." (Dec. 2, 1921).

Is it possible that the subtle-minded Gide did not read into Proust's pages the confession, and the readiness to confess, which I see staring from them? Perhaps Gide meant that he wanted Proust to make the confession frankly, "manfully," in defiance of the world. If Proust did not do it that way it was not for lack of courage. The reasons were artistic and involve much more than the treatment of homosexuality.

VIII

And all the time we must bear in mind that we can never know Proust in person; we can only know studies of him, works of art (as histories always are) in themselves. Mr. Painter's is thorough, honest, sympathetic, but it is Mr. Painter's, and he cannot help establishing associa-

*_The Journals of André Gide,_ translated by Justin O'Brien (Knopf). [M.S.]

tions which may be only his surmises. Of Proust's relation to his mother (wholly Jewish by birth) Mr. Painter says in one place: "His first attempt to love and be loved by someone other than his mother —that is, to escape from incest—had failed," and this, suggests Mr. Painter, was a contributory cause in Proust's sexual aberration. Concerning Charles Haas, the prototype of Charles Swann, Mr. Painter says:

But it may well be, as some have suggested, that he [Proust] saw Haas even at this early period as a hero and example, another self. Haas, like himself, was a Jew, a pariah by birth; yet by his own merits of intelligence and charm he had made society a career open to the talents. Proust set himself to do the same. Social acceptance was a symbol—though, as he was to discover, an illusory one—of salvation.

What deeper meaning, what added values, do we find in *Remembrance* when we have these facts and Mr. Painter's interpretation of them? And suppose we make our own interpretation, are we any the better off in respect to the meaning of the book? Contemplation of Proust's life as recorded by others (or even as witnessed by ourselves, if we were contemporaries), spiced with some slapdash psychoanalysis, is a fascinating occupation—and has nothing to do with the wisdom, beauty, and horror of *Remembrance*. Mr. Stephen Spender, in a recent article, says: "As Bernard Shaw, another Dubliner, well understood, Joyce's aesthetic egocentricity was largely the result of his early life of feckless poverty and uprootedness in Dublin." Perhaps it was, given that James Joyce was not his brother Stanislaus, which leaves the riddle where it was. But we are none the wiser for it about *Ulysses*. I have read most of what is obtainable on the life of James Joyce; I have marveled at his scrupulous and laborious reproduction of real-life Dublin; and by these studies I have added nothing to my speculations on the ultimate significance of *Ulysses*. Equally scrupulous and laborious is Mr. Painter's reproduction of all the details, personalities, and circumstances of Proust's life and their correspondences (to be amplified in a second volume—which I greatly look forward to) with details, personalities, and circumstances in *Remembrance*. The experience has been for me one more vindication of Mr. Hindus's apt reference to the genetic fallacy (though Mr. Hindus himself succumbs to it in several places!).

But if the facts of a writer's life, while remaining recognizable in his book, are so transmuted that they offer no key to the order of the new universe he has created, the work will often cast a sharp light on the writer. Stephen Dedalus is often the kind of Joyce whom the latter's biographers are trying to portray. Proust's treatment of the Jewish theme testifies unmistakably to a real-life inner struggle of the utmost cruelty. For at one and the same time we know (independently of the pointer in the homosexual-Jewishness link) that only an assimilating Jew working his way into gentile high society could have been capable of that treatment, and that the treatment bespeaks many moments of rage, frustration, shame, and self-hatred.

Swann, the "nice" Jew, enters the story very early (I, 11), an attractive, gracious, courteous figure, whose romantic connections with the highest society—the Comte de Paris, French Pretender, and the Prince of Wales are among his intimates—are unsuspected by Marcel's upper-middle-class family. Swann would be the last person ever to refer to them.* Proust simply can't get over the perfect tactfulness and charming simplicity of Swann. True, Swann has made a disastrous marriage, after the long love affair to be described further on; his wife is not "received," though he and Marcel's family are neighbors; but Swann himself, an old and valued friend, is a frequent, and almost the only, visitor on summer evenings; and his admirable bearing, his thoughtful little kindnesses, his wit, make up, with the above-mentioned qualities, a character as attractive to his hosts as to the reader.

Bloch, the "nasty" Jew (he heads a whole list, unrelieved except by Swann) turns up on page 68. The manner of his introduction is a prelude to his frequent appearances throughout the more than 2,200 pages of the two volumes:

I had heard Bergotte spoken of for the first time by a friend older than myself, for whom I had a strong admiration, a precious youth of the name of Bloch. Hearing me express my love of the *Nuit d'Octobre,* he had burst into a bray of laughter, like a bugle call, and told me, by way of warning: "You must conquer your vile taste for A. de Musset, Esq. He is a bad egg, one of the very worst. I am bound to admit, nonetheless," he added graciously, "that even he, and the man Racine, did, each of them, once in his life, compose a line which is not only fairly rhythmical, but has also what is in my eyes the supreme merit of meaning absolutely nothing. . . .

Great changes occur in Swann in the course of the story, before he dies in the middle of the second volume; Bloch, surviving to the end, is permanently fixed as introduced, or becomes more so: able,

---

*A typical Proustian confusion. Swann is at this time of his life recreating for himself a new position in society, on a very modest level, and has become an offensive name-dropper (I, 331 ff.). [M.S.]

brash, noisy, affected, fundamentally asinine, tactless, and careerist.

In Proust's introduction of the Jewish theme there is a cool detachment on the author's part which at this stage rules out the idea that the author is himself part Jewish and will later react in an unmistakably Jewish manner:

> My grandfather made out that, whenever I formed a strong attachment to one of my friends and brought him home with me, that friend was invariably a Jew; to which he would not have objected on principle—indeed, his own friend Swann was of Jewish extraction—had he not found that the Jews whom I chose as friends were not usually of the best type.* And so I was hardly ever able to bring a new friend home without my grandfather's humming the "O, God of our fathers" from *La Juive*, or else "Israel, break thy chain," singing the tune alone, of course, to an um-ti-tum-ti-tum-tra-la; but I used to be afraid of my friend's recognizing the sound and so being able to reconstruct the words . . . These little eccentricities on my grandfather's part implied no ill-will whatsoever toward my friends. . . . [I, 69–70]

I regard the suggestion (that the idea of the author's Jewishness might cross the reader's mind so early in the book) as ruled out because all the above is so harmless, so good-natured; though the author is afraid that his friends will recognize the tune (*afraid*, that is, he knows they will be made uncomfortable), his one-hundred-percent gentile withers are unwrung, and it does not occur to him that his grandfather is displaying the malice of the half-senile. Later, when we are convinced from the text that the author is in fact Jewish, this introductory detachment of his makes *us* uncomfortable. At any rate, it does me. If I were a mulatto and couldn't bring home a Negro friend without my all-white grandfather humming the tune of *Swanee River* or *Old Black Joe*, I shouldn't by any means absolve the old man of ill-will. In the book we are not, of course, told the degree of Marcel's Jewishness; we have to assume finally that it is one-half, at most, for if *this* grandfather is himself a Jew he is quite mad. (Nor, we take it, is his wife Jewish.) How, then, did Marcel's Jewish parent take "these little idiosyncracies"? And why doesn't Marcel add to "indeed, his own friend Swann was of Jewish extraction," "just like his son-in-law," or his daughter-in-law? Why, sensitive boy that he is, doesn't he in any case protest to his grandfather? We know the answer by now: because Marcel has to play the non-Jew as far as he can.

I permit myself a kind of prolepsis here. My examination of Marcel's and Proust's responses to the Jewish problem is far from the

*Marcel tells of no other Jewish friend he ever had and brought home. [M.S.]

kind of amateur psychoanalysis I dislike. I am dealing with responses recognized long before Freud was born. The escaping Jew aiming at a social career does what he can not to notice an anti-Semitic jibe, and while on the one hand he associates himself to the liberalism of the non-anti-Semitic Gentile, and also refuses to hear and see evil, he gives vent to his resentment at his own fate by speaking of "the wrong kind of Jew" with a savagery which apes and surpasses that of the most inveterate gentile anti-Semite. All this has been said by Proust—and here is Proust's description of Bloch, grown a man, entering the drawing room of the high-born Mme. de Villeparisis:

He had his chin pointed now by a goatbeard, wore double glasses and a long frock coat, and carried a glove like a roll of papyrus in his hand. The Rumanians, the Egyptians, the Turks may hate the Jews. But in a French drawing room the differences between those peoples are not so apparent, and an Israelite making his entry as though he were emerging from the heart of the desert, his body crouching like a hyena's, his neck thrust obliquely forward, spreading himself in profound "salaams," completely satisfies a certain taste for the oriental. Only it is essential that the Jew should not actually be "in" society, otherwise he will readily assume the aspect of a lord, and his manners become so Gallicized that on his face a rebellious nose, growing like a nasturtium in any but the right direction, will make one think rather of Mascarille's nose than of Solomon's. . . . Marvelous racial power that from the dawn of time thrusts to the surface, even in Paris, on the stage of our theaters, behind the pigeonholes of our public offices, at a funeral, in the street, a solid phalanx, setting their mark upon our modern ways of hairdressing, absorbing, making us forget, disciplining the frock coat which on them remains not at all unlike the garment in which Assyrian scribes are depicted in ceremonial attire on the frieze of a monument at Susa before the gates of the palace of Darius. [I, 851]

I submit that we have in this superb passage an ungovernable outburst of repressed malice; but for its high literary level it might have appeared in Streicher's *Der Voelkische Boebachter*. We have the same note again, in an absolutely unprovoked, irrelevant aside, *à propos de bottes*, on Swann, who ate a lot of gingerbread because "he suffered from a racial eczema and from the constipation of the prophets . . ." [I, 306].

I have mentioned how Swann, once a perfect gentleman, married the ex-prostitute Odette de Crécy, had to rebuild a social world on a lower level, and became a ridiculous dropper of socially third-rate names.

It will perhaps be objected here that what this really implied was that the simplicity of the fashionable Swann had been nothing more than a supreme refinement of vanity, and that, like certain Israelites, my parents' old friend had contrived to illustrate in turn all the stages through which his race had passed, from the crudest and coarsest form of snobbishness to the highest pitch of good manners. [I, 332]

In these three passages the author steps recognizably into the real world, our world, and without the announcement which heralds his tribute to the Larivières. It is no use to appeal to artistic power, to plead, for instance, that Shakespeare's overwhelming portrayals of Iago and Richard III do not point to a streak of villainy in him. It is not the power of the portrayal that is in itself decisive; it is a certain inside note. We would know with complete certainty that the author of *Huckleberry Finn* hates slavery, that the author of *Oliver Twist* is deeply affected by social problems, even if the books had been published anonymously. To step down somewhat, the author of *By Love Possessed, The Just and the Unjust, Guard of Honor,* must, whoever he is, be illiberal in his attitude toward Jews and Negroes. In *Remembrance,* which is called a continuous novel, and is a life-work, a series of novels, the stigmata of the author declare themselves as plainly as his genius. A good deal might be quoted in illustration; I confine myself to a few passages.

One day when we were sitting on the sands, Saint-Loup and I, we heard issuing from a canvas tent against which we were leaning a torrent of imprecations against the swarm of Israelites that infested Balbec. "You can't go a yard without meeting them," said the voice. "I am not in principle irremediably hostile to the Jewish nation, but there is a plethora of them. You hear nothing but, 'I thay, Apraham, I've chust theen Chacop.' " The man who thus inveighed against Israel emerged at last from the tent; we raised our eyes to behold the anti-Semite. It was my old friend Bloch. [I, 558–9]

The staggering unself-consciousness of Proust as he wrote this! And as he wrote the picture of the grandfather! I insist that only a programmatically assimilating Jew, moving in the world of *Remembrance,* could have produced the totality of this material. The more the writer struggles to free himself the more he becomes psychologically entangled. He writes: "I knew that, as deep, as ineluctable as is their Jewish patriotism or Christian atavism in those who imagine themselves to be the most emancipated of their race, there dwelt . . ." (II, 669).

This is an intellectual echo of Mme. Gallardon's primitive babble about converted Jews. By itself it could have come from a non-Jew; taken with all the rest it can have come only from a Jew. The same is true of the author's reflections on Swann in the midst of the Dreyfus upheaval.

. . . having come to the premature term of his life, like the weary animal that is goaded on, he cried out against these persecutions and was returning to the spiritual fold of his fathers. [I, 1130]

. . . this new loss of caste would have been better described as a recasting, for it made him return to the ways in which his forebears had trodden, and from which he had turned aside to mix with the aristocracy. [I, 1131]

What is, again, internally assimilating-Jewish here is the fact that nothing whatsoever is told of Swann to indicate that he was actually "returning to the fold of his fathers." Not a single gesture, physical or mental, is adduced. Implied, we must suppose, is that automatic response of the Jew empty or emptied of Judaism who, rebuffed and offended, takes refuge in: "Yes, I'm a Jew, and proud of it," and has no idea what there is to be proud of; unless, like poor Leopold Bloom when he is badgered by "the citizen," he suddenly bethinks himself: "Mendelssohn was a Jew, and Karl Marx and Mercadante and Spinoza. And the Savior was a Jew and his father was a Jew."

IX

It is useful to compare *Remembrance* with *Dr. Zhivago** in the matter of Jewishness and Jewish self-consciousness. That Pasternak, as in the quoted instance of Cozzens, makes his own views known through some of his characters is universally recognized. One of the curious twists of the Zhivago case is the failure of the Russian censorship to realize that the hostility to the Communist regime here expressed issues from intellectual attitudes so generally discredited that the book should have been welcomed by Communists with the delighted remark: "See the kind of person who doesn't like us?" For Zhivago and the others who are presented sympathetically are critical of Communism on grounds acceptable only to an insignificant and disesteemed minority.

When Zhivago protests: "Why on earth should I know and worry myself sick over everything? History hasn't consulted me. I have to put up with whatever happens, so why shouldn't I ignore the facts? . . . Whom am I to believe? And I have to go on living. I've got a family" he disqualifies himself as a critic of *any* regime (apart from the fact that, characteristically, he abandons his family).

---

*By Boris Pasternak, translated from the Russian by Max Hayward and Manya Harari, American edition, Pantheon. [M.S.]

When in the first winter of the revolution Zhivago at Varykino confides to his diary: "What happiness to work from dawn to dusk for your family and for yourself, to build a roof over their heads, to till the soil and feed them, to create your own world, like Robinson Crusoe . . ." he writes himself out of the social consciousness of the modern world.

And when as a doctor-prisoner of the Bolshevik partisans in Siberia, present at a skirmish with the Whites, he feels himself at one with the enemy ("All his sympathies were on the side of those heroically dying children. With all his heart he wished them success. They belonged to families who were probably akin to him in spirit, in education, in moral discipline [!] and values") and nevertheless takes up a rifle and starts shooting (though as a noncombatant he doesn't have to—only he just can't lie still while things are going on), and more or less accidentally wounds two Whites, perhaps kills one, the reader can only exclaim: "Good God! What a jumbled-up, indeterminable creature! Who cares about *his* views on Communism?" Similarly we have Lara, Zhivago's beloved, harking back to prewar, prerevolutionary Russia in phrases that automatically invalidate her criticisms of Communism:

I can remember a time when we all accepted the peaceful outlook of the last century. It was taken for granted that you listened to reason, that it was right and natural for your conscience to do so. For a man to die at the hand of another was a rare and exceptional thing, something quite out of the ordinary. Murders happened in plays, newspapers, and detective stories, not in everyday life.

Czarist Russia, with its cruelties, its brutalized peasantry, its oppressed workers, its pogroms, its intellectual repressions and dishonesties ("it was taken for granted that you listened to reason") as a lost paradise! Really now! What was the Communist censorship afraid of?

We have no doubts after reading *Dr. Zhivago* as to Boris Pasternak's mystic-spiritual identity. Does he in the same way disclose his Jewish identity, known to us from external sources? I can think of only two passages that might have alerted me. Pasternak is speaking of Misha Gordon, aged eleven, the Jewish, de-Judaized friend of Zhivago:

A feeling of care was his ultimate mainspring and was not relieved and ennobled by a sense of security. He knew this hereditary trait in himself. . . . It distressed him. Its presence humiliated him.

For as long as he could remember he had never ceased to wonder why, having arms and legs like everyone else, and a language and way of life common to all, one could be different from the others, liked only by a few and, moreover, loved by no one. He could not understand a situation in which if you were worse than other people you could not make an effort to improve yourself. What did it mean to be a Jew?

This has the flavor of inside perplexity, and one is inclined to hear the exasperation of the Jewish assimilationist in the following (Gordon and Zhivago, young men at the front, have just seen a Cossack tormenting an old Jew, to the huge amusement of the by-standers. Gordon is speaking of the persistence of the Jewish people):

What use is it to anyone, this voluntary martyrdom? Whom does it profit? For what purpose are those innocent old men and women and children, all these subtle, kind, humane people, mocked and beaten up through the centuries? Why didn't the intellectual leaders of the Jewish people ever go beyond *Weltschmertz* and ironical wisdom. Why have they not disbanded this army which keeps on fighting and being massacred nobody knows for what? Why don't they say to them: "Come to your senses, stop. Don't hold on to your identity. Don't stick together, disperse. Be with all the rest. You are the first and best Christians in the world. You are the very thing against which you have been turned by the worst and weakest among you."

Two such statements standing by themselves are not enough; besides, the Jewish subject is tangential to *Dr. Zhivago;* had it been as important as in *Remembrance* something might have come out. In *Ulysses* the Jewish subject is of great importance, and the extended utterances and portrayals of Bloom are wonderfully true to life; but independently of *Portrait of the Artist as a Young Man* we can see that Stephen's is the self-portrait in *Ulysses,* irreconcilable with the Bloom type, and it is Stephen's agonies that must mirror the author's defection from his religious upbringing. Stephen's relation to his past is a suffering one, Bloom's to his a comical one. Bloom does not, like Stephen, wrestle morally with his family and racial memories; he clowns with them sentimentally and tearfully. It would be unjust to say that the author does not feel for Bloom, but he does not feel for him as one would for oneself. And this is also what must be said of Pasternak and his observations on Jews. I would not have guessed that he was of Jewish birth.

The *Zhivago* criticisms of Communism are for the greatest part based on obsolete values, or else meaningless. The same may be said of the observations on Jews and Judaism. If Misha Gordon believes that the Jews "are the first and best Christians in the world" it is absurd of him to demand the dissolution of so exalted an example, and mean-spirited of him to ask: "What use is it to anyone, this useless martyrdom?" In this same speech Gordon says of the Jews:

Their national idea has forced them, century after century, to be nation and nothing but nation—and they have been chained to this deadening task all through the centuries when all the rest of the world was being delivered from it by a new force which has come out of their own midst. . . .

And Lara says to Zhivago:

Of course it's true that persecution forces them into this disastrous attitude, this shamefaced, self-denying isolation that brings them nothing but misfortune. But I think some of it also comes from an inner senility, a historical, centuries-long weariness. . . .

which is preceded by (it is Lara speaking):

It's so strange that these people who once liberated mankind from the yoke of idolatry, and so many of whom now devote themselves to its liberation from injustice, should now be incapable of liberating themselves from their loyalty to an obsolete, antediluvian identity that has lost all meaning, that they should not rise above themselves and dissolve among all the rest whose religion they have founded. . . .

And, going back once more, Misha Gordon says:

What are the nations now in the Christian era? They aren't just nations, but converted, transformed nations, and what matters is this transformation, not loyalty to ancient principles.

How, chained to a deadening task through all the centuries, fallen into an inner senility (Lara's and Gordon's views are much the same, Zhivago tells her—and they are by implication his, more or less), how can the Jews be "the best Christians in the world"? A befuddlement always results when the best in the Christian ideal is juxtaposed with the worst in real Jewish life; here the befuddlement is made quite desperate because the Jews are somehow offered as ideal human examples while exposed as a senile people loyal to an antedeluvian identity. The last touch is added when we reflect that, as Lara and Gordon and Zhivago and Pasternak well know, the nations are not "converted, transformed nations"; their nationalism is infinitely more important to them than their Christianity. (There are not a few Jews who assert that the Jews were infected, to their spiritual undoing, by the nationalism of the modern Christian nations, and that they ought to cleanse themselves—by becoming Christians!)

X

The statements just quoted so well typify the less intelligent Christian missionary to the Jews, and they seem to issue so naturally from the speakers, that, with the two exceptions noted, nothing in the book would prompt us to think of the author as a Jew. Pasternak has done a far better job of "assimilation" than Proust; and if I am to guess at the reason on the basis of *Dr. Zhivago,* it is because he is filled with the solvent of a mystical fervor alien to Proust. I find a resemblance between Pasternak and Ezra Pound, the non-Jew, and the former may be as gifted a poet as the latter; in both of them the talent of the poet is accompanied by a stultified view of Jewish and other matters.

We are now *en plein air,* noting the interplay between the books and our acquaintance, such as it is, with the authors as real persons. The reflections which follow are not "simply" literary. Whether just or wide of the mark they are tangential to the interpretation of a book as a book. But they do belong to a proper field of study, the topography and extent of which are not clear. We are concerned in it with the artist and his place in society, with his work and its place in the history of thought; with moral judgments and psychological analyses of books and men as influences. For that matter much of this essay has only an indirect bearing on *Remembrance* and *Dr. Zhivago* as works of art.

From this standpoint two phenomena of worldwide interest link *Remembrance*-Proust with *Dr. Zhivago*-Pasternak, namely, the Dreyfus case and anti-Semitism in Communist Russia. The first of these has a very large place in *Remembrance;* the second is never mentioned in *Dr. Zhivago.*

The bulk of *Dr. Zhivago* is placed in early Communist Russia. The last eight or ten years of Zhivago's life, which is vaguely indicated as having ended around 1930, are disposed of in 39 out of 560 pages. Then follows an epilogue of 16 pages bringing us down, in the closing paragraphs, to 1948 or 1953 ("five or ten years later"—i.e., after a conversation dated 1943), and 37 pages of the poems of Zhivago. From outside sources we gather that most of *Dr. Zhivago* was written long before 1943; the book itself tells us that the finishing touches were added not earlier than 1953. I do not know what revisions Pasternak made in the first parts when the finishing touches were added; but this much all of us know: that by 1953 the infamous record of Communist anti-Semitism had been climaxed by the "case of the poisoning doctors"; those doctors were cleared and released in the spring of that year, shortly after Stalin's death; and long before Pasternak offered his completed and corrected manuscript for publication in its present form—that is, while there was still time for a little revision—it was common knowledge that hundreds of Jewish leaders, novelists, poets, actors, publicists had been killed unjustly. Many were posthumously reinstated in Communist respectability; and queerly enough the accusation had often been "cosmopolitanism," another name for that "transformation" of the nations which Zhivago-Lara-Gordon-Pasternak are so fervid about. This is only part of the story; in its completeness it is something that should have shaken the soul of the mystico-religious Pasternak to its depths. He does not give a sign in *Dr. Zhivago.*

Some remarks by Lara shed a light on this insensibility. She says to Zhivago: "If you do intellectual work of any kind and live in a town as we do, half of your friends are bound to be Jews. Yet in times when there are pogroms, when all these terrible despicable things are done, we don't only feel sorry and indignant and ashamed, we feel wretchedly divided, as if our sympathy were more from the head than from the heart and had an aftertaste of insincerity."

The Dreyfus case as interwoven with *Remembrance* and Proust shows a wholly different design. It is recorded by Proust's biographers that he was very active as a Dreyfusard. In *Remembrance,* Marcel too is a Dreyfusard, with the ostensible objectivity of an intelligent and moral non-Jewish French patriot. The painful emotional reverberations in Proust the man were transferred to Swann. Proust obviously cannot get rid of his Jewish self-awareness. He is far more deeply involved in it than Pasternak, who has risen *au-dessus de la mêlée.* Proust-Marcel is, in his relationship to his Jewishness, pathological and tragic; in the same relationship Pasternak-Zhivago is adjusted and contemptible.

Even if he were a non-Jew one could not condone in Pasternak his handling of the Jewish issue. He might have omitted it altogether, and that too would have been dishonest when he spreads himself so willingly on the moral defects of the Communists. As it is he is doubly dishonest. His sanctimonious admonitions to the Jews are directed toward their Christianization; his indignation at their maltreatment is confined to the Czaristic period or to anti-Communists; and by his animadversions on their collective "senility" and "self-denying isolation" he makes them unpalatable to Christians and Communists alike.

Proust could neither "repress" the Dreyfus affair and the Jewish question nor "do" them offhandedly. There they were, looming enormously in the life of the France he was depicting. The concealments of Proust-Marcel are personal and transparent, for Proust is an artistic genius, and genius is among other things a compulsion neurosis of honesty in craftsmanship. When the genius is in bondage to his essential theme his compulsion will circumvent or rather ignore any *arrière pensée,* and his exertions will be as honest as those of a man swimming for his life.

Commentary, January 1960

31 MY FRIEND, THE LATE
MOSES HERZOG

I

The title of this memoir, or comment, or supplementary note—I hardly know what to call it—is not to be taken as a reflection on Mr. Saul Bellow's portrait of my friend, the late Moses Herzog. Far from it. My private information would not lead me to change a line or shading. The reflection is directed, rather, at the reviewers of the book and at friends with whom I have discussed it. What I make public here adds little to the picture but does, I hope, emphasize certain aspects of a record that has been widely misunderstood. As I shall show, the misunderstanding is largely due to Herzog himself.

I have kept silent till now because the inferences I invite the reader to draw would have depressed my friend. There is, however, no problem of the invasion of privacy. In setting down the story as told him by Herzog, Mr. Bellow has effected the fictional transference with a skill which cannot be too much admired. He has transformed the principal dramatis personae as to name, locality, occupation, appearance, etc., beyond possibility of identification; yet—the reader must take my word for it—he has retained their characters and relationships down to the finest details. This tour de force makes it possible for me to discuss them in Mr. Bellow's transposed terms without the slightest sense of falsification or frustration.

II

I have thought it better not to inquire from Mr. Bellow—with whom I am unfortunately not acquainted—whether the Joycean mode of narration he chose for *Herzog* means to him all that I have read into it. That it means much to him cannot be doubted. The name Moses Herzog is that of a minor character—a grocer in a small way—who pops up three times in *Ulysses*. Few readers of *Herzog* will know that, but to these few Mr. Bellow gives the insider's tip: "I know, and you know. . . ." He could not very well use, instead of Herzog, the name of the hero and/or anti-hero of *Ulysses*, Leopold Bloom, but he would have us understand that he is quite aware of an organic similarity of theme and protagonists. From a certain point of view *Ulysses* and *Herzog* may be regarded as two major modern studies in Jewish assimilation.

There are such striking resemblances between the two principal characters that one is tempted occasionally to think of Moses Herzog as Leopold Bloom with a Ph.D. They are both inveterate thinking men, interested in people, processes, and general laws: Bloom in his kindly, practical, commonplace, prolix, platitudinous way; Herzog bringing to bear on every subject an original, powerful, well-trained, well-stocked mind. They are alike in their concern for man's condition, and in their rejection of force and brutality; also in their appreciation of food. Bloom, simple, "ate with relish the inner organs of beasts and fowls, thick giblet soup, and most of all grilled mutton kidneys"; Herzog, sophisticated, appreciated the meals prepared for him by his mistress Ramona, the shrimp Arnauld which she served with Pouilly Fuissé, the prosciutto, the Persian melon, the white asparagus, and the flavored ice cream.

They have in common a strain of masochism. Bloom indulges his in fantasy; more exactly, Joyce plays on it in the phantasmagoric projections of the Nighttown episode. Bloom cringes blissfully before the terrifying whore-master-mistress Bello-Bella Cohen, bleating: "Exuberant female, enormously I desiderate your domination; I am exhausted, abandoned, no longer young. . . ." He goes into spasms of excitement before the classy, brilliantly-dressed society women who threaten him with whips and spurs. Herzog, not in fantasy, records: "There was a flavor of subjugation in his love of Madeleine. Since she was domineering and he loved her, he had to accept the flavor that was given." And he records further (that is to say, he had Mr. Bellow record for him) in what manner Madeleine demanded a divorce from him: "She had prepared the event with a certain theatrical genius of her own. She wore black stockings, a lavender dress with Indian brocade from Central America. She had on her opal earrings, her bracelets and she was perfumed; her hair was combed with a clean new part and her eyelids shone with a bluish cosmetic."

Thus in memory Herzog contemplated her, dressed to kill, and himself accepting execution submissively. "In the confrontation in the untidy parlor, two kinds of egotism were present (she had prepared the great moment, she was about to do what she most longed to do, strike a blow), and his egotism was in abeyance, all converted to passivity."

One cannot imagine a more complete dissimilarity than that between Bloom's wife, the hearty, beefy, aging musical trollop, Molly, and the young, ambitious, slightly demonic Madeleine, Herzog's second wife. But, as against this, their respective lovers are parodies of each other. Blazes Boylan, who cuckolds Bloom with such éclat on that memorable June day, is a loud, flashy bounder ("a bill-sticker, a bester, a boaster"), and the gruesome Valentine Gersbach, who displaces Herzog with Madeleine, is "so genial, so noisy, with those Scotch and Japanese imitations, and that gravel voice." Blazes Boylan is a concert impresario and Valentine Gersbach is a disc jockey in a small town near Boston before he moves (with Herzog's fatuous assistance) to Chicago, there to become a purveyor of culture to Hadassah and other organizations, specializing in Buber while he continues his affair with Madeleine. In line with his schematic concealments, Mr. Bellow has given Gersbach an artificial leg, but has more than restored the balance by making him friskier with one leg than most men with two.

III

The outstanding resemblance—and difference—between Leopold Bloom and Moses Herzog lies in their respective efforts to come to terms with their self-identification as Jews while trying to leave their mark on the world.

To all appearances there is little of the Jew left in Bloom (of Herzog's Jewishness I shall speak further on), and that little is something of a nuisance to him. Throughout his wanderings and encounters in the city of Dublin in the twenty hours from 8 A.M., June 16, 1904, to 4 A.M., June 17, Bloom is constantly being reminded of his half-Jewish origin. The conscious part of him usually has to get the nudges from the outside; his subconscious sends up promptings of its own. He is "subject to ancient and ancestral shadows," this Leopold Bloom, son of wholly Jewish Rudolph Virag-Bloom, of Hungary, who married the Irish Catholic colleen Ellen, without, however, reconciling himself to *tarfut* or failing to observe the Passover; Leopold Bloom, who, thrice baptized (once Catholic, twice Protestant), has only bits and snippets of Jewish information, fragments of Hebrew phrases and quotations, and no Yiddish at all, and has long been an agnostic; Bloom, the not-important advertisement canvasser for the Dublin *Freeman,* whom Joyce sees predominantly as the wandering Odysseus and I see as the Jew in the last stages of dissolution.

Soon after rising, Leopold Bloom goes out to buy a pork kidney to fry for his own breakfast after serving Molly's to her in bed. At Dlugacz the butcher's he picks up a piece of newspaper wrapping and reads idly: "The model farm at Kinnereth on the lakeshore of Tiberias. Can become ideal winter sanatorium." He is mildly interested. "Agendath Netaim,* planter's company. To purchase vast sandy tracts from Turkish government and plant with eucalyptus trees. . . . Orange groves and immense melon fields north of Jaffa . . .yearly installments. Bleibtreustrasse 34, Berlin, W. 15."

"Nothing doing," he decides. "Still an idea behind it."

Walking home in mild sunshine, stirred by the sight of a hefty servant girl crossing his path (like Moses Herzog he is highly concupiscent, but unlike him, impotent), he recalls pleasant days of old, evenings with neighbors, oranges and citrons coming all the way from the Levant. The train of associations is about to be submerged when a cloud covers the sun and a chill passes through him. The oriental scene undergoes a swift change. "A barren land, bare waste. Volcanic lake, the dead sea: no fish, weedless, sunk deep in earth. . . . Poisonous foggy waters. . . . Sodom, Gomorrah, Edom. All dead names. A dead sea in a dead land. Gray and old. Old now. It bore the oldest, the first race . . . the oldest people. . . . It lay there now. Now it could bear no more. Dead. . . . Desolation." He thrusts it all from him. "Grey horror seared his flesh. Folding the page into his pocket he turned. . . . Hurrying homewards. . . . To smell the gentle smoke of tea, fume of the pan, sizzling butter. Be near her ample, bed-warmed flesh."

This is the first visitation. Its meaning and purpose will be disclosed at the end of that long, long day (twenty hours representing twenty years). And in between there will be many other Jewish intrusions and evocations, some trivial, some profound, some like arrows in tangential flight, scarcely perceived.

In the composing room of the *Freeman,* Bloom sees the typesetter at work; the text reads backwards, like Hebrew; to the surface of his

---

*I use throughout the orthography and transliteration of the Modern Library edition of *Ulysses.* [M.S.]

mind float befuddled memories: "Poor papa, with his Haggadah book. . . . Next year in Jerusalem. . . . *Alleluia. Shema Israel Adonai Elohenu.* No, that's the other. . . . Then the twelve brothers, Jacob's sons. And the lamb and the cat and the dog and the stick and the water and the butcher and the angel of death. . . . Sounds a bit silly until you come to look at it well. Justice it means but it's everybody eating everyone else."

Stepping into the adjacent *Evening Telegraph* office, Bloom listens without participation to the conversation of the journalists. He hears Professor MacHugh deliver himself of a striking comparison between ancient Rome in relation to the Judea she destroyed and the British Empire in relation to the Ireland she had ravaged and was still ruling.

"We think of Rome," says Professor MacHugh. "Imperial, imperious, imperative. What was their civilization? Vast, I allow, but vile. Cloacae, sewers. The Jews in the wilderness and on the mountain top said: *It is meet to be here, let us build an altar to Jehovah.* The Roman, like the Englishman who followed in his footsteps, brought to every new shore on which he set his foot only his cloacal obsession. He gazed about him in his toga and said: *It is meet to be here. Let us construct a watercloset.''*

Bloom listens, and no thought of his own is recorded. A few minutes later Professor MacHugh takes up the Jewish theme a second time, and recalls verbatim an oration he once heard from the lips of an Irish patriot comparing young Ireland in revolt against British rule with young Moses in revolt against Egyptian rule; comparing also the lure of the two mighty civilizations, the British and the Egyptian, rejected respectively by proud young Ireland and proud young Moses.

There is no echo in Bloom. He goes on his way untouched. But he reacts painfully an hour or two later in Barney Kiernan's pub, where a convivial and thirsty group is assembled. The general conversation revolves about unhappy Ireland, her glorious past and her hopes for the future. Bloom, as he goes in and out, looking for an acquaintance who is helping him to collect the insurance for a poor widow, joins in the conversation here, joins in excessively, wearyingly, foolishly; talks at random, is at once Irish patriot, internationalist, humanitarian, Jew, authority on every subject that comes up. The atmosphere is hostile to Bloom, the more so as a false rumor is about that he has just won a packet on a horserace and is waiting to collect without offering the customary round of drinks, the truth being (the slandered, misunderstood Jew!) that he has won nothing and is only about his errand of mercy. During one of his absences the super-patriotic Citizen, who is setting the tone of the conversation, asks irritably: "Is he a jew or a gentile or a holy roman or what the hell is he?"

His acquaintance having turned up in a horsedrawn cab, Bloom is on the point of leaving when the Citizen, unwilling to let him depart in peace, shouts after him: "Three cheers for Israel" and makes an anti-Semitic speech to the loafers at the door. Thereupon Bloom calls back indignantly to the Citizen: "Mendelssohn was a jew and Karl Marx and Mercadante and Spinoza. And the Savior was a jew and his father was a jew. Your God." To this the Citizen responds, raging, with: "By Jesus, I'll brain that bloody jewman for using the holy name. By Jesus I'll crucify him I will." Bloom and his acquaintance depart at a sudden gallop as the frightened horse shies away from the tin biscuit box which the Citizen hurls at them.

The buried past rises more and more densely about Bloom as the day closes. In Nighttown, the red-light district, Bloom, always the worried do-gooder (Moses Herzog too complained of a weakness for good deeds), is in search of young Stephen Dedalus who, on a spree with riotous companions, has his month's pay as a teacher in his too easily accessible pocket. In fancy Bloom encounters his own dead father and mother: the former warns him against *"goyem nachez"*; the latter invokes for him the Blessed Redeemer and the Sacred Heart of Mary. Bloom then wanders into Bella Cohen's brothel, is approached by Zoe, one of the girls, sees her as an Eastern odalisque, and hears her (with his subconscious) sing: *"Schorah ani wennowwach, benoith hieru-shaloim."**

We need not list all of Bloom's mental collisions with the Jewish ideas whirling about him in Nighttown. It is enough for us to complete the trajectory of the Jewish theme. He fulfills his Good Samaritan obligation to Stephen Dedalus by taking care of him after a drunken brawl and inviting him home. When Stephen has left, Bloom reviews the incidents of the day and this tired man sinks into dreams of a happy future: not megalomaniac delusions such as pursued him in Nighttown, but reasonable anticipations within reach of his capacities, were those consistently employed. Why could he not leave the city and settle in the country? He had saved up nearly a thousand pounds, a respectable sum in the Ireland of those days. "Might he not become a gentleman farmer of produce

---

*This strange transliteration of the Hebrew passage from Song of Songs ("I am dark, but comely, O daughters of Jerusalem") may have been due to Joyce's ignorance or may have been intended to point up Bloom's. [M.S.]

and live stock?" How pleasant, restful, sleep-inducing are the fore-visioned gradations of his rise: "Gardener, groundsman, cultivator, breeder . . ." and, at the zenith of his career, fulfillment illumining his latter years, "resident magistrate of the peace with a family crest or coat of arms and appropriate classical motto *(Semper Paratus),* duly recorded in the court directory (Bloom Leopold P., M.P., P.C., K.P., LL.D. *honoris causa,* Bloomville, Dundrum) and mention in court and fashionable intelligence (Mr. and Mrs. Leopold Bloom have left Kingston for England)."

The soothing vision beckons to him from afar as he prepares to go upstairs and lay his tired body next to Molly's in the slight hollow left there that afternoon by Blazes Boylan. There is his refuge from ancestral importunation, from the assaults, insults, and snubs of uncouth *goyim* and from his own unaccountable twinges of uneasiness. And in token of his acceptance of this apotheosis, Bloom introduces it with a quiet farewell-and-rejection ceremony attended by incense-burning. "From an open box in the majolicatopped table he extracted a black, diminutive cone, one inch in height, placed his candlestick on the right corner of the mantlepiece, produced from his waistcoat pocket a folded page of prospectus (illustrated) entitled Agendat Netaim, unfolded the same, examined it superficially, rolled it into a thin cylinder, applied it when ignited to the apex of the cone."

The message from the ancestral home, delivered to Bloom the Jew in the morning through the agency of Dlugacz the butcher, is delivered that night to the flames by Bloom the prospective Irish country gentleman.

IV

Many of my readers will recall that Moses Herzog came from a thoroughly Jewish home, one that had known better days in Europe before he was born, and home memories were a strong motif in his makeup, perhaps the strongest and most abiding. It was not only that he thought of his parents, particularly his mother, with anguished love, and was unashamedly attached to his brothers and sister; he saw in his wretched childhood surroundings in the Montreal slum-ghetto the only possible ingredients of the right life for him. There he and his brothers had said their prayers together: *Ma tovu ohaleha Yaakov**—how goodly are thy tents, O Jacob; and with poignant fidelity Mr. Bellow records Herzog's thoughts: "Napoleon Street,

---

*As with *Ulysses,* I quote the transliterations in *Herzog* without change. [M.S.]

rotten, toylike, crazy and filthy, riddled, flogged with harsh weather —the bootlegger's boys reciting ancient prayers. To this Moses' heart was attached with great power. Here was a wider range of human feelings than he had ever again been able to find. The children of the race, by a never-failing miracle, opened their eyes on one strange world after another, age after age, and uttered the same prayer in each, eagerly loving what they found. What was wrong with Napoleon Street? thought Herzog. All he ever wanted was there."

Much, very much, was wrong with Napoleon Street, as he well knows. Nevertheless all he had ever wanted was there—only the filth and poverty had to be cleared away. He remembered his pathetically indomitable father, his humble, self-sacrificing, infinitely precious mother. "Whom did I ever love as I loved them?" He meets on a New York street a down-and-out friend of his Montreal childhood, Nachman, who owes him some money and runs away, pretending not to see him. They had last met in Paris, where Herzog had helped him, and Nachman had spoken of Herzog's mother. "A gentle spirit. . . . I was hungry and she fed me. She washed my hands and sat me at table. . . . I sometimes say a prayer for her." And a stifled cry rises from Herzog's heart, memorial words: *"Yiskor elohim es nishmas Imi"*— may God remember the soul of my mother.

He recalls how one day, on an outing, his mother had moistened a handkerchief at her lips and had cleaned his face with it, and the recollection is so piercing that he shrinks from it, suppresses it. There were times when he chided himself for loving the dead too much. "It was very bad indeed. He really believed in letting the dead bury their own dead." Did he really believe that? Sometimes, certainly. Nevertheless it was because of the dead that he laughed at himself in the role of the country gentleman when, at Madeleine's insistence, he bought with his inheritance of $20,000 (the sweat of poor papa Herzog's life) the New England estate which they occupied for a year or so. "There I was, myself, in Ludeyville as Squire Herzog. The Graf Pototsky of the Berkshires."

V

I made Willy Herzog's acquaintance in the fall of 1957 and at once took a great liking to him. He sat next to me on the dais at an Israel Bond rally which I addressed, and after it drove me to my hotel. He already had the reputation of a devoted worker in Jewish causes; he was well-to-do and a generous giver, though not among the big guns.

His concern for Israel, for Jewish communal affairs, was free from that pious self-consciousness which reminds one of the line: "What virtues, Lord, Thou makest us abhor." It was as natural to him as concern for his family. He knew his deficiencies and pleaded justification by works. "I don't go to *shul* every *shabbos,* let alone *daven* every morning. Still, *shabbos* is *shabbos* in the home, and the *yomtovim, yomtovim.* We eat *kosher,* but don't keep two sets of dishes. And my kids are more Jewish than I."

Willy Herzog is twenty years my junior, and I had to take the initiative in our friendship. He seemed to think it unlikely that I could find his conversation interesting, his company warming. He was surprised when I kept turning the conversation toward him, and when I questioned him insistently about his factory and his real-estate deals. I was continuously impressed by his shrewdness, patience, good humor, and alertness.

On one subject he was touchingly naive—his brother Moses, of whom he spoke to me in perplexity of spirit on our fourth or fifth evening together. He had invited me with some urgency to stop for a drink at his house on the way to my hotel. He had something on his mind, he would feel better speaking of it in his home. We would be alone, the family was away.

"We're three brothers, you know, we Herzogs," was the way he began. "My older brother Shura, Alexander, is very rich. But with him there's no hope—*farfallen.* He'll get richer and richer and every year I'll *shlep* out of him a thousand dollars for the U.J.A., and make him buy a bond, and *fartig.* But my kid brother, Moses." He paused. "*Ai,* our Moishele. I suppose you've heard of him. He's professor of history at Chicago University. He's written a book, *Romanticism and Christianity.* You've surely read it."

"Yes. Not too carefully, though."

"What do you think of it?"

"First-rate writing," I said. "Good thinking. And his knowledge! Also I like what he wants. But what more can I say? One third of the philosophers and historians he quotes I've barely heard of, one third I've dipped into at one time or another, and one third I've read and mostly forgotten. Perhaps two dozen men in America can give an informed analysis of your brother's book off the bat."

A gratified smile came into Willy's eyes. "Brilliant, eh?"

"Tops."

"If you can't give an opinion," said Willy, "how can I? And he's written plenty more. He's written a doctoral thesis, articles, papers, lectures, research he's doing for some foundation. But tell me"—the smile left his face, replaced abruptly by distress—"why has he never written a word about us, about the Jewish problem? I've said to him, just once or twice—after all, who am I to argue with him?—I've said: 'Why don't you give us a hand, Moishe? How many like you have we got?' He nods, with a faraway look, not No, not Yes, he doesn't want to hurt my feelings, but nothing happens. Why, Maurice, I'm asking you, why?"

I waved the question away vaguely.

"And why," asked Willy, with something like bitterness, "does he have to write *davke* about *Romanticism and Christianity? Vos tzum shvartzen yor* does he have to pick on that subject for? Never a line about the wonderful things we've done in Israel." His voice rose with the irritation of baffled love. "Or if not about Israel, then something about Jewishness, *stam azoi.*"

Seventy or eighty years ago, I thought, in some *shtetl,* Willy would have been *der feiner balabos,* Shura *der oyfgekumener gevir,* and Moses the *yeshiva bochur* gone wrong, *l'tarbut ra'ah.*

Willy's agitation, his wounded affection, prompted me to address him for the first time by his Yiddish name. "What can one do about it, Velvel?" I said, gently. "Here's a man of great ability who just doesn't care about his Jewishness. It's happened before."

"That's not so!" answered Willy, vigorously, almost hotly, as if I had unwittingly offended him. "He cares a lot. In a funny way, he's lots more Jewish than I. Do you know, he still visits our mother's grave. She's been dead, God rest her soul, more than twenty years. She wanted him to be a rabbi, and that's what he should have been. We need good rabbis, God knows." A wistful look came into his eyes. "Rabbi Moses Herzog, Ph.D. Don't you think that sounds just right?"

"Yes, Velvel. Perfect."

He leaned over. "Maurice, I'd like you to meet my brother."

"I'd be proud to."

"That's what I really wanted to talk to you about. I'd like *you* to tackle him, find out why he goes against his own nature so—so systematically. I'd like you to—well—sort of win him over."

I started so sharply that I almost spilled the drink I was holding.

"Good heavens, Velvel, what an idea!"

"What's wrong with it?"

I thought of the "dialogues" that were then coming into fashion. A "dialogue" is a tootle-word for a debate, and there's nothing like a debate for confirming the debaters in their opinions. In my young years I was a great one for debating, privately or publicly. Perhaps an audience might gain, but who ever heard of two debaters learning anything from each other besides, perhaps, better arguments for their respective sides?

"You don't have to win him over," said Willy. "Just meet him."

VI

The reader will of course bear in mind that when I met Moses Herzog I knew him only from his book and from Willy's observations about him. His confessions had not yet been given to the public by Mr. Bellow; their most important episodes had not yet been enacted.

We took to each other easily. He was prejudiced in my favor because of my fondness for Willy; I was drawn to him by certain resemblances to Willy. They had in common a deep vein of earnestness and a high degree of emotional sensitivity. They were both hard workers (I have an unreasoning detestation of lazy people), Willy consistently, Moses in tremendous bursts. Each on his own level, they loved ideas with the peculiar intimacy that I associate with Jewishness.

I suppose I need not mention that neither of us wanted a "dialogue" on Israel, the destiny of the Jews or anything else like that. Beyond a jocular reference he made to the hopes Willy had pinned on our meeting—"Aren't you supposed to convert me, or something?"—we tacitly stayed clear of that area. We found a great deal to talk about. I was delighted to find in him a fellow-Proustian with an excellent command of French and a special interest in the general problems of translation. We were soon capping each other's quotations from *A la recherche du temps perdu* in English and French, and testing each other's memories. We met for drinks at Willy's home on the North Side, but ended up at Moses', on the South Side. We had become entrenched in differing recollections of one of the many bravura passages in Proust, a treatment of "the little phrase" in the Vinteuil sonata, and Moses had at home, beside the Scott-Moncrieff translation, the original *Nouvelle Revue Française* edition, 1919–1922, of the complete work in thirteen paperback volumes. The *baal nitzachon* was touched off in both of us. Also, we were doing Willy a favor; he had wanted to bring us together and then withdraw; as he could not do this in his own home, it was for us to make a move.

When we got to Moses' home, his seven-year-old son Marco

was asleep. His wife, Daisy, exchanged a few words with us, excused herself, pleaded tiredness, and went to bed. If I had known the state of affairs between them I would not have barged into the house after ten o'clock, or I would not have stayed more than a few minutes. However, the original edition of the *Temps perdu* was something to see (and what a sight!—the miserable, browning paper crumbling to the touch, half the pages loose—he had to handle them as if they were Dead Sea scrolls); and there was, of course, the dispute, which we settled to our satisfaction, or rather to his, since I was in the wrong.

"Look at the perfection of that translation," he said, exulting as if he had done it. "And look at the frustration in it. The nearer it comes to perfection, the more a translation teases us with the suggestion of an ultimate, impassable barrier." He quoted again part of the description of "the little phrase," in French and in English. *'Elle passait à des plis simples et immortels, distribuant ça et là les dons de sa grâce.* 'It passed with simple and immortal movements, scattering on every side the bounties of its grace.' You can't get any nearer. But there's no English equivalent, in that context, for the simple word *plis; '*scattering on every side' is almost *'distribuant ça et là;* but *'les dons de sa grâce'* has a lightfootedness that defies translation. It's blasphemous to try."

"When the *Tanach* was translated into Greek," I said, "the Rabbis ordained a fast."

"Wise men," he replied. "They didn't have to wait for the Italians to tell them that translators are traitors."

He quoted other parallel passages in English and French, all dealing with "the little phrase," all pointing to the unbelievable ingenuity of the translator and to the impassable barrier. I remarked on the quality of his French. Had he ever lived or studied in France? No; in his early childhood in Montreal something of the language had lodged in him, to be forgotten but to have its influence on him in high school. I told him of my own, similar experience; but nearly fifteen years after my infant period in France I had returned for a few months before the outbreak of the First World War; and then again as an American soldier (how purely historical that must have sounded to him, much as the Franco-Prussian War does to me), when I had been demobilized there, had taken courses at the Sorbonne, and had stayed on for two years. He envied me that opportunity.

"You've done well enough," I said. "You must have a gift for languages."

"No. I've had to sweat for them. French. German."

That got us on to the Schlegel-Tieck translation of Shakespeare, one of the literary wonders of the world, and we recalled favorite passages. Moses quoted Hamlet's speech to the ghost: "Angels and ministers of grace defend us" and paused with rapture over the perfect rhythmic echo of:

> *. . . warum die Gruft*
> *Worin wir ruhig dich begraben sahn*
> *Geöffnet ihre schwere Marmorkiefer*
> *Dich wieder auszuwerfen.*

That was of course marvelous, I said, but there was more art in a simple phrase like: *"Mir ist schlimm zumut"* for "I am sick at heart." He nodded, and quoted the enchantingly neat: *"Mein Ehrgeiz geht auf eine bunte Jacke"* from *As You Like It.* "You can't conceive of a closer approximation," he said. "But look: *Ehrgeiz* is crammed with itself, and it's rooted in the language, whereas 'ambition' comes from the outside, and it's a fancy word. Nothing to be done about it." We went on to the general failure of the English at translation; half a dozen attempts had been made at Goethe's *Faust,* but the best of them was still Bayard Taylor's, a journeyman job. On the other hand there was the English Bible, an even greater miracle than the German Shakespeare. He didn't know enough Hebrew to make comparisons, but on general principles he guessed that the very magnificence of the language in the King James version implied a distortion. How could two such disparate races as the ancient Hebrews and the Elizabethan English possibly be at one in their conception of God and of human values? He asked me for the Hebrew of some oft-quoted verses in the Song of Songs, Isaiah, Psalms, Ruth. Many of the words were not strange to him; I gave him the literal equivalents of the others with, where I could, their etymology. Was I satisfied with the King James version, or others, Moffat's, Goodspeed's, Knox's? In this sense of course not, I said. "Once you've tasted Hebrew nothing else satisfies." But I would not place the same gap between English, French, and German as between any of these and Hebrew.

We chatted until midnight; then he insisted on walking me to my hotel. It had been an enjoyable encounter.

VII

I omitted to mention, that evening, the greatest gap of all, namely, between Yiddish and any other language I was familiar with; and I did not get a chance until my next visit to Chicago, on the occasion

of a lecture to the Hillel Foundation. I had written Herzog meanwhile, having bethought myself of some particularly captivating bits
in Proust and Shakespeare. We met for a late lunch. (He did not ask
me to his home, and I never set foot in it again, nor did we ever come
together again at Willy's. His life was becoming difficult and complicated, and he wanted to keep me out of it.) In this and in later talks,
in Chicago, in New York, and finally in Europe, we more than made
up for our initial omission.

I was astonished by the quality of his Yiddish. He had, in spite
of his disclaimer, a great gift for languages. He caught at them like
a musician at melodies. In his love of Yiddish he also heard his
parents, particularly his mother. Gersbach's coarse, butcher's boy
maltreatment of the language offended him, as he told Mr. Bellow.
It was disrespectful, impious, dishonoring, a kind of *chilul ha-Shem.*
Willy's Yiddish, though greatly inferior to his brother's, was never
that of a *grobyan.*

Up to the time he fled to Europe following Madeleine's dismissal
of him, I must have met Moses more than a dozen times. Our talks
were not exclusively of literature and translations, nor did we altogether avoid contemporaneous problems, though by mutual consent
we always skirted Israel. But I am concerned to impress on the reader
Herzog's intimate relation to Yiddish, which, though clearly enough
indicated in Mr. Bellow's transcription, has not been sufficiently
evaluated by reviewers and readers.*

Speaking of the hopelessness of reproducing the flavor of authentic Yiddish—Sholom Aleichem's, for instance—in a translation,
I once expressed the opinion that the most intractable language in
this respect was German; and when scholarly ignoramuses, usually
prejudiced, talked of Yiddish as a debased German dialect, they made
me think of those accomplished philologists who know everything
about words except how to put them together in readable sentences.
It was precisely the German "physical" origin of nine-tenths or so of
Yiddish words that made German particularly alien to Yiddish; the
purely structural similarities led to fatal misunderstandings.

We amused ourselves looking for some of them, and imagined
a German reading the Yiddish: *"Er hot gehat a groysen durchfal oyf der*

---

*Mr. Bellow does not quite keep pace with Herzog's Yiddish. Herzog would
never have translated *"ausvurf"* (Mr. Bellow's spelling) as "outcast"; the meaning is
"libertine" or "scoundrel." *"Beth Olam"* is not "house of the multitude" but "everlasting house" or "house of eternity." In giving this literal translation of the word for
"cemetery" Mr. Bellow has evidently been misled by the predominant Yiddish conno-
tation of *olam* (*"a groysser oylem," "der oylem iz a goylem."*) [M.S.]

beeneh" as: "He had a tremendous attack of diarrhea on the stage," instead of "he was a tremendous failure." Or trying to make sense of *"Geyt, vasht zich,"* which is only a way of inviting a man to table. Or: *"Men zol im ton zein recht"* as "do right by him," instead of "give him proper burial."

"Even the genius of Heine," I said, "couldn't make a Jewish thing sound Jewish in German." I read out to him Heine's *Prinzessin Sabbath* and Bialik's Yiddish adaptation of it. The very opening rang false in German:

> *In Arabiens Märchenbuche*
> *Sehen wir verwünschte Prinzen . . .*

when placed side by side with:

> *In die alte bobbe maisses*
> *Kummen for gilgulim printzen . . .*

while in many places the alienation was simply grotesque. Heine thus contrasts the meretricious beauty and intellectual pretentiousness of the Queen of Sheba with the wise and loving gentleness of *Prinzessin Sabbath:*

> *Schöner war*
> *Nicht die Königin von Saba*
> *Salomonis Busenfreundin.*
>
> *Die, ein Blaustrumpf Äthopiens,*
> *Durch Esprit brillieren wollte,*
> *Und mit ihren klugen Rätseln*
> *Auf die Lange fatigant ward,*

which Bialik turns into:

> *Ver mir, vos mir Malke Sh'vo*
> *Di vos iz gefelen Shloymen!*
>
> *Yene kusher shtreimel kligt zich*
> *Un farmogt a moyl oyf shreiflech,*
> *Est sich ein mit ihre chochmes*
> *Un fardrayt dem kop mit chides.*

Bialik's adaptation, further, included practically new passages, based on hints from Heine, and over one of them Herzog paused, making me repeat it and murmuring it after me:

Sha! Di kinigin, di Sh'chineh,
Bensht, farmacht di oygen, licht.
Gold'ne licht fun trayst un k'dusheh
Oyf dem ventl fun dem omed
Glentzt ir, vi a shterntichl
Oyf der mame's libn shtern.

It took him back to the lost paradise of his pitiful, love-encircled childhood.

He noted once that the rich seasoning of Hebrew words was not the only major source of the difference between Yiddish and German. There was, for example, the unpredictable transformation of verbs under Russian influence but with German-origin prefixes, a dazzling display of folk inventiveness.

"You take *kumen,* with its *onkumen*—itself divisible into the neutral *di post iz ongekumen,* and the pathos of *onkumen tzu kinder;* and *tzukumen,* also divisible: *ich vel tzukumen tzu eich,* and: *a shtik gezund iz mir tzugekumen:* and the boast attributed to the Hasid: *Got iz take Got, ober tzum rebn kumt er nit;* and *opkumen*—there's the lovely: *opkume mit shrek;* and *iberkumen.* And so many of the German uses have dropped out of Yiddish, or never entered it, like *kommt mir nicht so,* and *an eine Sache gekommen* and *in das Fleisch gekommen*—we would say *bichovodo u-v'atzmo.*"

I agreed. "There's a transformation quite independent of the infusion of Hebrew words or any other purely linguistic factor. The difference between *goyish* in its detractory and Yiddish in its approbatory sense shows in certain modesties. A well-brought-up *shtetl* Jew will not eat, *er vet toyem zein,* he'll partake of something; he won't actually sleep, *er vet zich tzushparen,* doze off, snatch forty winks."

"And things that have accumulated," he broke in. "You take a straightforward, objective designation: *Dem rebns shnur,* and you translate it: *Die Schwiegertochter des Rabbiners.* Well, to begin with, a *Rabbiner* isn't a *rebbe,* and though *Schnur* is classical, archaic German, it isn't our Yiddish *shnur,* with its richness of Jewish family connotation. *Shnur* oozes *mishpocheh.* The English is no better than the German: The rabbi's daughter-in-law. *Opgeshmat!*" He laughed sharply. "These relationships have entered our blood, like our detestation of violence, our disesteem of the fighter, of Esau the hairy one, no matter in what elegances and gallantries he drapes his primitive hunter's lust." He shot off in the new direction. "In our heartbeats we hear ancestral voices prophesying peace. We fought, in ancient days, without glorifying the warrior. Would a Jew ever have said: 'War is the father of everything?' When the joy of battle is celebrated in the *Tanach* it's by a horse. 'He saith ha! ha! among the trumpets.' *Nu, a ferd nebech,* what can you expect? And David the warrior, the giant-killer, who saved his country, forbidden to build the Temple because he was a shedder of human blood. All his psalms didn't help him. That strain has come down to us across the ages."

I wondered then at his repeated references to a kind of genetic Jewishness and was therefore not surprised when I met them again in *Herzog.* To his one-time schoolmate Shapiro, now a scholar who put on genteel Anglo-Saxon airs, he wrote: "You are too intelligent for this. You inherited rich blood. Your father peddled apples." And again, derisive of himself because he had entertained the idea of shooting his wife and her lover, he exclaims: "Ancient Herzogs, with their psalms and their shawls and beards, would never have touched a revolver. Violence was for the *goy.*"

I remember an evening when he came to see me in my hotel on West Seventy-Fourth Street. He was negotiating for a job in New York (I know now that his break with Madeleine was imminent. He had not yet "met up," as they say, with Ramona; he was making do with what he called "vile amateurs") and he wanted an escape from himself, which he found in conversation with me. He had been reading, with much excitement—his mind never took a rest—some of the physicists, Bridgman, Gamow, Dyson, Bohm, and was especially intrigued by the last, who, he said, was by far the most imaginative of the group and presented a vision of the universe which could have occurred only to a Jew. It was the prophetic concept of infinity couched in the neutral terminology of the laboratory. "The infiniteness of God," said Herzog, "in contemporaneous nonreligious terminology. Job expressed it for the prescientific world as no Greek ever did, though there were perceptive-monotheists among the Greeks. The modern Jew brings Job's cry of wonder into scientific physics and cosmography."

"Have you any idea," I asked, "whether Professor Bohm has had a Jewish education, or knows the Bible?"

"I don't believe that matters. All you've got to do is read his *Causality and Chance in Modern Physics.* Einstein had no Jewish education to speak of, but his theory of relativity, which should really be called the theory of the absolute, is the greatest and most Jewish modern revelation beyond the flesh. Beyond the flesh, and therefore of God."

He walked back and forth, looking at my bookshelves and paying no attention to me.

"What science has done in the last hundred years is liberate our intelligence from the flesh, from the tyranny of the sense organs. We've transcended the sense organs, our animal equipment. As animals we are limited in sight to a narrow slit of the electromagnetic spectrum midway between the longest radar waves and the shortest gamma rays. As animals we live in a tiny bottleneck of temperature near the absolute zero; and as animals we are acquainted only with slow motion, in which relativistic effects are not perceptible and the universe is Euclidean. Science has opened up all the range of electromagnetic rays, all the range of temperature, and has enabled us to measure great speeds with such delicacy that we've learned how time and space are fused into a unity."

"Wait, Moishe. The new vision began with Maxwell and the field theory."

"Granted. The Jews weren't the first monotheists either. Even the Bible tells us that long before Abraham 'men began to call upon the name of the Lord.' But the Jews were the preeminent monotheists. In the modern world it was Einstein who most effectively demolished the notion of a world of duality, matter, and energy, and demonstrated that matter and energy are only two perceptions of the single underlying substance—I use 'substance' here as Spinoza used it. It was the same fixation in the Jew that made him preeminent in the moral field. Here!"

He had snatched down a copy of Edmund Wilson's *To the Finland Station* and was turning its pages rapidly. "Here: 'The characteristic genius of the Jew has been especially a moral genius . . . and even in the case of those great men among the Jews who do not occupy themselves with religion proper it is usually a grasp of moral ideas which has given them their peculiar force.' And here: 'Furthermore Karl Marx had inherited from his rabbinical forebears a tradition of spiritual authority . . .' Karl Marx had absolutely no Jewish education. His parents were baptized."

It would be irrelevant for me to present here my objections—they are very strong—to this thesis of hereditary Jewish predisposition to moral perception. I refrained from mentioning them to Moses, thinking I would wait for a better time, when he would be more relaxed and receptive.

VIII

At a certain period Moses lost contact with his brothers and I saw more of him than they. Willy was dreadfully unhappy about him on two counts, that he should have left Daisy and the child, and that he should have done so for a woman like Madeleine, about whom he spoke with great bitterness. "I haven't met her, and I don't want to meet her; but I know all about her. She's hard; a taker, not a giver. Conceited. But that's nothing. She's turned Catholic!" He said these last words helplessly, as if a disgusting medicine were being forced down his throat. "A Jewish girl turning Christian these days! Can't think of another way of worshipping God. But to hell with her! She's none of my business. But Moishe!" He broke into a kind of wailing. "How can he do that? It'll kill him. I have to say thank God mother isn't here to see it. It's driving my father out of his mind. He'll marry her in a church and he'll baptize the children. He began with *Romanticism and Christianity* and he'll finish up with a Jesuit son or a daughter a nun."

"He'll never marry in a church!" I exclaimed. "Never. He *can't.* If he tries to he'll fall into a hysterical paralysis."

"Don't you know what new converts are like?" said Willy. "She'll make him. She'll tear his guts out and make him."

I was profoundly convinced, from what I already knew of Moses, that the worst of Willy's fears were unfounded. Moses Herzog baptizing his children! His tongue would cleave to the roof of his mouth.

"He was carrying on with a Japanese girl," said Willy. "For God's sake, can't he find a Jewish girl to suit him? There's plenty of them with looks and brains and good character. No. Orientals and *meshumodim!*"

I quoted from the chapter in Judges following my Bar Mitzvah *haftorah:* " '*Ha-ein bivnoth*—is there never a woman among the daughters of thy brethren, or among all my people, that thou goest to take a wife of the uncircumcised Philistines?' That was Samson."

"Yes," said Willy. "That's not such a good omen. But he wasn't famous for brains, was he? A long time ago I saw an old movie with Marlene Dietrich. She was a circus performer, I think, and a professor was in love with her."

"The Blue Angel."

"I remember she made him do such humiliating things that I was ashamed to look at the screen. She made him crack an egg on his head and crow like a rooster. If that woman doesn't understand what she's doing to Moses, she's an idiot; and if she does she's a murderer."

I too had not met Madeleine at that time, but I too had heard about her passionate Catholicism. It was a mysterious business to me, and Moses never spoke to me of his personal affairs.

"It won't last long, Willy," I said.

"How long does it take to ruin a man?"

I said something about the difficulty of ruining a man like Moses, but Willy had touched a chord in my mind with "turning Christian these days." The thought of a Jew dissociating himself from his people at this historic juncture, and dissociating himself with a public flourish, precisely to enter the Christian communion, was, I knew, abhorrent to Moses. The six million were an abiding memory with him. I remembered once reading to him from the Yiddish literature of the great calamity, some lines from Chaim Grade's *Rays of Extinguished Stars:**

> As once from nightfields of Bethlehem,
>   weeping goes up in the night from the ruins of Cracow;
> Lublin! You were steeped in the Torah of Yavneh!
> You, the adept in the maze of *toseftas,*
> Who will now *daven* and learn in your ancient *yeshivas?*

And another kind of protest from Segalovich:

> My stomach turns at the thought of man and his deeds:
> He is repulsive to me, intolerably repulsive.
> And not only the coldblooded Prussian flayer,
> The manufacturer of human soap,
> But all the two billions of all the continents
> Who looked on at the greatest murder of the ages.
> My spirit faints with disgust at the thought of the son of man,
> The words choke in my throat.

Moses then said, in a low voice: "They talk admiringly of the ghetto fighters and the Jewish partisans. I suppose it's all right. My idea of a memorial for the six million is something else. I see the father holding his little son in his arms on the brink of the mass grave and comforting him up to the moment of the fusillade; *not* turning on the butchers in the hope that he takes one of them with him. He has infinitely more serious business. The child's last moments on earth must have some loving words in them, words of God in the midst of chaos." And in the same low voice, now edged with a kind of fury: "Those who have written and spoken—they had nothing better to do at such a time!—of Jewish passivity, complicity, cooperation with the murderers, what are they? The sneer in the charnel house. And those that choose to turn Christian at such a time. . . ."

---

*These and following passages I translate, however inadequately, in order to make them at least partly accessible to the reader who has no Yiddish. I have left in the original only passages which would have no point at all in translation. [M. S.]

It was on such words, or others like them, that I based my assurances to Willy. Later, when the book appeared, I verified my impressions and found them valid. I quote again his unmailed letter to Shapiro—one of the hundreds he wrote to the living and the dead during his half play-acting nervous breakdown (none the less real for all that): "We are survivors in this age, so theories of progress ill become us. To realize that you are a survivor is a shock. At the realization of such election, you feel like bursting into tears. As the dead go their way, you want to call to them, but they depart in a black cloud of faces, souls. They flow out in smoke from the extermination chimneys . . ." And there was a quiet, annihilating contempt in what he said to his and Madeleine's Protestant-existentialist psychiatrist: "Do you think that any Christian in the twentieth century has the right to speak of Jewish Pharisees? From a Jewish standpoint, you know, this hasn't been one of your best periods."

IX

For a long time after his marriage to Madeleine I saw nothing of Moses. He settled briefly in Chicago, then was persuaded to give up his professorship and buy the Ludeyville estate in Massachusetts— "Herzog's folly." Then I ran into him and Madeleine in Cambridge. I had gone up for a week to look through the Russian stacks of the Harvard library, and one day, on the steps, I saw them. Moses was so obviously embarrassed as he introduced me to Madeleine that I hastened away, mumbling about an appointment. Ten minutes later Madeleine joined me in the Russian section. I was looking for Korolenko, the elder Nabokov, the 1914 annuals of *Rech* and *Novoye Vremya*, and other contemporary material on the Beiliss case, and she was looking for material on early Russian Church history. We exchanged a few words, but I was infected with Moses' embarrassment. It was not till our second meeting in the same place that we walked out together. She had an appointment with Gersbach, who, to my astonishment, invited me to join them at lunch. I was not quick-witted enough to frame a plausible refusal.

It was an extremely uncomfortable three quarters of an hour. They were working on me all the time. Madeleine seemed to be probing while alternating between polite curiosity and little bursts of gushiness. She apparently wanted to know how friendly I was with Moses and his family, and whether Moses had spoken to me of her. Was I one of the people who disapproved of the marriage? These and other questions were in her manner. As come on, she explained what she was doing in Cambridge; from time to time she took a few days off from her duties as housekeeper and mother to return to research. She could of course have come in by the day, it was only twenty-two miles from Ludeyville to Boston; but it was so exhausting to switch rapidly between housekeeper and student; she had to do it in lumps. Their good friend Valentine Gersbach usually drove her back and forth, as they were neighbors and he had to be in Boston frequently. She brought the baby with her and hired a sitter; thus Moses was free to pursue his own work.

In response to this unnecessary rigmarole I made little of my acquaintance with Willy and Moses and talked instead about my lectures and the book I was writing. Gersbach helped me out by his extraordinary *Blitzkrieg* on my goodwill. What an honor to meet me! And what a stroke of good luck. It had been unforgivable on the part of Moses never to have mentioned that he was on friendly terms with me. "Listen, Maurice—you don't mind if I call you Maurice?—I feel I've known you for years. Why, I grew up on *Sholom Aleichem and His World,* and I've read *The Gentleman Is a Jew* a dozen times. Say, while you're here in Boston, would you tape a talk with me? Just fifteen minutes. We don't pay much, but it's good publicity," and so on and so on.

That was the last I saw of either of them: but I was convinced from that moment on that they were lovers.

X

I lost contact with both branches of the Herzogs. I was abroad for nearly a year and on my return had few occasions to be in Chicago. On those occasions Willy was out of town and I would not call Moses, who had resumed his professorship at Chicago University. It is irksome to keep up a friendship with a man whose wife you dislike, unless he dislikes her too. Then I heard from a common friend that it was all over between Moses and Madeleine. Finally I came face to face with him in New York less than a block from my hotel, and he tried to avoid me as his childhood friend Nachman had avoided him. But Moses owed me no money, so I felt free to run after him and grab him by the arm.

He was a shocking sight. As we say, *a sheneren bagrobt men*: they put better-looking ones in coffins. Not down-and-out in the ordinary sense—no sign of hunger, and his clothes spoke of neglect, not poverty—but just plain miserable, defeated, distraught, life-weary. Forcibly accosted, he gave up. I was very glad to see him, and it must have got through to him, wherever he was.

In reply to my: "Moses! In heaven's name! Where are you off to?" he said: "Good, good. And you? Yes! I was going . . ."—he pulled back, as on the brink of an indiscretion, or as if it suddenly occurred to him that he had not been going anywhere. He scrutinized me, establishing my identity, weighed me up, deliberated, nodded acquiescence, modified it by pursing his lips. Yes, I will. Should I? Why not? What for? It was as visible as if written out. He wanted to talk to me, wanted to hold his tongue, not unpack his heart with words, keep our relationship unspoiled by confidences. And I, like him, was of two minds, entirely for his sake. I asked him up to my apartment for a drink. I had just bought two volumes of Jacob Glatstein's poetry; here, I said, was a man whose work he ought to know; he did things with Yiddish that had never been done before, revealed in it an unbelievable range of styles. I had also recently acquired Itzik Manger's *Songs and Ballads.* Moses ought to know him too.

"Yes, I'd like that," he said. "And I'd like a drink. Nice of you," and for some reason I felt like scolding him.

He asked me to read to him while he sat sipping his drink. At first he listened with half an ear; his eyes wandered over the bookshelves or unfocussed and became blank. He sighed heavily, the authentic Jewish sigh, fetched all the way from the pelvis. Then he gave me fuller attention and when I made a tentative stop said: "Go on."

Gradually he reassembled himself. He smiled at Manger's picture of fuddy-duddy Grandfather Abraham expostulating with his bibulous nephew Lot, the scandal of the village. He sat up, as if jolted, at certain lines in Glatstein's *Der Reiseman.* "Dazzling!" he exclaimed. Then I read him Glatstein's Nachman Bratzlaver cycle, pausing, here and there, long enough to let him start talking. He only said: "Please go on."

I read next what I regard as one of the most moving poems of modern times, Jacob Glatstein's *Tzvay Berglech*—"Two Mounds"—and when I had finished he leaned forward, his face dark and heavy, and said: "Will you read that again?" At the end of the second reading he stood up violently. "I can't stay," he said, in a strangled voice. "I would like you to lend me that book. Please. I'll be sure to return it."

"Keep it," I said.

"No. I'll return it. Please excuse me. Things, you see. And thank you, oh, thank you very much."

He left the book at the desk a few days later, and it was another year before I saw him again. This time it was in Paris and the meeting was not accidental. I had his address on the rue Marboeuf from Willy, who begged me to take out a day or two on my way to Israel and hunt up Moses.

It was late in March, and a sweet heralding of the spring, a *b'surah,* hovered over the city, so that the hours I loitered in the street outside Moses' apartment have become set apart in my memory as one of those unpredictable, unearned experiences which more than make up for the equally unearned injustices of life. And what was it? Just a mood! Nothing but a mood! An uncaused *Verklärung,* transfiguration, unintelligible in terms of reason, one of those experiences in which we approach God through commonplace persons and things. O lovely street, lovely sunlight and shadows, lovely corner café from which I kept watch part of the time, lovely shuffling waiter who obviously wondered whether I was a *flic* in plain clothes, or a collector of bad and doubtful debts, or a jealous and suspicious old husband.

In the late afternoon Moses got out of a taxi and I charged across the street. Because of what I had just been thinking he did in fact look to me, for a moment, like a criminal, an absconding debtor, or an illicit lover surprised respectively by a detective, a sheriff or a wronged husband. I had to explain the sudden laughter with which I greeted him.

He was booked for flight to America in thirty-six hours. As the reader of *Herzog* will remember, he had just finished his six-month tour of Poland, Czechoslovakia, Greece, Turkey, Israel, Italy, France. He was going back to clean up the mess, take his little daughter Junie away from the impossible Madeleine and start life anew. He saw all his mistakes, saw also how to rectify them, and was determined to do it. That was what he told me that evening, for at last he unburdened himself to me, at length, in depth, and unsparing of himself. I would almost say that, somehow foreknowing that we should never meet again, he decided to break through the pattern of our relationship and reach out to me.

I proposed dinner at a Jewish restaurant on the rue des Petits Blancs Manteaux; he counterproposed the Place des Tertres, objecting that the old ghetto would be noisy and the enchanted wind would not reach us. So we took a taxi up to Montmartre, and to my surprise and delight the Place des Tertres had burst its winter cerements and put out the tables and chairs and was doing a gay out-of-doors business, with the fake painters hawking their dreadful products and the street minstrels singing their sentimental ballads.

Before sitting down to a drink we loitered in front of the Sacré Coeur and looked out over the rampart at the spread of Paris breaking into a million lights under the pure arch of the diminishing day. It had not the beauty of Naples seen from the Castle of St. Elmo, of Haifa seen from Carmel, or San Francisco from Nob Hill, or Montreal from Inspiration Point, or Cape Town from Table Mountain; its beauty was of the mind, of historical association, more than anything else the history of ideas and personalities.

"But for me," I said, as if he had been reading my mind, "Paris has chiefly personal associations. Until I was forty-five or so, this" —I swept my arm in a semicircle toward the Trocadero and the Left Bank—"used to bring back the months I spent here before the start of the First World War, when I was nineteen. Paris when you're nineteen, and a genius, and there hasn't been a world war, or a Buchenwald, or an atomic bomb. The delirium of it! I used to go mad remembering. And now it's nothing to me, or rather, foolishness, pose, conceit, the dishonesty of loud-mouthed adolescence. Now I am overcome instead by memories of my fifth and sixth years, which we spent here before going on to England, and my father and mother and I and a brother and two sisters lived on the rue Joseph Dijon— it's down there, a fifteen-minute walk—in a room and a half, the half being my father's workshop. And in that shoemaker's workshop my mother set the table for the *seder.* My father, bashed about by fate since the age of eight, when he became an all-round orphan—*a keilichiger yosem. Yosem, yatom,* our peculiar feeling for the pathos of the world has been with us since Sinai. What my father went through! And he held on all the time to the line from Sinai. I think of my childhood days in Paris, those hungry, squalid days, with over-whelming love." Without knowing it, I was saying to Moses what he had said, or was to say to Mr. Bellow about Napoleon Street in Montreal.

"That's what Paris is to me now. Not *la ville lumière,* not revolution and artists and thinkers; but Isaac Samuel of Macin, Rumania, and his wife Fanny, and the *seder,* the world they carried with them, hunted and poverty-stricken, faithful custodians of my heritage. They never heard of *Liberté, Egalité, Fraternité,* but they had the original version, never equaled in translation."

"Your childhood sounds much like mine," said Moses, as we turned back.

"A man doesn't get the full memory-taste of his childhood," I answered, "until he's in the sixties."

"Some people grow old faster," said Moses. "Whenever I go to

Montreal I taste my childhood as you taste yours here. But for me, here—it's my first visit to Paris, you know—of course I can't think of it personally, or in a Jewish connection."

"Heine is buried here. And Herzl wrote the *Judenstaat* here."

"You know what Balzac said of Paris? A city where great ideas perish, done to death by a witticism."

"They couldn't get the better of Herzl," I said.

We interrupted the conversation to order dinner. When the waiter withdrew a singer with a guitar approached. He sang, not at all badly:

J'aime le son du cor le soir au fond du bois.

I gave him something.

"Like the gondoliers singing Tasso in Venice," said Moses. "Only I have Shaw's complaint about that. During my visit, too, the practice was, for some reason or other, suspended." He listened as he spoke. "I suppose we Jews are the authentic world-lovers. We have nostalgic memories, sweet and painful, of so many places."

Encouraged by the tip, the minstrel began a new song, somewhat below de Vigny's level, a back-home-again song:

J'irai revoir ma Normandie,
C'est le pays qui m'a donné le jour.

"Why is it," asked Moses, "that when the world has become slightly thoughtful about us—for how long?—the revulsion from Hitler, and all that, why is it that just at this point the English language is *empesté* with all that's vulgar and shmaltzy in Yiddish? Why is it that the words that have passed over make up a sort of thieves' jargon, a low vaudeville slang? We used to give the world such words as *hallelujah, cherubim, leviathan, Eden, amen.* Now it's *chutzpah,* and *shlock,* and *tzorres,* and *kibitz.* And there are some idiots who think of this as the Yiddishization of American humor."

"The reason," I said, "is that in the *golah* most Jews can't stand the thoughtfulness you mentioned, having so little Jewishness, and so they respond ingratiatingly with comicality, the grin of the insecure. And the majority of Gentiles respond on that level. Deep calls unto deep, Moses. *Macht* Rashi, deep calls unto deep means the lowest appeals to the lowest. But we're giving the world a few good words nowadays; only so far they come from the Jewish homeland. *Chalutz, kibbutz* (not *kibitz*), *shalom.*"

"It's time we had writers," answered Moses, "who can use Yiddish and Hebrew without self-consciousness; who can describe an attractive Jew without a gurgle of complacency and a repulsive Jew without implying an attitude, without making one feel they're working off a grudge."

"We have some," I said. "But the masses on both sides prefer the others."

Another street singer stationed himself at our table. He sang *Le Temps des Cerises,* which I had not heard for perhaps fifty years, a period piece, charming in a small way, if you are in the mood. Moses seemed to be listening with peculiar intentness. At the words:

> *Quand vous en serez au temps des cerises,*
> *Si vous avez peur des chagrins d'amour,*
> *Évitez les belles . . .*

he looked down at his plate, his hands on the edge of the table. Then he called the singer over, tipped him, and waved him away, saying: *"Ne vous en faites pas, mon vieux. J'ai quelque chose à dire à mon ami."* And to me: "There's something on my mind. But not here."

When we had eaten we walked back to the platform before the Sacré Coeur and there, leaning his elbows on the parapet above the city, Moses recited by heart the whole of Glatstein's "Two Mounds":

> *Die Mame fun altz vos lebt iz geshtorben,*
> *Nor zi baklogt zich nit.*

The mother of all that lives has died.
But she does not complain.
For all that lives she takes with her.
This is the secret of the end.
To join one's mother is not punishment.

The whole pitiful squabble
Shot up into a tiny, smiling flame
And with thanks stretched out to me its
five-fingered hand:
You have performed a good deed;
More than visiting the sick:
Visiting death while he blossoms
Like a sapling. It is well that the leavetaking
At least has a tongue, and speaks.
Tomorrow or the day after I shall lie
Near my mother.

A deep sigh brought a passing stammer into his speech.

> To be gathered in,
> That means to accept with love,
> Unlamenting,
> Even with praise,
> This grassy eternity,
> This crumbling into dust
> Of my firm, massive, characteristic self—
> —God save the mark!
>
> He held me in a bony handshake:
> This means homecoming,
> In peace, in goodwill, not at odds.
> To lie near one's mother means
> To be cradled to sleep.
> I no longer have the strength for heavy
>   thinking,
> Not even the desire for the last tottering step
> Toward God.
>
> My thoughts kindle like fireflies,
> A flicker and a falling into blackness.
> There waits for me, foreordained,
> Warm sanctity,
> Holy earth.
> How can a man be so vile
> As to begrudge his life
> When his own mother has died?
> There is your purpose in death,
> To die for your mother's death.
>
> Two little mounds, a shining of grace.
> You understand it well,
> God of Compassion.
> Last pains torment
> The rebellious flesh.
> To all, greeting,
> L'hitraot,
> You and you and you.

Ingathered to merited rest.

"Soon," said Moses, "in a little while. But first I have to put some order into my life, and before that some order into my thoughts. *Chagrins d'amour!* The paltriness of it. I've played the fool, handed myself and my dearest possessions over to my enemies. I can't die young, like my mother. I must live and look after the kids. I know Willy has told you something, my good, decent, worrying brother. I want to tell you the rest, *aropreden fun hartzn.* Listen for his sake, if not for mine."

He spoke in long and short spells for four hours, while we sat on the cathedral steps, or strolled about the square, or leaned against the parapet. He could not, even in four hours, make his account as complete as he has made it to Mr. Bellow. Compared with the record it had many lacunae; apart from the limitations of time there were certain things he could not bring himself to speak of to a much older man, at least, at a first confession. On the other hand, he told me nothing essential not to be found in the book.

XI

From this last meeting with Herzog I went on to Israel, while he returned to America. I will recapitulate here what happened to him there up to the closing point of Mr. Bellow's narrative. (Herzog's subsequent trip around the world and his death on a safari out of Nairobi lie beyond the narrative and are not relevant to this memoir.) He proceeded to Chicago, filled with determination, as he thought and proclaimed, to get his little daughter, Junie, away from Madeleine, whom he considered a pathological case, unfit to be trusted with a child, particularly his, a typical Herzog. That Gersbach the buffoon should have a hand in the upbringing was an additional guarantee of Junie's ultimate ruination.

He came back to New York from Chicago, crushed by his failure to get the cooperation of various persons he had counted on, including his own lawyer, who seems in fact to have let him down completely, if not sold him out. In New York he went into a sort of craze—this was his wild, compulsive letter-writing period—without becoming certifiable. He ran hither and thither, found consolation in likeable, attractive, and experienced Ramona, fled from her, returned to her, then made another dash for Chicago. This time he *had* to get the child away from Madeleine.

In Chicago, at the nadir of his condition, he switched impulsively from rescue to revenge. He was going to shoot Madeleine and Gersbach. On an icy winter's day he went with a loaded revolver to his former home, where Madeleine still lived and where Gersbach spent as much time as at his own home. Peeping in through the window Moses saw Gersbach bathing the child, and suddenly everything seemed normal, domestic, acceptable. Gersbach handled the child in an affectionate, playful, fatherly way, while Madeleine looked on. What the devil was he doing there, the idiot, lurking outside the house with a loaded revolver? Was he, Moses Herzog, going to shoot someone? "The intended violence turned into *theater*, into something ludicrous."

Rapid reconsideration followed and a new light flooded on his plan. The likelihood of his getting legal custody of the child was very small. But what was so bad about letting Madeleine and Gersbach bring up Junie? Sure, they weren't married, and Madeleine was abnormal, and Gersbach was vulgar, preposterous, intellectually repulsive. But who was to say that he, Moses, no shining example of stability, would do better by the child?

He stole back to his rented car and drove away.

A day or two later he was allowed part of an afternoon with Junie, and then, as he was driving about with her, occurred that extraordinary accident which demonstrated beyond cavil that he was not fit to be trusted with the child. Not that he was to blame for the accident, which was fortunately minor. If he had been, it would at least have shown that in accidents he took the initiative, and was therefore only a *shlemiel.* He revealed himself as a *shlimazel,* one who is accident-prone. One does not have to be a cynic or, what is worse, an amateur psychoanalyst, to perceive that he had made this dash for Chicago in order to rid himself, once and for all, of the responsibility for Junie's upbringing.

This achieved, he dashed back east, to his rundown and abandoned estate in Ludeyville and there, as brother Willy and sweetheart Ramona come to visit him, the story ends. What he felt at that moment I shall consider later. Meanwhile other matters must be puzzled out.

XII

Until I had the record before me I had no idea of the tormented and tormenting love Madeleine had awakened in Moses—the kind that cries for assuagement at the cost of a man's last sanctities and sweeps before it his instinct of self-preservation together with his self-respect. I shall perhaps be told that I ought to have known; Madeleine was very beautiful and I had met her. Yes, she was extremely good-looking; no doubt she made people stare and turn round; yet she was not besieged by suitors. Why should only Herzog have fallen for her so violently? (We don't know the quality of Gersbach's love for her.) They were not well suited sexually; Herzog never found in her the physical joy offered him by Ramona, or the Japanese girl Sono.

Madeleine seems to have belonged more or less to the class of "vile amateurs."

In what, then, was the violence of the attraction rooted?

Before I try to answer this question, let me establish the facts.

I knew from Willy that Moses had after all not married in church, and that their little girl had not been baptized. I assumed, therefore, that report had exaggerated the seriousness of Madeleine's Catholic phase; hence I assumed further that Moses' struggle with himself had been less severe than I had anticipated. The assumptions were wrong. The record establishes the seriousness of Madeleine's Catholic phase, the bitterness of Herzog's struggle with himself, and the pathological character of the attraction Madeleine had for him.

Let us begin with the scene in the bathroom, when Madeleine is making herself up to look fifteen years older, "sober and mature," for the sake of her job at Fordham University and her Catholic superiors. Moses sits on the edge of the bathtub, watching, fascinated by her skill, her rapid, slashing movements, and her beauty. "The pity of the whole thing!" He, the worn, unshaven, sinful Jew, was endangering her redemption. But "she had her white convert's face and Herzog couldn't refuse to play opposite."

They go out for a hasty breakfast, and Madeleine lays down the law: "You and I have got to marry in the Church, otherwise I quit. Our children will be baptized and brought up in the Church." What is the reaction? "Moses gave a dumb half-nod. Compared with her he felt static, without temperament. The powdered fragrance of her face stirred him (my gratitude for art, was his present reflection, any sort of art)."

She is not satisfied with the dumb half-nod. She repeats: "It'll be these rules or nothing." And "Moses watched her as though he were submerged. 'Do you hear me?' 'Oh, yes,' he said. 'Yes. I do.' "

What was happening here? Was he lying and gambling? Anything as long as he could hold on to her? Or was he sure he would never be called to book and could play opposite her safely? Or was he simply refusing to think it through? He could have pleaded to himself that in this matter Madeleine was sick, because she was not religious by nature. She was sick, he was waiting for her to get better, he would help her to get better. He never offered this plea. When he accompanied Madeleine to church he sat in the pew wondering at himself: "What was he doing here? He was a husband, a father. He was married, he was a Jew. Why was he in church?"

The clearest and most unquieting expression of his sense of guilt is the letter he began to write to his mother—began, and got no further than the opening—when he was passing through his crisis, getting Madeleine out of his flesh: "Dear Mama, as to why I haven't visited your grave in so long . . ." There it stopped. How, indeed, could he have continued? "You see, dear Mama, I was taken up these last few years with a Jewish girl who had turned Catholic, and I had promised to turn Catholic too, and have your grandchildren baptized. I guess I didn't mean it, but I couldn't tell you about having made that promise, even though I didn't have to keep it in the end. I guess you wouldn't have understood, you who wanted me to be a rabbi, how I could make such a promise even if I was only pretending."

He could not tell his mother what he told his chronicler, namely that he had fought Madeleine's apostasy "in the sack," and had won her away from the Church. From every point of view it was too crude a joke. We see that in nothing did Moses take the lead except in self-abasement. Madeleine entered the Church and left it, accepted (tolerated? liked? loved?) Moses and rejected him according to the rhythm of her own needs. If the Catholic episode had lasted a year longer Moses would have had to face a test beyond his capacity. As it was, he became someone who could not face his own beloved dead.

Hardly less depressing is the havoc Madeleine wrought in his common sense. Granted that husbands, wives, lovers resist to the last gasp the evidence of an infidelity, there is after all a limit to gullibility this side of the lunatic asylum. If it were not Herzog himself who told this story we should denounce his attitude toward Madeleine and Gersbach as a silly and offensive invention. Not only did these two often stay together at a hotel in Boston, not only did they tell Moses about it, but Madeleine actually sent Gersbach to the house for her diaphragm and Gersbach picked it up while Moses was looking on. Whereupon—but as the reader will perhaps think I am exaggerating I refer him to page 192 of the hard cover edition, page 238 of the paperback—Moses asked Madeleine for an explanation and was told that it was petty of him to ask, and that he had lost the right to an explanation! He wasn't to think that she was having an affair with Gersbach, whom she found repulsive except as the brother she had never had.

We are brought back to Bloom. In the Nighttown fantasy projections Joyce shows Bloom to have been the eager pander to Molly and Blazes Boylan, peeping in on their sexual engagement with erotic glee, and gratefully accepting a tip for his services. Joyce may have meant that Bloom actually got a feeble thrill from the contemplation of the probability that Molly and Boylan were in bed together while he was wandering about the city. Joyce did not mean that Bloom had promoted the adultery. But Moses Herzog, with his unbelievable, cooperative gullibility, did play the pander to Madeleine and Gersbach. Yet there is no hint that Moses belonged to the type which finds an aphrodisiac in such fancies. We must look elsewhere for the motive, just as we must look for the source of his love-frenzy to something other than Madeleine's beauty or the sexual happiness she offered him.

XIII

I believe that Moses Herzog made a mess of his life because he did not realize that his Jewish feelings were much too powerful for the minimal practical role he assigned to them. There was a disastrous struggle between his concept of his public duty, the non-Jewish thinker's career to which he committed himself (I use "career" in an inoffensive sense), and a great inner need which he would not satisfy even in his private life; pushed and pulled by forces he refused to understand and therefore could not reconcile, he broke himself.

We can see his trouble more clearly if we return to the parallel with Leopold Bloom, who had to reconcile his image of himself as a world-betterer with his (partial) identity as a Jew. His Jewish attachments were, as we have recalled, fragmentary and uninsistent. He dismissed them with a symbolic gesture. His father had already broken the back of the problem for him, bringing him up in an advanced stage of assimilation. But Moses Herzog had to do all of his assimilating himself, and he was burdened with a particuarly rich emotional Jewish heritage, besides being endowed with piety and sensitivity.

Leopold Bloom, an advocate of universal brotherhood, but for all that an Irish patriot, dreamed of finding a personal base in his identity as an Irish country gentleman, and his residual Jewishness offered no resistance. But where was Moses Herzog to find a personal base? In Ludeyville? He laughed at the idea—a "monument to his sincere and loving idiocy, to the unrecognized evils of his character, symbol of his Jewish struggle for a solid footing in White Anglo-Saxon Protestant America."

But given that he was, emotionally, the kind of man who needed a footing, where was he to find it? In his Jewish self? Powerful, indeed fateful, as that was, it was out of kilter with the material of his thinking, his working material, so to speak, which was wholly non-Jewish. Psychologically he was Jewish, culturally universal via America. It might have been different if he had received a Jewish education commensurate with his capacities. But by the time he was married it was too late for him—or so he thought—to equip himself with the requisite Jewish knowledge.

We get a glimpse of him taking out his children after he had given them up. What does he talk about to them? The Hamilton-Burr duel, fishes' scales, fairy tales about a boy freckled with the heavenly constellations, Big Dipper, Little Dipper, Orion. Never Jewish fairy tales, Noah's ark, Jonah and the whale, Joseph and his brothers, Sholom Aleichem's "The Penknife." He does not ask himself what kind of Jews his children will be. Since his own Jewishness has no share in his lifework, his philosophic system, his communication to the world, he (deliberately?) refrains from imposing it on his children.

He told Mr. Bellow that "it was painful to his Jewish family feeling that his children should be growing up without him. But what could he do?" By the time he uttered this plaint, he could do nothing. But how had the situation arisen?

He began by leaving his first wife, Daisy, and his son Marco, to whom he was deeply attached. "I gave up the shelter of an orderly, purposeful, lawful existence because it bored me, and I felt it was simply a slacker's life." But he had done his best work during that period and did almost none after he left Daisy. "Bored" he undoubtedly was, and he *may* have felt he was leading a slacker's life, but it grew much slacker after the change. What he does not observe is that he had rid himself of the burden of helping his son to acquire an identity. He left that to the mother.

Then he met Madeleine during his affair with the Japanese girl Sono. The material for an explosion was stored up: the middle-aged man, the *reveil du lion,* and also the need to make his private life consonant with world enterprise. He might have fallen in love with a non-Jewish girl, but Madeleine's apostasy was the ingredient which at once set off the explosion and gave it its abnormal temperature. The unreasoning and unjustifiable emotions are the strongest. It was precisely the aspect of her which he disavowed that produced the mortal effect. This was what made him cringe, besmirch his soul, put on a spurious humility which was at bottom a shameful servility; this, and not her beauty or the sexual satisfaction she afforded him.

He saw in Madeleine release and renewal; and she did in fact release enormous energies, only to absorb them all, and more. Between them, she and Gersbach simply emptied Moses. Allowing for a touch of hysteria in his account, there is something weird in their manipulation of him—with his acquiescence. "My idiocy"—as he calls it—"inspired them, and sent them to greater heights of perversity."

Love has its momentum. The initial propelling force dies, the motion continues with steady deceleration in an agony of shame and confusion. It became a life and death necessity for Moses to free himself from Madeleine; it was also necessary for him to be rid of his second unmanageable commitment, his and Madeleine's daughter. He could not do it by simply walking out; that would have been a frightful comedown. He could not, for shame's sake, after such wild protestations and acts, become the repudiating party. He could not play the wife-hopper, initiate divorce proceedings; it made him look in his own eyes like a Tommy Manville. The repudiation had to come from Madeleine; it was the only seemly way he could shake off his second wife and his second child. He had to go down fighting "injustice," and he did.

In all this he had to laugh at himself occasionally, calling himself "that suffering joker." It helps such a man, committing such self-betrayals, to do a little clowning vis-à-vis himself and potential intellectual spectators. It soothes a certain perverse self-respect.

XIV

He was in Ludeyville, a free man again. That woman was no longer in his flesh. "He was surprised to feel contentment . . . contentment? Whom was he kidding? This was joy! His servitude was ended and his heart released from its grisly heaviness and encrustations." And again: "It was a delicious joy to have her removed from his flesh. . . ."

In a final series of adjustments—final, that is, as far as his record extends—he addresses letters in various directions, the most important being to his son, God, and his mother (his daughter was too young). To his son he writes: "Dear Marco. I've come up to the old homestead to look things over and relax a little. . . . Perhaps you'd like to spend some time with me here, only the two of us—roughing it—after camp. . . . Do you remember the talks we had about Scott's Antarctic expedition. . . . Maybe you and I could take a trip at Xmas to Canada. . . . I am a Canadian, too, you know. . . ."

For his daughter, to whom he could not write, he had a present, a little toy piano. And he thinks of what he can leave his children: "The patrimony of his children—a sunken corner of Massachusetts for Marco, the little piano for June painted a loving green by her solicitous father. That too, like most other things, he would probably botch."

To God he writes: "How my mind has struggled to make coherent sense. I have not been too good at it. But have desired to do your unknowable will, taking it, and you, without symbols."

And to his mother (this he did not actually write, but only thought of writing): "The life you have given me has been curious, and perhaps the death I must inherit will turn out to be even more profoundly curious. I have sometimes wished it would hurry up, longed for it to come soon. . . . But . . . I still have certain things to do. . . . I may not turn out to be such a terrible hopeless fool as you, as I myself, suspected. I want to send you, and others, the most loving wish I have in my heart. This is the only way I have to reach out— out to where it is incomprehensible. I can only pray toward it. So . . . Peace!"

The letter to his mother carries strange echoes of Glatstein's "Two Mounds." He believes himself to be free to address her again, but does not explain why he has not visited her grave for so long. Perhaps he never intended to visit it again. Would he not, after all, have to bring her greetings from her grandchildren? And what had he done with them? What memory of her and of his father and of their forebears had he planted, would he plant in them? "I am a Canadian, too, you know," he writes Marco.

In the *al chet* with which he opens the account, all the sins he can think of are neatly listed: "He had been a bad husband—twice. Daisy, his first wife, he had treated miserably. Madeleine, his second wife, had tried to do *him* in. To his son and daughter he was a loving but bad father. To his own parents he had been an ungrateful child. To his country an indifferent citizen. To his brothers and his sister affectionate but remote. With his friends, an egotist. With love, lazy. With brightness, dull. With power, passive. With his own soul, evasive."

It is all, somehow, touched with self-satisfaction, as if he had really emptied himself, in a sort of *tashlich* ceremony, to the bottom of his pockets. It was not so, either then, or later. Was it enough to say in summation, that he had been a bad father, an ungrateful son, and evasive with his own soul? Every man can say that of himself;

a generalized confession is no confession at all. He had avoided the admission into his life of the vital Jewish ingredient: he had dealt treacherously with his children in withholding from them (and it was a crime if only on prudential psychological grounds) the knowledge that to be Jewish has certain meanings; he had destroyed the posterity of his parents.

The essence of his sinfulness, obscured by the complacency of a rhetorical moral accounting, is compressed into a single word. At Ludeyville, in the exultation of his reestablished freedom, he exclaims *"Hineni!"*

Hineni! It is the word with which the infant Samuel answered God's call; and with the same word Abraham answered God in token that he was ready to bring any sacrifice God asked of him. *Hineni, here I am,* said Moses Herzog, in imitation. But where in fact was he, and what was he prepared to do? Whom, to use his own words, was he kidding?

He was a man close to fifty, used up by his struggles with himself. Had he the strength to build a new life? Was he going to marry again, beget more children? Was he going to retrieve those he had already begotten and abandoned? Was he going to reach a great new synthesis of thought?

Since with God all things are possible, Moses Herzog might, if he had lived, have contrived to resolve the contradiction in his psychological needs. As it is we can only say that we sorely miss a recording of what went on in his mind during the year of wandering which preceded his death. For his mother's sake, *yitzror bitzror hachayim et nishmato,* may his soul be bound up in the bond of eternal life.

Midstream, April 1966